This book
but it may

1.

14. A

25. J
27. J

24. A

25. N

2

24.

THE PEACOCK'S TAIL

ENGLISH TATTOO DESIGN STILL IN USE

The Peacock's Tail

by

PEARL BINDER

author of
"Odd Jobs" "Muffs and Morals" etc.

*With 4 plates in half-tone and 204 illustrations in the
text, 178 by the author*

GEORGE G. HARRAP & CO. LTD
LONDON TORONTO WELLINGTON SYDNEY

To my friend SAH OVED *with love*

First published in Great Britain 1958
by GEORGE G. HARRAP & CO. LTD
182 High Holborn, London, W.C.1

© *Pearl Binder* 1958

Composed in Bembo type and printed in the City of Oxford at the Alden Press.
Made in Great Britain

CONTENTS

Upon the reconstitution of the British Cabinet in January 1957 Mr John Taylor, the Editor of the *Tailor and Cutter*, commented: "Sartorially speaking, Mr Macmillan is to be preferred to Sir Anthony Eden. Mr Butler wears his hat on the back of his head – and that makes him look more like a plumber than a Prime Minister."

PLATES IN HALF-TONE

ACKNOWLEDGMENTS

I am deeply indebted to and wish to thank the following people, who have helped me gather material for this book: Professor François Boucher; Professor Raymond Firth; Sah Oved; Miss Gertrude Ely, of Bryn Mawr, Pennsylvania; Mr F. Bermingham, the Editor of *Esquire*; Mr Tom Lyon, the Librarian of Eton College; Messrs Jaeger, Ltd; Dr Walter Voegelin and Dr V. L. Hefti, of *CIBA Review*; Mr Jay Leyda; the tailoring firms of Messrs Henry Poole, Ltd, Court tailors, Messrs Whitley, and Messrs Moss Bros; the staffs of the Friends' House Library, the British Museum, the Victoria and Albert Museum, the Museum of English Rural Life, Reading, the American Library, the India House Library, the Museum of English Costume, the National Maritime Museum, Greenwich, the Imperial War Museum; the Museum of Modern Art, the Museum of the American Indian, and the Museum of Natural History in New York; the University Museum and the William Penn Museum in Philadelphia; Mrs Jermayne MacAgy, of the Contemporary Arts Museum, Houston, Texas, and Mr Douglas MacAgy, of the American Museum of Modern Art, New York; Professor L. A. Mayer, of the Hebrew University, Jerusalem, for particular information on Muslim dress; Miss Beatrice Saxon-Snell, for information about George Fox; the Serjeant at Arms, House of Commons, for permission to copy wall-paintings in St Stephen's; and the late Cardinal Griffin, for information on the use of symbolism in the Roman Catholic Church.

I particularly wish to thank Mr John Taylor, Editor of the *Tailor and Cutter*, for allowing me to consult the files of his journal and for permission to reproduce seven plates.

To my patient family also I wish to say thank you.

P. B.

A BRIEF BIBLIOGRAPHY

Book of Sufferings (Kingston Friends' Meeting House) (seventeenth and eighteenth centuries).
BOORDE, ANDREWE: *The Breuiary of Helthe* (1547).
BURTON, MAURICE: *Animal Courtship* (1953).
BYRON, LORD: *Letters* (1832–33).
 Parliamentary Speeches prepared by his Lordship for Publication (1824).
CANTLIE, DR JAMES: *Physical Efficiency* (1906).
CAVALRYMAN, A: *The Whole Art of Dress* (1830).
COOK, CAPTAIN JAMES: *An Account of a Voyage round the World* (1809).
CORELLI, MARIE: *Mrs Maddenham* (1897).
Coutumes de Toulouse (1296).
CRUMP, LUCY: *Nursery Life 300 Years ago* (1929).
DARWIN, CHARLES: *Beagle Journal* (1834).
DISRAELI, BENJAMIN: *Endymion* (1880).
EBENSTEN, HANNS: *Pierced Hearts and True Love* (1953).
EDGEWORTH, MARIA: *Tales of Fashionable Life* (1809).
ELLIS, HAVELOCK: *My Life* (1940).
FALVY-BOURDON, MARIE DE: *De Paris à Samarcand* (1880).
FOX, GEORGE: *Journal* (1694).
GRONOW, CAPTAIN: *Memoirs* (1860).
HAMILTON, A.: *Mémoires de la vie du comte de Gramont* (1713).
HARDING, E.: *Costume of the Russian Empire* (1803).
HAWES, ELIZABETH: *It's still Spinach* (1954).
HONNECOURT, VILLARD DE: *Designs* (1250).
JAMESON, STORM: *Decline of Merrie England* (1930).
LAHONTAS, BARON DE: *Suite de voyages en Amérique* (1704).
LE ROI, PÈRE: *A travers le Zanguibar* (1863).
LECKY, WILLIAM: *History of European Morals* (1869).
LECONSFIELD, MAUD LADY, and JOHN GORE: *Three Howard Sisters ... 1825–33* (1955).
LEHNER, ERNST: *Picture-book of Symbols* (1956).
LIBRON, F., and H. CLOUZOT: *Le Corset* (1923).
Manual of Good Behaviour and Polite Accomplishments (1855).
Manuel de la Toilette (1828).
MAYER, PROFESSOR L. A.: *Mamluk Costume* (1952).
MEMBER OF THE ARISTOCRACY, A: *Manners and Rules of Good Society* (1902).
MORRIS, WILLIAM: *The Decorative Arts and their Relation to Modern Life and Progress* (a lecture delivered before the Trades Guild of Learning) (1878).
 Hopes and Fears for Art (1882).
 News from Nowhere (1890).
POWDERMAKER, PROFESSOR HORTENSE: *Hollywood the Dream Factory* (1950).
ROUSSEAU, J. J.: *Émile, ou de l'éducation* (1763).
RUNDELL, MRS, and MRS E. BIRCH: *A New System of Domestic Cookery founded upon Principles of Economy* (1847).
SAND, GEORGE: *Elle et Lui* (1858).
SHAFTESBURY, SEVENTH EARL OF (LORD ASHLEY): *Parliamentary Speeches* (1842).
Strangers' Guide to Paris (1819).
STUBBES, PHILIP: *The Anatomie of Abuses* (1583).
VINCENT, J. M.: *Costume and Conduct in the Laws of Basel, Bern, and Zurich, 1370–1800* (1935).
WEEMS, M. L.: *Life of William Penn* (1850).

CHAPTER ONE

THE SITUATION TO-DAY

*We have lost the art of living and in the most important science of all, the
science of daily life, the science of behaviour, we are complete ignoramuses.
We have psychology instead.*

D. H. LAWRENCE, *Etruscan Places* (1932)

THIS is a book about men's dress. It is an attempt to discover why
modern man has renounced the art of dress. To try to find the answer
to this question I propose to travel both in space and in time. What I shall
have to say will not always be directly about man's dress, but it will always
be about man, how he has thought and behaved in the past and how he
thinks and behaves to-day. For dress is but the outward expression of
man's state of mind, and it is in his attire that he tells the world what he
thinks of himself.

If I pay particular attention to the dress and adornment of primitive

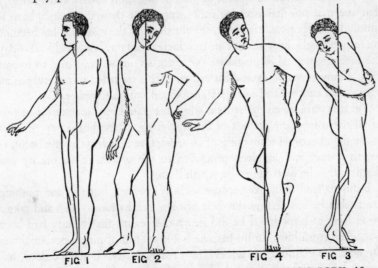

"THE CONFORMATION AND ATTITUDES OF THE HUMAN BODY AS
TOUCHING TAILORING"

Tailor and Cutter, 1881

people in this book it is because I am writing from the point of view of the artist, believing that it is among primitives, and to-day almost exclusively among primitives, that we still find vitality in sartorial creation.

Also, being a woman, I must make my comments on male dress from the point of view of a woman. This, I am well aware, is a delicate task, demanding no little skill and temerity. Yet it is a task that urgently needs to be undertaken. Let me say right away that I am not out to win a battle against men. On the contrary, this is a battle I, and every other woman, want men to win for themselves. I greatly esteem the male sex, and would rejoice to see all men looking as gallant and beautiful as they could look, and would look if only they would adopt a dress which did them justice. And several hundred million women agree with me on this point.

Men dress drably in our modern Western world because beauty has no real place in our everyday lives, which are increasingly machine-dominated. Beauty is not something that can be switched on and off like the radio, but, on the contrary, beauty is something that we must seek out and cherish, and which must permeate our whole civilization, or else our civilization will wither.

Our machine civilization, in which, so far, beauty has been sacrificed, has not yet succeeded in giving man the full and happy life he wants, and which he could enjoy if the machines were used intelligently—that is, used *for* man instead of against him. The situation to-day shows clearly that the machine has become more important than the man whom it should be serving, and the artist, the antithesis of the machine, has become correspondingly insignificant in our increasingly robot world. To-day the machine is used to plagiarize the artist, to outwit him, and to bypass him; almost never to extend his values. Art is regarded impatiently as an 'extra' that can be, and usually is, dispensed with altogether.

Yet it is only when the artist is truly integrated into society (as he was in all the important periods of the flowering of the human spirit) that every man becomes something of an artist, that his everyday life becomes worth living, and his dress proclaims to the world, in its beauty and dignity, that he feels life to be worth living.

Industrialized man has become so busy pressing buttons and pushing levers that he has neither the time nor the inclination to stop and take a good look at himself. If he did he would realize that beauty had been wrenched from him. In his bath he is a man, full of magic potentialities. Dressed, the glamour has gone. He is Mr Nobody. Dull in colour, unimaginative in cut, distinguished from the dress of his neighbours in no particular, his clothes might be a prison uniform. Indeed, that is precisely what they are, for his spirit is in gaol.

Heir to so rich a past, possessor of such vastly greater wealth than the ancients could command, disposer of such fabulous present power, he should feel godlike. But he does not feel godlike, for his dress tells us clearly that he feels unmanly, unimpressive, and bored.

"Man's earthly interests are all hooked and buttoned together and held up by clothes," declared Thomas Carlyle. The question that must be asked to-day is, just what are his earthly interests? What is wrong with his daily life that causes him to shroud himself in his present mud-coloured garments, which neither cling revealingly to the body in golden youth nor drape the mature body with dignity? Why is he in perpetual mourning? What sin is he expiating? What is he doing penance for? What makes him dress thus in sackcloth and ashes?

On the crowded streets of our great cities, in the bus, the train, the plane, the eye is saddened by the same dreary male uniform, shapeless and lacking colour. Rich men, poor men, labourers, intellectuals, bankers, barrow-boys, old men, young men, all to-day dress like robots. There is a terrible cancelling out in their attire, a neuter quality which can only be described as an emasculation.

Yet this sad cipher which is Western man is master of such magic power that the wildest dreams of mythology appear contemptible beside his achievement. He has but to touch a button to move mountains, to summon the world's greatest singers, dancers, and actors to entertain him. He even knows how (by film and recorder) to call them back from the dead to entertain him as they did in life. He can outstrip the wind when he chooses to fly. He can penetrate beyond sound. Without moving from his chair he can converse with people at the other end of the world, with people in the sky, and with people in the depths of the oceans. He knows how to explore every element and make himself at home where no man before him has ever trod, swum, or climbed. He can do everything, it seems, except dress himself, and all his wonderful achievements seem to have brought him no thrill of pride, or he would not dress like a beetle.

His ancestors, whose scientific and industrial efforts were puny compared to his, dressed with sumptuous arrogance and dazzling variety. Yet to-day, when everything around him moves with such velocity, his dress has slowed to a dismal standstill. Sartorial paralysis has set in. This paralysis has not descended suddenly, but has been encroaching upon him for 150 years—the years of our industrial development. To-day, muffled, shackled, cramped, and pinioned from head to foot in ugly discomfort, he seems unable even to summon the will to protest.

Why does he, a creature no less vain than other creatures, accept ugliness as his portion, when the meanest housefly can flaunt rainbow-hued wings and look beautiful after its fashion? Why? For there must be a reason. Tailors, like dressmakers, can only interpret what is in the minds of their clients, and what is in the minds of their clients is the social climate of the times they live in.

As V. S. Pritchett truly says, "We live by our inner life and our illusions." Man dresses as he feels, as he wants to appear, as he would *be*. In his dress he puts his hopes — and not only his hopes, but his fears as well. If to-day he dresses with dull anonymity that is the way he is feeling. It is his heart which is speaking, and his heart is filled with endless ennui and fear of appearing different from millions of other robots. He is turning himself into a machine-made man.

The American student of dress Hilaire Hiler asks, "Does the disappearance of dressing up indicate the passing of Western civilization?" A century ago Captain Gronow, dandy and friend of dandies in his Regency youth, was already deploring the decay of art in male dress. In the eighteen-seventies Verlaine spoke of "Madmen walking the streets all dressed in black." The picture has not brightened since then. Even man's symbols of social success lack colour. Motor salesmen report that out of all the brilliant range of colours available by far the greatest number of cars sold are hearse-black, despite determined efforts from America to cater for female preference for other hues.

Doctors tell us that Western man to-day is full of fears and resentments. He sleeps badly. He has nervous breakdowns. Professor Mottram, of the University of London, blames this state of mind on the tension of modern living. Never have doctors, it is certain, recorded so many stomach ulcers. Never have lawyers had to deal with so many divorces. The vastly expanded and expanding services dealing with psychological and psychiatric therapy in our hospitals are occasioned by the fact that no less than 50 per cent. (more in America) of all hospital cases are mental cases. Even these expanding services, however, are unable to cope with the demand for their aid, and the waiting-lists of mentally sick patients are very long.

Obviously something is deeply amiss with Western man. He is not happy. He is unable to find the comfort and reassurance he needs either in the various creeds of the various Churches or in politics. Despite his vastly increased understanding of the forces of nature and his greater ability to control them, he has lost confidence in himself. He is frightened. It would be foolish to blame this fear on the threat of atomic warfare, for this threat is only part of the general picture of modern life, and it is modern life itself which is amiss, and man's fear has been growing for more than a century.

Man wants to belong to a stable community. He wants to make his little impression. He wants to love and to be loved. He wants to feel that his job has some significance. And in his spare time he wants to have some fun. These apparently simple desires appear to be impossible to realize to-day, especially the last, though he pursues entertainment as never before. It is, however, not fun that he finds to-day, but boredom, and this state of affairs he shows in his attire.

Here the reader may well ask what is meant by beauty in dress, since the conception of what is beautiful varies with every epoch and in every country, and what was admired and slavishly imitated yesterday to-day is

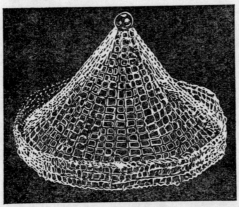

CREATIVE DRESS (PRIMITIVE MARINE ORGANISMS)
Radiolaria. "These take up silica and secrete it around their bodies in the form of amazingly beautiful glassy skeletons.... So far as we can see, the making of this skeleton confers no particular benefit on the animal that makes it ... it merely satisfies some creative impulse."
Maurice Burton, *Animal Courtship* (1953)

detested and neglected. Beauty can assume endless shapes, in art as in nature, but there are only two ways of dressing the human body with beauty. Clothes may be cut to fit the body closely, revealing its shape, both at rest and in movement. That is one way, often the best way for the long, supple lines of youth. The second way is to make no attempt to fit the body, but to wear garments of the extremest simplicity and looseness, wherein the body itself makes the shapes from within. In these two categories, including the infinite varieties of duets which can be played between them, are to be found all that has ever been beautiful in dress and all that ever will be.

In the first category male dress includes such garments as tights, close-fitting high-necked jerseys and doublets, trousers of Spanish cut, and so on; in the second category cloaks, long gowns, chitons, and all forms of drapery. What is inadmissible and always ugly is dress which fails to qualify for either of these two categories, such as our present male dress, which is too loose for the first category and not loose enough for the second.

Apart from the vital question of the shape, or, as we say to-day, the 'cut,' there are such other questions to be considered as colour, texture, and decoration, but if the fundamental shape is no good nothing can redeem the dress from banality. To-day there is a stirring among the tailors, especially in America. There is the Teddy-boy phenomenon and much talk of brighter dress for men. But to add colour (sadly lacking though it is in man's dress to-day), while retaining its present ugly shape, would only make the dress worse than it is already. It would not bring man's dress back to life, but merely be painting the corpse. The contemporary lounge suit in bright scarlet or gold brocade would look no better, as Liberace's lamé lounge suits show only too clearly. Indeed, it would look worse, for a sack is best left the natural colour of a sack.

Since dress is nothing but a moral mirror, reflecting man's opinion of himself, it must be obvious that our dress-reformers to-day are working on the wrong lines. They might be more successful if they first turned their attention to how man lives to-day, for when man can look upon his life with pride and hope he will, without any prompting from outside, insist on wearing a dress which reflects that pride and hope. It is not the tailors who are at fault—it is Western man's spiritual values.

To-day man in the Western world is technically better housed and better fed (and in Great Britain also better doctored and more socially secure) than his splendidly dressed ancestors. Nevertheless he has lost belief in himself because his life does not make sense to him. He realizes that his wonder machines have outpaced him and are rapidly unmanning him. And he has no moral authority with which to control them.

Man's physique, designed by nature for conditions very different from those prevailing in his machine-ruled world, is unsuited to his present life, and is saying so in no uncertain terms. His jawbones and teeth, designed to gnaw bones and hard substances, are to-day malformed and crumbling, the dentists warn us, because of the softness of so much of his diet. His muscles are so rarely called into sufficient action to keep him healthy that many men find it necessary to buy 'rowing' machines and mechanical exercisers. Even farm-workers to-day spend much of their time driving machines and working levers, to the detriment of all muscles other than the muscles of the wrist. Small wonder then that Western man is having trouble with his bowels, suffers from migraine and nervous depressions, and is so often overwhelmed by a sense of his own futility. Wherever he looks, in town and in the country, he is confronted by machines that can do his work a great deal better than he can himself. As to the work which the machine cannot do, the arts, he finds there is so little interest taken in them that he hesitates to seek comfort in their exercise.

Nature has not yet been successful in evolving the right type of man for the machine age. The right type of man will have to be without interest in or pity for human fallibility. He will have to be extremely well co-ordinated within very narrow limits. He will have to be quick at dodging traffic, non-speculative, without temperament, without a feeling for the past or curiosity about the future, and asking nothing better than to spend his working life and leisure pulling levers and pressing buttons. Above all he will have to be blind to the arts.

It is because modern man has not yet reached the stage when he can ignore the arts without suffering a sense of loss that he feels futile to-day. He can buy Hi-Fi, but he himself no longer sings. He cannot relax enough to dance without the aid of alcohol, and even then he has to borrow his dances from American Negroes. His knowledge of the world is brought to him by machinery, in the form of newspapers printed with smudgy photographs, or the eye-watering flicker of the television screen, or violent colour photogravure exhorting him to spend his earnings on this or that.

The subtle and beautiful rhythms of nature, in whose image his body is formed, are unknown to him. He eats what the shops sell him, regardless of the season. He sleeps according to his work-shift, not according to hours of darkness and light. His five senses have degenerated pitiably, and, worst of all, he has lost his sense of wonder in the universe and with it his gods.

In the smog-hued industrial world of to-day man too has grown smog-coloured. He dresses in smog-coloured clothes, losing himself, since he cannot hope to find himself, in the multitude of similar drab raincoats, dark flannels, thick, ungainly shoes. Mediocrity being respectable, and as such desirable, he dare not think differently nor dress differently from his fellows. Beauty has become suspect and art the word he associates with pornographic photo-magazines.

Samuel Butler, in the preface to *Erewhon* (1872), marvelling at the wonders of the vapour engine and the flywheel, warned his readers of the increasing perfection of machinery in "the next hundred thousand years, and the accumulated progress they will bring." Little did he realize that within eighty years automation would have become a *fait accompli*. He foresaw, however, that man's spiritual progress would be negligible in comparison:

We cannot calculate on any corresponding advance in man's intellectual or physical powers which shall be a set-off against the far greater development which seems in store for the machines. Some people may say that man's moral influence will suffice to rule them, but I cannot think it will ever be safe to repose much trust in the moral sense of any machine.

This was considered exquisitely far-fetched eighty years ago. To-day one begins to wonder.

Though man to-day dresses like a mouse, in his heart he still craves to look as beautiful and distinguished as nature and art can contrive. For man, to-day no less than yesterday, ardently desires to make a good impression on his fellow-men and on women. To-day, it must be said, however, that he gets absolutely no help from his clothes. A young man of our time must be handsome indeed, must be exceptionally well made, not to appear to positive disadvantage when he is dressed. The middle-class youth, bound by iron convention to the white-collar employments (and the middle-class, with its infinite social gradations, now includes a huge proportion of the population), is possibly in the most desperate sartorial plight.

His utmost achievement must be 'respectability,' meaning to dress, usually on a paltry income, in a manner intended to make it quite clear to beholders that he does not work with his hands. He cannot hope to pull himself upward into the moneyed leisure class, and he is haunted by fears of slipping downward into the class below, which does work with its hands—a class to-day which frequently earns more money than he does. The aloof, baffled face of the young bank clerk, frozen above his correct, dull dress, symbolizes our present impasse. Like other youths of his age, he is probably dreaming of girls and wishing he were rich.

He is dreaming of girls and longing to make a favourable impression on them, and we may be sure the girls are just as eager that he should, yet the dreariness and uniformity of his dress works against him. It is noticeable to-day, in America possibly even more than in England, how young women, normal heterosexual young women, look with real interest not so much at the opposite sex as at their own. They look at other women to see what they are wearing and what effect they are creating by their dress. They do not look at young men with the expectation of being charmed by their apparel, because for over a century men's clothes have ceased to exert any charm.

If, then, the garb of Western man is unfair even to golden youth, how much crueller to the loosened contours of middle age, the breaking lines of old age. Our era, for all its scientific marvels, is surely unique in history

GENIUS AS GENTLEMEN

WILLIAM CONGREVE   WILLIAM SHAKESPEARE

This is how they would have looked in modern dress.

WISHFUL THINKING

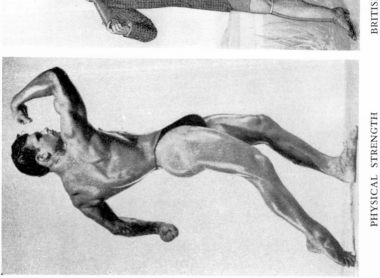

PHYSICAL STRENGTH
Illustration from *Adonis*, the art magazine of the male physique (U.S.A.)

BRITISH SUPREMACY
Sporting attire, 1881
Tailor and Cutter

MILITARY PRESTIGE
"My word! I don't know how they looked at Austerlitz, but they couldn't have looked better than this."
Lithograph by Daumier

insofar as our present male dress is consistently ugly and ungracious from the cradle to the grave. There is positively no age that looks well in it.

Observe how amateur operatic and dramatic societies (a popular meeting-ground for respectable suburban courtship) prefer to produce costume plays. It is the only chance the young women will ever get to see the young men in a more favourable light than in their normal dress. How many young women, staring at their boy friends dressed up in the costumier's idea of Tudor doublet and hose, are thrilled at the revelation that men really do have legs which are not grey cylinders. Thrilled and amazed precisely as were their great-grandfathers to learn—though, save illicitly, not until their bridal night—that beneath the crinoline encasing their bride existed legs, real legs. Man's present dress is, in fact, so prudishly concealing that his true shape is impossible to guess.

Film-producers, who make money out of films by a shrewd understanding of the dreams and desires of ordinary people, are concentrating more and more on costume films, though these are notoriously difficult and expensive to mount. They are concentrating on epic dramas of Tudor, Roman, or cowboy-American epochs, because the male film-stars, displaying their manly bodies to best advantage in the appropriate costumes, prove an irresistible lure to movie audiences. The women will rush to the cinema to see their film heroes dressed in something manlier than a lounge suit, and the men will rush to the cinema to dream-substitute themselves for the same film heroes.

It has not been the stagecoaches, the lurid battles with bogus Redskins, the tawdry fracas in the fake small-town bar-rooms, in themselves which have made Westerns such good box-office, nor even the spectacle of splendid horses endlessly galloping, though this last is a pleasure no one ever tires of. It has, to a great extent, been the more subtle spectacle of well-built men in dynamic action, wearing trousers of extreme tightness, set off by loin-emphasizing double belts; men crowned with hats of noble dimensions and shod with high-heeled decorative boots of extreme elegance.

This is why Europe and America, and much of the Eastern world too, are offered endless epics of film cowboys in skintight riding-chaps and sexy riding-boots, Hollywood heroes in Hollywood Tudor tights, and panoramic Roman orgies wherein, blown-out, concaved, and stereoscoped into godlike dimensions, current film idols display their manly arms, manly legs, and as much of their manly torsos as the censor will permit. This is sexually healthier for the film-fans, no doubt, than the murder orgies and horror films which are the usual alternative, and which, curiously, have much less difficulty in passing the censor, in whose opinion, it seems, sex is much more dangerous to public morals than murder.

That modern man is obliged by his present dress to uglify and conceal his charms must be a source of deep discontent to him, though it is not considered manly for him to admit it. Psychologists tell us that their male patients often reveal intense rancour against women, whom they accuse of supplanting them in every sphere, taking their jobs, earning their incomes, becoming financially independent of them, and wearing the fine feathers they themselves are denied. It does not do to underestimate the depressing effect of dreary dress in the formation of a thwarted outlook on life, because we know that the effect of dress on the wearer is of the most enormous importance. It has always been so since history began, and it is still so to-day.

Man dresses sadly because he is the victim of the machine society he has created, and in which he now finds himself but a poor cog. His sad dress in turn depresses him, and thus adds to his male humiliation. He does not know how to break out of this vicious circle, nor what he can do in order to feel like a man again, and in his despair he blames women.

But women would be delighted to see their menfolk differently dressed, for if their present dull dress is dispiriting for men to have to wear, how much more dispiriting is it for women to have to look at, to make allowances for, to tell themselves, against the evidence of their eyes, that inside the triste cocoon is really a man? It is certainly not women who have willed dull dress on men, though the decline of male dress follows the same line as the rise of female emancipation. Every woman knows that a world ruled by women would be no better than a world ruled by men. What is wanted, of course, is balance, a quality which seems almost impossible to achieve in our present lives.

Women cannot feel womanly unless men feel manly, and that so many drably dressed men do not feel manly to-day is a source of anguish no less painful to women than to men. Every woman in her senses prefers her menfolk to swagger, to display *panache*, even effrontery, rather than to subside into their present apathy. But what *panache* can a man possibly display when he is dressed in a city suit?

At every Highland gathering the splendid dress of the men dominates the scene, to every one's delight, and the women are happy to be eclipsed in so worthy a cause. At Westminster Abbey on the occasion of the Coronation of Queen Elizabeth II the notably gallant appearance of men in Court dress, male guests from the East in their sumptuous costumes, and African potentates in their dazzling regalia were highlights in the total spectacle, and it was obvious to the onlookers what dignity and pride these fine clothes bestowed on their wearers.

Those who assist at the Lord Chancellor's ceremonial induction of new 'silks' each year are fascinated to observe the cluster of nervous, middle-aged, and sometimes sagging barristers in dim everyday dress disappear into the dressing-room in the rear of Messrs Ede and Ravenscroft's establishment, presently to emerge, like butterflies metamorphosed from caterpillars, larger, taller, resplendent, magnificent, in flowing silken gowns worn over dignified eighteenth-century dress, and full-bottomed wigs. They are no longer anybody like everybody else. They have become somebody. And this new dignity their dress has given them has something curiously in common with the dignity of the fisherman's jersey and tarpaulin jacket and the working engineer's blue overalls with their strategically placed pockets. Like the Redskin's sartorial battle honours, the appropriate dress signifies that the wearer has earned the right to wear it by being master of his trade.

SANITARY WOOLLEN   SELF-ADJUSTING
SLEEPING PANTS   SOMATOMETER
Jaeger Catalogue, 1884   *Tailor and Cutter,* 1883

In our sartorially deprived male world we can only be thankful for these vestiges of former glamour and point out that Britons not only love dressing up, and are very good at it, but that they sorely need to dress up. No less than a successful actor a successful Q.C. needs the assurance of his distinguished dress to play his part impressively. Would not robes and gowns, it may be asked, add to the dignity of the American courts of justice, not to mention other countries where democratic ideals express themselves in not dressing up at all?

A democracy which is expressed by everybody dressing down is surely a spiritually impoverished democracy. A democracy which really revered the potentiality of the common man ought, on the contrary, to give every one a chance to dress up. Instead of the moral and artistic error of kings dressing like stockbrokers, how much pleasanter if all men dressed like kings. Nor is it likely that the tonic effect of such fine dress would soon wear off and men long for tedious garments again. All the experience of history points to the contrary.

But the situation to-day is even worse than it appears, for the dull dress of Western man is no longer confined to the West, but is spreading all over the world like a blight, and is even having an effect on women's dress as well.

The sartorial decline of Western man, which coincided with and was conditioned by the Industrial Revolution, accompanies the machines wherever they go, and to-day there is hardly a corner of the world where they do not penetrate. The enormous industrial expansion of the nineteenth century, involving the creation and administration of a vast British empire, made it inevitable that British dress should be slavishly copied, for the successful nation, in peace as in war, is always the one which is imitated. All over the world men of every race and colour have tried to adopt the garb of the machine-owning conqueror, of the successful modern merchant.

The unbecoming dress of the Victorian industrialist, gloomy, concealing, and stiff, has become the coveted garb of Indians, Africans, Asians, even of Oceanians. Top-hats, bowler hats, striped trousers, black jackets, the boring lounge suit, proliferate in East and West Africa, Malaya, Russia, even penetrating into China and the torrid zone of India, places where the climatic conditions and way of life are totally different and the native dress infinitely more manly and becoming, more suitable in every way.

Mulk Raj Anand, the Indian novelist, has related how as a little boy he was so impressed by the importance of the white sahibs in his country and the deference shown them that he made himself a white man's dress out of paper, carefully copying an advertisement in the sahibs' trade catalogue. It was this attitude of mind that Gandhi tried so hard to combat by decreeing a deliberate return to homespun Indian cotton as patriotic wear. He believed that Indian politicians and businessmen, no less than scholars and writers, could not throw themselves wholeheartedly into the struggle for

Indian independence while dressed like members of the British Stock Exchange.

As nationalist movements arise in one Asiatic country after another, so inevitably does this question of Western dress. Subject peoples begin their fight for independence by tearing off the garb of the conqueror and replacing it, if they can, by what was there before. But as this also brings up the problem of sartorial class strata the situation becomes an extremely complicated one. Eastern merchants, however patriotic, often prefer to dress like merchants of the West rather than demean themselves by dressing like peasants of their own country. High-ranking lawyers and leaders of commerce of the East, Asiatic royalty and their diplomatic service, now almost invariably wear Western dress. The great numbers of students who come to the West to study usually relinquish their native dress as soon as they arrive, if they have not done so already before they left their own countries.

Freya Stark reports a Baghdadi schoolteacher in Asia grumbling about European dress which he was wearing. "There is not an Arab who does not take refuge with Allah from the discomfort of your socks." Nevertheless he wore the socks, for though they chafed him they also raised his social status. Despite the strong emergence of Indian nationalism, many Indian barristers in India still go to court in a temperature of 110 degrees dressed in the heavy black jacket and airless striped woollen trousers of the English law courts. Even Russian peasants are demanding English woollen suits, though their own traditional padded or sheepskin jackets are warmer and suit their way of life better. In a recent comedy by the Soviet playwright Korneichuk a young tractor-driver interrupts an ideological lecture by the secretary of the Regional Party Committee to demand, "Will there be plenty of suits of navy-blue cheviot under Communism?"

Singapore's first Labour Government began with a world shock when Chief Minister David Marshall, the Singapore barrister, wore local instead of European dress for the inaugural session. Despite the tropical heat, the ardent nationalist sentiments of the Assembly, and Mr Marshall's polite behaviour, his open-necked bush shirt and white trousers caused a scandal. Angry letters flooded the local Press, asserting in the strongest terms that if Mr Marshall wished to uphold the dignity of Singapore nationalism and make clear to the world Singapore's freedom from white domination he must dress in the garb of Whitehall.

"As Chief Minister he should show more decorum," protested Y. B. Ong, in a letter to the *Singapore Times*. "How can we show respect to our rulers if they choose to dress like clowns?" Another correspondent, signing himself "Anti-Bush-shirt," wrote:

> Is it not possible for our newly elected Chief Minister to occasionally appear in public decently dressed? . . . Come, come, Mr Marshall, by all means dress how you like at home, but just because you are a member of the Labour front doesn't mean that you have to attend public functions dressed like a labourer.

To those of us who prefer to see beautiful clothes rather than ugly clothes — and beautiful clothes include the infinite varieties of dress different countries have evolved in the course of their history—the domination of the London city suit is dejecting. Worse still, in this perturbing rout of the beautiful, the suitable, and the individual by the ugly and the anonymous, is the fact that increasing numbers of women in the Western world to-day are abandoning their privilege of dressing with colour and variety, and copying their menfolk by shrouding themselves in black or dark grey.

The 'little black suit' is fast becoming a world uniform for women, especially those wealthy and celebrated women so assiduously copied by poorer women and the women of other countries. Though the cheaper dress-shops still show some bright colour, the expensive dress-shops go out of their way to insist on the snob value of black simplicity and to abandon colour and fantasy as vulgar. As every dressmaker knows, black may well be chic, just as any colour and any style may be chic, on a woman who has chic. Conversely, a woman who has no chic will certainly not acquire it by the mere act of putting on a little black suit.

It may well be that women too are feeling the hypnotic effect of industrialism, and wish to cast off their individualities in order to merge themselves in the colourless multitude. Women, however, have had to work in factories ever since there were any factories to work in, and they have acquired a long experience of combating machine mentality by their female intuition that it is wrong as much as by their innate hatred of regimentation. But the student of dress must recognize a tendency—and there is no doubt that to-day there is a strong tendency, especially among the educated middle class—for Western women to put on a plain dark suit in the morning and feel dressed for the day, and often for the evening as well. Is this a premonition of the brave new world of to-morrow?

Few men in the Western world will to-day admit that their dress is bad, whatever they may secretly think. Instead they immediately advance four reasons in favour of it as it is. These reasons are: first, to dress more brightly, they say, would look effeminate; second, dark colours, they say, do not show the dirt; third, their present dress, they say, is both functional and comfortable; fourth, anything different, they say, would be more costly.

Let us examine these reasons, or excuses, one by one.

Reason Number One: To dress more brightly would look Effeminate

Never, in the entire course of history, has brilliant and elaborate dress been a sign of unmanliness or homosexuality. There is, indeed, every evidence to the contrary. Sir Walter Raleigh, whose devotion to his wife and child is no less a matter of historic fact than his learning and seaman- ship, conducted his famous explorations in dress studded with precious stones and bedizened with lace, wearing tight corsets, and bombasted round the loins into the shape of a pumpkin. Such notable soldiers as Marlborough, Prince Rupert, and the Duke of Wellington delighted in flaunting the extremest modes of their dashing eras. Samuel Pepys, whose preoccupation with his wardrobe has proved such a godsend to dress his- torians, was certainly no pederast. On the contrary, they believed that brilliant and dashing dress helped them to keep up their military and social morale and to make a good impression on the opposite sex.

Pirates (hardly an effeminate profession) were notoriously addicted to brilliant colours and jewellery. Even the Puritans, who for so long (and, it must be admitted, not without some justice) have been blamed for the decline in the art of dress, did not condemn luxurious and gallant dress because of its homosexual associations. They condemned it because they considered it wanton and ungodly—quite another matter. And, compared to present-day male dress, the garb of the Puritans and the dress of the early Quakers appear extravagantly form-fitting and luxurious. So reason number one is hardly acceptable.

Indeed, the argument might well be pushed the other way. It is curious how fearful the Western world has become (England and America in particular) of any accusation of homosexuality. Is Western man in fact protesting too much? Men whose jobs are too heavy for women to tackle (navvies, dockers, and coalminers, for instance) are never afraid to brighten their dress with gay handkerchiefs and bright jerseys. Butchers (whose job is hardly one for a woman) love to wear fancy rings as they wield the heavy chopper. The tough nature of these employments gives them the right not to be suspect.

It is precisely the sedentary types—the clerks, insurance salesmen, accountants, for instance—who fear to invite the taunt of effeminacy, knowing only too well that their jobs are not essentially manly jobs, but can be, and often are, done by women. These are the men who therefore cling to dull, respectable dress. This does not make the dull, respectable dress manly, but merely shows that the wearer knows that his job is not a manly job.

Reason Number Two: Dark Colours do not show the Dirt

Of all futile reasons this is the least admissible. First of all it is not true. Dark colours show up dirt and dust just as much as, if not more than, light colours. Black is notoriously difficult to prevent looking dusty. In an era so hygiene-conscious as our own is it, then, men's intention to carry about with them on their clothes the accumulation of days and weeks and months of dirt? To-day there are cleaners and laundries everywhere, even in the poorest districts. Moreover, science has placed at man's disposal all manner of fascinating new materials which can be washed easily overnight and will be dry and in precisely the same shape in the morning. Men wear light shirts, and particularly white collars and cuffs, to-day in order that they can display their cleanliness. To be clean is no longer the privilege of a Regency dandy, but is within the means of the least well paid. Reason number two, then, can be dismissed.

Reason Number Three: Their Present Dress is both Comfortable and Functional

Do men really believe that their strait-jacket dress and very limited choice of colour is functional? That to be subdued to the point of extinction makes life easier for them? Grey, black, fawn, can be attractive colours, just as potatoes can be attractive fare, but if one were forced to subsist on nothing but potatoes, and those cooked exclusively *à l'anglaise*, how rapidly loathsome would they become. We can only describe men's choice of colour to-day for his suitings as an extraordinarily large range of fiddling subtleties, none of which can be distinguished from the others at very short range. Colour becomes colour only by contrast with other colours. If there are no other colours, then there is nothing.

The shape, the cut, from any æsthetic point of view is deplorable; from any functional point of view no better. The body of man is abruptly cut in two where the jacket ends, at the least interesting point, *pudeur* dictating the shrouding of the posterior and vital organs, but stopping short of sufficient length to give dignity. Then the legs—man's proudest assertion over the animal world, his noble ability to stand upright on his two legs—muffled into a grotesque semblance of the limbs of elephants, two uneasy monoliths. The crease in the trousers—a tacit acceptance of their ugliness—makes the situation even worse, for it necessitates the nervous fidget of trouser-hitching, every time the wearer sits down, in a vain attempt to preserve the crease.[1] The narrow hips and long legs of man are his chiefest

[1] Though Australian scientists have now perfected a method of putting a permanent crease into wool, Savile Row scorns such subterfuge, nor will it appeal to young Englishmen, who prefer trousers too tight to hold a crease.

beauties. How can he thus efface them and pretend that his life is thereby improved?

From the point of view of beauty, comfort, or function present-day neckties are hardly worth the trouble of putting on in the morning and taking off again at night. They are neither big enough to look romantic nor small enough to look elegant. All that the conventional necktie of to-day can do is to draw the boredom of the dress nearer to the face and decrease the appearance of height. Men's shoes to-day are too stiff and clumsy to be comfortable, if we may judge by the numbers of male patients at the numerous foot clinics. Men's socks, with their paraphernalia of suspenders or built-in garters, are undignified, if not ludicrous.

As to men's headgear, at the same time heavy, head-marking, and uncertain of itself, can any male hat worn to-day pretend to beauty or comfort, still less usefulness? The answer to this is surely the fact that so many younger men are to-day resolutely going about hatless—it may be both as a protest against discomfort and in order to express distrust of class distinctions, which the hat once proclaimed.

Worst item of all, in man's penitential sartorial catalogue, is the universal raincoat—culminating depravity of colourless ennui and shapelessness. Surely man can protect himself from the rain more æsthetically than this? How has he done so the last several thousand years?

Men assure women that the stiff city collar is much more comfortable than it looks. We must hope for their sakes that it may be so. It remains, nevertheless, icy in winter and galling in summer. If it is so easy to wear, why are men increasingly adopting the soft collar?

Male underwear is such that most men are embarrassed to be seen therein even by their own wives—certainly in the early days of marriage, when they still wish to look their best. It is worth noting that the better English boarding-schools for boys to-day do not include undervests as a necessity in their school clothes list.

The jacket of the lounge suit is heavy and signally inflexible. In America and on the Continent it is still worse—too big and too square for the trousers, as though the wearer were trying to blow himself out like a frog. The elephant-leg trousers are perhaps the least comfortable, as well as the least æsthetic, of all garments yet devised to cover man's nakedness. In winter the wind pierces the material and blows icy draughts up the legs from the ankles. In hot weather the trousers are airless and clammy. The mystic crease, as jealously guarded as a Hindu caste-mark, needs more attention than a woman's complexion—and, despite the use of a trouserpress by night and continually hitching during the day, never really stays in.

For more than a century artists have despaired because trousers are un-rewarding to paint and heartbreaking to sculpt—so much do they dis-figure the male body. One Victorian sculptor—and he badly needed the money the commission would have brought him—went so far as to refuse the commission if his client insisted on contemporary dress. A gallant but hopeless gesture. One cannot carve the man of our times in a Roman toga, or naked, as Napoleon's sculptor did. Or, "for the sake of beauty and truth," clap a contemporary head on some one else's naked body, as did Pigalle, the sculptor of Voltaire, much to the indignation of that stormy petrel, who protested bitterly against thus being depicted *en singe* instead of in full-bottomed wig and satin breeches. The curious statue is still preserved, however, in the French Academy, a tribute to Voltaire from all the writers and savants of his day, his toothless old head looking curiously Presbyterian above the withered body of an old sailor who had been enlisted as the model for the rest of the statue. "Ni beau ni vrai," was Voltaire's outraged comment. So much for stone trousers. Sculptors to-day are just as baffled by this problem.

To dress himself each morning a man to-day has to fasten no less than thirty-one buttons, if we include overcoat and gloves. Is the result achieved worth so much time and effort?

Reason Number Four: Anything Different would be more Costly

This is perhaps the greatest illusion of all. Outfitters have to live, and they will provide whatever clothes their clients will pay for, from the cheapest to the dearest clothes. What modern man needs to ask himself to-day is just what he *is* paying for. Camouflage? Snobbery? He is pay-ing a lot for them.

A well-dressed Englishman, turned out to the best ability of the top-rank English tailors, with a wardrobe extensive enough to meet their approval, may spend upwards of £1000 a year on his clothes, including hats, hand-made underwear and shirts, hand-made shoes, and such abso-lutely inconspicuous but costly jewellery as convention to-day permits in good society. At the other end of the social scale, the poorest section of the male community buys its clothes second-hand, or buys odd items of surplus war uniform, or pays for its new clothes on the instalment plan. None of these clothes are cheap, and there are to-day thousands of Englishmen and Americans who have never in all their lives owned a complete suit, but have only known odd jackets and trousers, which were never intended to match, being bought item by item according to which item was most desperately needed. But none of them, from the point of view of service or appearance, can be called economical.

From the æsthetic point of view there is no doubt at all that a poor fisherman in a thick knitted jersey and patched cotton trousers looks more manly than the most perfectly tailored product of Savile Row, and there is more essential male dignity even in the crude dress of working miners. But dignity and manliness are beside the point. The creation of Savile Row is not intended to make its wearer look like a man, but like a gentleman. In our present world both gent and spiv pay more than they can afford—not to dress becomingly, but to dress in a way they consider looks socially superior. It is this snobbery which boosts the price of men's dress to-day. There is no reason to suppose that different dress would be more costly.

And now let us take a look at the male dress which has been the envy of the world for the last century and a half, that miracle of sartorial understatement, the Savile Row suit.

ENGLISH SHIRT EMBROIDERY, 1630
Red silk on linen
Victoria and Albert Museum

CHAPTER TWO

THE SAVILE ROW SUIT

A period when fashion has placed at the disposal of the tailor the most hideous material that could possibly tax his art. . . . The coat may have a long tail or a short tail, a high collar or a low collar, but it will always be an ugly garment. The modern hat may be spread out at the top, or narrowed, whilst the brim may be turned up or turned down, made a little wider or a little more narrow. Still it is inconceivably hideous.

CAPTAIN GRONOW, *Memoirs* (1860)

DISCRIMINATING Americans, too busy to come to London to be fitted, still prefer to leave their measurements with their London tailors, who will make their clothes for them in their London workrooms and dispatch them to their American clients by air without the American clients even putting in an appearance. This is confidence indeed. For America to-day has herself attracted some of the most skilful tailors in the world, emigrated from England by the temptation of fabulous wages and perhaps the seductions of a more democratic atmosphere. But the products of these top-rank American tailors are still more expensive than those of the top-rank English tailors. And it may be that the English *cachet* still confers its magic.

In the seventeenth and eighteenth centuries English noblemen regarded France as the true arbiter of male dress. The reason England became the home of the best tailoring in the nineteenth century was because of her increasing industrial power and wealth. Since money has become all-important in our society to-day, more important than social rank, art, or virtue, the English ideal has come to be symbolized by the successful stockbroker or company promoter, on whom the finest tailors of Savile Row now lavish their skill and experience.

The bowler hat and rolled umbrella, the exquisitely prosaic city suit, express to perfection the man whose mission in life is to make money. The task of Savile Row is to create this uniform. And how supremely well Savile Row does this. If endless patience, long experience, and perfect co-ordination sufficed to produce a work of art, then the Savile Row suit would indeed be a work of art.

But, the pursuit of money being spiritually negative, the dress of the

pursuer cannot but express negation, and the dress the English city man
has evolved is therefore essentially lifeless and can never be dynamic. It is
a protective colouring suitable for the financial jungle. Costly sobriety is
its hallmark: costly to show that he is financially successful and can afford
to have his suit made in Savile Row, sober to show that he is respectable.

The irony is that English tailors have learned the science of cutting
better than any other tailors in history, precisely at an artistically sterile
period which (by the cramping confines of modern dress) prevents them
from exercising their knowledge to any purpose. Wit, *panache*, sentiment,
melancholy, audacity, bombast—how much can be expressed with a
flourish of the scissors. But our fine tailors may not flourish their scissors.
They may run the gamut only from A to B.

The tailors of the eighteenth century, who made such breathtaking
clothes for men, did not know how to cut. They were clumsy amateurs
compared to the contemporary magicians of Savile Row. But they were
not afraid of brilliant colour, varied texture, and rich embroidery, any
more than were their clients. To-day taste in male dress has degenerated
into restraint and restraint only. The craft has become entirely divorced
from the art, and Savile Row leads the tailoring of the Western world in
expending infinite trouble, skill, and expense on the confection of a style
of dress in which desiccation is deified.

Let us examine this infinite trouble and skill. I have chosen the firm of
Henry Poole as representative of the small class of superlative English
tailors whose renown is world-wide. Their London establishment is
large, impressive in an extremely quiet manner, and of cathedral solemn-
ity. People there speak in hushed voices.

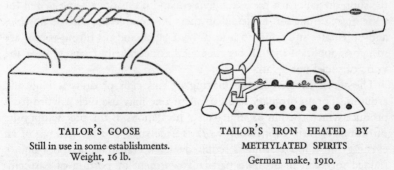

TAILOR'S GOOSE
Still in use in some establishments.
Weight, 16 lb.

TAILOR'S IRON HEATED BY
METHYLATED SPIRITS
German make, 1910.

The large entrance hall is lined with gilt-framed testimonials from past
and present Royalties and Ambassadors and noblemen of all countries,
for the firm of Henry Poole has been celebrated for 150 years. This firm
was Court Tailor to her Majesty Queen Victoria, and the liveries of her

servants, which had to be as impeccable as the dress of their sovereign, were always made here.

Not a few of the thrones whose kings were dressed by Henry Poole in the past are no longer in existence. Tsars, Kaisers, Shahs, and Emperors have given place to presidents, and their fading testimonials exhale the nostalgia of a closed chapter of history. Sturdily, however, stands the British throne, and Queen Victoria's licence reads thus:

To hold, exercise, and enjoy the said place, together with all rights, profits, privileges, and advantages thereunto belonging. Given under my hand and seal the 11th day of March 1869 in the 32nd year of Her Majesty's reign.

Here is a testimonial from the Shah of Persia, dated 1906:

By Appointment: Fournisseur to S. A. Le Khédive
Whereas Mr Howard Gurdey, trading as Henry Poole, who are the most famous tailors in England, has for many years past received orders from the Imperial Legation in London, always exercising the greatest skill and devoting the most earnest attention to their execution, the merits of the said Mr Gurdey having been brought to the notice of his Imperial Majesty the Shah, it has graciously pleased his Majesty to commend this warrant, by virtue of which Mr Gurdey receives the Honour and Right of styling his firm from this date as Court Tailors by Special Appointment to his Imperial Majesty the Shah of Persia. *6th day of the month of Ramadan 1324.*

Here to-day, in Henry Poole's stately ateliers, contemporary English male dress is created, with all its complicated ritual processes, according to the gospel of George Brummell. Henry Poole is renowned to-day as the supreme tailor for the older gentleman, his creations being prized for their quiet distinction no less than their impeccable fit. Asiatic notables and potentates still come to him to be garbed, and his fitting-rooms are still cosmopolitan, though his clientele has necessarily changed over the years of social upheavals.

The work entailed in the making of this class of dress is long and arduous. For an ordinary lounge suit (if one may use such a word for a product which, within its strait-jacket limitations, is the precise opposite of ordinary) forty-four hours' work is necessary. For the making of an evening suit a longer time is required. Each craftsman here is a highly trained specialist in his own particular garment or portion of garment. The waistcoat, the jacket, the trousers, are each entrusted to none but the confident and experienced hands of master tailors.

The process begins when the customer calls by special appointment to discuss the suit he proposes to order. A middle-aged salesman, with the manners and the appearance of a courtier of the Court of St James's, helps the customer to choose the cloth for his suit. This is a most delicate process, involving the careful balancing of an infinity of considerations in the selection of one out of a multitude of varieties of only microscopically dissimilar patterns and materials, all extremely subdued in pattern and texture. It is, indeed, only by means of the refinement of subtlety that the English gentleman may to-day express himself sartorially, if at all. If the resulting dress should prove too subtle to register with ordinary people, so much the worse for them. Like the Emperor's new clothes, it should not be beyond the capacity to appreciate of other gentlemen who wear Savile Row suits.

The cloth being chosen for the suit, the cutter then takes the customer's measurements. The cutter is the key man in top-class tailoring, where every craftsman is a master of his craft. In an establishment such as this he earns a salary of at least £1000.

A paper pattern is now mapped out and cut from the cutter's measurements. This paper pattern will be filed and kept for twenty years or more, to be brought out when required and carefully adapted to the changing measurements brought about by the passage of time. Henry Poole's customers, however, are expected to exercise gastronomical restraint, so that their vital statistics should not deteriorate—or, at least, not deteriorate much—for this august firm would never think of exposing themselves to the vulgarity of aping youthfulness. What they do supremely well is to dress the older gentleman with the perfection of conventional distinction, for in the financial-social circles for which they cater it is the older men who have attained distinction.

The trimmer now takes over from the cutter. The trimmer's task is to be responsible for linings, buttons, canvas, twist, the horsehair which shapes the breast of the coat and the padding which gives shape to the shoulders. His also is the responsibility for the sewings for the waistcoat and trousers and the important jigger button. A written ticket has already been compiled to instruct him in the particular requirements for this particular suit. A special buttonhole sewn nearer to the edge of the lapel to accommodate the Légion d'Honneur, for instance, is a not infrequent consideration at Henry Poole's.

The élite, or those who consider themselves so, who have their clothes made at Poole's, to an extremely discreet point set the fashions in high circles—that is to say, they launch the minuscule variations on the same theme, which is as far as English tailoring allows itself to go to-day. Therefore the firm is not averse to such infinitesimal adaptations of the classic style as may be desired by gentleman who really are sure enough of themselves to know what they are about. Every suit turned out by Poole's, though this may hardly be perceptible to the untrained eye, is in point of fact an entirely new and individual creation.

The cutter now gives the craftsmen who will assemble the suit minute instructions for their task. No less than three fittings are usually required of the customer, each fitting lasting as a rule about fifteen minutes. Making a suit in this class has something in common with painting an expensive portrait, in that the result must fit perfectly and bring out the best points of the sitter, without obvious flattery. It must be at the same time highly individual and perfectly well-bred—so well-bred that it will pass unnoticed, except to the trained eye.

The education and training of tailors for this high-class work is long and difficult. Five years' apprenticeship is required for a coat-maker, and Poole's prefer to train their own men. To qualify as a cutter seven or eight years' apprenticeship is necessary, and the cutter must first qualify as coat-maker before graduating to the greater responsibilities of the scissors. No cutter, however gifted and diligent, would ever be considered under the age of at least thirty, because he could not have had enough experience of his craft. Every cutter is aided by an assistant cutter known as a 'striker.'

The work of the Savile Row cutter is, of course, the key to fine tailoring, for it is his skill which makes it possible to suggest, and within permitted limits even to produce, the illusion of the distinguished male

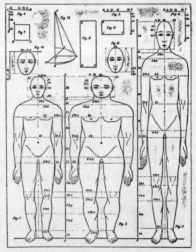

"ANTHROPOMETRY, OR THE MEASURE-
MENT OF MAN"
Tailor and Cutter, 1883

MANLY (NOT GENTLEMANLY) DRESS

GARIBALDI
1860

CZECH PEASANT
Contemporary.

LONDON COSTERS
Plaistow, 1946.

THE ENGLISH GENT

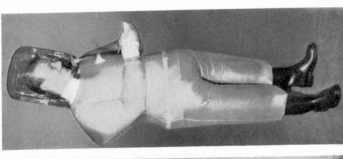

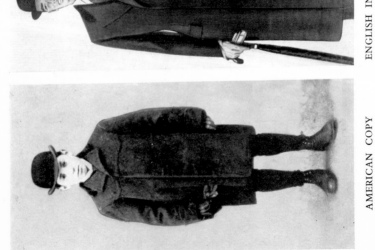

AMERICAN COPY
Harpo Marx, aged fourteen.

ENGLISH INTERPRETATION
Moss Bros dress-hire
advertisement.

NEW VERSION
Teddy-boy, 1954.
Hulton Picture Library

NUCLEAR MODEL
Protective dress for
atom worker.
By courtesy of the B.B.C.

elegance the customer pays for. What is provided by nature he can ever so slightly enhance; what nature has failed to provide he can ever so slightly supply; and what nature has provided too much of he can ever so slightly delete. These adjustments, of course, must be made within the most rigid limitations of austere good taste and muted discretion.

No client of Poole's is believed to practise any kind of waist-suppression by belt or corset. Restraint at table and careful exercise alone are supposed to aid the task of the cutter in producing the illusion of well-preserved slenderness. Poole's, moreover, are of the opinion that even were waist-suppression by corset or belt attempted it would do no good at all, but merely push up the diaphragm and so make matters worse, for a pouter-pigeon breast would be in deplorably bad taste to-day. They prefer the type of customer who is naturally tall and slender and who naturally carries himself elegantly, but their very long experience of clients of other races and less athletic dispositions has given them the delicate skill necessary to circumvent nature in a gentlemanly way when nature has not proved too kind.

What is the price of the exquisite product resulting from so much effort and combination of skills and experience? In the autumn of 1957 Poole's prices, including purchase tax, were as follows:

For a lounge suit	£49 16s. 0d.
For a dining-suit	£58 2s. 0d.
For an evening suit	£61 4s. 3d.
For a winter overcoat	£48 15s. 9d.
For a summer overcoat	£44 12s. 0d.

Diplomatic dress costs £130 to £140, and it is a reflection on our increasingly unceremonious times that Court dress is no longer being ordered. This does not mean that it is not sometimes hired elsewhere, though such a possibility is never even mentioned at Poole's.

Though changes in good-class male dress over the years seem almost negligible, changes there have been. Men's clothes are less tight-fitting on the whole than they were twenty years ago, the tendency towards looseness having started after the 1914 War when officers returning to civilian life wished to feel more at ease. More recent tendencies have been towards a looser jacket, which fashion, having been started in expensive tailoring, was immediately taken up and grossly exaggerated by the cheap tailors and consequently at once abandoned by the expensive tailors.

To-day men dressed by Savile Row may allow themselves only the very faintest Edwardian tendency in their dress, and this must be slight indeed, for the top tailors must by some means contrive to keep above the

B

possibility of being aped by inferior tailors. Subtlety is their only armour against invasion from below.

The social upstart cannot to-day be kept out by sumptuary law nor publicly rebuked for his pretensions, as he sometimes was a century ago. All the top tailors can do to-day is to hope to lock him out by the self-denial of sartorial expensive sobriety, unless, as nowadays may happen, he is rich enough to patronize the top tailors himself. "In a mercantile country like England," warns a social guide-book published in 1830 under the title of *Hints on Etiquette*,

> people are continually rising in the world. Shopkeepers become merchants and mechanics manufacturers. With the possession of wealth they acquire a taste for the luxuries of life, expensive furniture and gorgeous plate; also numberless superfluities with the use of which they are imperfectly acquainted. Such persons are often painfully reminded that wealth alone is insufficient to protect them from the mortifications a limited acquaintance with society will entail upon the ambitious.

"Gorgeous plate" and "numberless superfluities" suggest less the aristocrat than the already arrived *nouveau riche* trying to keep out the next wave of social claimants from below. To-day the power of wealth alone is much greater than it was, and hardly any social circles are proof against money if claimants can boast money in sufficiently large amounts. Certainly Savile Row is happy to welcome the millionaire to its clientele, and to turn him into a gentleman by dressing him according to its famous formula of sedate propriety.

Poole's are resolutely opposed to the introduction of any colour or dash whatsoever into male dress, and earnestly dissuade their customers from attempting the slightest gaiety, for instance, even in their waistcoats, a fashion they are content to leave to commoners with no head for the arid heights of first-class tailoring. The utmost Poole's will consider in the way of colours for waistcoats is dark green, and possibly beige. Further than this they refuse to go.

Poole's have equally firm views about evening wear. Tails—and Poole's cater for the élite class who still attend social functions where tails are *de rigueur*—must reach to the knees, and none but the severest cut is tolerated. Poole's are of the strong opinion that nothing is so distinguished for the evening as black and white, or provides so good a foil to the bright hues of the evening dresses of the ladies.

Here, however, it may not be inopportune to point out that the smartest ladies to-day are also of the opinion that black and white are the most distinguished colours for the evening, and they also tend to confine themselves to one or the other. Thus they are in no position to take advantage of the good foil their escort offers them, being good foils themselves. Our great balls, in fact, are becoming increasingly magpie in hue, if not dead black, and colour retreats rapidly from the only social occasions left to display it.

For hours of male relaxation at home Poole's have no objection to the wearing of velveteen smoking-jackets, provided they are of the finest possible quality in the most sombre colours. Dark blue, dark green, or deep maroon are permissible, though they prefer black. Silk facings on these smoking-jackets are the one aspect of the disastrous (from their standpoint) Edwardian revival not so far taken up and vulgarized by the cheap tailors, and therefore still possible for the best tailors to offer.

Evening waistcoats are more enterprising, being now made like a bib, slipping over the head in the fashion of a halter, thus ensuring cooler wear and a better fit. This break with tradition may be ascribed to the fact that the clients of the cheap tailors rarely demand tails, and there is less chance of the good tailors being copied in this respect.

The average wardrobe of the well-dressed man, according to the firm of Henry Poole, should contain at least fifteen suits, including two for evening wear. Nothing less than twenty suits would be proper to be truly well-dressed, and no suit should ever be worn more than three years if the wearer wishes to keep his sartorial reputation untarnished.

The economic position to-day of those Englishmen who care to uphold such gentlemanly standards of sartorial elegance is unfortunately not too promising. Money is passing into different hands, and men rich enough to have their clothes made in Savile Row are to-day rarely the type to be interested in this aspect of the art of living. To-day no less than 60 per cent. of Poole's business is export trade, to Spain, South America, North America, and the Continent.

Now let us look at a different but no less distinguished tailoring establishment. Whitley's, an old and famous firm of tailors who cater for the top ranks of the younger men about town, are also advisers to the Men's Fashion Council, which introduces new fashions for gentlemen, an extremely delicate and tricky business to-day. Whitley's used to dress the Duke of Windsor when he was Prince of Wales, and greatly miss his presence to-day in English tailoring, for his immense popularity and debonair figure made him an admirable fashion-setter.

Whitley's clients include several film-stars, among them Errol Flynn, whose proportions they consider pretty well perfect (vital statistics: chest, 44 inches; waist, 25 inches; seat, 42 inches) for a well-exercised man in his forties. This firm favours squared, but not too squared, shoulders, nothing to excess. Even for the younger man with legitimate pretensions to dandyism the suggestion of the illusion must suffice.

Whitley's is the firm which was instrumental in introducing the Edwardian waistcoat, an innovation whose resounding success (and rapid vulgarization by the cheaper shops) obliged them to drop it themselves from their own repertoire. This awkward impasse has made them decide that the best and only way to keep British tailoring — that is, good tailoring as distinct from mass-production — at the top of the sartorial tree is to keep it so conservative and costly that imitators will be discouraged, because the sobriety and subtlety of the best English tailoring cannot be cheaply copied. Moreover, the spivs, whose adherence immediately wrecks an interesting new fashion, are fortunately not interested in inconspicuous dress.

Quality and discretion cannot, indeed, be imitated. They are the last privileges left to the English gentleman or to the South American millionaire who has his suits made in Savile Row in order to try to look like one. The trouble to-day is that increasing numbers of gentlemen who ought to be dressed by Savile Row are becoming less interested in what they wear, so that soon it will be only South American millionaires who dress like English gentlemen. English social barriers are rocking. There are few royal families and emperors and scions of noble houses left in the world for Savile Row to dress.

Whitley's, in pursuance of their policy of expensive sobriety, use only the very best and most costly materials, such as pure vicuña wool which costs at least £30 a yard. (It may be said that few fashionable ladies wear materials which cost more, or, indeed, so much.) Whitley's do not insist on black for evening wear, but venture into dark blue, which, they claim, looks richly black by artificial light. The usual evening dress they make for their customers is dark blue barathea, and they find that tails are out of favour with the younger men, who regard them as faintly *démodé*.

As leaders of the Men's Fashion Council Whitley's are well known for their experiments, within the narrow limits permitted, in designing new styles which they hope will prove impossible to copy cheaply. The most daring of recent attempts is a coloured dining-jacket, unchanged in silhouette, of maroon vicuña with heavy satin facings. Hardly what could be called revolutionary, but what would be the use of producing something truly novel only to have it delightedly taken up and popularized by the cheap tailors and thus to court another obligatory renunciation of a good idea, as with the ill-fated Edwardian waistcoat? A top London tailor to-day dare not be popular. He must remain exclusive or go out of business.

Thus Whitley's make an exclusive and magnificent evening coat, absolutely plain and simple in design, of black super-cashmere, which costs about £100 or more. They also make a few superb black evening cloaks, lined with white or crimson satin. But these beautiful garments seem out of step with the upper-class young dandy of to-day, whose liking for an Edwardian flavour in his dress does not seem to extend to cloaks, and these cloaks are almost never asked for.

It must be noted that this firm, in common with other top-ranking English tailors, are finding it increasingly difficult to engage staff with the high qualifications they require. Old, experienced hands are dying off, and new apprentices are not entering the trade. For it is a *de luxe* trade,

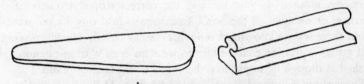

TAILOR'S KNEE IRONING-BOARDS
The skill in top tailoring lies in the hands. The tools are extremely simple.

which appears to young people deciding on a career not to have much future. In the past the prestige of English tailoring attracted apprentices from Sweden, Italy, Holland, and Germany, besides plenty of English youths. But to-day there are many more lucrative and apparently steadier and less seasonal professions with brighter prospects, and which do not require so long and arduous an apprenticeship.

Before 1914 good-class tailoring was notorious for its bad working conditions, and, though this is now different (and the best English firms to-day pay 25 per cent. more than the official trade-union rate for the job in order to attract the most skilled workmen), the bad odour still lingers. Eighteen pounds a week and upward for a working tailor, £1000 to £1500 a year and upward for a cutter, may seem good pay; but other industries to-day offer more enticing conditions and better prospects, and in this increasingly mass-produced age expert tailors are on the decline, and will do everything they can to keep their own sons out of the trade, though they themselves are proud of their own skill.

Cutters with seven years' intensive apprenticeship are becoming absorbed by the big multi-tailors, and learning to adapt their subtle personal skill to monster cutting-machines which spit out millions of quick clothes for the masses. Even their occupational diseases are changing. Their muscular cramps of former days are giving way to wrenched spinal discs due to the different motions they employ for their new work.

Mass-production of English male dress, though the exact opposite of the Savile Row suit, nevertheless still bases itself on the Savile Row ideal, for snobbery and conservatism seem inextricably bound up with Englishmen's clothes, no matter in what social circles they are worn. Indeed, it is to-day particularly that section of the community which in England works with its hands which has become interested in dressing in the grand manner, and it may well be that the ideals of Savile Row will finally be upheld only by a determined effort by manual labourers not to let them die.

I was recently at a public reception, for instance, where the speech of the evening (an extremely witty speech, if lacking in grammar and delivered in a richly Cockney accent) was given by a working docker who was impeccably dressed in admirably fitting black coat, stiff collar, perfectly adjusted discreet tie, and the correct striped trousers of the barrister or member of the Stock Exchange. Until this docker actually spoke there was no knowing from what class he hailed. His fine physique and genial expression enabled him to wear his dress with distinction. He looked as though he might have belonged to the Guards' Club.

Similarly to-day the dress of Tory and Labour M.P.'s is identical, with the tendency to dandyism often coming from the Labour rather than the Tory side of the House.

The new lords of the new Western society which is now emerging are the famous technologists and atom scientists and inventors of synthetic materials and wonder machines. These men are notoriously poor dressers. They are interested neither in displaying the staid *chefs d'œuvre* perfected by 150 years of English tailoring skill nor in creating an artistic new male dress altogether — which would be more in keeping with the new age they are busy preparing.

Now is the moment when these scientists should begin to work together with artists to create, not merely new materials and techniques, but beautiful new styles of dress for men. For "Orlon," "Dacron," "Acrilon," "Terylene," and all the amalgams of new synthetic materials, to be used alone or in combination with present materials, now being invented, and others still to be invented, may well change men's dress altogether. Artificial heating may replace wool. Sewing may be replaced by casting or moulding in ready-made shapes, and it is not impossible that Western man may presently find himself covered (he will not be "dressed" according to our present meaning of the word "dressed") with no-crease, non-iron compounds never before seen on this earth. There is no reason why such new dress should not be becoming to man if the artists are brought in to design it, for there is potential beauty in everything except crass imitation and pretentiousness.

However, man is still suspicious and conservative when his dress is in question, and it is likely that his future dress of different materials will go through the unpleasant process of copying his dress of to-day, just as early linoleum imitated parquet and Turkey carpets. What we shall soon see, no doubt, will be an imitation of the Savile Row suit moulded complete like a jelly, and corduroy, now renounced as a class stigma by manual workers and adopted instead by sportsmen and sculptors, synthetically cast and dust-proof, rust-proof, non-tear, and unstainable.

In this period of ours, a period of stress and social change, any English gatherings of any consequence, from a provincial wedding to the great ceremonies of Court and State, are still notable for the numbers of meticulously dressed men apparently turned out by Savile Row. With English income-tax what it is, and the cost of good tailoring what it is, how can these men afford to dress as they do?

The secret is that most of these expensive clothes are quite simply hired for the occasion. From the correct morning dress of the provincial bridegroom (not to speak of the elegant white satin wedding-dress of his bride) to the full panoply of Court ceremonial dress, sword, orders, and all, every item can be hired for the occasion, and most of them are.

Peers of the realm, whose lineage is longer than their entailed stately avenues, sit patiently in the reception-rooms of Messrs Moss Bros, together with their fellow-peers, waiting to be fitted for their hired crimson mantles and gold and velvet coronets, before each State opening of Parliament. Goodwood sparkles and shimmers with hired top-hats and silver-mounted sticks which do not belong to those who carry them except for just this one day. In the world of sport there is a lively trade in hired hunting pink. Even ski-suits can now be hired. Every one thinks it all rather a joke, and every one does it.

Englishmen like to believe that it all began with the 1939 War, wherein moth waged so violent a destructive private war on such ceremonial clothes as the enemy did not directly destroy that there was nothing left to wear afterwards. The War over, clothing coupons prevented the purchase of all but the most elementary sartorial necessities; thus hiring was devised in order to solve the problem without loss of face.

This plausible explanation, however, is not altogether true. The hiring of ceremonial dress was already doing a pretty brisk trade well before 1939. Most impecunious young barristers were accustomed to hire morning dress and grey top-hat for the famous garden parties of the Inns of Court long before the Second World War. They have continued to do so, and have been followed by thousands of others, for all occasions which need ceremonial costly dress. The Buckingham Palace garden parties, for instance, are enabled to present their impeccable sartorial appearance largely because 90 per cent. of the males present, if not more, hire their fine dress.

The English are indeed snobs. They are, however, logical snobs. This hiring of correct dress is an excellent example of the English genius for compromise. Is it not better to hire than to dress all wrong? What Englishman would dare spoil the general appearance of a grand occasion by unsuitable dress? Informality of attire is never the Englishman's way out of a sartorial dilemma. And herein lies an important clue to our national character and, it may be, some hope for the future of male dress.

The advantages of hiring are many. The clothes are well tailored, and they can afford to be, for trade is brisk. There is a size to fit every applicant. The delightful accessories of proper gloves, correct cane, suitable tie, and so on are not lacking. A gardenia can be arranged. The clothes are cleaned after each hiring. Above all, the atmosphere in the hiring saloons is as respectful and soothing as in Savile Row. The hiring firm, indeed, has taken on the psychological functions of the best private valet. *Amour-propre* is cleverly saved, and the show goes on.

CHAPTER THREE

UNSPOILED MAN

Ces hideux sauvages, ces êtres rebutés, ils sont par bien des points supérieurs au prolétariat abîmé de nos grandes villes. Ils savent chanter, danser, rêver. Ils ont des langues magnifiques. Ils ont, nous affirme notre auteur, de grands poètes.

PAUL CLAUDEL, in the Preface to Father André Dupeyrat's *21 ans chez les Papous* (1952)

DESPITE Savile Row, man is not born with sober and restrained tastes. Like any magpie or mackerel, he has an inborn craving for colour and glitter, and even anthropoid apes show a distinct aversion to the colour black. It has been our industrial civilization, grafted on to a puritanical fear of pleasure, which has suppressed the Englishman's perfectly natural instinct for colour and gaiety, and at a terrible cost.

If we want to learn how man dressed before he was corrupted by the joyless worship of money we must seek out savage communities where the white man has not yet set his destructive mark, and peasant communities not yet engulfed by industrialization.

In primitive man art is associated with his gods, his personal valour, every detail of his domestic and his tribal life. The machine, and the pursuit of money which has turned the machine into man's enemy, are alike unknown to him, and he is bubbling with creation. He has no separate word for art because he creates it all the time in his everyday life and it is part of him.

Savages to whom the use of metal, of the wheel even, are unknown delight in creating fantastic and beautifully made objects of the most intractable materials, and it takes some time before contact with machine civilization destroys their innate instinct to please the eye and the soul by the work of their hands. They sing, they dance, they make patterns, as naturally as they breathe, and they do so at all times and every day of their lives.

Primitive man uses whatever he finds in nature to weave, carve, embroider, and make patterns, and these he does because they please him, not to make money. Once money is introduced into his consciousness his

41

conception of life changes and his own arts begin to deteriorate. We smile to-day at Rousseau's romanticized conception of the noble savage, but there is no doubt that in music, in movement, and in applied art the savage has taught much to civilized man, who has now been civilized out of his own inheritance in the arts.

It is interesting that the eighteenth century, which in its early part at least, had more respect for the arts than the industrialized nineteenth century, was fascinated by the art of primitive men, whereas the nineteenth century was chiefly interested in blotting it out — stopping native dancing, abolishing their heathen idols, and destroying their barbaric handwork. Thus nineteenth-century Britain filled its tradesman's sitting-rooms with Indian brasses and ivories and African carvings (usually draped for decency) as so much curious loot. It is only now in the twentieth century that primitive art is being appreciated for itself, a more enlightened opinion by no means shared, it must be confessed, by all white men, though ethnologists and artists have led the new appraisal. Since the early nineteen-twenties, when African carved wooden masks first began to appear on the walls of cultured Bloomsbury and Montparnasse flats, there has been no looking back. Only to-day such carvings are becoming increasingly difficult to procure, as Africans, under white influence, cease to desire to express themselves in carving.

It is a chastening experience to contemplate, in the anthropological museums of our great Western cities, the superbly decorated objects wrought by humble peoples, whose daily lives are frequently a grinding struggle to exact the barest subsistence from unsubdued and often hostile nature. The eye is entranced by big and little masterpieces, at the same time ingenious and ingenuous, painstakingly wrought in wood, bone, stone, fishbone, tree-bark, shells, feathers, spiders' silk, seeds, beetles, the vertebræ of snakes, fur, hide, quills, hair, the scales of fish, and the claws of animals, even the cast-away scraps from the white man's industrial plenty, such as safety-pins, bits of telephone wire, and beer-bottle tops. Strung together on animal sinew, glued with bison-bone adhesive, adorned with brilliant and subtle colours laboriously scraped from the earth, pounded out of rock, squeezed from wild berries, and boiled down from flowers, these objects display, each of them, a fertility of invention strictly controlled by skilled craftsmanship and informed with the understanding which denotes the true artist.

Missionaries may deplore the savage for his lack of Christianity, colonists may deplore his listlessness as white man's employee, politicians may deplore the un-European workings of his un-European mind, but artists, who meet him on common ground, have nothing but admiration for the creations of his hands. For in primitive man, as in uncorrupted children,

WEST AFRICAN SCEPTRES OF
POWER

Steel-headed. Used by kings and chiefs
(Dahomey). The same respect must be
paid to these sceptres as to the sovereign.

Musée de l'Homme, Paris

WEST COUNTRY BRASS
STAFF–HEADS
(FRIENDLY SOCIETY)

English, nineteenth century.
*Museum of English Rural Life,
Reading*

perception, imagination, and memory are at their keenest, each person is an artist, every design has meaning, and values have not yet become debased into prices. Every activity of his daily life must be embellished, and time and trouble taken over the least as over the greatest object in daily use. Religion gives meaning to everything and shapes and sharpens every pattern. In its own right it all makes sense.

Primitive man has more frequent and more elaborate religious ceremonial than we have, every action in his life being given meaning by his gods. For him decoration, godliness, pattern, and piety are inextricable. He is much nearer and in more direct contact with Nature, and, though he greatly fears her power, he also loves and understands her moods and her beauty more than we do. Living in closer communion with the birds and beasts and insects, he contrives garments and ornaments for himself from their hides, scales, and feathers, believing that the powers of the creatures with which he dresses himself will enter into him. Thus primitive dress is full of meaning and full of magic. But he who would win the right to the finest and most powerful dress must show himself worthy by deeds of valour to deserve it.

Professor Raymond Firth has recounted to me how, revisiting Polynesian Tikopea, where twenty years previously he had pursued his anthropological studies, he decided to take with him a quantity of bead necklaces as gifts for his old Polynesian friends, though hardly hopeful, after so long an intervention of white influence, that these islanders would still care for baubles. He was wrong. The beads were seized upon with cries of joy. In the sharing out Professor Firth observed that the brightest and largest beads were allotted, by honourable right, to the bravest tribesmen, whose valour would have been disgraced not to be thus distinguished. The men were all more avid than the women to bedeck themselves with the new treasures, and grandfathers disputed with their little granddaughters the right to every trinket.

With American Indian tribesmen the right to wear each feather in the headdress and each ornamental marking of the dress and the body had to be fairly won in battle or on the hunting-ground. To dress like a brave meant qualifying as a brave, and sumptuary law was dependent upon the valiant exercise of manhood — birth and wealth counting as naught against this aristocracy of physical valour. Among the Blackfoot Indians only those braves who had indisputably killed an enemy in war and taken scalps, for instance, were privileged to paint horizontal stripes (a primitive symbol for death) on their jerkins and leggings.

The working of feathers, one of the most difficult of all natural materials to manipulate, is often remarkable among primitive people, who are eager to adorn themselves with bright plumage, not only because it is

beautiful, but also because they believe it will confer upon them the swift-
ness and keen eyesight of the birds from whom the feathers come. Australian aborigines, perhaps the most primitive of all known tribes in existence
to-day, practise a highly individual form of body-decoration intimately
associated with their totemistic religion. They cover their bodies in close
patterns of magically significant horizontal stripes and perpendicular lines
made from the down of certain birds and applied with an adhesive formed
by pricking the skin. Amazonian Indians, whose culture and religion are
closely associated with the brilliant bird-life around them, make necklaces,
bracelets, turbans and boas, cloaks and breast ornaments, entirely from
feathers, securing them by weaving or knotting by means of fibre. Even
their working axes are adorned with feather tufts.

The Arawak Indians decorated their naked bodies, for their dances,
with quantities of tiny vivid feathers applied to the skin by adhesive
balsam, the Master of the Ceremonies being distinguished from the other
tribesmen by brighter feathers. The young exquisites of the Orinoco
Baberre Indians used a different system of applying feathers to the body.
They covered themselves with gum, upon which they blew clouds of
down collected from different birds.

One Amazonian tribe has evolved a novel method of ensuring the
supply of toucan feathers they so greatly prize. They use blunted arrows
dipped in a specially weak solution of curare poison to shoot at the
toucans, and so merely stun them, thus making it possible for the toucans
to grow a fresh crop of feathers in place of those they take.

No amount of trouble is spared by primitives to make the dress they
are preparing as handsome and enduring as possible, and time does not
count. The great war chiefs of the Marquesas were entitled to wear the
ta-avaha, or huge ceremonial headdress made from the tail-feathers of
cocks. For this headdress only the two longest tail-feathers from each
cock were suitable, so that a single headdress necessitated the supply of
250 cocks at least. In Hawaii the aristocracy reserved for themselves
ceremonial shoulder capes made entirely from the red and yellow feathers
of the oo bird, feathers so rare and of such great value that subjugated
districts were obliged to contribute oo feathers as tribute.

Captain Cook noted in his log in 1777 that the Maoris were wearing
aprons of close-wrought fibre cloth entirely covered with red feathers,
dog-skin and shell being used for additional ornament. "Their common
clothing," he reported,

is very much like thrummed mats that are made of rope yarns. Another
softer material is stout as strongest sail cloth and not unlike it.
To one end of every piece is generally worked a very neat border of

different colours (Taniko) of four to six inches, and they very often trim them with pieces of dog-skin or birds' feathers.

Sir Joseph Banks reported a Maori dress entirely made of the red feathers of parrots. Ling Roth, in *A Monograph on Maori Mantles*, published in 1923, throws further light on this culture, explaining how magic enters into the method of weaving, odd numbers being considered very unlucky.

Feathers were introduced into the texture by a method of close over-lapping (almost indeed as the feathers grow on the bird in its natural state). Kiwi feathers were the most costly and the prerogative usually of Chiefs.

The chiefly headdresses of the American plains Indians, with their sweeping pendants of power-conferring eagle feathers, set off by subtle embroidery with different feathers worked in coloured sprays and loops and tasselled with brilliant tufts from the plumage of other birds, are authentic works of art. The feathered apparel we see to-day in the Musée de l'Homme, the New York Museum of Natural History, and the British Museum are still as bright and intact as when they were newly created, though under glass for decades and far from new when first acquired for the collections. They were magic-conferring garments, made to last.

Another aspect of primitive dress which is highly prized is the noise the dress makes in movement. Swishing and rattling sounds, tinkling, the gentle thumping of heavier portions of the garments during dancing, are relished greatly, and ensured by all manner of ingenious sound-producing ornaments, such as pendant seeds and nuts or bits of shell or bone. G. F. Angas reported in 1847 that the Maoris covered their mat dress (*waikawa*) with flax leaves, rolled into tubes and dyed black, bristling like the quills of the porcupine and producing a loud rustling noise with every movement of the wearer.

As with more sophisticated people, that which is rare and difficult to obtain is correspondingly prized, and the Maoris used precious dog-fur as expensive embroidery. The fur of white-haired, long-tailed dogs was so particularly precious that such dogs were reared in careful luxury, under the care of a member of the aristocracy, a commoner not being considered important enough for so proud a task. These dogs had special mats woven for their use, and their tails were shaved regularly so that none of the precious hair should be wasted.

Another aspect of primitive dress, liable to be overlooked because its gorgeous qualities so often dazzle us to the exclusion of its other merits, is its practical value. Each tribe contrives dress for its particular needs, and if magic is frequently evoked for aid with major problems, the ordinary everyday contingencies of life are also not forgotten. The fringed ends of the Redskin jerkins and leggings, for example, as with the Maori dress made from the leaves of the flag, are devised as rain-conductors, the drops of moisture running down these artificial gutters and falling to the ground, instead of soaking through to the wearer's skin.

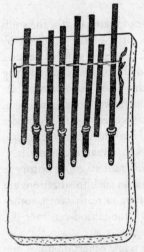

ZANDI HARP

Made from a discarded wooden toilet-paper holder, whalebones from a missionary's corset, and strips from a sardine-tin. Sudan, 1900.

By courtesy of the Pedoe family

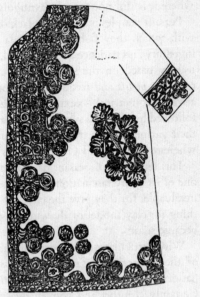

PEASANT GREATCOAT

Black silk braid on white felt. Timi-soara region, Rumania. Contemporary.

Peasants no less than primitive people delight in brilliant jingling dress, and even among the world's poorest peasants there is immense effort bestowed on making the humblest garments beautiful by embroidery, for peasant wealth is in their fingers, and the skill with which the embroidery is contrived is valued as highly as the effect. Peasant ceremonial dress, worn on Sundays, for weddings, and for galas, has been in the past so richly adorned and so lovingly embroidered that a garment would be handed down from father to son, and from mother to daughter, like heirloom jewellery.

Before the days of saving up to buy a socially superior but artistically inferior ready-made garment from the city, richly intricate patterns were embroidered on stout homespun or sturdy local linen, the dress being cut roomy enough to give the embroiderer plenty of scope as well as to give the wearer plenty of room to dance in. Lace, worked in every degree of coarseness and fineness, galloon, sequins, beads, tiny bells, and gold and silver coins were introduced to add to the gaiety and richness. Before the dour garb of moneyed respectability smothered the peasant's natural love of life and colour peasant gala dress was indeed something worth looking at. In India to-day beetles' wings, tinsel, and bits of looking-glass adorn peasant gala dress. Happily there are still pockets of Europe left where it is still not entirely extinguished.

Peasant peoples make up for lack of diversity of materials (for the stuffs with which they fashion their gala dress are often of the simplest) by ingenuity and patience and, above all, by a superb natural sense of pattern, usually based on the shapes of nature around them, often introducing religious *motifs* and frequently combining both. The oldest patterns are always geometrical. Next come stylized fruit and flowers, of pagan origin, followed by religious symbols. Rumanian peasants even to-day embroider their garments with traditional patterns dating back to remote antiquity, wherein barbaric and Oriental *motifs* mingle with Byzantine symbols.

This tendency of peasant dress to embody different stages of history is one of its many fascinations. To the dress historian such fossilizations are invaluable, for they give the effect of the real thing as really worn, something no clay model or drawing or painting of the period can ever do, because static.

Why particular items of dress should survive while others do not is one of the mysteries of sartorial history. No doubt stubborn local pride, national sentiment, and the hypnotism of custom all play their part. Certainly comfort and convenience are not the reason, for those items which do so survive are likely to be in the most extravagant styles. We need only point out the fantastic headgear of some of the peasants of Brittany and other parts of France, fossilized in the Middle Ages, shrunk to doll-size but retaining its original form for five centuries or more. Polish and Slovak peasants still wear male gala dress which is rich in items unchanged in form for hundreds of years. Some Slovak villagers on Sundays wear bonnets of the sixteenth century, ruffs of the seventeenth century, petticoat breeches which recall the times of Louis XIV, and rich lace flounces from the sixteen-sixties.

It is, however, where the basic dress is of the simplest form, such as a simple straight shirt and trousers, or long gown, that the rich peasant embroideries are seen to best advantage. Bands of embroidery riot round the throat, the cuffs, the hem, down the front and the back, and across the shoulders. Even parts which are normally concealed in wear are thus enriched, so strong is the impetus to adorn. Thus the gorgeously patterned toes of Kurdistan stockings, never seen except in privacy. Some Hungarian dress, indeed, is so richly ornamented both without and within that it is almost ruinous, being uneconomic to keep (so much wealth and time has it consumed to create) and painful to sell.

In the Carpathians each village still retains its own sartorial specialities. The embroidery of their sheepskin waistcoats and leather jackets, and those of their womenfolk, is usually the work of shepherds. In these districts even nightshirts are elaborately embroidered. We must be thankful that industrialism so far has not destroyed these village riches, as it has or is in process of doing elsewhere. The finest garments here are those reserved for days of gala, but even everyday dress is bright with embroidery.

Here dyes from natural sources are still in use, and, though some aniline dyes are employed, they have not yet driven out the older softer dyes. Red is obtained from the leaves of wild crab-apple, yellow from the osier, black from birch and alder—all fixed with the aid of common salt.

Peasant dress, history teaches us, cannot survive apart from its associated pleasures of singing and dancing, feasting and festival, of which it is but one cultural facet. In our present generation we have begun tardily to try to preserve these rich manifestations of national life before it is too late, for it is not in a dusty city museum that these treasures show to best advantage, but on the living, breathing body in a living, breathing culture. History cannot be made to stand still, however, and our insidious Coca-Cola civilization is the antithesis of peasant dress and peasant pleasures. Yet it is still not too late. Galas, festivals, fairs, and the like still mean something, could still be something more than a purely commercial enterprise if artists and those of artistic goodwill are made responsible for their organization. In our day we are beginning all over Europe to create and re-create such festivals, and these I will deal with in a later chapter.

European peasant dress, once so richly varied and brilliant, each village contributing something individual and delightful, has long been in decline. Already in 1803 the artist Edward Harding, who was compiling a book of drawings of national costumes for the awakening romantic taste of his own countrymen, observed sadly:

> Characteristic national dress is already disappearing from the European peasantry. The different races of people which form the principal nations of Europe have long assimilated each other and gradually adopted the same garb and outward appearance.

He felt himself to be writing a requiem. Though he was more pessimistic than the facts warranted, he marked an accelerating tendency. In conditions of industrialism, where the sons of peasants tend to seek work in the cities or emigrate to lands overseas where there seems more hope of earning a livelihood, what is remarkable is not that so much peasant dress should have disappeared, but that not a little stubbornly remains.

When Harding was preparing his book of costumes the Industrial Revolution was sinking its claws into English life and already beginning to affect the rest of Europe. Harding hoped his book would please in England precisely because of English nostalgia for the bright dress she herself was losing.

What this can mean to the happiness and self-respect of peasant people we can see for ourselves in the extraordinarily rich indigo-print culture of Slovak villages—a culture of hand-printed dress material and furnishing linens which arose in the eighteen-eighties and has flourished ever since.

Industrialism means a plurality of the same thing. Peasant dress is exactly the opposite. Peasants who retain their bright home-made dress do not in point of fact have a large wardrobe. One working-dress for every day and another dress for Sundays and galas suffice them. But the Sunday dress is glorious indeed, no pains and no expense being spared to make it as sumptuous as possible. It is when there is enough money to buy lots of ready-made clothes that the glamour and distinction of Sunday Best ceases. Too easily come by, the dress signifies nothing and looks like it.

The gloomy Sunday, without fun and deprived of gay raiment, is rooted in commercialism, as I shall hope to prove in the next chapter. The conception of an austere, beauty-fearing deity is as alien to peasant as it is to primitive minds. Peasants have no doubt that in dressing themselves resplendently on the Sabbath their Lord will be pleased with them, for they have dressed up in His honour. Their Lord is closely concerned with the blessings of fertility, and will, they know, appreciate gorgeous apparel for weddings. Though He can be terrible, He is never arid, and the Protestant Sunday, they believe, is no compliment to Him for the creation of the richly coloured world.

Austerity makes no appeal to the peasant mind, which adores plenty and fears scarcity. It may be said, indeed, that it is only wealthy and highly sophisticated communities, who have no conception of want, who think of dieting and admire extreme slimness in their women and despise brilliant dress as vulgar.

The traditional peasant beauty is robust and full-breasted, the favoured festival Harvest Thanksgiving. The conception of restraint (limiting of crops to keep up the price, limiting of families to afford social elevation of fewer children) is outside peasant understanding. Feasting and plenty, large families, fertile fields, these are the desired blessings of life. That is why peasant gala dress often makes use of such fertility *motifs* as suns, ears of corn, flowers and seeds, and such colours of ripeness as yellow, russet, and crimson.

Richard Cobbold in 1845 still remembered the pagan pleasures of the Suffolk harvests of his childhood:

> The last load of corn was conveyed into the barn or stockyard and covered with green boughs, with shouting and the blowing of the merry harvest horn, with the prettiest girl riding on top.

INDIGO PRINT PATTERN (10 INCHES):
THE RESURRECTION
Bratislava, Czechoslovakia. Contemporary.

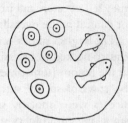

HARVEST THANKSGIVING
LOAF
Penshurst Parish Church.
Contemporary.

There followed the harvest supper for the fourteen farm-hands, their wives and children:

> smoking puddings, plain and plum. Piles of hot potatoes, turnips, carrots, cabbage, and every kind of vegetable the farmer's lands could produce. Beef roast and boiled, mutton, veal and pork, everything substantial. A rich custard and apple pies. Brown ale to drink.

And afterwards a touch of gentility which marked the changing times: "The wives and children drank tea and ate cakes in the best parlour."

Even to-day in England, where the Civil War and the Industrial Revolution have destroyed so much, the Harvest Festival brings all the village altars suddenly to glowing life. Even the most austere and tight-lipped of Low churches and chapels shine with offerings of brightly polished apples, sheaves of corn, carefully washed bunches of parsnips and carrots, baskets of the largest, brownest eggs, and wreaths of un-teetotal hop-plants, in pagan profusion.

In Penshurst Parish Church, which was founded in 1177, I was enchanted in the autumn of 1955 to observe among the Harvest Thanksgiving offerings a large round loaf with a beautifully designed raised pattern in dough of the five Biblical loaves and the two fishes. Baked no doubt by one of the old women of the village sitting devoutly and primly in the congregation that evening in her dull Sunday black, the loaf would not have looked out of place on a pagan altar dedicated to Ceres.

Now that English farm-workers dress like everybody else we may well ask ourselves what there ever was distinctive about their dress in the past? It was in particular the smock, which was once the traditional garb of the English farm-hand, and a sensible and handsome garment in every respect. Until the 1939 War Gardiner's of Whitechapel, in London, still sold such agricultural smocks, for which there was still a brisk demand. To-day they sell sweaters and jackets suitable for driving and servicing tractors in, or clinical white overalls suitable for supervision of the electric milker.

The English smock was a loose, wide shirt made of strong linen, usually square-necked to be easily slipped over the head. It was closely gathered at the bosom (sometimes also at the back), the gathers being held in place by rows of special stitching known as smocking. Sometimes the full sleeves were similarly smocked at the wrists. The thread used for the smocking embroidery was either the same colour as the smock or a shade or two darker. A variety of smocking stitches were used, traditionally worked into symbols indicating the wearer's particular skills. The smock thus formed an embroidered testimonial. Pride in manual skill informed the smocking which wife, sweetheart, or mother embroidered — pride in the man's skill and in her own. Tree-fellers' smocks, for instance, were smocked in circles representing cross-sections of a tree-trunk, and so on. This symbolism is in the true tradition of primitive art, where every design has its meaning.

Love of pattern was evident in all aspects of village life, and Hannah More relates how the wives of the humblest labourers, too poor to afford richer material, took pride in drawing patterns of flowers with a burnt stick on the whitewashed walls of the chimney corner.

As is to be expected of a country like England, whose agricultural skill has long been high, the domestic arts of the English countryside were also correspondingly high. Excellent in quality, and cooked with a cunning simplicity suitable to good ingredients, English country cooking was famous before land enclosures and the Industrial Revolution drove the women as well as the men into factories, when there was no time left for country girls to learn the culinary art from their mothers, and in one generation it disappeared. For country people, then largely illiterate,

handed down their recipes by word of mouth and practical demonstra-
tion, cookery books being for grand city folk. Observers at the period
reported that there was hardly any more cooking done in the cottages,
for every one was working in the factories. Meals were snatched from
ready-cooked bought victuals. There was scarcely time to eat. Still less
for the fine country crafts, including dress-embroidery.

The tools and utensils, as carefully made and gaily decorated as the
things they made, stood idle until they decayed, and were no more made.
The old patterns of English wooden butter-moulds, comparable in charm
with the finest Polish gingerbread moulds, were abandoned, and to-day—
such is the irony of our times—have become antique-shop treasures,
while farmers who would like one for their dairy (and one or two
highbrow farmers to-day, we know, do have such yearnings) have to go
without.

Horses provided an excuse for a thousand curious and agreeable fancies
in brass harness-ornament which the tractor has never pretended to evoke.
Magic crescents, good-luck charms, even portrait heads of King Edward
VII, were gauds dear to the carrier before the motor-lorry drove the
horse off the road. Horse-brasses too are collectors' pieces to-day—indeed,
so popular with city flat-dwellers that they are manufactured specially for
fireplace ornaments.

Straw lent itself to many village ingenuities while there was still leisure
for the making of pleasing contrivances. It was separated into as many
as five strands, and handsome edgings and embroideries were made from
it. Here we have village art in its purest aspect, the working of the
simplest raw material into something of beauty by skilful hands informed
by a natural talent for design. Such patient, proud skill would amaze the
young bored people of our present cities, accustomed to buy and discard
ready-made rubbish from multi-stores, and who look back on the peasants
who made these objects as belonging to the age of the dinosaurs.

English baskets, from the feather-light strawberry pokes to immense
baskets intended for logs, have been a splendid English craft, made precisely for each domestic and agricultural requirement in strangely necessary shapes and weights of local materials, and made to last as long as was
needed. Thatching too, which to be seen in good heart means going to
Essex or Suffolk, makes a trustworthy and long-lasting roofing pleasing
to the eye, though thatchers complain that present-day straw, which
comes from fields fertilized by artificial fertilizers, does not endure anything like so long as former thatching.

No less than Red Indians in the wilds of North America English farm-
hands (wonderfully pagan beneath their respectable Sunday-observance)

loved to bind themselves together into secret societies from which their womenfolk were rigidly excluded. Such English societies existed ostensibly for the declared purpose of gathering funds to help members in misfortune, for there was then no State provision for sickness or old age. But the ceremonial had much older significance. With pomp and ritual the members marched to their annual banquet in the village tavern, preceded by their sacred emblem, a large brass totem borne before them by a privileged member. Clasped hands, crowns, a wide-open eye, the oak leaf, a bell, such are the commonest ensigns. Sometimes a maypole gay with ribbons and flowers was also carried.

Dress, well made, brightly embroidered, was part of all this enjoyment of everyday things and pleasure in making them, and if the men no less than the women in England's agricultural communities now wear the dull dress of the cities there are still a few districts in Scotland where beautiful material is still skilfully made by hand. Tweed woven by the work-seamed hands of peasants on the storm-tossed Hebridean islands off the coast of Scotland, tweed to which the aromatic heather scent of the islands still clings, has become world-renowned for its strength and resistance to damp no less than for its handsome appearance. Once woven only for local wear, it is to-day esteemed in all social circles; nor has familiarity blunted its desirability.

Scottish fisherfolk and shepherds are notable knitters, and they have become so because Scottish fishermen and shepherds need stout jerseys for their work. When the B.B.C. Television Service sought the best knitter to be procured in order to demonstrate to their viewers it was a Scottish shepherd who easily surpassed all other claimants.

In the Scottish coastal villages the traditional wedding gift, knitted by the fisherman's sweetheart, is a sturdy, high-necked jersey of black wool. Black because Calvinism has set its mark on the villages, but knitted in a splendid variety of patterns which predate and outwit Calvinism, patterns symbolizing magic-religious desires, which vary from village to village. Thus the jerseys of Broadsea are knitted in a diamond-and-ladder pattern. The girls of Whinneyfield knit theirs in a pattern of diamonds and anchors, and the girls of Buchanham in diamonds and hearts.

In the Aran islands tremendously strong sweaters are knitted from the heaviest natural wool, with the grease left in its staple, for better protection against the cruel sea-winds. These sweaters are worked in richly raised patterns of stripes and twisted cable, and, though in constant strenuous use, often outlive their wearers.

How much longer will such superb hand-knitting be kept up? And what is our throw-away mechanized civilization going to substitute for this kind of handsome durability? Modern factories offer greater leisure than in the past, it is true, but mechanical amusements are eroding both manual skill and the desire to exercise it.

In my Staffordshire childhood there was much knitting and crocheting of lace for pillows and sheets and petticoat edges, and every little girl was eager to learn and show off her skill. Odd moments, outdoors as well as

PATTERN FOR ITS
OWN SAKE

Toe of knitted sock. Kurd. Contemporary. In ordinary wear the prettiest part of the pattern is hidden by the shoe.

Musée de l'Homme, Paris

A TRADITIONAL PATTERN:
FISHERMAN'S JERSEY (ARAN
ISLAND)

Oiled wool, knitted 1903; still in use.

indoors, were beguiled by the soothing manipulation of the crochet-hook, and there was something to show for time thus expended. I have seen to-day, in the Catalonian fishing village of Cadaqués, apparently modern misses happily working at pillow lace in between serving customers in the little shops, though the Cadillacs rush past the main street and Coca-Cola is on sale at the local café. Cadaqués girls, especially the poorer ones, still make the lace for their own cotton petticoats. Nor are they girls with time to kill, but, on the contrary, work much longer hours at their domestic tasks than English girls. To make and wear lace is a cherished aspect of their lives, and they never sit with idle hands. How much longer will it be thus?

A happy survival in England, from more brightly coloured and individual days, is the coster with his cart and donkey. The motor-van has not yet supplanted him in the outlying edges of London and the older suburbs. The coster's cart, which he prefers to paint himself, is a gallant display of bright-hued lozenges, circles, squares, and oblongs, intricately interwoven, non-representational—though curves are preferred to angles, as more feminine and shapely. The favoured colours are brilliant green, blue, scarlet, and yellow, the owner's name being prominently introduced in grandiose flourished script.

Sunday, in flat defiance of Puritanism, is the coster's chosen day, and on his suburban rounds he dresses himself in an oddly nautical jacket, a cap on the back of his head, and bright kerchief, crying vegetables to the good householders on their way home from chapel, and also crying such delicacies as cockles and winkles.

For such a man—and there are not many left—the factory, the garage, and the toolshop hold absolutely no appeal. He loves the city, on his own street terms, and he relishes the freedom and the chaffering with housewives. He is never in a hurry, and he enjoys being his own boss and showing off his nag and his gay cart, even if he does not earn much of a living. Almost the last English individualist left, his is the roaming instinct, though he roams on concrete roads, and he is brother to the shirt-sleeved watermen who man the narrow boats, painted with roses and castles, on our English canals.

The coster has his sovereign, like other Englishmen; his is the Pearly King, in whom, in a curious manner, some flavour of merry England survives in his audaciously brilliant dress and sparkling gaiety to match. It is true that the London bus conductor is also a man of parts and wit, but he, alas, is defeated by the dowdy uniform of his profession, a sad decline from the caped splendour of the old stagecoach driver. To the costers of the eighties dull dress was anathema, and so they evolved, with peasant-minded ingenuity, a gallant and glittering garb for themselves from what came most readily to hand on the East End haberdasher's stalls. The suit they made so famous was of black velvet for preference, though often enough velvet was too expensive for them, and they had to make do with worsted or shoddy instead. Cut in the tight-waisted style of the eighteen-seventies and flaunting the masher's nautically widened trouser-bottoms, the Pearly King's suit was decorated all over with pearl buttons, patterned into symmetrical fancies of his own designing, and in effect strongly reminiscent of the jewelled Elizabethan doublets. It was a costly dress to make and enormously heavy to wear, the number of pearl buttons thus sewn on being prodigious. Here we see, in its bounce, flamboyance, cheerfully noisy show-off, and strident masculinity, the vulgar answer to the Savile Row Suit.

The Pearly King, of course, had his consort, or Donah (from the Spanish doña), who glittered beside him in a snowstorm of pearl buttons patterned equally on to black velvet, sumptuously gathered and draped in a long skirt, and with flaunting great ostrich feathers in her hat. The Pearlies came into their own, rightly, on the important English festivals, especially Bank Holiday, and Hampstead Heath was their spiritual home. Of course, there was always a yearly turn-out for the best donkey-cart.

There still is, though all that survives of this cheerful and indomitable group of Dickensian individualists to-day are a few elderly costers and their families, who dress up in their pearlies and go out to collect for charity. They still make their own dress, covering ordinary lounge suit, bowler hat, boots, and tie with thousands of pearl buttons, so close sewn in patterns that only a strong man can carry the weight of the dress. Let

RED SILK EMBROIDERY ON CUFFS AND NECK OF MAN'S SHIRT
English, 1630.
Victoria and Albert Museum

us not underestimate the Pearlies. They belong to that rich, pulsating stratum of London life which produced Charlie Chaplin and the splendidly positive music-hall songs sung in the East End pubs of the late nineteenth century; in their zest for life and love of glitter they have much in common with Tudor England.

The Pearly King is traditionally a cheerful, impudent fellow with a taste for sentiment and a heart of gold, nearly always illiterate, always a superb pattern-maker. When we study him more closely we can see that he was more truly English than Beau Brummell, and that his roots tapped a purer source of refreshment than the tainted well of Brummell. The Pearly King, like his coster subjects, wasted no time trying to be a gentleman, being fully occupied enjoying himself as a man.

We are beginning to understand in this generation that it is not only in Blue books and serious Parliamentary Reports, and the library findings of closeted scholars, that we must search for clues to our English history. What the common Englishman has read, when he has been able to read, what he said to other chaps in the local in the evening, and the songs he has sung to cheer himself up by their melancholy, these also have something important to tell us about ourselves. One or two old women east of Aldgate Pump still remember the sweet, nostalgic tune of this early coster music-hall ballad, which recalled the vanished joys of the English country lanes:

> When the spring-time comes again
>   And the pretty flowers are growing,
> When it's sunshine after rain
>   And the summer breezes blowing,
> We will roam about the country
>   With a moke what's always willing.
> You shall buy,
> I shall cry,
>   "Three pots a shilling!"

CHAPTER FOUR

THE PURITAN REVOLUTION

In their double anxiety to obey a given ethical code and to get on in profitable business, the typical men of the new age overlooked some of the other possibilities of life.
PROFESSOR G. M. TREVELYAN, *English Social History* (1942)

TWO revolutions were necessary to make England into the great industrial Power she still is and to cause Englishmen to dress like mice. The first of these, which introduced Puritan dress, was the upheaval led by Cromwell in the seventeenth century. The second, which ushered in the top-hat, was the Industrial Revolution towards the end of the eighteenth century. Cromwell's revolution set the English middle class on its feet, and gave it such deep inhibitions about art that it has not yet shaken them off. The second made it rich and still more inhibited. In this chapter I will try to deal with the effects of Puritanism.

What was life like in England before the Civil War? From plays, music, documents, poems, legal enactments, and the descriptions of travellers, we know there was colour and gaiety, fun and bravado; there was also corruption and cruelty, disease and sometimes famine. Shakespeare's England was daring, restless, vulgar, avid, and the tempo of life, all accounts agree, was enormously invigorating. It got and it spent heartily. No false refinement stopped the magnificoes and their womenfolk from overdressing and overeating. Daring and intelligence might rocket a man to high office, whatever his birth. The women spoke up for themselves with no uncertain voices.

Religion was brightly coloured, and much pagan jollification went on in the villages. The theatre, professional and amateur, was a general passion. Music was all-important. Sport and dancing claimed all classes. The money and treasure looted from Spanish ships made a dazzling display at Court, and some of it trickled lower down the social scale.

The merchant adventurers (unlike the dour English tradesmen to come) were as extravagant in their dress as the courtiers. Those who went to meet King Philip of Spain on his entry into Antwerp in 1549, it was recorded, wore livery and buskins of purple velvet and paned hose

DIVINE AID
Wall-painting, thirteenth century.
St Stephen's, House of Commons

embroidered with silver, doublets and puffings of purple satin, purple velvet hats with gold bands, fine brooches and white plumes, rapiers, daggers, spurs, stirrups, and bridles, all gilt. Nor were their horse trappings any less splendid, being of purple velvet to match, embroidered with gold and green silk, and with white and green plumes for their horses' heads.

Not only were the fashions costly and extravagant, but they changed continually. Anything newfangled was sure to find customers. Colours carried fancy names like pease-porridge, tawny, popinjay blue, lusty gallant, devil-in-the-hedge. There was no end to the glorification and variety of the ruff. "Treble-quadruple Dædalian ruff, the rabato ruff, ruffs that have more arches for pride to row under than can stand under five London bridges," complained a critic. "Twelve, yea sixteen lengths a piece, set three or four times double and is of some fitly called three steps and a half to the gallows," protested the Puritan Stubbes, adding spitefully, "and in rain it becomes as limp as a slut's dish-clout." Worse still, the same critic vowed that "Chaste and sober matrons" were aping men by wearing doublets with pendant cod-pieces and galligaskins to "bear out their bums."

If dress was so fine one reason was that there were plenty of occasions to wear it. Banquets, festivals, plays, and occasions in the grand world were echoed by equivalent merrymaking in the villages. Much of it had a pagan flavour, though it centred round the Church, and there was a general fear of witches. The Catholic Church had taken over all sorts of pagan holidays and renamed them after its own festivals, thus wisely preserving the continuity so important to peasants. Midsummer Day rites, for instance, had been celebrated in England since before the time of the Druids. December 25 was the great Mithraic festival. Certainly Easter, with its fertility symbols of eggs and seeds, as old as mankind, meant an older than Christian resurrection in the villages.

The night before May Day would be entirely spent in the woods, the youths and girls of the village singing and dancing till daybreak, returning laden with birch branches. Their chosen Lord of Misrule with his hundred followers, all bedecked in light bright livery gay with ribbons, laces, and glass jewels, belled garters jingling, hobby-horses prancing, would dance after their drummers and pipers in procession to church, and set up bowers in the churchyard, where they would dance and feast all day and through the next night as well. Pagan it was indeed. And so was the maypole, much venerated and drawn by teams of twenty or forty yoke of oxen, themselves decorated with sweet nosegays and followed by crowds of excited villagers and their children, who helped to rear it on end and then danced round it. Pagan too were the bonfires lit in the fields at midsummer, over which the boys and girls would leap joyfully, and into which they threw sprigs of verbena and violets.

Puritans were loud in their denunciations of these frolics. "Wanton," "filthy," "Sodomical," were the terms used against them.

TREE OF LIFE
Polish papercut. Contemporary.

HOLY POWER: PATĀRĀ KAPĪSA
Triumphant Buddha at Gravalsi. Flames rise from his shoulders, and torrents of cold water flow from his feet. Greco-Buddhist. Carved stone. Afghanistan. Third century.
Musée Guimet, Paris

The Christmas revelries aroused their particular fury. "More mischief," growled Philip Stubbes, "is that time committed than in all the year besides."

What masking and mumming! What dicing and carding! What eating and drinking! What feasting and banqueting! is then used ... to the great dishonour of God and impoverishing the Realm!

Church-ales, the equivalent of our present more staid church bazaars, were for the same purpose of raising money for the repair of the church fabric. For the church-ales the churchwardens, together with the parishioners, provided twenty quarterns of malt, which was brewed into strong ale and sold and drunk in church, those who paid most for their drink being reckoned the godliest. It must be said that neither magistrates nor bishops were over-partial to these church-ales, believing them to cause a certain amount of disorder and contempt of the law. Puritan critics went farther than this and claimed they produced "other enormities, great profanation of the Lord's sabbath, the dishonour of almighty God and increase of bastardy and dissolute life."

The greater number of holidays—for saints' days were thus counted—meant more frequent breaks from the grind of hard manual toil. In the fields in the summer, and working indoors on the production of farm tools, wooden ware, rushlights, spinning, weaving, and straw-plaiting all the winter, the villagers were never idle. They worked hard and they enjoyed themselves hard. And they centred their pleasures round the church, as they centred their aspirations and devotions. In the cathedrals masons worked on the statues of angels and holy figures, carving them into the likenesses of their neighbours, and thinking it no sin to shape God the Father in the image of the simple devout old man who was their own father on earth, and to fashion cherubim in resemblance to their own children, before they grew up to carry on the work. Every one belonged and had his place. Thus it had been for many centuries. Time stood almost still. They did not have to work against the clock. Nor were they listening for the whistle.

The Gospels were very real to the common people, and the Church did not consider it sacrilegious to allow God the Father to be carved in stone or presented in the flesh, dressed up in fine clothes, on the stage. Right from medieval times onward, until Puritan enactments stopped them in 1657, every English town and village had delighted to stage its own versions of stories from the Bible. Mystery plays drew in amateur actors from every trade, who dressed themselves up and enacted saints and demons with much enjoyment, while every one gathered to applaud the performances.

No doubt from such amateurs the professional theatre recruited its members. No doubt Shakespeare and the humble originals of Snug, Peter Quince, and Bottom began thus. These centuries of amateur drama, with regular rehearsals of noble words well spoken, brilliant dress grandly worn, and dramatic gestures carefully delivered, had immensely important influences upon the lives of ordinary people in England. Perhaps they themselves did not appreciate how important they were until the stage was banned. Certainly in 1657 something vital was amputated from our English life, which we could and can ill do without.

The drama is a wonderful means of self-expression. Combining as it does dance, speech, music, emotion, and costume, the theatre is the most important of all the arts, and perhaps the most satisfying. When all Englishmen regularly took part in dramatic performances they were enlarged and enriched thereby, and individually fulfilled in a way unknown to the shy and reserved Englishman of our own times, who keeps his hands in his pockets because he does not know what else to do with them, and who queues for hours in the drizzle to use up his spare time watching a film in darkness. His ancestors did better for themselves than this. Today, though we can boast of a theatrical genius like Sir Laurence Olivier, and few actors in the world can surpass the finest contemporary English actors, nevertheless noble speech, assured gesture, and the proud wearing of fine dress do not come easily to Englishmen in general any more.

Yet Englishmen, despite their puritanical inhibitions, still love dressing up, and for a grand occasion will brace themselves heroically, to dress and look and behave splendidly.

Though the mystery plays which for centuries enraptured Englishmen, and in which at some period in their lives practically all of them took part, have vanished from the scene, we know something about them from the careful expense accounts which were kept. The accounts of the Chester mystery plays, which, starting in 1300, continued without a break for over three hundred years, give us a vivid picture of what these plays must have looked like.

In Chester, as elsewhere, the plays were presented both in the open air and in church on the Monday, Tuesday, and Wednesday of Whit week. In addition to these, special plays were performed at Christmas. Every craft and guild performed its own particular play. The Drapers, for instance, were entrusted with *The Fall of Lucifer*, the Water-carriers appropriately performed *The Deluge*, and the Cooks *The Harrowing of Hell*.

Tricked out in brilliant costume, bewigged and brightly painted, the actors were paraded about the city on decorated carts prior to the first public performance, which always took place in front of the abbey gates. The second performance was given before the mayor of the town and the town council.

The mystery plays were expensive to produce, and at first the fine costumes were provided by the Church. Later, as they grew rich enough to afford the outlay, the cost of the production was defrayed by the trade guilds. "Our Lord" wore a large gilt peruke and a brightly painted sheep-skin coat. Lucifer wore horns, a tail, cloven feet, and a long red beard. Red hair represented evil, and therefore not only Lucifer but also Judas Iscariot always wore a red beard and red wig. Players were paid for their services to make good the money lost in wages during their absence from work at rehearsals.

The Chester accounts include the following items:

Payd to ye players for rehearsals 1 imprimis

To God	*2 shillings 8 pence*
Item to Pilate his wife	*2 shillings*
Item to the Devil & Judas	*1 shilling 6 pence*
Paid to Fauston for coc-croying	*7 pence*
And to Fauston for hanging Judas	*5 pence*

Scenes like "Hellmouthe" and "Setting the world of fyer" are frequently mentioned. At first the cart theatre was vertically divided into three, to form heaven, earth, and hell. Later this was altered into a triple horizontal division, with heaven at the top, earth in the middle, and hell down below. Even after the Church withdrew its patronage in 1577 these mystery plays did not die out, but were transferred to St Bartholomew's Fair in the form of a short opera called *The Creation of the World*.

To the Puritan mind all this stank of idolatry, and they looked upon actors as criminal parasites. Fear of gaiety and distrust of beauty it must, be said, was no new attitude in religious life. St Augustine himself had roundly denounced "delight in beautiful and varied forms, in shining and agreeable colours." Throughout the history of the Christian Catholic Church Popes and bishops had striven to turn people's thoughts away from earthly pleasures by trying to confine ceremonial splendour and gorgeous dress to the Church and kings, together with the great ruling nobles. This had held together the social structure for centuries, for to defy class bonds was impious and made the transgressor liable to severe punishment. The Catholic Church, however, with its long experience of human weaknesses, did make provision for outbursts of jollification and temporary dressing up. If the daily life of the common man was hard, uncertain, and without prospect of earthly betterment, there were frequent distractions.

The Catholic Church understood perfectly that ordinary people love gorgeous ceremonial, brilliant processions, and splendid theatre. It realized that the poorer and more obscure people's own lives were the more they sought colour and excitement outside, never seeing evil in extravagant display and asking only that they might be permitted to look at and to take part in it and absorb something of the glory for themselves by association.

History reveals that there were plenty of abuses of the permitted opportunities for rich display, the worst abuses perhaps taking place among the clergy themselves. Popes were constantly having to denounce their own bishops and prelates for shameless pride in dress. The Anglo-Saxon missionary Boniface declared that in his day the dress of the Christian clergy was so besotted by luxury as to foretell the coming of Antichrist. Priests were not wanting who thought nothing of letting their hair grow long enough to cover their tonsures, while the lower clergy had to be forcibly restrained from growing beards.

By Papal law ecclesiastical gloves had to be pure white. By the fourteenth century, however, they were widely being worn dyed purple, scarlet, green, and even in gay patterns, besides being adorned with forbidden fringe and thick-sewn with forbidden pearls. The Pope was obliged to issue a special Bull on the subject.

Colours and jewels were associated with, and should have been confined to, certain states of grace and holy ritual, restrictions which unauthorized priestly luxury chose to ignore. Joy and virginity, for instance, were symbolized by white, the Holy Spirit by the colour scarlet; black was for Good Friday mourning, violet for penitence, green for hope, blue for the Blessed Virgin's mantle, yellow for confession. Similarly every jewel was allotted its own special meaning and holy curative

Left: MONK ATTENDING A DYING MAN
From a painting by Paolo di Stefano, 1450.
Fitzwilliam Museum, Cambridge

Right: HAT AND VEIL OF THE ORDER OF MISERICORDIA, TUSCANY
Waxed black linen.
Smithsonian Museum, Washington

C

properties. In dressing out of their permitted context extravagant priests not only brought dangerous worldly thoughts into the minds of their congregations, but also brought the Church ritual itself into a state of confusion.

By Chaucer's day such unlawful priestly luxury was so general that in denouncing it Chaucer was only expressing what most Englishmen felt. The proud prelate, too preoccupied with his fine apparel and social pomp to bother himself about the needs of his poor flock, was a recurrent lament in the annals of Christianity.

One reason for this priestly passion for fine dress was that, since the rigid social pattern allowed no way of rising in the world except in the service of the Church, ambitious youths of humble birth were obliged to seek their careers in the Church, vocation or no. Often enough their real vocation was not the service of God at all, but the pursuit of worldly success. An example of this was the butcher's son Wolsey, whose ambition can hardly be said to have been governed by piety, and who nevertheless was almost in the running for the papal throne. To ambitious youths the chance to wear sumptuous vestments must have presented immense temptation, because outside the Church strict sumptuary laws denied them the opportunity for indulging in sartorial splendour.

There were other abuses also, which were inevitable in a system which had to outlaw scientific curiosity in order to maintain its authority. For instance, the only text-books on anatomy permitted in the Middle Ages were those compiled for the use of the Inquisition, and compiled for the express purpose of revealing where most pain could be inflicted.

Despite the efforts of the humanists, the formative struggles of the Reformation involved great cruelty. Torture of every kind was frequently invoked during the struggles of the Reformation in England, because religion and politics had become so confused that a religious deviation could easily be punished as a crime against the State. Fearful for its own security, the State constantly intervened in questions of religious conscience, and when poor Anne Askew was put to the torture in the Tower in 1546 it was the Lord Chancellor himself who administered it. Throwing off his gown to get a better purchase of the instrument, it was recorded by eyewitnesses, he drew the rack so severely that he almost tore her body asunder.

Witches continued to be burned after the Reformation, as they had been before it and during it. An iron glove, heated red-hot, was generally used to obtain confession, as had been the practice for centuries, and both sides employed it. In the reign of Queen Elizabeth the rack seldom stood idle, being popularly known as "the Duke of Exeter's daughter," after the nobleman who introduced it into England from Spain. A special "press-yard" was built to accommodate this instrument of torture, which was sited between the Court-house and Newgate Prison.

John Milton described the Puritan Revolution as "the reforming of [the] Reformation." Like a volcano which threatened to erupt, there were prophetic rumblings long before it broke out. The intoxicating new idea that each man might find his own way *directly* to God was in the sixteenth century already giving rise to deviations in Church ritual that alarmed Queen Elizabeth, who saw therein not the distant prospect of democracy, but the immediate danger of anarchy. In 1577 she was protesting:

> We hear to our great grief that in sundry parts of our realm there are no small number of persons presuming to be teachers and preachers of the Church, though neither thereunto lawfully called nor yet fit for the same, which do daily devise, imagine, propound and put into execution new rites and forms in the Church as well as by their preaching.

Pagan maypoles she had no objection to. Indeed, she enjoyed them herself. But the slightest rearrangement in the Church service aroused her worst suspicions.

All civil wars are cruel. In the English Civil War so much venom was engendered, so much damage done to the older fabric, such hatred and bitterness were aroused, that it is almost impossible for any English writer to be impartial on the subject. Certainly our English schools have been unable to teach partiality, for they themselves are heirs of one side or the other, mostly of the Puritan side, as the fact that Englishmen to-day dress with such drab propriety bears witness.

History reveals that every revolution tries to obliterate tangible evidence of the faith it is trying to replace. It is only the more astute revolutions of our own days which sometimes attempt to preserve ancient monuments to placate the sensibilities of world opinion, and also, cunningly, "to serve as witnesses of past oppression." In our distress at the wanton destruction and sackings inflicted on English churches and cathedrals by the Puritan armies we must not fall into the sentimental error of regarding everything from the past as priceless, either. Vulgarity and a passion for rubbish are not the prerogative of our own times. Wealthy men with bad taste have existed in all ages, though certainly not in such numbers and with such riches as the Industrial Revolution was to make possible in England.

Vandalism in the name of righteousness was certainly unselective in its destructiveness. Puritan iconoclasts declared that they were faithfully obeying the Bible, which commanded them to stone idolaters to death, when they destroyed visual symbols of the Christian faith in the English churches. They smashed up holy images and crucifixes and tore to pieces every surplice they could find, calling such vestment "the ragged smock of the whore of Rome." They made the use of holy water a crime by Act of Parliament. Yet so devout were they that oaths incurred heavy penalties and blasphemy was punished by life imprisonment. It was a period of passionate, exalted destruction. Roundheads stabled their horses in churches and in the crypt of the House of Commons, where the lovely wall-paintings of the life of St Lawrence had been hastily whitewashed over, and among the irreparable damage done at this time were the smashing of many of the holy statues in Canterbury Cathedral and the destruction of much of its wonderful stained glass.

Minister Culmer himself climbed up a tall ladder in order to break the Thomas à Becket window, shouting loudly, "My master whipped the living buyers and sellers out of the Temple. These are dead idols which defile the worship of God here, being the fruits and occasions of idolatry."

Exquisitely balanced people are rare in this world. Not only rare, but also likely to be inactive at times of crisis. Especially is this so during revolutions. In the English Civil War it was the extremists who triumphed, pushing zeal to excess. There was much to blame on both sides, for Puritans were as intolerant and priggish as Royalists were intolerant and dissolute, and both armies were destructive. The tragic victim, the first attacked, the worst damaged, and on whom the scars rested longest, was unfortunately the arts.

If the artists had been respected by the Puritans many treasures would certainly have been saved during the Revolution, for, though the Puritans hated the use to which the arts had been put, they would nevertheless have loved the beauty and skill of the works of art themselves, and in time they themselves would have produced new works of art with a different theme. But the arts were swept aside as wanton and unnecessary, and the artists denounced as "sturdy rogues," no better than actors. Dress was one of the arts which early suffered severe "cleansing," extreme Puritans banishing every stitch of embroidery from all their garments, with the sole exception of their underwear, which was neatly embroidered with Biblical texts.

Oliver Cromwell himself, however, was much less fanatic than some of his lieutenants. He played bowls and football, enjoyed practical jokes and listening to music, and sometimes even wore a red sash. It was his personal intervention only, we must not forget, which saved the Hampton Court Palace statues from destruction. Many of his followers, unfortunately, were narrower and more bigoted, and the more bigoted the more destructive. Transport was slow in those days, and once an idea had taken hold of part of the country a counter-order could not arrive more quickly than a man could ride, and by then much damage could already have been done. But in the sickening story of destruction of works of art and the subsequent repression of personal liberty it must never be forgotten that Milton and Bunyan also belong to Puritanism, and, in their white-hot integrity and passionate belief in man, expressed all that was noblest in Puritanism.

LIFE

Mohica pot used in rain-making and fertility rites. Peru, A.D. 500.

DEATH

Coloured plaster funerary figure. Eighteen inches high. Paris. Contemporary.

Puritanism, indeed, began nobly with belief in man as an individual capable of shouldering the heaviest spiritual and moral responsibilities and no less capable of the highest intellectual self-development. John Milton wrote proudly of his fellow-countrymen as "a nation not slow and dull, but of a quick, ingenious and piercing spirit; acute to invent, subtle and sinewy to discourse, not beneath the reach of any point the highest that human capacity can soar to."

The Puritans who fought and won the Civil War were men who believed passionately in themselves and in their destiny. They were men of England's rising middle class, many of them merchants and tradesmen. They had been seeking a creed suited to their political and commercial aspirations, and this they found in Calvinism. Hard work was their way to salvation, for they remembered only that man had been cast out of Eden and preferred to forget that he had ever lived in it.

The older Church had not only encouraged frequent holidays, but welcomed gaiety of heart as a virtue and denounced usury and the pursuit of money as sinful. The Puritans, on the contrary, were determined to put an end to the time-wasting jollification and financially unprofitable merriment, and set England to work as she had never worked before, for the good of her soul and the profit of the realm. They were essentially getters, not spenders.

We know now that what went wrong with the Commonwealth was not the Puritan preoccupation with God, but the Puritan's increasing preoccupation with Mammon. We actually owe the survival of some stained-glass windows in village churches to the prudent Puritan consideration of how much money it would cost to replace the large windows with plain glass afterwards if they smashed them. Even more significant, perhaps, is the fact that during the orgy of destruction of pictures some marked for burning as "lewd," were instead sold abroad at a good profit.

The Puritans began with self-confident pride in man and a sense of individual responsibility which was eventually to lead to political democracy. But if the arts, which man creates for man's enjoyment and which are the supremest work of his hands, are not respected, sooner or later man himself becomes an object of contempt. Before long the Puritan régime had replaced English love of beauty and zest for living by love of power and zest only for making money. The slate they had ruthlessly wiped so clean to enable them to worship God more directly and more spiritually was very soon covered with financial calculations. People who love money have no time for the arts and come to distrust and hate beauty. England's reformation of the Reformation finally ended in a victory for the Bank Account, and doomed Englishmen's dress to joyless obscurity.

In Cromwell's armies, and in civilian life afterwards, hard work and long sermons were the order of the day. Many preachers were enrolled in the ranks of the Roundheads, and there were several 'pep-talks' preached to the troops every day. Cromwell trusted his "plain russet-coated captain that knows what he fights for and loves what he knows" to win the war, and history was on his side. Instead of the drinking and wenching that distracted the Royalist troops the soldiers in Cromwell's regiment flung themselves into passionate political and religious discussions, for they were on fire to win the war quickly and rebuild England according to their new conception of human dignity and responsibility to God.

The real nature of the new way of life was a problem which only really began with the ending of the Civil War, when hordes of vagrants and beggars, disbanded soldiers, robbers, cut-throats, out-of-work actors, and a host of would-be prophets and minor Messiahs roamed the country.

The liberty of conscience the Puritans sought expressed itself in an outbreak of curious new sects. Some of these sects (such as the Levellers, who anticipated the Welfare State by three centuries, and the Quakers, whose conception of a united, peaceful world was even more premature) were true historic precursors. Others were simply outbreaks of hysteria.

For there were now no arts. There was no drama, no entertainment, nor pastimes nor sports of any kind permitted, wherein the human emotions could release themselves. During this time of anguished soul-searching the Church of England was so distrusted by the Puritan Government that even the use of the Book of Common Prayer was regarded in the same light as fornication and tavern-haunting. People felt choked up. They had no outlet except religion, and this drove them mad, for they now had no ritual to express it with. Thus, in St Paul's Cathedral during a sermon on the Resurrection at this time, one evangelical lady in the congregation threw off all her clothes and rushed upon the preacher, crying "Welcome the Resurrection!"

The Puritan Government, faced by this alarming upsurge of new sects, tightened its grip and enacted still more restrictive legislation. Saints' days and holidays were banned. Fasting and days of prayer and humiliation were imposed, such as March 10, 1647, set apart "for public humiliation for national errors of popery, superstition, heresy, schism, and profaneness." The Blasphemy Act of 1648 decreed death without benefit of clergy for denial of the main Christian tenets, and life imprisonment for suggesting that infant baptism was unlawful or that the Presbyterian Church was not the true Church.

An increasingly fanatical bureaucracy exercised thought-control of the population of England by means of spies and informers. Above all, the people had to be put to work and denied distractions so that they could be kept at work. One reason for the severe restriction on amusements was undoubtedly to prevent the assembly of crowds of people, which, in the general state of discontent, might well have led to serious rioting.

Especially condemned were taverns and stage plays. All actors were accounted rogues and liable to punishment as such. Magistrates were held personally responsible for the destruction of all theatres, and for the prevention of any arrangements of seating which might enable a play to be seen by several people. They also had to supervise the whipping of actors as "incorrigible rogues," and, besides, were held responsible for the collection of the five-shilling fine (then an enormous amount of money for ordinary people to afford) mulcted from every spectator who, despite all the restrictions, did manage to witness a play somehow.

Bear-baiting and cock-fighting were simultaneously outlawed, not because of any sudden tenderness towards dumb animals, but owing to distrust of crowds. The attack on pagan pleasures, combined with the desire to exact some extra days of work from the people of the country, led to the Act of Parliament of June 1647, which decreed the abolition of Christmas Day, Easter, and Whitsun. Among the recreations banned at this time were gaming, tippling, animal-baiting, dancing, bell-ringing, the singing of secular music and the playing of all musical instruments, wrestling, leaping, running, shooting, and even walking in a churchyard if a sermon were in progress.

It is true that the second Tuesday of the month was set aside for recreation, and that day only. But there was absolutely nothing left to do with it that could lawfully be done. The taverns were all shut. It was a crime to play tipcat. It was a serious offence to flirt. Dancing was a punishable offence. The only pastime which might safely be indulged in was religious introspection, and even that only with the proviso that such introspection must not lead to unlawful sectarian thought. To prevent this possibility Parliament ordered private catechism twice a week, with another day a week earmarked for repentance and humiliation.

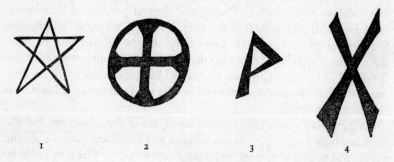

MAGIC SIGNS

1. Celtic: witch's foot. 2. Germanic: Cross of Wotan. 3. Celtic: madness-inducing.
4. Nordic: protection against poison.

Adultery being a crime punishable by death, and fornication a very serious offence, and there being much disparity in numbers between the sexes as a result of the Civil War, there was at this time serious talk in Parliament of legalizing bigamy, which some members pleaded was standard practice in the Bible.

Englishmen, to their credit, did not take kindly to all these Puritan enforcements of godliness. The Commonwealth was not shaping the way most of them wanted. In Canterbury the mob drove the clergy, together with the magistrates and the mayor, right outside the city walls and bolted the gates on them. Riots broke out in many large towns during the Christmas of 1647, and the irrepressible populace played football defiantly in the streets. In London valiant citizens decorated their churches on Christmas Day with forbidden pagan evergreens, and afterwards chased the interfering magistrates' officers from the streets.

This defiance did not stop the Government from pouring out a flood of fresh legislation ordering further restrictions. At this stage, in peculiarly English fashion, the agencies of the law, by ca'canny means, also began to express their opinions. Thus, when in 1650 adultery was decreed a crime to be punished by death, English juries proved reluctant to convict. The magistrates themselves hesitated to send still more prisoners into the already overflowing prisons for the wicked sin of morris-dancing, or for having anything to do with the "utterly pagan" maypole. Some of the new Acts, too, were clearly impossible to enforce, such as that specially enacted against the Thames bargees and lightermen, forbidding them, under heavy penalties, to curse and swear.

It seems that the people were better balanced and more reasonable than their Puritan Government, and it appeared no less strange to them then than it does to us now that their Government should have clapped so many people in gaol at the very time when they were most anxious to have everybody hard at work to rebuild England's shattered economy. For although the prisons were cold and foul they were costly to maintain, being always crammed with such culprits as actors, men who had been overheard to swear, poachers, fornicators, and criminals convicted of sinful indulgence in sport.

It was to rid themselves of the burden of the upkeep of such "sturdy rogues" that the Government decided to transport them to the colonies; and, besides these offenders inside the gaols, they wanted to rid themselves of the offenders outside—those Englishmen who offended by reason of their poverty.

It is here, perhaps, in their ruthless attitude towards poverty, that we can best understand the Puritans' growing reverence for riches. The old Poor Laws, bad as they had been, had collapsed during the Civil War, when money had sometimes been provided instead of work. By the time the Commonwealth had established itself the whole parish machinery of administration was in a state of decay, and the thousands of unemployed ex-soldiers thrown on to the parish at the end of the war had totally wrecked the old system.

The Puritans had nothing new to suggest for dealing with this problem except increased severity. They identified hard work with piety, and therefore blamed the poor for their shiftlessness in being poor, declaring that their poverty was an act of Divine retribution, because they were too lazy to amass wealth. Therefore, since they had displeased God by being unsuccessful, they must be further punished by whipping. All unemployed beggars were well whipped, and this did at least give employment to one man, the official parish whipper, if it did little to cure unemployment in general.

Though England's middle class was growing much richer at this time, there was an actual decline in private charity, for Puritans did not believe in alms. Never spenders, without a profitable return for their outlay, they believed they pleased God by hoarding their money when it was not out at interest. Authorities complained at the lack of small change, pointing out that those who might have given a farthing or half a farthing to charity would not offer a penny or twopence. But it was those who could best afford the penny or twopence who gave nothing at all on principle.

The situation worsened so gravely that the city of London swarmed with beggars, who pursued respectable citizens right inside the churches, which were the only places besides their business premises they ever went to. The workhouses and orphanages the Government reluctantly set up were so ill-financed that they were totally unsuccessful, no instruction being given, nor any money to buy teaching material. Instead still another Act of Parliament was passed in 1657, decreeing that anyone at all found on the roads without means of subsistence, *even though not begging*, was liable to severe punishment as a sturdy beggar. Puritans hated giving charity, which they described as "bribery and the encouragement of the idle dissolute." Englishmen were to be whipped into making money whether they would or no.

Their failures they shipped off in thousands to America to provide the manpower to develop the new colonies. Those transported had to pay back their passage money in the form of indentures of four, five, or seven years' labour. This, in practice, meant a temporary slavery, all the more cruel because, being temporary only, the planters made a practice of forcing as much work as they could out of the transported men during the time they had the use of them. By all accounts bought slaves were treated better because they cost more, and therefore had to last longer. One such transported English prisoner named Burton kept a diary in which he wrote of "the most insupportable captivity in grinding-mills, furnace-work, digging in tropical heat, feeding on nothing but potatoes and water. Sold from planter to planter and whipped at the master's pleasure." He declared real slavery a thousand times preferable.

Such ill-treatment of English citizens at the very time when Cromwell was raising the name of England to a great height of respect among the nations of the world can only be explained by the fact that the Puritans believed wealth to be an infallible sign of personal goodness and Divine approbation, and, conversely, poverty to be the stigma of Divine displeasure at failure to succeed. Puritans came to regard poorer men,

however honest as employees and hard-working as labourers, as spiritually
inferior to freeholders and tradesmen, and this philosophy took root and
flourished mightily in American soil and had a vital influence on the
development of that great continent.

Shakespeare, in his portrayal of the Puritan Malvolio, with his disapproval of cakes and ale and his ambitious schemes, glimpsed how the
movement might go wrong. It was no part of the destiny Milton had
prophesied that some Englishmen should become millionaires at the
expense of the rest, for no man knew better than Milton that no great
civilization had ever risen nor ever would rise whose highest objective
was riches. And it was precisely in deifying wealth that the Puritans be-
trayed themselves and their reformation, setting a grim and joyless pattern
of life without relaxation and without art for themselves and for the
industrial era which followed.

Their utter concentration upon getting rich was both a cause and an
effect of their utter rejection of the arts. People who are happy and
creative, like the Greeks, for example, are not acquisitive of money. They
are the givers out, not the takers in. It is the uncreative people who hoard.

Puritanism did not start off on the wrong foot. It got out of step later.
When we look upon Puritan dress beside our present sartorial failure it is
not its dourness that strikes us, but its dignity. No dripping limp laces and
cascading ribbons mar the effect of male pride. The body and legs are
firmly outlined by well-fitting breeches and close-fitting hose. The square-
cut shoes are essentially masculine. In its height and stiffness the Puritan
hat expresses more personal authority, not to say arrogance, than the

BURNING A WITCH
(1296)
French illuminated
manuscript.
Bibliothèque Nationale,
Paris

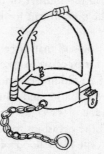

SCOLD'S BRIDLE
English, seventeenth century.

supine sumptuousness of the Royalist hat. If Puritan dress did away with colour it also swept male dress free of accumulated clutter, and its wide linen collar was kept cleaner than the lace flouncing favoured by the Royalists.

Puritan costume, beginning so well, could have been an excellent fresh start, instead of merely the beginning of a long desiccation, which has resulted in the present dull, deadlocked dress of the English business-man. But it went wrong, and we know now why it went wrong.

The early Puritan virtues were corrupted into vices as they waxed richer. What had begun as simplicity soured into narrowness; their thrift hardened into greed for money, their honesty into expediency, and their godliness into a passion for financial success. They overworked their employees mercilessly. When Parliament had finished abolishing "pagan holidays" there remained only one free day a month for rest and relaxation; as compared to Catholic France English labourers had lost fifty holidays annually. This loss benefited their employers, who used all the former free days to get more work out of their workmen. In such ways did the Puritans deny themselves pleasure and take any hope of it out of the lives of those in their employment.

Human beings cannot live under such restraints without breaking out somewhere. During the fifteen years of Puritan rule there was a sharp increase of witch-hunting, wife-beating, and monstrously brutal punish-ments relished instead of sport. Reports from Calvinist Scotland in 1650 recounted increased lying and swearing which accompanied the holy talk and sermonizing, and there was so much secret fornication that it was not until a woman had given birth to her sixth illegitimate child that she was there considered to be irrevocably sinful. In 1651 reports showed a heavy increase in the murder of bastard children by their mothers in England, where the punishment for loss of chastity was severer.

It may be said that fifteen years is too short a time in a nation's history for new forms of art to take shape. But that is not the reason why no new forms of art did in fact emerge. The heightened tension of the era which produced Milton and Bunyan must inevitably have produced great painters and playwrights and actors and sculptors and musicians, had these arts, and the occasions for their use, not been torn bodily out of English life. Except for a flood of sermons and tracts Puritanism produced no literature either, with the two mighty exceptions of Milton and Bunyan, the humanist poet and the inspired tinker, both of whom pointed the way which Puritanism failed to take.

There is much romance in commerce, and no lack of colour and excite-ment in trading, as any street market will show. But if the trader is only interested in making as much money as possible as fast as he can, the colour fades and the excitement and romance wither. Work, however hard, can always make sense and be enjoyable, if for the general good and tackled as well as possible and performed like an art. Happy people sing and whistle at their work when life makes sense and there is something to look forward to besides wages. In stopping people from singing Puritanism killed something very important, for English music had been so rich and so varied and delightful that every foreign visitor for centuries had remarked upon it, no less than upon the gaiety and liveliness of English dancing. It was not the concentration upon trade and hard work, therefore, but the denial of the natural arts as "impractical and time-wasting," in order to concentrate upon the acquisition of wealth, that corrupted Puritanism.

When Charles II returned to London in 1660 John Evelyn recorded how all the long-silent bells were set wildly ringing, how the streets were strewn with flowers, and how the fountains ran with wine; how the Mayor and aldermen, the lords and ladies, were all splendidly dressed for the occasion in cloth of gold and silver, and how the triumphal procession was so long that it took seven hours to pass.

There was, he related, some disorder and a little rioting and a good deal of drinking and drunkenness. The theatres and fairs hurriedly reopened, and in Southwark monkeys and apes tricked out in modish raiment danced on the high rope, and acrobats performed their tricks. But one thing was missing from the gaiety. There were no viols left in England nor any English musicians left who knew how to play them. Any music they wanted had to be imported from abroad.

Puritanism had set its teeth too deeply into the lives of the English middle class for the marks ever to be erased. There was something forced and weary even in Restoration debauchery. Samuel Pepys, with his desperate sartorial vanity and his close attention to money, his guilty prurience and his social push, gives us a wonderful picture of post-Puritan England. The old mould was broken, the new mould not yet set. But the coming shape is clear enough. He seems the typical *nouveau riche*.

The Puritan sense of guilt and fear of enjoyment lingered on in England until, in the eighteenth century, the advent of John Wesley fanned it to flame again. British self-righteousness outlived its Puritan creators, and the spoiled Sunday is still to some extent with us, that gloomy Sabbath which is the despair of the provinces and the ruin of our tourist trade. So used are we by now to making a virtue of our deprivation that we look down our noses at any display of emotion as 'foreign,' any appearance of enjoyment as unmanly and not quite the thing. Walter Scott related how, as a young child, he once timidly remarked at breakfast that the porridge he was eating tasted nice. His outraged father immediately ordered the servant-girl to add a pint of cold water to it.

This tight-lipped rejection of pleasure was the spirit with which middle-class England went into the Industrial Revolution when it came, determined to make a good thing financially out of it. It is this spirit, suitably clad in black top-hat and dour frock-coat, which informed the conquering and the colonizing of so much of the world, in order to remould it on Puritan lines, with a Puritan Jehovah presiding over the Union Jack and all the natives decently covered up in Manchester cotton. Typical of this point of view is the children's primer of instructive verse, published in England in 1832, in which a picture of a Hindu bears the pious words:

> O that Britannia's God His word may send
> To men like these and bid their errors end!

Perhaps the poor heathen might have been less puzzled had there been but one missionary to instruct him in one British religion. But that sturdy individualism and respect for healthy competition which we owe to Cromwell's revolution obliged as many different sects as could raise the funds to send a missionary each.

To-day, with the sole exception of the United States of America, where Puritanism was and is even stronger than in our own country, no country in the world has so many different religions and religious deviations as England. Besides the multiplicity of orthodox and unorthodox religions there is an assured place in England for other forms of approach to the supernatural. England to-day has not only her atheists, but also her witches. A retired inspector of schools reported to the British Medical Association in 1955 that witches were still in practice in Devonshire:

> There are definitely black and white witches still practising in Devon. I have known of doctors advising patients suffering from warts to visit local white witches. It is still done in Exeter. I believe black and white witches have power over neurotic people, by hypnotism and auto-suggestion.

In remote Devonshire villages, he declared, the seventh child of a seventh child to-day automatically becomes a witch.

Free-thinkers too exist in other countries than England, but they do not usually write their own epitaphs and insist on being buried in the local churchyard. Typical of English free-thinking is the severely plain, cross-less gravestone in Kingston churchyard thus inscribed:

James Smith aged 63 Died in 1875
He worked out for himself the Problem of Life
And no man was the keeper of his conscience.

A final result of Puritanism in England has been to denigrate the clergy-man and lower his status to that of a poor relation. Once the power in the church came from the pulpit. To-day it comes from the principal pews. The Protestant parson, hard-working, impoverished, genteel, is nervous and uncertain of himself in a community where wealth and business are of such importance. He tends to anxious jocularity, especially about his cloth, such as could happen with no other priesthood, in no other religion. The following letter was written to *The Times* in 1956:

In the doldrums between Christmas past and Lent still to come, a firm of clerical outfitters has once again sent me its catalogue of robes and clothing for the clergy. This they do every year. No doubt in the hope that I shall order a new cassock, though they make them so well that this is only my second one since I bought my ordination outfit from them twenty years ago: and I might add that I am one of those who wear the cassock fairly regularly and not only for Christian service: for a cassock is a seemly garment, affording warmth in winter, and such as will hide a pair of shorts in the hottest days of summer.

CHAPTER FIVE

THE INDUSTRIAL REVOLUTION

From childhood I have believed in progress. Common sense and justice tell me that there is more love for man in electricity and steam than in chastity and abstinence.

ANTON CHEKHOV, in a letter to Maxim Gorky

Is money to be gathered? Cut down the pleasant trees among the houses. Pull down the ancient venerable buildings for the money that a few square yards of London dirt will fetch. Blacken the river. Hide the sun and poison the air with smoke and worse, and it's nobody's business to see to it or mend it. That is all that modern commerce, the counting-house forgetful of the workshop, will do for us.

WILLIAM MORRIS, in a lecture

To the descendants of Cromwell's Puritan merchants, who regarded gaiety and beauty as sinful and the acquisition of wealth as godly, the Industrial Revolution offered a magnificent opportunity which they eagerly accepted, undisturbed, for the most part, by qualms as to the human suffering involved, since they too believed that poverty was caused by

DEMON FROM ENGLISH BESTIARY
Late twelfth century.
Cambridge University Library

thriftlessness and pauperism was a crime. Daniel Defoe had said that it was impossible for tradesmen to be Christians, but they were convinced that their increasing riches were a direct mark of God's approval.

The Industrial Revolution, which made England so powerful among the nations of the world and clapped her men into the dullest dress known to history, was also productive of much tragedy and human waste. After 1760 many former farm-hands were already drifting into the new factories. Towards the end of the century many more were impressed into the

Army and the Navy to fight in the war against France, (Rowlandson gives us unforgettable pictures of England's green countryside, the swaggering enlistment officers, the bewildered yokels, and the frightened girls.) Enclosures were speeded up, and the lands neglected because the smallholders were away fighting disappeared from their possession. The cottager lost his right to graze his cow and his poultry on common land, and he was no longer allowed to seek his fuel there. "Instead of taking the goose off the common," it was said at the time, "the common was taken off the goose."

Bigger, more scientifically run farms needed fewer men as farm-hands. Differences in wealth began to increase rapidly. As the old order changed many empty cottages testified to the plight of former owners who were broken in the process. Landlords began to pull such cottages down and raise the rent of the rest. The dispossessed crawled into mud hovels. They had no scrap of land left to grow food for their dependants. Nothing could be made at home any more, for the little cottage industries had also been engulfed. Food, clothing, everything, had to be paid for out of wages, and wages had to be earned somehow from somewhere, for now the former potato patch, the home wool clip, the grazing rights, even the old gleaning rights, were all gone.

By the end of the eighteenth century in England the trickle of country lads and country men into the towns had become a flood. There they worked in the new factories, together with their wives and children, whose competition brought their wages down very low. Conditions were such that when Sir Frederick Eden was preparing his Industrial Survey in 1795 he found that almost all the workers in the districts round London were clothed in second-hand garments. A man's hat cost 2s. 6d. A coat, which needed 4 yards of cloth at 2s. 6d. a yard, cost 3s. to make. A waistcoat needed 1½ yards of cloth, and leather breeches cost 3s. 6d. These prices and stuffs were well above the reach of the factory-hands, who were all, in bitter winter weather, wearing ragged flannel or cotton.

First the land-enclosures drove the smallholders to the city; then the new machines took away the livelihood and the self-respect of the hand-worker. The factory, as the nineteenth century developed, increasingly consumed him. He had no time to live, no leisure to relax. He lost the rhythm of the seasons in the "Satanic mills"; his religion changed to whining self-abasement; and he lost the right to look upon his two magic hands with pride.

When simple pastoral communities become industrialized their previous culture disintegrates, as we see to-day all over Africa. So it was in England. The remnants of merry England that had survived Cromwell, or revived in patches in the villages after the Restoration, were now utterly destroyed.

There was more behind the blind rage of the Luddites than frenzy against their metal dispossessors. There was also the bitter spiritual protest of the humiliated man, of the deprived artist. For it was immediately and patently clear that the proprietors of the new machines were not proposing to use them to further the general welfare, but to make themselves rich as quickly as possible. England, as we have since realized, started her Industrial Revolution on the wrong foot, morally speaking, nor has she ever since been able to regain her balance.

The machine, which we now believe to be the key to a high standard of living for everybody, was first used in a way which actually worsened the standard of living for the vast majority.

In England more land was already being set aside for game and less food cultivated, since the poor could not afford the high prices, and there occurred a series of food riots all over the country. Half-starved women held up carts of provisions on their way to market and forced the owners to sell more cheaply. The swift and savage punishment for such rioting, moreover, did not put a stop to it. It was against this background that the steady installation of machinery in factories provoked serious industrial rioting and threw a new word into the language—"Luddism."

For damaging machinery—and to the alarmed mill-owners inadvertent damage due to nervousness and inexperience counted as Luddism—the death penalty was demanded, and a Bill was hastily brought before the House of Commons and rushed through the House of Lords. Here Lord Byron, just returned from his first tour abroad, made his maiden speech in 1812 in defence of the Luddites. He knew what he was talking about, for his own county, Nottinghamshire, was the scene of bitter industrial rioting. Forty frames had been damaged, he said, in one recent evening, and not a day passed without further outbreaks. Declared Byron:

> But whilst these outrages must be admitted to exist to an alarming extent, it cannot be denied that they have arisen from circumstances of the most unparalleled distress. The perseverance of these miserable men in their proceedings tends to prove that nothing but absolute want could have driven a large and once honest and industrious body of people into the commission of excesses so hazardous to themselves, their families and the community.

He protested that their crimes, which were rendering them liable to conviction and punishment, were the capital crime of poverty and "lawfully begetting several children whom, thanks to the times, they were unable to maintain."

A workman thrown out of work by a machine had nowhere to turn for relief — or other work. Byron went on to say:

> Considerable injury has been done to the proprietors of the Improved Frames. These machines were to them an advantage, insofar as they superseded the necessity of employing a number of workmen, who were left in consequence to starve. By the adoption of one species of Frame in particular one man performed the work of many and the superfluous labourers were thrown out of employment.

An interesting point was that the new machines were producing inferior work, which in itself angered the workmen, who had always been proud of their skill and reputation. The duplication of large quantities of shoddy was, in fact, the first-fruits of the Industrial Revolution, and the workers hated it, whether they were retained to supervise the machines or thrown out of work on their account. Said Byron:

> It is to be observed that the work thus executed was inferior in quality; not marketable at home and merely hurried over with a view to exportation. It was called in the cant of the trade "SPIDER WORK."

His Lordship then permitted himself a jibe at the mill-owners for which they never afterwards forgave him, though he spoke but the simplest truth:

> The rejected workmen, in the blindness of their ignorance, instead of rejoicing at the improvement in Arts so beneficial to mankind, conceived themselves to be sacrificed to improvements in mechanism. In the foolishness of their hearts they imagined that the maintenance and well-doing of the industrious poor were objects of greater consequence than the enrichment of a few individuals by an improvement in the implements of trade which threw the workman out of employment and rendered the labourer unworthy of his hire.

Byron also pointed out that the machines were being introduced at a time when trade was almost at a standstill, the prospect of export nil, and when the workers, because of the long war and increasing unemployment, were unable to buy on the home market.

> It must be confessed that although the adoption of the enlarged machinery, in that state of Commerce which the country once boasted, might have been beneficial to the master without being detrimental to the servant, yet in the present state of our manufactures, rotting in warehouses without a prospect of exportation, with the demand for workers and workmen equally diminished, frames of this description tend materially to aggravate the distress and discontent of the disappointed sufferers.

He described the culprits as "wretched mechanics famished into guilt," and declared that "these men never destroyed their looms until they were become useless, till they were become actual impediments to their exertions in obtaining their daily bread." It was, he pointed out, the general poverty resulting from the eighteen years of war which rendered the situation so desperate in England.

> I have traversed the seat of war in the Peninsula. I have been in some of the most oppressed provinces in Turkey, but never under the most despotic of infidel Governments did I behold such squalid wretchedness as I have seen since my return in the very heart of a Christian country.

He ended his speech by protesting vehemently against the infliction of the death penalty for even the accidental breaking of a lace-thread, due to inexperience with new machinery. There was, as he well realized, fear behind this ferocious legislation, for the French Revolution was not long since over, and there had been a series of disastrous harvests in England, which was even then in a state of near-famine. In this February of 1812, when he defended the Luddites in the House of Lords, there were over 30,000 unemployed in Glasgow alone, vainly seeking relief, and the situation in both Lancashire and Yorkshire was alarming, while in parts of Nottinghamshire it was desperate.

Lord Byron did not endear himself to the mill-owners by voicing what was already in their minds and causing them no little uneasiness.

> Are we aware of our obligations to a mob? It is the mob that labour on your fields and serve in your houses, that man your navy and recruit your army. That has enabled you to defy all the world *and can also defy you when neglect and calamity have driven them to despair.*

As the rumble of social unrest grew louder in England demands for Parliamentary reform were added to the demands for work and for bread. The mill-owners tightened their hold on their possessions and, like their Puritan ancestors, dug in their heels. If the noise of angry people penetrated the exquisite Queen Anne windows of the great houses of the aristocracy, however, it made no very perturbing impression. Or, if it did, the grand folk who lived there believed everything would soon be all right again. Society in England had always come out on top of every upheaval, and their lives would surely go on just the same, whatever happened.

Lady Howard, whose family were closely concerned in the Government, wrote in a letter to her sister in 1830:

> The state of begging in large numbers in Lilleshall has been very unpleasant. But we had a good account yesterday of people returning

to their work. If this were not so all feeling of comfort in every sense of the word would go. It would be impossible in a state of starvation a long discontinuance of work must bring.

She then proceeded briskly to the more entertaining and more important gossip about the ball she had just been to:

> Harriet was in a new gown, a black net with white blonde flowers at the bottom and on the *séduisantes*. Over this, pink satin with a pink rose in her hair was very pretty and *distinguée*-looking, though not much like mourning.

The wretched hand-workers who blindly attacked the stocking-frames in Nottinghamshire, knowing that the punishment would be death or transportation, were attacking not only the threat to their livelihood, but also the threat to their manhood. Competition from flesh and blood is stimulating, but from a steel monster it is annihilating.

In the early factories conditions were grim and unhealthy. In leading the world's Industrial Revolution England paid, and is still paying, the penalty in blackened, sordid towns, belching poisoned smoke from factory chimneys, and mile upon mile of slums. In nineteenth-century factories the hours of work were very long. There was no nonsense about paternal direction; the employees were there to work, and every ounce of effort was extracted from them.

There was no time or spirit left to contrive the former pleasant fancies from straw, or whittle wood into agreeable shapes, or embroider a smock handsomely, or stitch a dashing waistcoat. In the dirty towns the days of the week and the months of the year lost their rhythm and meaning, and one season of the year was not to be distinguished from another. There was no time for the pleasures and relaxations of family life for the factory hands. No time for passing on the secrets of manual dexterity in the formerly manifold cottage arts, or for teaching the children the songs and dances learned from grandparents—for parents and children alike were utterly engulfed by the factories and the mills.

The deprivation of the arts which had bereaved Puritan England, and which had affected the middle classes so profoundly, now affected the labouring classes even more destructively, and what they had saved of their songs and dances and artistic manual skills from the years of Puritan repression, and had treasured through the eighteenth century, was now doomed to perish in the factories.

To make things well by hand needs time and thought, needs a pattern of life which the country had favoured and the town now destroyed. In one generation the cottage arts of England were gone, and among these cottage arts was the art of English peasant gala dress, sobered down by the years of Puritanism, but nevertheless an art, which had combined delight in wearing fine dress, though made of humble material, with the skill, experience, patience, and interest in making it slowly and carefully by hand to individual taste.

Such dress required time to make, and the drudges in the new factories had no time. They were never able to relax, being worked such long hours at such intense pressure that, when not actually in the factories, they sought oblivion in the momentary warmth and glitter of the gin-palaces or in opium, the startling rise in the consumption of which tells its own tale.

THE SEVENTH EARL OF SHAFTESBURY

In the factories, the mills, and the mines of England children were worked to such an extent and in conditions so bad as to excite protest from other countries. Workhouse officials sent barge-loads of their charges out as 'apprentices' to the mills and the mines, no conditions being laid down or questions asked afterwards. These children died off so rapidly that such openings for apprentices seemed limitless.

Sited next to the factories were the 'apprentices' houses, where the beds were never allowed to get cold, as day and night shifts of child workers succeeded each other. The competition for 'orphan waifs' was so keen that one Northern manufacturer allowed one idiot child to be thrown in with every score of normal children. Twelve or fourteen hours' work daily was usual in the factories, and the children were taken at very tender ages. In the manufacture of tobacco, for example, children as young as seven years of age were confined in unhealthy conditions of work for more than twelve hours daily. In the bleaching factories boys of eleven years of age or younger worked in an atmosphere of 120 degrees most days of the week and frequently all night as well. In the weaving of Brussels carpets children were obliged to start work at three or four o'clock in the morning and continue at work for sixteen or eighteen hours. In the iron-mines children of five years of age worked from five or six o'clock at night until eight in the morning.

Themselves hopeless and brutalized by work in the mills, and without a franchise, parents had no means of struggling for better conditions for their children. Nor perhaps, in the general degradation of the human spirit, did they care, so long as something was being earned. In the calico-printing mills, where a great deal of the night-work was done by children, mothers could be seen taking their weeping children of five years old to work at midnight in the depths of winter. Children of both sexes were commonly employed as beasts of burden in the mines and collieries, working naked in the heat and moisture.

Lord Ashley (later Lord Shaftesbury), reporting to the House of Commons in 1842, declared:

In South Staffordshire it is common to begin at seven years old. In Shropshire some begin as early as six years of age. In Warwickshire the same. In Leicestershire nearly the same. In the West Riding of Yorkshire it is not uncommon for infants of even five years old to be sent to the pit. In Halifax and the neighbourhood children are brought to the pit at six years of age and some are taken out of their beds at four o'clock. Near Oldham children are worked as low as four years old, and in the small collieries some are so young they are brought to work in their nightgowns.

He described the method of coal-hauling thus:

The child has a girdle round its waist to which is attached a chain which passes under the legs and is attached to the cart. The child is obliged to pass on all fours and the chain passes under what therefore in that posture might be called the hind-legs; and thus they have to pass through avenues not so good as a common sewer, quite as wet, and often more contracted.

The coal-bearers, as well as the haulers, were usually female, often very young.

One little girl, only six years old, was found carrying half a hundred-weight. Fathers had ruptured themselves in lifting loads on to their children's backs.

(This seems indeed a nightmare from another age. Yet a sergeant from Carmarthenshire in his seventies, can recall his grandmother showing him the terrible scars on her body caused by the chains of the coal-trucks she had thus been obliged to haul in her infancy.)

The results of such conditions on the health of the children were every-where discernible, and Lord Ashley specified stunted growth, crippled gait, asthma, and all manner of afflictions of head, back, and feet. He described the children as "dying off like rotted sheep, and those who survived drugged until the quantity of opium consumed almost staggers belief."

The American slave-owners of the Southern States (in the years of agitation against slavery which preceded the American Civil War, agitation in which the voices of English crusaders were loud) were able to point very effectively to these conditions in England, protesting, and not without reason, that their Negro slaves on the plantations were very much better off than the free English child factory slaves.

Reformers were not wanting who criticized the right of mill-owners to make their money out of so much human misery, and as early as 1802 Sir Robert Peel introduced a Bill into Parliament for the better treatment of pauper children in the mills. In 1815, in 1819, in 1825, and in 1830 further attempts were made by reformers to get Parliament to do something about the scandal. It was hopeless. Both inside the House of Commons and outside the mill-owners and overseers strenuously opposed all reform as a "wanton interference with the rights and liberties of the employers." Medical men were bribed to give evidence against the children, one declaring to the Commission that it was impossible to form any idea of the number of hours a child of eight might work in a mill without hurt, another doctor swearing that he did not see that infant employees had any need for recreation, and so on.

The reason Parliament was so hostile to factory reform, according to Lord Shaftesbury, was because it was held firmly in check by "the preponderating influence of the manufacturing influence in its midst." Cromwell's revolution had given political power to this very class, and at the same time hardened their hearts, in their narrow preoccupation with money-making, against the suffering their greed was causing.

"Fear of foreign competition" and "fear of loss of trade" were the reasons they advanced for their opposition to reform, protesting that social legislation would not only be wanton interference with their liberty as employers, but would also be interference with the liberty of their employees to work themselves and their children as long and as hard as they pleased. Even as late as 1878 a Member of Parliament named Fawcett proposed in the debate in the House of Commons on the Factory Acts that "Adult women should not have their liberty interfered with by Parliament."

It would be fanciful in such conditions to expect Englishmen to produce anything beautiful in any of the arts, least of all that of dress. The manufacturers, who were growing enormously rich, presided over a period of hideous design in dress, which managed to combine sanctimonious respectability, dull pomp, and fussy officiousness. Just as Cromwell's Puritans, in their preoccupation with personal cleanliness, seemed to be trying to wash off stains of guilt, so the manufacturers of the nineteenth century, in their deacon's black and funereal top-hats cast in the shape of their belching factory chimneys, seemed to be mutes following the funeral of the civilization they had destroyed.

The money-box, the counting-house, and the ledger had become their Trinity. And, just as thieves are careful to lock up all their own possessions, so we find the manufacturers and their wives ever suspicious and on the alert against the slightest possibility of threat to their wealth.

The opportunity wealth offered for social climbing was responsible for the outburst of books on etiquette in the nineteenth century. It was also responsible for the cultivation of female physical fragility, intended to make clear to the world that the wives and daughters of mill-owners could be just as delicate and overbred as any blue-blooded aristocrat. Organized charity was taken up by the wives of manufacturers, who had discovered that it might be instrumental in bringing them into contact with titled ladies, who sometimes sat on philanthropic committees

Charity balls with enviable social openings were one thing, the actual dispensation of domestic charity quite another. In the latter we catch a glimpse of the tight-lipped realities behind the genteel churchgoing and artificial altruism. The middle-class mother who could teach her daughter how to feed the poor from the scourings of the family dishes was applauded as the best of mothers in the cook-books of the period. Here, for example, is a useful hint from a book on domestic economy published in England in 1850:

> Cut a very thick upper crust of bread and put it into the pot where salt beef is boiling and nearly ready. It will attract some of the fat and when swelled out will be no unpalatable dish to those who rarely taste meat.

The preparation of large quantities of soup was always recommended, water, its chief ingredient, being not very costly.

> Put in pieces of bread that come from the table on the plates. It will afford better nourishment than the laborious poor can obtain, especially as they are rarely tolerable cooks and have no fuel to do justice to what they buy. 10 or 15 gallons of soup could be dealt out weekly at an expense not worth mentioning. Ladies should tell their cooks not to throw away the feet and necks of fowl, unripe celery, fishbones and fish-heads. Use all for the poor-soup.

The careless kitchens of the eighteenth-century great houses were a thing of the past. The mill-owner's wife spied on her servants, to be certain they did not steal the spoons nor eat too much, and she was careful to lock up her husband's brandy-carafe between meals, lest the butler should forget himself. A brandy-carafe was, indeed, invented at this period which actually had a lock and key incorporated in the design.

Economy was practised, significantly, not by decreasing the retinue of domestic servants thought essential to maintain social face, but by paying them very little in the way of wages and giving them less to eat. The nineteenth-century cook-books are full of hints on how to be thrifty without the guests' noticing; how to keep a tab on dishonest servants; how to test every commodity for short weight and foreign matter. Nothing, nobody, was to be trusted. The servants must continually and unceasingly be restrained from eating too much. "Every loaf of bread must have its own ticket and a tally kept to avoid cheating."

This hard-fisted outlook produced the hypocrisy so typical of the period, for the female face it presented to the world was advised to be "of a delicate reserve, a rosy diffidence, and of a sweetly chastened deportment" according to *The London Journal*. A dove in the drawing-room, a vulture in the kitchen.

The Puritan attitude towards the theatre as the abode of sin persisted. The Puritan fear of the flesh developed into positive prurience, which took the form of substituting such a word as 'inexpressibles' for trousers, and swathing the mahogany legs of tables, chairs, and grand pianos in pantalettes, because, though of inanimate wood, yet they were legs.

English middle-class commercial values spread upward and downward like a blight. The aristocracy dressed like the manufacturers, and the poor tried desperately to copy the sartorial respectability of their masters. In the chilly, encaustic-tiled, low churches throughout the country recipients of the 'poor soup' and petty clerks lifted up their voices on Sundays and intoned Isaac Watts's hymn:

> Though I am but poor and mean,
> I can teach the rich to love me,
> If I'm modest, neat and clean
> And submit when they reprove me.

Here it is in our brave island history that the art of male dress came to a dead end. It had become a money-grabbing dress, a salesman's dress, not a creative dress any longer, but a constipated and introverted dress, prurient in its concealments and miserly in its absorption of dirt which was not supposed to show. Here the English peacock's tail was trapped helplessly in the door of the counting-house, nor has it ever since managed to free itself.

In outline, in colour, in material, the dress of the businessman of the

Western world has not since materially changed, except that it has become a little less self-righteous and more self-conscious, as well it might, after two world wars.

What the possession of great wealth, divorced from either artistic integrity or humanity, can achieve we have only too many examples of in our country. London, with its endless rows of slums and street after street of pretentious, chilly houses, with their mausoleum fireplaces,

LINCOLNSHIRE CHIMNEY-SWEEP,
1914
From a photograph.

DANCING PEASANT
France, fifteenth century.
Illuminated manuscript.
Bibliothèque Nationale, Paris

ugly tile surrounds, draughty attics and sordid basements, is the ugliest capital city in the world. The horrible industrial towns of the North of England and the Midlands, the steel and coal towns pock-marking the whole country with ramshackle, smoke-racked slums, are monuments to the enormous wealth of the nineteenth century.

Greece at the height of her fame, Egypt herself in the days of the pride of her Pharaohs, were but poor relations compared to the monetary riches England's Industrial Revolution brought her. How was the money spent? Shelley had pleaded that something of lasting good and beauty be brought to life with so much money. But he was not talking a language the owners of the wealth understood. The wealth was dissipated in Stock Exchange ventures, in the creation of more smoke-blackened towns on other continents, in tasteless jewellery and hideously pretentious houses, and above all on wars. Some of it, saddest of all perhaps, was invested in grim philanthropic enterprises such as the ugly and draughty Peabody tenements which still infest the East End of London.

To-day we of the atomic age are having to think very hard as to what kind of future world we are preparing. The world has shrunk within reach of a plane-flight, and the radio to-day takes no account of latitude or longitude. We have long passed the point of accepting the machine, and with the advent of automation it is now a question of the machine accepting us. Man began without the machine. It looks as though the machine will now continue without man.

The modern factory is a far cry from the horrors of the early Industrial Revolution. It is a palace, large, well lit, and airy, with geraniums growing in rows outside, and spacious green sports grounds beyond. The hours of work are strictly regulated, and cups of tea come round on trollies. There are music while you work, social insurance, and meal vouchers and bonuses. And if the worker feels the strain of performing one simple routine action hour after hour and day after day, there is a sympathetic welfare officer he can confide his troubles to. And soon there is going to be automation, so that he won't have to be there at all.

Why, then, is there so much uneasiness? So much neurosis? So much boredom? The answer is that it is the machine which is having the fun of making something, not the employee. He is enslaved by the machine he is assured was designed to relieve him from slavery. This is true of industrialized Europe, and still more true of America, which is more highly industrialized than Europe.

Everything the factory employee does is mechanized, both at work and at play. His leisure and his thoughts and even his sex life are dominated by machinery. Radio, T.V., domestic gadgets, fruit-machines, cars, the farce of do-it-yourself hobbies, the Holiday Camps, organized down to the last communal cheer (camps where he presents himself like a coin put into a slot, and the rest follows automatically), where does he himself count? Count as a male, an individual, and a person unlike every other person?

For he is physically still more or less as nature made him. He has two arms and two legs, ten fingers and ten toes. He has his masculine muscles and his cunning human brain (not just the same as every other man's brain, but capable of individually different thoughts which should be helping him to contribute something to society). And he has, like the most primitive man, a deep desire for beauty and order of his own making, a desire which to-day in his mechanized work and mechanized leisure he finds no means of gratifying.

Void, bored, he sits in darkness (like a mole, though without the mole's handsome jacket) in the cinema, or in front of a hire-purchase T.V. set, night after night, and through the week-ends, watching exciting things being done by others. Or, greatly adventuring, he buys a ticket to sit with thousands of other bored men, seeking diversion watching other men kick a football or watching a mechanical hare being pursued by greyhounds. Or he spends his leisure brooding over the week's permutations of football pools in the hope of winning a fortune. He needs this dream of something to look forward to every bit as much as his degraded ancestor who slaved in the foul early mills needed opium to keep going.

No one could honestly call his present life much of a life. He clearly does not think much of it himself. And now, owing to our improved medical and social services, he has every expectation of living at least ten years longer than his parents lived, twenty years longer than his ancestors of less enlightened ages, perhaps fifty years longer than the poor Indian coolie, who, nevertheless, despite the shortness and the hardship of his existence, yet perhaps manages to experience, in his panoplied religion and his creative manual skill, moments of glory our Western man will never know. And not only moments of glory, but a feeling of belonging, of being part of something human and social which is greater than himself. For it must be obvious that our mechanized workman of to-day is increasingly lonely.

Small wonder, then, that he looks without enthusiasm upon the promised land of milk and honey which he is assured automation will bring him. Is he soon not going to be even a machine-nurse? If machines are going to nurse other machines, where does he come in? For more than a century he has steadily been deprived of his natural tendency to create things with his hands. He no longer trusts his artistic vision. He has been coaxed and bullied into believing the machine can do everything better than he can. He has been turned into a knob-twister, and he knows it. The prospect of further leisure, when he finds that which he already has turning sour because it has become so uncreative, fills him with despair.

Small wonder that the murder motive has become necessary to arouse a flicker of interest in his entertainments. Perhaps the individual murder is the last gesture of individual self-assertion left to him to understand. It would appear so. Crime and killing are more popular than sex in the newspapers and cheap paper-backs he reads. The *Evening Standard* complacently advertised in its 1956 story page "A murder a day."

But the gangster of to-day has moved a long way from the Gentlemen of the Road of the eighteenth century. Gone are the silks and laces, the affectation of fine manners, and the winning way with the women of

Captain Macheath. To-day's cut-throat is terse—a streamlined cut-throat with no fancy trimmings. He kills silently, or with nothing more eloquent than a grunt. He is joyless and takes no pleasure even in his women. He dresses drably in a mackintosh and dull felt hat. He looks like anonymity itself.

It is worth noting that the film hero of the youth of two continents, the late James Dean, was in life and played to perfection the mixed-up modern youthful neurotic—directionless and given to blind rages and alcoholism, a being without social roots as without purpose, who can find —and, in fact, actually did find—nothing better to do with the marvels of scientific industrialism than to drive himself to death in a fast motor-car. His biographers tell us that he never knew what to wear, never wore the right thing, whatever the right thing was in Hollywood. He did not know where he stood or what he stood for.

CHAPTER SIX

THE INFLUENCE OF AMERICA

The American oyster is reputed to lay 500,000,000 eggs per year, of which, under normal conditions, only one on an average will reach adult proportions.

MAURICE BURTON, *Animal Courtship* (1953)

TOLSTOI, in *Anna Karenina*, mentions a fashionable Moscow restaurant named the England. This was in the eighteen-seventies, when anglomania was still spreading over Europe, when Paris still named her cloaks after Queen Victoria and her colours after London fogs, still boasted 'tea-shops' where coffee was poured from teapots and tea (so called) from coffee-pots and horrid pudding was offered under the name of 'plum-kek.' To these snob teashops fashionable French ladies were driven in pseudo-English tilburies attended by French grooms called by English names, the very ponies, bred obviously in Normandy, being supposed to come from County Meath. To appear British on the Continent in those days meant to be rich, correct, and very smart indeed.

As to Frenchmen, such was the awe in which English tailoring was held, such the adulation for the British way of life, that the least athletic clanked about the boulevards in riding-breeches and spurs, smoked a big pipe, were studiedly cold to the ladies, and even tried to speak French with an English accent. The "distinguished elegance of restraint" in their dress, which their would-be-English French tailors assured them was modelled on Savile Row, was such as to be described by Balzac as mistaking "la morgue pour de la dignité."

"Mais elle a un goût exquis," breathes Mme Alvarez to the sugar-beet millionaire Gaston Lachaille, in Colette's *Gigi*, complimenting him on the Englishness of his costume, at the turn of the century. "Mon Dieu, que votre complet est donc d'une belle étoffe! C'est distingué au possible, cette rayure fondue."

To-day all is changed. Paris night-clubs advertise *les streap-teases*; the *grands boulevards* are dotted with *les snack-bars* doing a roaring trade in *les hot-dogs*. French Senators, whose *complets* are now cut after the style of Fifth Avenue rather than Savile Row, fall over themselves backward trying to please the Pentagon, and the youth of France devours American films and American comics and rushes to buy cotton overalls labelled *le véritable jean-New-Yorkaise-Pittsburgh* and French brassières ticketed *le véritable busty-look Americain*.

The heroine, Dominique, of Mlle Françoise Sagan's second wildly successful adolescent novel, *Un certain sourire* (1956), pursues her love affair with a married man in "Sonny's" night-club and in American bars in the Rue Marbeuf, where, in the American fashion, "nous commençames à boire méthodiquement," their drink being whisky.

Crew-cuts look odd above Gallic faces, but they are numerous and increasing. The day of the rich English milord is over. Paris worships the American millionaire instead.

In the nineteen-twenties, when America began to be fashionable in France, it was not the America of big business, but the America of the American Negro. With her sensitive nose for new artistic trends it was American jazz that then seduced Paris, as it now seduces the entire world. It was the authentic voice of black Africa, beating up through New Orleans and Chicago and out of Harlem, to electrify the weary white world.

To-day the American influence is quite different. Jazz has long been accepted and claimed its devotees of all heights of brow. What France and much of the rest of the world are inspired by is the America of big business and glossy Cadillacs. In Paris the post-Occupation despondents are slavish in their adulation of New York. *Le Cocktail*, that most un-French form of *apéritif*, is now so important that in Paris special furniture is being designed round it.

"These imported mixtures are becoming so successful with us," declares Jacqueline Foolot complacently in a popular French magazine of domestic arts, *La Maison Française*,

> that it is true to say that they have become an indispensable element in our receptions. The *coin-bar*, how whisky should be served, etc., are now part of the rhythm of our modern lives, and cocktails have now become not merely acceptable, but indispensable, almost a necessity. *Le plus anodin* of cocktails [she goes on reassuringly] will give you in a few seconds *un petit kick*.

It is, unfortunately, not always the noblest aspects of a culture which spread the fastest and the farthest. The America so much of the world is trying so hard to copy is the "Coca-Cola" America, the America of the horror comics, machine-worship, the passion to get rich quickly no matter how or at whose expense, the America of the sexy but sexless girls, the rootless America of the rapid boredoms and long neuroses, the crew-cut

AMERICAN SOLDIERS IN WORLD WAR I
Drawing by Fish, 1917.
This drawing originally appeared in *The Tatler*.

'Do you think it's the Spring, Alice, or has Throgmorton Street really gone mad?'

AMERICAN SOLDIERS AFTER WORLD WAR II
This drawing by Sprod appeared in the *News Chronicle* in 1954.

D

America of uncertain men in loud ties and lingerie-pink shirts whose wives buy their suits for them.

What is splendid, what is worth while, in America—the classlessness, the devotion of huge sums of money to research and to scholarship (at least on the highest levels), the deep-rooted and unshakeable belief that men are fundamentally equal and the optimism and immense *élan* such belief imparts even to the humblest of American citizens, the belief in and practice of hard work, the real lack of snobbery, the refreshing willingness to try out new ideas, the bubbling and ready humour, the belief that life can be good and the determination to learn how to make it so, the blessed lack of cynicism—these splendid American concepts, so vital for the tired world of to-day to believe in, are not exported.

Europe knows America chiefly through her comics and her films. The Americans known to Europe are the American tourists, always in a hurry, so busy taking photographs that they have no time to use their eyes, irritated (and understandably so) because Europe is nothing like what the American advertisements said it was going to be, and for ever darting on somewhere different in the decreasing hope of finding American sanitation in the next place.

Since America to-day sets a world pattern, in men's wear as in so much else, we must try to understand not only what she is, but what has made her what she is. Two characteristics of the present-day American way of life must be noted. The first is its instability, the second its uniformity. The instability is that inseparable from something in process and unfinished. The pattern has not yet hardened, and much is still fluid and uncertain. Things, places, people, homes, marriages, style of trousers, change overnight. America likes to move on somewhere else and has the means to do so. She is a nation on wheels.

The uniformity is the result of the instability, a desperate attempt at homogeneity in a nation without homogeneous roots. So many different cultures are involved, so many different social and moral standards, so many different bloods, that the only possible way to create a quick national identity is to cast everything away and try to conform to a single rigid new standard, to create, dress, and act the part of 'an American.'

It would indeed be ridiculous to generalize about so vast and varied a continent as America if it were not for the fact that radio, T.V., and advertising are hard at work day and night seven days a week trying to teach Americans how to play this part of 'an American,' and, it must be admitted, with notable success. Americans do strive, and strive passionately, to be alike, to act alike, to submerge their individual personalities in order to appear alike. Writes Dr Helen Witmer in *Personality in the Making*: "They are ably abetted by advertisers as well as by well-meaning magazines who describe in great detail the means by which uniformity can be achieved."

As is beginning to happen already, now that America has become so financially powerful, much of the world's male dress will copy American male dress. Therefore we have to study carefully just what the American

THE LANDING OF COLUMBUS
Print from a book of voyages published in 1601.

male stands for and what he is trying to say about himself in his clothes. We have to find that elusive identity which American men are so painfully seeking for themselves. It is easy enough for them all to dress exactly alike to gain cohesion, but just what costume is the model they are all going to copy?

To find a clue to American identity it would be best to glance at American history, to trace, if we can, the sources whence American men derive their concepts of the art of dress.

The raw material for all the arts, particularly the art of dress, has abounded in America. It is a country of surpassing and richly varied beauty, widely diverse native population, many of notably handsome appearance, and all passionately devoted to the delights of dress and adornment. Besides these, colonists and immigrants have come from every corner of the world, bringing with them the skills and arts of every continent. In addition to all these, a large Negro population contributes its racial inheritance of music and movement and its love of colour and fiesta. All these artistic riches America has had, and has still in abundance, and if to-day her artists tend to escape to Europe and her American designers of male dress tend to seek inspiration in every country but their own there must be a good reason.

The reason, we shall find, is the same reason as that which impoverished the art of male dress in England: Puritanical fear of finery as sinful extravagance, on to which was grafted the ideal of the pursuit of financial wealth as the highest good, wealth produced the last hundred years by the large-scale use of machinery. America to-day has strong influences in addition which affect her alone, and are affecting male dress. The strongest perhaps is the extremely powerful position of American women, who are courageous, well organized, most energetic, and in possession of much of the wealth of the country.

The first white men to settle in America were adventurers, followed by merchant adventurers and colonists seeking religious freedom—Catholics, Protestants, every variety of Christian sect. They found the country in all its wild original beauty, for the Redskin inhabitants did not seek to bend Nature to themselves, but rather to adapt themselves to Nature, coming and going in the woods without sound and almost without trace. All early accounts agree that the Blackfoot, the Iroquois, and the Sioux Indians, in particular, were a physically superb race, as, indeed, they must have been to thrive in such cruel extremes of climate, handsomely decorated but practically naked.

Pagans, with reverence for Nature and understanding of her different aspects, they were devoted to sports, to dancing, to religious ritual, and to the decorative arts. They adorned their simple skin dress, or their naked bodies, with magnificent patterns, always based on Nature. Though in time they acquired from the white invader such things as buckets, nails, mirrors, blankets, axes, beads, and, unfortunately, syphilis and alcohol as well, they were well suited with their own religious beliefs, and liked their own way of life so well that they did not propose to change it.

The earliest white settlers in America astonished them no less than they astonished the white settlers, but the two races were not mutually hostile to begin with. On the contrary, the Redskins welcomed the white men with music, feasting, and ceremony, for, as with all primitives, hospitality was part of their faith. They taught the white men their methods of cultivating maize, squash, the potato, and tobacco, showed them how to tap for maple syrup, and how to make snow-shoes and canoes. They also taught them how to play lacrosse. Perhaps the most important thing they adopted from the white men was the horse.

The ways of life of the two races were too totally dissimilar, perhaps, for there ever to have been complete understanding. But there could have been at least trust and tolerance, and at the beginning, in some settlements, there were, to the mutual benefit of both races. There were even a few exchanges of children, in a friendly competition of confidence, to see which system produced the best result.

General Lafayette, in the eighteenth century, thus adopted a Red Indian boy, who created a sensation in the fashionable Paris *salons* when he was taken to France, where he quickly learned the deportment and conversation of a French *seigneur*. To the amusement of the General's friends, however, the lad, on his return to America, cast off his European civilization like an uncomfortable shoe, went straight back to his own tribe, and 'readopted the rug.'

Now that we can see the whole American story in perspective, it becomes clear that all the different cultures which later streamed confusedly into America could have blended more coherently together, and could have fused into a more harmonious whole, had the Red Indian arts formed a sound basis for them, for additions and interchanges enrich, and do not impoverish, all cultures.

Unfortunately for America, however, this did not happen. The reason why it did not happen was that the Red Indian culture was destroyed by the settlers before its importance had been understood. Calvinist colonists, impatient to seize the rich Indian lands to put them to profitable use, and despising the Indian arts as sinful and pagan, did not hesitate to break up the traditional Indian way of life. Catholic colonists, though they appreciated the visual imagery of the Redskins in a way the Calvinists could not, felt themselves obliged to try to convert the Redskins to their own religion, and thus also helped to break down their culture and way of life.

Yet the Redskin, in a way that has proved impossible to repeat, was America. The Red Indian tribes understood and loved America, knew exactly how to live in it and not just on it. They were an essential part of the American picture. And the price of the destruction of these native American tribes is even now being paid for by contemporary America in its frantic and unsuccessful efforts to conjure American art out of thin air.

One or two significant straws show which way the wind might have blown to better purpose. There were, in the early days, not a few red-white marriages, the most famous, that of the Virginian settler John Rolfe with the Princess Pocahontas, sealing an entente which lasted for many years between the two races in Virginia and producing, from the one child of their union, a remarkable American family whose descendants still retain something of the stature and high-nosed dignity of their ancestress's race.

Though Pocahontas, on her only visit to England, soon sickened and died, away from the pure air of Virginia, she had already taught her

CARVED LADLE (WAMPANOAG)
Massachusetts, 1681.
Museum of the American Indian, New York

husband the secrets of the cultivation of tobacco, and he became a successful and well-to-do planter. What neither Pocahontas nor any other Redskin ever understood, however, was the white man's passion for cultivating more tobacco than he could ever smoke himself or hand round to his friends. The lavish exchanges of gifts was an essential part of Redskin culture, but commerce as we understand it, with a profit motive to power the enterprise and make it worth undertaking, was completely outside their conception. So was the buying and selling of land. The Indian ideas in this matter were those of the early Christians, or the seventeenth-century Levellers who were trying to copy the early Christians. They had no conception of the meaning of the private ownership of land, believing the earth to belong to God, Who merely loaned it to man that he might enjoy the usufruct thereof during his few years in the world.

Thus the red man signed contracts for the sale of miles and miles of rich territory and teeming forests for a few mirrors and a bag of beads, without any idea of what the white purchaser understood by purchase, believing that he would do as the red man did, hunt and grow a row of corn, since there was plenty of room for both. Records show that some Indians sold the same land to several different white purchasers in all innocence, having absolutely no understanding of territorial possession—indeed, believing that the chief purpose of the transaction was the feast with which the transaction was celebrated, and turning up yearly with gifts and furs for more feasts.

Unscrupulous traders soon discovered that Indians were especially attracted to blue beads, because they were the same colour as the sky, which they held in great reverence as the abode of their Great Spirit, and pushed up the price of blue beads accordingly.

There were many possibilities of misunderstanding. The Indian conception of stealing, for instance, was that of the Spartan warrior. Skill and expedition made of it a merit. To be whipped for having stolen a bucket from a white settler was to the Indian brave much worse than death or torture, which would have afforded him an opportunity for displaying his manliness and courage in fortitude. When this theft ,which to him was no crime, was punished by whipping he would revenge the insult by killing a white man, and, since to him all palefaces looked alike, it was usually not the same white man as the one who had whipped him.

It must also be remembered that the early colonists were of all kinds. Some were upright and diligent people who had left the Old World in search of religious tolerance, and who were prepared to grant it to the natives. Others were educated gentlemen, whose classical knowledge gave them an appreciation of the beauties of pagan ways of living. But there were many other types of white men coming to the New World. Many were transported criminals, or riff-raff younger sons, too feckless for anyone to bother with at home. Not a few colonists were really turbulent adventurers, who thrived on fighting and looting and did not seek far for an excuse.

The immeasurable stretches of the vast American continent seem to have intoxicated the settlers, fresh from the overcultivated, haggled strips of Europe and for the first time in their lives feeling themselves independent and with land within their grasp. They could hardly devour it fast enough. Unlike the careful and thrifty Indians, who thanked their spirit god for every grain of corn and wasted not even the smallest strip of skin when they killed a buffalo, the white newcomers snatched crops out of the rich soil without manuring, hacked down trees without a thought of replanting, and when they had exhausted the soil moved on to snatch more, abandoning the ruined earth and leaving a terrible inheritance of erosion behind them for those who came after. Wastefulness has been part of the picture of white settlement of America—wastefulness of land, of lives, and of indigenous arts.

In the bloodstained history of white settlement in America, wherein the Redskins were ruined and their arts thereby denied their white successors, one attempt at least was made towards a policy of reconciliation instead of extermination.

It was in exchange for an old debt of £16,000 that Charles II bartered to William Penn, the English Quaker, the province of Pennsylvania, which is about the size of England. Penn resolved to establish there a colony for those seeking religious liberty, whatever their creed, and was determined that the original Redskins of the district should also receive fair treatment and an honest price for their furs.

Penn was a trained lawyer and a skilful statesman, and he took the trouble to learn to speak to the Redskins in their own language. He was also a fine athlete, and won the respect of the Iroquois when he outjumped them in their own games, as a Quaker eyewitness testified. What drew Penn close to the Indians, above all, was their deep religious inspiration. Their affection was mutual, and he conducted a series of successful parleys and treaties with the Conestoga, the Ganawa, the Shawnee, and the Iroquois. An interesting wampum belt now preserved in the Philadelphia Penn Museum records one such treaty. Upon it the natives have worked in shell the figure of Penn in unity with a Redskin.

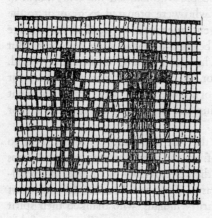

WAMPUM BELT GIVEN TO WILLIAM
PENN BY THE INDIANS

IROQUOIS DANCE MASK
Plaited corn-husk with trade bells.
American Museum of Natural History,
New York

Penn always came unarmed to these parleys, though the Redskins wore the dignity of full war-paint and were, at the early ones at least, heavily armed. His good faith and hatred of bloodshed prevailed, and during his lifetime and for long afterwards there was no conflict between white man and red man in Pennsylvania that was not settled amicably.

"It is not our custom," he announced at his first parley, "to use hostile weapons against our fellow-creatures. Our object is not to do injury and thus provoke the Great Spirit, but to do good."

In reply the chiefs and their sachems promised to keep the friendship "while creeks and rivers run, while the sun, moon, and stars endure."

Customary to Quaker practice, no oath was taken, and of this treaty Voltaire later declared that it was the only one ever taken without oath and the only one to be kept.

Had Penn's principles prevailed the Indians and their culture and their arts would have survived, and the dress of present-day American men would doubtless be very different from what it is.

As it was, Penn's admirable beginning was kept up for seventy years and when, the Quakers no longer governing Pennsylvania, war against the Indians at last broke out history records that Indian warriors never molested any Quakers. Three generations had not effaced the memory of Penn's good beginning.

When, after the fighting of 1780, the Redskins were driven from their Pennsylvania territory some wandered up into Canada, others into the Southern and Western parts of America. But they took with them the parchments of Penn's treaties, and in their meetings in the woods used to repeat over and over again his speeches to them during their ceremonies.

They wanted to believe in the good faith of the white man, and here was one white man, if only one, in whose faith they had been able to trust. Indeed, Penn was better treated by his Red Indians friends than his own compatriots, for he was so cheated by his own bailiff that, though he had been a rich man before the Pennsylvania venture and the colony was exceedingly prosperous, as an old man he was obliged to go to prison in London for debt.

Penn's methods were simple. He said what he meant, kept his word, respected their different way of life, and did not try to change them. Though, as a Quaker, he held strong views on the subject of extravagant dress, this did not affect his easy relations with the brilliantly adorned Redskins. He stopped the sale of alcohol to them on the earnest plea of their sachems, who declared:

When we drink it makes us mad. We do not know what we do. We then abuse one another and throw each other into the fire. Seven score of our people have been killed by reason of drinking it since the Dutch first sold it to us.

He made strict laws to ensure that they were never cheated in their dealings with the colonists.

Seventy years is not a long time in the history of a people, but Penn's successful experiment showed what could be done by reason and tolerance. The traders who followed Penn, however, were actuated by no such sentiments. They were out to make money as fast as possible, and did not hesitate to ply the Redskins with alcohol, under the influence of which they gave away their furs and everything they had. As the picture darkens, the Redskins, chiefs, sachems, and tribesmen, were alike eager to drown their misery in the white man's liquid oblivion.

Penn had been greatly impressed by the fine physique of the Redskins, describing them as "generally tall, straight, well built and of singular proportion. They tread strong and clever and mostly walk with a lofty chin." This splendid physique could no more stand up to the unaccustomed alcohol than to the colds, the measles, and the smallpox the white colonists introduced. After having survived the rigours of the extreme American climate for thousands of years the red men succumbed to the destructive way of life of the white man in two centuries.

Yet, though they destroyed the Redskins, the brilliance and romantic appeal of their splendid dress has never failed to fascinate their conquerors, as it still fascinates all white children. And this magnificent attire is more truly American than any other dress that has been worn in America ever since. For it belongs essentially to America and to nowhere else. In every detail it was an American product. The skins, the sinew with which it was sewn together, the bright colours made from earth and berries, the glorious feather headdress, the shell and bead ornament, the porcupine quill-work, and the particular symbolism of the decoration, all were native American; and no prouder nor more masculine American has yet been evolved on the American continent than the Iroquois chieftain. His loss is irreplaceable, and no amount of imported finery, however far the bustling American buyer ranges, and however many dollars he pays for it, can make good this loss. Here was the basic American identity Americans have been looking for ever since they destroyed it. But it has gone, and gone for good.

Meanwhile the early French settlers were reacting in their own manner to the Redskins of other provinces. Fresh as they were from their own highly stratified society (where sumptuary laws held the classes in place with a grip of iron), the feather crowns and proud bearing of the natives made an enormous impression on them, and from the enthusiastic reports they sent back to France Rousseau and Voltaire drew the conclusions that they wanted to draw and their readers wished to learn. All savages, they concluded, must be wise and good, simply because they lived away from the pernicious cities and the corruption of courts.

In 1704, in his book *Suite de Voyages en Amérique* Baron de Lahontas reported with relish the words he claimed to have been spoken by the Huron Chieftain Adana:

> Really you weary me with your talk of gentlemen, merchants and priests. Would you see such a thing if there were neither mine nor thine? You would all be equals as Hurons are. Those who are only fit to eat, drink, and amuse themselves would languish and die; but their descendants would live like us.

From such inflammable material as this philosophers in France began to pile up ammunition for the French Revolution that was to come.

America needed populating, and substantial dowries were offered in France to Christian girls prepared to go out to America and marry colonists. There was also a good deal of intermarriage between the French settlers and Red Indian girls from the Canadian and Louisiana

REDSKIN MILITARY ENCOUNTER (DAKOTA-SIOUX)
Painted on chief's deerskin robe. Nineteenth century.
Musée de l'Homme, Paris

tribes, helped by the fortunate French freedom from colour prejudice. But still more marriages were required, and somewhere about 1800 the senator Patrick Henry introduced, and nearly succeeded in getting through Congress, a Bill providing good bonuses for the intermarriage of whites and Red Indians.

Such intermarriage on a large scale might have saved more of these physically fine native people, and, as is often the case, strengthened the white race as well, spiritually and physically. We can only speculate on what might have happened. Certainly the arts must have benefited had such intermarriage taken place, for we have a few notable examples of the offspring of such unions. Paul Robeson, for example, is descended on his mother's side from mixed Negro-Red-Indian and Quaker stock, and the three outstanding American ballerinas, Maria and Marjorie Tallchief and Rosella Hightower, are all of mixed Indian-white blood.

But these are exceptions, and history records little but tragedy for the original inhabitants of America and their arts. Here, as elsewhere, the white man's firearms gave him supremacy. Already in 1834, in La Plata, Charles Darwin was writing in his *Beagle Journal*:

> Santa Fé is a quiet little town and is kept clean and in good order. The Governor Lopez has been 17 years in power. The Governor's favourite occupation is hunting Indians. A short time since he slaughtered 48 and sold the children at the rate of three or four pounds apiece.

In 1854 the Indians of the Blackfoot tribe were the most powerful of all the Indians of the North-western plains, dominating the whole area between North Saskatchewan and Yellowstone, Wyoming. They lived on buffalo, which provided them with meat for food, skins for their tepees and dress, sinews for thonging, and fuel for their fires. After the careful records of the United States Indian Service the Northern buffalo herds in 1874 numbered at least four million head. By 1879 these herds had been practically exterminated by white settlers.

Buffalo skins were in demand for fashionable rugs and trophies. There was also hatred against the now hostile Redskins and the desire to despoil them of their livelihood. The close-packed herds offered lust-stimulating targets. So the white men shot and shot. The mighty herds of buffalo vanished from the prairies, and covered wagons, going westward during those five years, encountered mountainous piles of buffalo bones whitening under the hot sun.

Without the buffalo the Blackfoot Indians had no food, no fuel, and no shelter, and during the twelve months between 1878 and 1879 very many of them died from starvation. Those who survived kept themselves alive by devouring dogs and making a wretched soup from the rotted buffalo bones on the prairies. In 1883 the broken remnants of this once splendid tribe were rounded up without too much difficulty and driven into Government reservations. They were by then totally destitute. But the reservation proved only a different place of deprivation, and during the following year there were many deaths among those left—from typhus resulting from starvation. Much too late Government rations of beef and flour were doled out.

It had taken only a few years to destroy a whole people. To-day there is practically nothing left of this fine tribe, and their intricate and beautiful culture is a receding flutter in history.

Much on the same lines could be related of the other American Indian tribes, whose skilled and imaginative handwork and whose splendid raiment we can gaze upon to-day, dusty and useless, behind glass in city museums, as we gaze upon the obsolete bones of the brontosaurus: the Piegan tribe, of whom one-quarter starved to death, the Cherokee, the Creek, the Shawnee, and the rest.

Photography was already in existence in the eighteen-sixties, and in the fascinating plates of the explorer-photographer Jackson, who followed the tragic trail westward, the marks of death can already be seen on the strange Redskin faces.

When Longfellow published *Hiawatha* in 1855 he based his style on the Finnish epic *Kalevala*, so little understanding was there, even on the part of America's foremost poet, of native Red Indian metre. In our own day the American Indian has already become a legend, cruelly distorted and exploited by the movies and the comics and frequently traduced by more responsible authorities.

Thus, when those in charge of the designs on American dollar bills decided on a series of engravings of important American historic figures, the Sioux Chieftain Onepapa ("Running Antelope") was invited to sit for his photograph for this purpose. Onepapa arrived at the studio in Sioux costume, wearing his chiefly headdress with its traditional three long feathers. This headdress proving too high for the camera frame, Onepapa was given the short headdress of the Pawnee tribe to wear instead. The Pawnees being the hereditary enemies of the Sioux, Onepapa refused to wear their headdress. The matter was settled when an employee of the Bureau of Engraving posed in a Pawnee headdress, which was super-imposed over the photograph of Onepapa. "White man always double-cross Red man," commented the *New Yorker* genially.

Is it possible that so richly decorated and completely indigenous a way of life as that of the American Indians could be so utterly destroyed in so short a time and leave no traces behind? Traces there are, undoubtedly, to be found in America to-day, but they must be sought patiently. They are certainly not to be found in the bogus revivals and commercial attempts to make money by selling quack 'Indian' beadwork to tourists, bead-work that to-day has lost its roots and its meaning.

An authentic easiness of soft-skin footwear, worn for sports by contemporary Americans, derives undoubtedly from the Indian moccasin. Also Red Indian is the traditional finishing off of leather jackets by cutting the edges into fringe. Certainly the tight American male trouser-seats owe their origin to the Red Indian dislike of covering the male buttocks. Their own leg-coverings had no seat at all, and when the Redskins borrowed trousers from the white men the first thing they did, in order to feel at ease in them, was to cut out the seat. Tailors in England with American clients, well aware of the American insistence on tight trouser-seats, attribute this fashion either to the more thickset American male body or to the American mode of wearing the trouser-belt below the hips for comfort, so that, in order not to fall down the trousers have to be cut tight across the buttocks.

Both these explanations may contain a grain of truth, but the real origin of the custom derives from Red Indian dress. The white colonist dared not copy the Redskin directly in his display of manly virility in the form of the exposure of lean and muscular naked buttocks. But he has done the next best thing in wearing the seat of his trousers so tight that he can reveal their shape as closely as nature itself.

AFRICAN SLAVES BEING SENT TO THE COAST
Engraved from a drawing made on the spot by Père Le Roy, French missionary.
(*A travers le Zanguibar*, 1863)

One thing the white colonists never succeeded in doing to the American Indians of North America was to enslave them. If the red man had consented to work for the white man he might have survived, though but as a helot, and American history taken a different shape altogether. But slavery was against all Redskin traditions. The Redskin could not and would not demean his manhood by submitting to menial tasks. Death was to him much to be preferred to working the white man's plantations, for if he died bravely resisting white domination his creed promised him a respected life in the hereafter. The cultivation of tobacco and corn had always been the work of Indian women, and for a red man to do such work was to suffer the utmost humiliation.

There were repeated attempts on the part of the colonists to force the Indian men into field work. They always failed. Since, therefore, the

Indian proved useless as a field worker the colonists had to search else-where for manpower. They used all the transportees they could get, but as the indentures lasted usually no more than five years (seven at most) this was not enough. So the colonists early turned to Africa to supply them with the slave labour they needed. There the fertile lands of the Congo and Nigeria had long been a source of supply for slaves to Arab countries, to England, and to wealthy early colonists.

The journey from Africa to America was long, and conditions for the fettered prisoners in the hold were so grim that many died on the voyage. But the strongest, who did survive, fetched a handsome profit on arrival, and the traffic soon grew into a vast enterprise. Here another and most important strand was introduced into the web which has formed the American way of life. The gifts of music and rhythm which the slaves brought with them, gifts which no hardship nor economic misery could deprive them of since they were innate, have produced in our own time the one distinctive art to emerge from America—jazz.

Before the advent of the big machines American prosperity depended largely on slave labour. It was worth while for colonists to invest in as many Negro slaves as possible, and even the poorest settler strove his ut-most to save up and purchase at least one slave. Indeed, there had been a special law in Pennsylvania preventing Negro slave field-hands from marrying, because this made their sale more difficult for the purchaser who could afford to buy only one. It was the misery and promiscuity resulting from this law, and the hordes of black nobody's children thrown on the slave market at the mercy of speculators, which goaded William Penn into a campaign to get the law changed.

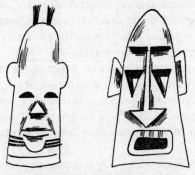

MASKS OF WHITE FOREIGNERS
Dogon, French West Africa. Contemporary.
Musée de l'Homme, Paris

By another Pennsylvania law, which under the guise of benevolence hid callous lack of responsibility, Negro slaves were to be granted their freedom after serving fourteen years' slavery, and with their freedom also given a small parcel of land, two suits of clothes, and three agricultural tools, on condition that they paid back to their former master two-thirds of the produce from this bit of land, plus, from the remaining one-third, the price of the two suits of clothes and the three tools. In effect this law kept the released slaves destitute and in debt for the rest of their lives, while releasing their former master of the necessity of maintaining his ageing slaves. This law too Penn managed to have amended.

If these harsh laws could apply in benevolent Pennsylvania the conditions under which Negro slaves lived in less tolerant provinces may be imagined. The American newspapers of the eighteenth and the first half of the nineteenth centuries abound with advertisements offering "likely Negro slaves capable of all sorts of plantation work" and "sturdy Negro wenches fit for all sorts of housework."

Though conditions for house Negroes was often not bad, the lot of the plantation-hand was frequently deplorable. Slaves cost money to buy, and excessive punishment rendered them unfit for work. But many of the planters were ignorant and brutal men, rendered callous by the very traffic that was enriching them, and the times themselves were callous, transported white men, too, being used as slaves in America and elsewhere. Darwin in his *Beagle Journal* records, for instance, how odious he found the use of white convicts as slaves in Australia, and how it sickened him "to be waited upon by a man who was flogged from your representation of some trifling misdemeanour the day before."

If white men had so little regard for others of their own race, what hope was there for the Negro slave? "The less intelligent a white man is, the stupider black men seem to him," wrote André Gide, after travelling in the Congo. And there is no doubt that the American planters, many of them of English origin, regarded their Negro slaves as another species of animal creation altogether, certainly not human.

Yet it is from the Negro slaves of America that the only authentic American art has sprung since the destruction of the original American Indian cultures. Ignorant, illiterate, superstitious, wrenched from their own African patterns of life, these Negro slaves poured their spiritual integrity into their masters' desiccating religion and brought it to throbbing life.

From the cotton-fields where they toiled in the scorching sun, and from the cruel prisons of the Southern states, rose the Negro spirituals, those burning appeals to the white man's god, who had supplanted their own tribal deities; rose spontaneous work-songs whose anguish, valour, and wit were expressed in amazing and subtle rhythms; rose such tribal coun-sels in music as the song of *The Grey Goose*, bidding the black man to hold on and to multiply, for only thus could he survive slavery and eventually achieve his freedom.

In New Orleans the Negroes poured their intense musical vitality into the white man's strange brass instruments and tired respectable dances, and created the phenomena of jazz.

Nor was it only in North America that the enslaved Africans were sweated, and yet created music. Conditions for Negro slaves in South America were still worse than in the Northern states. In all his travels, Charles Darwin reported in his *Journal*, he found nothing to compare with the cruelty inflicted on the Negro slaves of South America by their Christian white owners. One instance will suffice:

> Near Rio de Janeiro I lived opposite to an old lady who kept screws to crush the fingers of her female slaves. I have seen a little boy, six or seven years old, struck thrice with a horsewhip on his naked head.

Such is the background whence emerged the second form of American Negro music, the South American mambas and the rumbas, which to-day, along with jazz, has set the youth of the entire world quivering. There seems nothing which has vitality, colour, and rhythm in America to-day but owes its source to its coloured population.

Though to-day on the shabby New York underground railway, used only by the unsuccessful who cannot afford a car, one sees respectable elderly Negresses extinguishing themselves in dull garments of black, though the better-off Negro loves to dress himself up in the white man's prestige-granting sober city suit and hard shoes, the irrepressible African passion for musical movement and bright colour lies not far beneath these sterile surfaces. It is impossible not to be struck by their very manner of wearing the white man's dress. American Negroes, natural dancers, invest it with something of themselves, an inner swagger which makes it look startlingly different. It becomes a performance, not merely a dress.

The millions of European peasants who poured into America through-out the nineteenth century in the hope of bettering their lot at first retained something of the arts and crafts of the Old World, though their children have decisively rejected the Old World in order to strive after American identity. Among these peasant immigrants there were many artistic skills and, perhaps even more important, a sense of values which included the practice of the arts.

Grandma Moses is no new phenomenon in American life. There were thousands of her in America before the machine killed domestic handwork. America has always abounded in nimble-fingered old women with sturdy and original personalities. Though we look back on the log-cabin days, and the patchwork-quilting bees held in them, as far removed in

Lightning

Horse tracks
(prowess at
horsestealing)

Dragon fly

Arrow
points

Feathers
denoting
rank

Cloud   Tepee   Leaf   Mountain

AMERICAN INDIAN SIGN-WRITING

time, in fact they took place not so very long ago. Mrs Ann Catherine Milne, an old lady who died in October 1956 in Salt Lake City at the age of 107, actually walked the whole way from Boston to Utah as a child of eight in the Mormon migration of 1855, a distance of a thousand miles. It was such women as this, who helped their families to build the log cabins in the wilderness, and who were nearly as close to the wild beauty of America as were the Redskins, who gave something distinctive in their handwork to the culture of the country, though all too frequently what they had to give was stifled and narrowed by the restraints of their art-fearing religious creed. Nevertheless the peasant delight in pattern-making surmounted the hardships of the log-cabin life, and at first, before

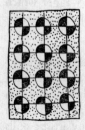

AMERICAN PATCHWORK-QUILT PATTERNS (NINETEENTH CENTURY)
From left: Steeplechase, shoe-fly, flock of geese, windmill. Note links with Indian patterns.

prosperity stifled the manual arts, turned the crafts brought from the Old World into something new and American.

American patchwork, though Welsh in origin, derived its being from the simple economic necessity to make something warm and interesting out of nothing. The earliest American patchwork quilts were cobbled together from anything at all that could possibly be used in the way of material. Not only were the sounder portions of worn-out dress cut up and used, but also bits of old Civil War uniforms and portions of burlap, often dyed with the aid of local plants and nuts. One old patchwork quilt even contains patches from the crimson robe of a former Lord Mayor of London. The fascinating patterns which the American patchwork developed were chiefly religious in *motif*, such as the handsome "Star of David." Others were inspired by political events, such as the "Radical Rose," whose black patches refer to the Negro problem. Others again were geometrical, with no particular sentiment, such as the popular "Lend and Borrow"; and others, in their geometrical arrangement, display distinct Red Indian influence, the same basic patterns and even the same names for the patterns being used. For until the wars of extermination ruined all possibilities of friendship there was some friendly traffic between the log cabin and the tepee. The Indian method of ornamenting hides and working dyed porcupine quills and beads presented similar geometric problems, and their imagery, rich and pleasing, was instinct with poetic meaning which the early settlers did not disdain to borrow.

Like the Indians, the early settlers had to make everything by themselves. They had to build up from nothing or go without. They were not grand city folk who could afford to import and set up a costly *salon*, patterned on St James's, in the fashionable quarter of New York, nor import a handsome Dutch home ready made from Amsterdam. These patchwork quilts were not the pastime of idle hands, but the toil of calloused fingers and sewn in precious time snatched from onerous daily chores. They were quilted for warmth during the bitter American winters, and they were attractive and pleasing in design because here, as elsewhere, simple people in touch with nature are creative. What is particularly interesting in the light of the frantic competitive system that America later developed—a system which has helped to make her so rich and has made individual Americans so lonely—is the fact that the patchwork quilts, like corn-husking, apple-ringing, and so many of the chores of early pioneering days, were co-operative efforts. The patterns were held in common, exchanged, lent about, added to, enriched by mutual understanding and willingness to share. Each housewife worked on her own units, and when she had assembled sufficient all her neighbours would come along to help her with the quilting, a score or more working together on the material, which was stretched tightly between two chairs or planks.

The quilting usually ended in a party, and it is interesting, too, that though the sewing of a gay patchwork was not regarded as wicked—especially if the *motif* happened to be a religious one—not a few of the square dances at the party had to be enacted in the form of a game, instead of danced, as dancing was considered irredeemably sinful. It was this puritanical element, rather than the scarcity of material available, which determined the choice of American decoration and style of dress.

CEREMONIAL WOODEN MASK
PAINTED WITH RED CUMULUS
CLOUDS

Haida Indians, British Columbia.
Museum of Natural History, New York

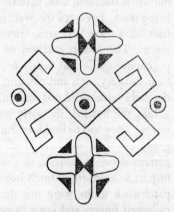

PAINTED PATTERN ON GOATSKIN
CUSHION PETTICOAT

Matto Grosso, Brazil. Contemporary.
Musée de l'Homme, Paris

American patchwork quilts continued to be made by hand until the eighteen-seventies, when the machine undermined and finally killed the art. The pioneers were growing prosperous enough to afford to buy horrible ready-made bed-coverings and dour black suits. Instead of painting the bare boards of their cabins with patterns or scattering speckles of paint like a thrush's egg, a thrifty and economical early floor decoration, they could afford lino printed with Turkey-carpet patterns or imitation-parquet patterns.

To-day the American yearning for something lost since the early pioneering days, some understanding and social kindness, some unvarnished spiritual integrity, some plain human dignity, has stimulated enterprising American businessmen, eager to cash in on the yearning while it lasts, to manufacture bogus, machine-made patchwork quilts wholesale, on the principle of what the hand could do the machine can do better, quicker, and cheaper.

The great-grandchildren of the women who made the original patchwork quilts have to-day infinitely more time on their hands than their ancestors. But they make nothing with their hands, for they consider their time too precious to waste thus, though, in fact, they do nothing very much but waste it going very fast to nowhere in particular, motion being regarded as having meaning in its own right. Thus the proud announcement in the *Saturday Review* (March 1955):

> It is estimated that airborne passengers travel approximately 25 miles while they toy with their appetiser, 110 miles while they savour their first course, 40 miles for the salad, and 55 miles more through the dessert and beverage; 250 miles to the dinner.

Now that the machine makes him rich the American wants and seeks the good life as earnestly as the early Christians ever did, but by totally different means. He hopes for salvation by the use of machinery, even at the cost of his personality and individuality, and to doubt the value and omnipotence of the machine in the America of to-day is plain heresy. Yet the wastefulness, the strains, the very speed of American life, are making him increasingly aware of himself, his frustrations, and the problems of his puzzling identity; and he therefore seeks the aid of psycho-analysts to explain himself and his impasse to himself, as an engineer is summoned to correct the faulty workings of a penny-in-the-slot machine, and to procure him reassurance, for he is not sure where he is going any more than who he is.

In frantic getting and no less frantic spending the part played by machinery in present-day America is vital. No people in the world are so conditioned by the machine as are the people of America. And this important fact, no less than their inhibiting Puritan tradition, is responsible for their anxiety and uncertainty as to how to dress their menfolk.

V. S. Pritchett has remarked, with truth, that Americans are soothed by machinery. Not unexpectedly, since they are so greatly attuned to and conditioned by the use of machinery, Americans find machinery easier to handle than human beings. Not only easier but more dependable, less unpredictable, more easily replaced by scrapping if not satisfactory, and capable of steady improvement in design and performance in a way that real people are not.

To the contemporary American automation beckons as enticingly as the Californian goldfields once beckoned to his ancestors. *The Scientific American* (1955) suggests that it would be—and, in fact, already is— "best to provide the machine with the best sense organs that money can buy, and then teach it to understand and speak English. This process could follow the normal teaching of a child."

Indeed, the machine should prove much more receptive than the American child, who, according to American educational statistics, is having immense difficulties with this very subject.

"Reading is a problem to well over a quarter of our school children," reports Director Joseph Grassi, of the North Carolina Psychological Clinic. Would not the machine do this much better, and not need the expensive attentions of reading therapists and psychiatrists?

The paradox of American life is that the machine, created to liberate the pioneers, who opened up their hard, beautiful continent, from sheer physical drudgery, and developed since then by engineers of genius to its present omnipotence in order to support America's huge population, now appears to have totally enslaved the people of America. Yet this slavery is voluntary, for one and all adore their mechanical fetters and daily seek to add to them. For millions of Americans culture means machinery.

To do even the smallest action by hand that a machine can be bought to do instead is socially disgraceful. Abercrombie and Fitch, the sporting-equipment store in New York, for instance, now sell an electric fish-scaler (110-volt AC/DC) for the use of anglers who do not wish to lose face.

Bigger machines ensure bigger kudos—especially in the matter of cars, which show no sign of ever halting in their expansion. "*The Big Mercury* for 1957 is even bigger—with the biggest size increase in the industry. Mercury is now close to two-tons big! Extra weight, length, width," boasts a Ford advertisement. Yet this "million dollars' worth of velvet," which sticks out so aggressively before and behind, is intended to carry only one family—say, three people—for the people next door have their own car. Maybe, indeed, just two or even one person, for Mom may well have her own car, not to speak of Junior having his own car. Junior must also have big things to make him feel successful. A toy plush giraffe sold at Schwartz (Christmas 1956) was $8\frac{1}{2}$ feet tall and cost 225 dollars.

To have an enormous car and to be seen in it continually means so much to contemporary Americans that some are prepared to eat less to afford it. And the continual use of the motor-car so shapes the American body that often it cannot stand properly upright when released. There is a noticeable slackness of deportment to-day even in privileged and well-nourished undergraduates due to the over-use of the car. It used to be observed of cowboys that they were reluctant to dispense with their mounts, even for the most trivial few steps. To-day the same applies to the car—with the difference that riding a horse exercises certain muscles of the body, whereas driving a car exercises only the eyes and the hands.

John B. Kelly, U.S. Olympian champion and Director of Physical Fitness, declared in the *American Magazine* (March 1956):

> Despite better nutrition and medical care, American youngsters to-day are weaker and flabbier than those in many other countries, and they are growing softer every year. 57.9 per cent. (compared with only 8 per cent. of European children) of American youngsters failed in basic strength and flexibility tests.

He blames this physical decline on too much "riding in autos and buses, instead of walking or pedal-cycling, machines to do all the chores," and on passive entertainments such as "radios, T.V. sets and movies, which leave no time for active sports."

The American housewife (target of millions of dollars' worth of high-pressure advertising) is becoming a machine-minding cipher in her dream kitchen filled with gleaming steel servants; a mere button-presser, the last lever in a complicated mechanical process whereby her family is cleaned, fed, and laundered. The drudgery is being extracted from the American kitchen, and the creative activity as well. For once it is possible to substitute a lever for the human equivalent nobody knows where to stop.

As in England, many housewives in America go out to work to be able to afford the payments on the hire-purchase of these mechanical marvels. On their return they assemble a hasty meal sold them ready to serve, and their evening is completed with the mechanized amusements of T.V. or radio. There is almost no time left for human conversation, and what little there is concerns itself largely with talk of machines, their performance, upkeep, and price.

For machinery has become America's supreme mode of social expression and social enhancement. To own a lot of costly machinery signifies financial success, and is believed to be the way to make sure of attracting respect and love, for to be unable to afford such machinery is proof of financial failure deserving nothing but scorn and contempt—the old Puritan belief. While it is socially embarrassing to dress differently from others in one's professional class, every American does his utmost to outdo his neighbour in the acquisition of machinery—the aristocrat of the democratic way of life being he who owns the most, the biggest, and the costliest. That is why American cars grow steadily longer and longer. "Designers to-day," says Raymond Lowey, the American industrial designer,

> are being briefed to give the public what it wants, and what the public wants is being translated into the flashy, the gadgety, the spectacular. Bulk . . . a sorry choice. To-day's dreamboat is a vehicle that's too big for most people, too expensive, too costly and too gaudy.

AMERICAN HOBO SIGNS

Key: 1. Man with gun. 2. Be prepared to defend yourself. 3. Danger. 4. Keep quiet. 5. Wealth. 6. Tell pitiful story. 7. Halt. 8. Be good — religious. 9. All right. 10. Don't give up. 11. Very good. 12. Dog. 13. Telephone. 14. Officer. 15. Gentleman. 16. Afraid. 17. You will be beaten. 18. Gaol. 19. Doctor. 20. Safe camp. 21. Kind-hearted woman. 22. Judge. 23. Unsafe place.

It is also too dangerous. One out of every ten American hospital beds at the present time is occupied by the victim of an automobile accident. In 1954 36,000 or more people were killed on the roads of America. In fifty years' time we may expect as many as 120,000 people killed annually.

Just as in the history of sartorial fashion once a trend begins it persists to the uttermost limits of exaggeration, so American cars, replacing the historic long-trained gown and vast retinue of servants as prestige-bestowers, continue to push out their distended hindquarters farther and farther. In theory if a conveniently small car could be made very costly indeed it should be able to induce a fashionable drive in the opposite direction—that is, towards the aristocratic, prestige-bestowing distinction of exclusive smallness instead of common bigness. So far, however, America is still deeply in love with bulk—sheer, useless, even dangerous bulk. No doubt, too, the American car industry is tooled to produce size and dare not quickly change. Of the 1956 automobile models the Lincoln Capri Coupe was 222.8 inches long, the Chrysler New Yorker Hard Top 224.2 inches long, the Fleetwood Limousine 235.7 inches long (that is, nearly 20 feet). Measurements are always given in inches to look more impressive, and such is the importance of extra length that the Studebaker Sky Hawk, classed as a small car, lists with precision its length as $203\frac{15}{16}$ inches, immeasurable prestige being involved in the struggle for every sixteenth of an inch.

Next to sheer size virility of performance is demanded, even though the car may never be used flat out. "Zooming with power" follows closely in advertising American cars, on "Money can't buy more flashing style" and "A foot and a half longer than any other low-priced car."

Not surprisingly, with such large cars and with such social prestige attached to the possession of them, the streets of American cities present grave problems of space. Double and treble parking causes the authorities no less trouble than the car-drivers, and the streets of New York are often choked up so solidly with cars that it is infinitely quicker to walk. "The violent snarled congestion of the bursting streets costs the city at least 1 million dollars a day," reports John Gunter. The new highways being hastily cut all over the country cannot keep pace with the increasing size and numbers of new cars to fill them, and cab-drivers are computed to suffer from the highest rate of duodenal ulcers in America. Prestige, in America as elsewhere and to-day as since the dawn of history, outweighs convenience, for man is still governed not by reason, but by emotion. The American car, so often jammed in traffic blocks, so much in occupa-tion (if not, for reasons of traffic congestion, in actual movement), is a home from home, often more important than the real home, and designers fall over themselves to offer within the car itself all the amenities of the drawing-room. "Sound-conditioned ceiling," "colour-keyed interiors," are as common as built-in radios and built-in phonographs; and built-in television, despite a feeble protest from some worried pedestrians, is making brisk headway. In the *Atlantic Monthly* Mr Loewy, forecasting the future, declares:

> Near-certitude developments are more people owning two or more cars which will be air-conditioned, move laterally, have steering-wheels which transmit the metabolic and neuro-electric variations to correct faulty dangerous driving and stop automatically when the driver becomes helpless through sleep or alcohol.

(This is the automation automobile, and a startling confirmation of Samuel Butler's wildest prophecies. It seems pertinent to wonder how much longer such intelligent and infallible machines will put up with stupid and only too fallible humans?)

Drive-in cinemas, meals handed into the car on trays, obviate the irksome necessity of dismounting at all, so that Americans are becoming a machine-age centaur—half man, half motor-car. The importance of the car is more than part of the American way of life. It *is* the American way of life. In 1955 nearly seven and a half million new cars were sold in the United States, and the traffic in second-hand cars is immeasurable. ("Our car gives you the biggest trade-in value," is one surprising advantage advertised at the moment of sale.) All this, which is true of America, is slowly becoming true also of the rest of the world where the dollar reaches. The signs of a slump in the American car industry are watched with no less anxiety in far-off countries than on the New York Stock Exchange.

Paramount in the American machine-obsession is the yearning for social prestige, the snobbery of things replacing the snobbery of birth, and the North Carolina Negro families who proudly install their washing-machine on the front porch, so that every one can see they can afford to buy one, are no less logical than those white citizens who put up T.V. masts on their roofs and radio masts on their cars strictly for show, having neither T.V. nor radio within.

The advent of the machine has deeply affected family life in America more than elsewhere precisely because America expresses and invests her greater wealth in the acquisition of machinery, the "higher standard of living" being reckoned not in higher education or wider spread social services, but in domestic machines.

"Of course," states an educational expert,

> with radio and now television, parents devote less time to reading for their own enjoyment and also for the benefit of their children. Many parents bother little with nursery rhymes, poems and stories. Rather they purchase recordings of these for the children to enjoy. There is no objection to this.

In fact, if the parents can't be bothered to read in this machine age, why should the children? America is pointing the way towards an epoch wherein the printed word no less than the word spoken to the direct hearer, will have altogether decayed, so much are pictorial and sound-recorded methods of imparting information preferred. The eye and the ear will in the future, at this rate, be attuned only to metal and plastic teachers and mothers.

"I have observed," says John Steinbeck (*Reporter*, March 1956),

> the symptoms of Television-looking on children as well as on adults. The mouth grows slack. The lips hang open. The eyes take on a hyp-notised or doped look. The nose runs rather more than usual. The backbone turns to water, and the fingers slowly and methodically pick the designs out of the brocade furniture.

Reading is difficult and takes too long. The radiogram and the tape re-corder are here, and only the scientists can speculate as to what even better people-replacers may soon be invented. Not surprisingly, therefore, America, with all her vast population and colossal wealth, actually reads fewer books than England.

One kind of book, however, still sells briskly in the United States. The twenty-five-cent manuals which teach how to be a success are steady best-sellers. For Americans are curiously lonely people, and believe that to achieve success means to be loved and to be popular. To become financi-ally successful, they are certain, will ensure social prominence, and that is the recognized way to attract love and avoid the shame and anguish of loneliness. Even those far from financially prosperous are urged to behave as though they were affluent, and it is particularly for those who are not well off, by American standards, that the handbooks on etiquette are written and sold by the million. This sympathetic magic is no newcomer to democratic American life. One of the most comprehensive etiquette books ever compiled was published in New York in 1855, *The Manual of Good Behaviour and Polite Accomplishments*, and achieved phenomenal sales, and no wonder, for it offered sound advice on every aspect of life from how to choose a tie to how to conduct a duel. "In this land of Free-dom," the author begins democratically, "of ambition and energetic self-hood, every aid is demanded which can contribute to the highest social achievement." He is adamant about table manners: "Do not use a fork for olives and cherries." "Do not fill your mouth with water and spirt it into the finger-glass." The author (unlike the author of contemporary manuals) is unfailingly gallant to the ladies: "So long as courtship is the pretext and marriage the object, almost all liberties are permitted. Young ladies may receive their presumed admirers at all hours."

He is a bitter opponent, however, of amorous dalliance between those of the same age. "First attraction between a young man entering society and a lady of mature age is a great good fortune . . ." he declares. "The true and natural mode of completing an education. She will polish his manners, refine his taste and understanding, and open his heart."

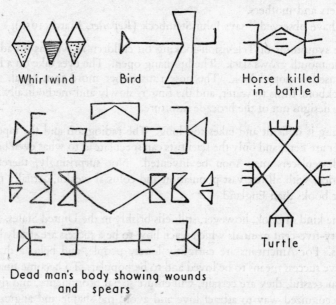

AMERICAN INDIAN SIGN-WRITING

Old men had much to thank the author for, in that he decisively reserves the young girls for them. "Prize the company of elderly men," he implores American débutantes, "if they are good and simple-hearted. Prefer the company of mature and even married men to young beaux and coxcombs . . . a manly bald head is something very becoming."

Dash and delicacy are his slogans. When the first method is inappropriate he advises the second. Thus, "The ceremony of bedding the couple," he counsels, in a long chapter on how to conduct a wedding, "which may have been well enough in the good old times, is utterly inconsistent with our present ideas of refinement." Indeed, he goes further. "There is at the very best," he suggests coldly, "enough in the marriage ceremony that is repulsive to the pure instincts of a modest pair."

There are helpful chapters on the acquisition of foreign languages and of music; chapters on how to travel and what to wear and how to behave on Mississippi steamboats; chapters on how men should dress their hair

and apply their cosmetics; and intensive chapters on how ambitious democratic Americans should conduct a conversation in order to attract
approval and invitations into higher social circles. Among other recommended subjects for such 1855 drawing-room chat he lists "The modern
sciences of phrenology, Galvanism, Magnetism and psychometry, this
last a very interesting and instructive subject for conversation."

Where this charming handbook differs chiefly from the American
etiquette handbooks of to-day is in tempo and lack of anxiety. The
pressure that the machine was to bring is notably absent. The author
appeared to have all the time in the world to enjoy his life and teach his
readers how to do the same.

To-day it costs no more than twenty-five cents for equally ambitious
Americans to learn how to do everything successfully, how to write
better letters, how to build up a more powerful vocabulary, how to meet,
infatuate, hold, or divorce a husband or a wife. These little booklets
replace universities for those who have neither the time nor the money
but only the passionate desire to improve themselves; and in examining
the American way of life and its effect on American male dress we must
remember that only a very small section of Americans go to college, and
of those the number who go to Yale and Harvard is very small indeed.

Glibness is always advocated as an invaluable social asset, in the easy
rules of thumb guaranteed to steer the novice past every social quicksand.
For the modest outlay of twenty-five cents the little booklets promise
SUCCESS, with its certain consequence of attracting LOVE. Popular film-
stars and newspaper personalities, for whom such booklets are 'ghosted,'
act as successful examples of the methods they advocate, and make a strong
appeal to both sexes, for these lessons in how to get on in life are studied
as avidly by young men as by young women.

Enormously popular with both sexes are the cultural quizzes with their
compulsive self-marking.

Is it acceptable to cut lettuce with a knife?   YES.   NO.
Do we sit in a chair from the right of it?   YES.   NO.
Should the drinking-glass be held near the top? YES.   NO.

More specifically directed at male youth (though the girls also buy them
to enjoy the pictures) are the cheap physical-culture magazines for sedentary young men, sold on the New York bookstalls and throughout
America and vying with Superman in the personification of adolescent
dreams. Such a magazine is *Adonis* (*The Body Beautiful*), which describes
itself as "the champion of the Male Physique."

Herein the problem of reading is sidetracked by the lavish use of photographs and the employment of very easy captions showing what grit, determination, plus the use of the advertised aids to manhood, can do for a boy.

There is something almost pathetic about this physical braggadocio, some deep felt American yearning to achieve (without the aid of dress, for in America, as elsewhere, the rich can buy grander than the poorer can afford to buy) a democracy in nakedness. A poor and not very intelligent youth from a district with no social prestige, it suggests, can, by exercising his body, achieve renown and distinction, no less than a rich and privileged youth with every advantage of education and social background.

Thus the galaxy of photographs showing carefully posed, heavily muscled adolescents in showy stances, armed with such manly weapons as fencing-foils, axes, dumb-bells, and ox-wagon wheels. There is a cosy intimacy, a get-together cheeriness, in the captions cunningly calculated to draw in the lonely male reader. Beneath the heroic, frozen-faced young athlete on the muscle-bound photograph is such gossipy information as:

Arthur Gold of Brooklyn, champion gymnast and hand-balancer. Arthur has the most unusual red-gold hair, very blue eyes, and is always deeply tanned. He is 5 feet 8 inches tall, weighs 168 lb., and is seventeen.

The advertisements in such magazines are revealing: "Posing straps," described as "professional (price one dollar)," also "Posing trunks." "Don't spoil your Physique [always used with a capital P], by wearing poorly fitting trunks." Other offers on the back pages include a bottle of reducing tablets, a twenty-four-hour course for overcoming embarrassment from pimples, another course in toning up the muscles of young but already sagging faces, "How to gain up to 50 lb. and look and feel like a real man," and a surprising number of guaranteed cures for the confirmed bald. There is an article, however, inside, entitled "Toupee or not Toupee," which brutally advises wigs for those without hair:

Hair pieces, rugs, doilies, trapezes or broadlooms. Some of these examples of the wigmaker's art-craft are real works of art. Some are so natural that they defy close inspection. *And some are actually an improvement on nature herself.*

This last is the *coup de grace* of all American salesmanship, for if that won't sell it nothing else will. But of course it will sell it.

Here must be noted the national passion to outwit nature, to do her job better than she can, with the result that artificiality in America is admired as a desirable end in itself. This may perhaps be traced to the fact that Nature in America, though so beautiful, is full of menace. Rattlesnakes, typhoons, floods and droughts, black-widow spiders, and whirlwinds have driven the American of to-day into working himself into early death from heart-failure to provide himself with air-conditioning so cold and central heating so hot as to cause his equally early decline from debility.

SENECA INDIAN MASKS

Left: Wooden mask hung on tree facing wind to direct storm. *Right*: Mask cut into living tree for curing illness.

Museum of the American Indian, New York

Fashions in artifice here are pushed to extremes too, to the detriment of real art. Nature must be, Americans believe, always rearranged and improved. This Hollywood approach to life is responsible for the brisk sale in green dye to dye lawns greener, artificial butterflies of plastic and clockwork to flutter to order over these dyed viridian lawns, and the widespread boosting of the word 'simulated.' In England this word still carries a taint of faint shame, but it is used as a virtuous selling-point in good-class American advertising. Thus: "Like Wedgwood are these Made in Japan copies of the distinguished English Ware," boasts an advertisement for switch-plates of faked porcelain. "Every lady who loves tradition will want one for every room in her house." The *New Yorker*, reporting on the new wallpapers, remarks: "Probably the most successful of the lot are two remarkably lifelike photographic reproductions of a red-brick wall and a white-brick wall, which it is hard to believe are not three-dimensional." Also selected for approval are a plastic material patterned in "Various coloured marbles, and a knotty pine that might well put an awful crimp in the business of the authentic knotty-pine people." And, following this line of æsthetics to its logical end, "One of the most expensive wallpapers offered is copied from an old French *toile*, with simulated rust-spots of age (extra)."

Who could resist paying extra for those simulated rust-spots? Plagiarism, like insincerity, is a poor basis for art, and disastrous for the art of dress, as we shall see. Encouragingly, there is, at the same time, enough real interest in art and history to enable the magazine *Life* to publish splendid series of costly and technically superb reproductions of the world's masterpieces, which the fabulous circulation enables the magazine to include in its pages at no extra cost to the public. Such beautiful, and often otherwise inaccessible, pictures must be cut out and pinned up from one end of America to the other, for America is a picture-loving country. In this sort of popular education (in which America's most distinguished historians also collaborate by explaining the pictures in careful, simple language) America is unique in making the best kind of sense out of democracy in the machine age.

When he faces the problem of how to dress himself for the role of 'an American' the American male is pulled all ways. He desires to express dashing virility, but in this his Puritan background impedes him; he desires to express financial supremacy over his fellows, though here his democratic upbringing forbids him sartorial show-off in the slightest degree different from that worn by his fellows; he desires to dress to attract women, when he feels himself so hamstrung by their domination over him that he resents and sometimes hates them; above all he yearns to dress with youthful insouciance, since youth is worshipped in America, yet the very basis of his material success is an early assumption of the carking cares of competitive business, which ages him prematurely.

He can therefore, in his dress, express only the strain and confusion of his life. The very quality he is most in need of, in fact, is the very quality most notably absent from his dress, as it was the quality most noticeably present in the dress of his Redskin predecessors—that is, dignity. Let us see just how his present conflicts express themselves in his dress. The most interesting items of contemporary American dress, the lumber-shirt of bright plaid, the tight trousers and dungarees, derive from the garb of common people fulfilling themselves in tedious and dangerous jobs. Though to-day glamorized out of recognition of this basic truth and worn by men who may never leave their office all day, such was their origin. These clothes belonged to and were conditioned by their jobs. The glaring pattern of the lumber-shirt was obligatory in order that the lumber-jack wearer might stand out in the gloom of the forest, so as to avoid accident from falling trees, and in order to be instantly visible in the turbulent currents of the unfreezing rivers, in times of accident during dam-breaking. The loud plaid lumber-shirt was a protective dress, and, as Oscar Wilde pointed out, as always what is suitable for its purpose is beautiful in its own manner.

Similarly every item of cowboy dress, to-day so staled by exploitation, derived originally, not from passion for the picturesque (though the real cowboys liked colour and dash), but from grim necessity. The romantic ten-gallon hat was used as sunshade, sou-wester, water-carrier, and pillow. The bright kerchief was there to be pulled over the face in dust-storms. The broad leather belt was a corset to offset the intense physical strain of the lasso, and the elegant high heels were essential for better grip on the stirrups.

Dungarees display the dignity and simplicity of all unpretentious working dress. The cut is easy. Blue is universally the cheapest of all dyes. The pockets, strategically placed and shaped to contain tools, are right because they are there for a purpose and belong to the dress. Such is the plain honesty of dungarees, conveying the essential dignity of the readiness to employ physical effort, that their manliness cannot be denied. Perhaps it is just this manliness that contemporary American youth, brought up on cars and a packaged existence 'untouched by hand,' are desperately seeking when donning dungarees in and out of season, like a fancy dress.

Rushing willynilly into the totally mechanized future, the youth of America turn their heads backward to find a flesh-and-blood hero of their own to emulate, for Superman has definite disadvantages in the age of the supermarket and atomic fission. Here Walt Disney came forward to supply them with exactly what they were dreaming of. Davy Crockett has made trapper dress the rage not only of America, but of every country where the film has been shown, a rage cunningly stimulated by the sale of copies of this trapper dress at prices to suit all purses.

The Times (May 8, 1956) reported this curious result:

Domestic cats are being killed for their skins, Lord Scarsdale, President of the Derby and District Branch of the RSPCA, claimed at the annual meeting to-day.

He said that the fur was being used to make Davy Crockett hats popular amongst the children, since the recent film on the American Pioneer of that name.

These tails, however, were not those of stray cats but of "Domestic cats roaming at large instead of sitting in the house." They were being collected and killed.

"Anyone making the hats should be suppressed from doing it unlawfully and do it lawfully," there being plenty of real stray cats the R.S.P.C.A. in Derby had had killed out of kindness. "The hat-makers must get their fur from somewhere," said Lord Scarsdale "and I think my idea would put an end to any suggestion of back street cat-snatching."

These cat-snatchers, stalking the domestic tabby by night on the concrete pavements of English provincial towns, are the real Davy Crocketts of to-day, but they themselves wear no more romantic a hunting dress than raincoat and trilby hat.

Davy Crockett, lumber-shirts, and dungarees, however, are all very well for the dreams of youth, and nostalgically for the vacation wear of the very rich, but America is the land of enterprising businessmen, bankers, promoters. Such men must dress differently, must wear the garb of respectability, and this means the European city suit, with such distinctively American improvements as a more blown-out jacket, a louder necktie, and different materials, though, it should be noted, heaviness and darkness are still respected more than lightness of hue and weight.

The American dress-designer Elizabeth Hawes points the finger of scorn at this American business dress, declaring that it "shows up the timidity and unaggressiveness of American males . . . If the U.S.A., as some say, is turning into a matriarchy it can only happen because most of the men are in reality mice."

She blames the Puritan fetters and fears for this unenterprise: "Puritanically they deny themselves their rights to the pursuit of all the mental and physical satisfaction women can get from dressing." And she asserts that the reason for conservatism in dress is the same as in Europe: "What a lot of snobbery there is in our great democracy. Is it a sign of the aristocracy we aren't supposed to have here to wear four thicknesses of material about the neck?"

"Men of America! If your forefathers could get rid of George the third, surely you can arrange the necktie situation . . . don't let the necktie be your boss!"

The influence of women in America must not be underestimated. They have money, they are deeply interested in æsthetics and eager to learn and to experiment. Their influence on male dress in the future may be the determining factor.

Certainly, bad as is the lounge suit in temperate Europe, it is infinitely worse in a country so much hotter and so much colder, as is America. But comfort is not a serious consideration in the latest American efforts towards a different male dress, for those men who cannot find salvation in "that lean, restrained, Patrician look" of men's shoes (price 20 dollars

ILLUSTRATION FROM AN AMERICAN
COMIC
Contemporary.

AMERICAN MASTER BLACK-
SMITH IN HANGTOWN,
CALIFORNIA (MID-
NINETEENTH CENTURY)
From an oil painting.

95 cents), or be certain that their evening will be "far more *enchanted* when you go elegantly formal," as is urged for such men as have "fashion adventure in their blood," and who, having this, are invited to purchase "relaxed formals with masculine magnetism."

Just what is this hybrid "relaxed formal," a contradiction in terms, a contradiction which is apparent in many aspects of American male dress? It is a neurotic attempt to do two different things at the same time, to be democratic-aristocratic, easy-tight, dashing-secure, traditional-untraditional. Uneasiness about the "sack suit, sign of the successful businessman ... the jacket worn rather tight with uncomfortable trousers and heavy shoes," which Miss Elizabeth Hawes condemns as unmanly, and the psychologists (who, however, wear such dress themselves) stigmatize as thwarting, is causing American male dress to veer to-day towards the "informal" and "relaxed." Sportive imports from Europe to meet this demand are specially done up for the American market, and transformed into such fantasies as the Broadway "conversation piece in new walking shorts of character [intended for the two-car class of buyers] made in bold-striped lustrous cotton." "Authentic Black Watch Tartans" are offered "also in brown and green," with no sense of anachronism. The *New Yorker* male-dress advertisements offer fascinating mixtures of sentiment and snobbery such as "Authentic Ascot cap, soft yet robust, for perfectionists" (price 7 dollars), and "Unusual Shetland jackets," of which the high selling point consists in the claim that they are "woven on primitive hand-looms in stone cottages," and they cost the not inconsiderable price of 75 dollars. Five-dollar ties are boasted to display patterns "purloined from antique music boxes," and woollen socks sell because it is claimed that "In England a gentleman is judged from his feet up."

Such innovations flourish as flowered Hawaiian shirts in city offices, on the weary backs of middle-aged salesmen; and the enthusiastic adoption of Italian shorts intended for children's wear, or English shorts intended for *safari* in Africa, as the business dress of elderly merchants proceeds merrily.

The bank clerks of the Tompkins County Trust Company in Ithaca, in Central New York State, in the summer of 1955, for instance, were all clapped into white Bermuda shorts during business hours, or else plaid shorts with a loose white shirt and open throat. Conventions of tired and pot-bellied salesmen, with the sagging diaphragm and varicose veins of their profession, all suddenly appear in tight black shorts and bright, youthful knee-socks (though still wearing the heavy black shoes which infuriate Miss Hawes), still smoking the fraternal cigar and exchanging the customary badinage, with no sense of unease since they are all still dressed the same. The doormen of the Raleigh Hotel in Washington in the August of 1956 were similarly thrust into shorts and socks, which, it was observed, the disconcerted elderly commissionaire on morning duty surreptitiously attempted to pull up over his ageing knees.

America is eager to adopt no matter whose or what garments, from no matter where or what country, and to make them her own, for she must find herself somewhere, now that her own past, when she knew very well who she was, is gone beyond recall. Japanese robes, Indonesian slippers, Spanish cummerbunds, English hunting-jackets, German *Lederhosen*, South Sea Island shirts, all are eagerly advertised, eagerly bought, and eagerly worn, without, it must be added, any perceptible advance so far in the establishment of a real American sartorial identity.

I had the pleasure of an interesting interview with the handsome Editor of *Esquire*, Frederick Bermingham, in the spring of 1955. Mr Bermingham, the arbiter of American dress for men, was wearing, with a delicate sense of social position, a well-cut jacket of Black Watch tartan with huge embossed silver buttons, in his New York office. "But," he assured me, "I would not, of course, permit my salesmen to dress like this. They have to wear conventional dark suits."

Mr Bermingham grouped American male dress into three sections: first, dress remarkable for extremism of cut, design, and colour; second,

DANCE MASK
Carved wood with feathers.
Esquimo.
Philadelphia University Museum

WOODEN CERE-
MONIAL MASK
Haida Indians,
British Columbia.
The bars represent
the ribs of a bear.
*American Museum of
Natural History,
New York*

HOPI INDIAN DANCE
MASK MADE OUT OF
WHITE MAN'S DIS-
CARDED FELT HAT
*Philadelphia University
Museum*

dress displaying quieter and more restrained taste (typical, he declared, of the professional classes); and, third, the dress of the younger men for whom *Esquire* caters, a class more enterprising than the second class and better off than the first.

Such younger men are demanding more colour in their dress, insists Mr Bermingham, "without sacrificing their prestige or their virility." There is plenty of money to be spent on male dress, a real if confused interest in the subject, and no foolish embarrassment about trying what is new, no matter how often the styles change.

"We are 20 per cent. on the way to a male renaissance in dress," Mr Bermingham prophesies. He says he is hopeful of the result because he considers that American men to-day have advantages over their ancestors as they are able to purchase such figure-aids as elasticized shorts and to diet intelligently, and therefore are in better shape than their ancestors, and in consequence have a good figure to dress.

This may be questioned, however, for the constant use of the car and the nervous rush of the lives city Americans have to live largely offsets both the diet and the elastic shorts. Diet, elastic shorts, psychoanalysis, twenty-five-cent know-how handbooks, all these are very well in their various ways, and make the American man feel not so bad when he feels not so good, but none of them can give him the quiet assurance of absolute confidence in himself he really needs to dress really well—and to express in his dress what he means by 'American.' He may have money, but he is not yet morally and emotionally adult. The second-hand clothes that early marked the depredations of the English Industrial Revolution, moreover, had their counterpart in America, and lasted longer.

The dollar-aided world keeps its eyes on what America wears and copies it, willingly or no, because America is financially very powerful. If the American identity (driven by the machine to nowhere) is uncertain and the dress the American wears an awkward mixture borrowed from other countries, that uncertainty is reflected back as in a mirror. Clothes that don't look easy on Americans in the first place because they don't belong there are going to look worse still one degree farther removed.

The dark and sombre nineteenth-century city suit, depressing as it is, avoids the embarrassment of flagrantly unsuitable dress meant for the young and fair, and which is to-day in America so often worn by the old and ugly. Those flowered shirts (very like the loose covers on settees in English country drawing-rooms) are so often worn by massive men on the streets of American cities that the simile is even more marked. They belong by rights on slender brown bodies on burning coral beaches in the South Seas.

The Spanish cummerbund, that relic of the former true corset, worn by pale-faced, worried insurance men, does not look so appetizing as when worn by a slim-waisted Spaniard with proud head and noble carriage—and worn, moreover, with a short, wide jacket above and skintight elegant trousers below. Worn by unco-ordinated adolescents with acne and a stoop, or weary old brokers whose waistline has long gone, it becomes a mockery of manhood.

America is slowly and unwillingly finding that it does not pay æsthetic dividends (though it pays in abundance the other sort of dividends) to borrow bits from different cultures without the culture that informs them. The traditional method of putting on the cummerbund (which may have a Moorish origin) is by a skilful pirouette. This gives a subtle personal control over the degree of tightness, no less than the arrangement of the folds, that nothing can replace, just as no mechanical means of pressing the juice out of grapes to make wine has ever been able to compete with the delicate nervous subtlety of the human foot.

Of course, modern America has neither the time nor the inclination to perform such a pirouette, and the cummerbunds sold to Americans are all ready-made, with six small buttons in front or back hooks (and a ready-made tie to clip on quickly to match), not to mention further 'improvements' in the way of a vast range of fancy colours, particularly phoney plaids. Thus the cummerbund, all life and spirit filched from it, is made up to date and killed simultaneously.

The American attraction to Spain and things Spanish is understandable for all sorts of reasons. Spanish-saturated Mexico is near to them. They are fascinated by the domination and dignity of the Spanish male in his own country, and the *mystique* of the bull-fight has always meant more to Americans than to Englishmen. They feel the Spaniard manages his women better, and they are impressed by the way he wears his clothes no less than by the clothes he wears. The gaucho of South America, with his dignified dress and demeanour, represents something that rich Americans are vainly searching for. What they find instead, however, are such things as mink neckties sold in "The New York Shop for smart men" and worn by other rich romantics searching vainly for something their money prevents them from buying.

When Oscar Wilde lectured in New York in 1882, after travelling across the United States, he told his smart audience:

> The only well-dressed men I saw were the Western miners (and in saying this I earnestly deprecate the polished indignation of your Fifth Avenue dandies). Their well-brimmed hats which shaded them from the sun and protected them from the rain, and the cloak which is by far the most beautiful piece of drapery ever invented, may well be dwelt on with admiration.

> The high boots too were sensible and practical. They wore only what was comfortable and therefore beautiful. As I looked at them I could not help thinking with regret of the time when these picturesque miners should have made their fortunes, and would go East again and assume the abominations of modern fashionable attire.

CHAPTER SEVEN

THE YOUNG IDEA

Crepe-soled creepers and drainpipe trousers are out *for the really smart boy nowadays. We wear trousers with turn-ups 18 inches round, and black leather shoes with highly-polished toe-caps. Long hair is finished too. The favourite cut to-day is a short-crop "Marlon Brando" or a short style with a quiff falling on the forehead.*

"EAST ENDER," in a letter to the *Daily Mirror*, February 26, 1956

Baby boys, as every parent knows, delight in colour and pattern every bit as much as their sisters, and take the keenest interest in their appearance, which they like to be as gay and bright as possible, until society clamps down its grey conventions upon them, which in England happens at the age of four or five years. (Even in America there is a distinct tendency for the richest boys—therefore the most admired and envied and copied—to try to adopt middle-class English conventions in their dress.)

As they go to their first school English boys are hurried into these shapeless, sombre garments, and thus sentenced to sartorial death in life right at the beginning of their male life.

"Grey is practical. It doesn't show the dirt." This is the reason given for the sudden deprivation of one of the major pleasures of life, the enjoyment of beautiful dress. Behind this reason lies the curious fear that to be interested in dressing becomingly would be unmanly. In fact, parents infect their sons with their own puritanical fears, and the garb bequeathed the fathers by the Industrial Revolution is visited upon their children.

Parents, in the relentless struggle for social prestige, a struggle that goes on in every home in all income groups, try to educate and dress their children according to their own ambitions. The struggle is usually keenest in the poorest circles, who so often dress their children above their social circumstances. It is against the fierce passion of parents to dress their children according to the rank they want them to occupy that sumptuary laws invariably crumble. Kindness, comfort, convenience, count as naught beside social ambition, and generations of boys, not to speak of girls, have been martyred to parental pride in dress so stiff, heavy, tight, cumbersome, and costly as to take all the pleasure out of childhood.

Harshness to children, in fact, by the wearing of painful dress no less than in other ways, has been the rule rather than the exception throughout history, and no child, however highly placed in the social scale, has been exempt. Harshness was for centuries regarded as the only decent Christian

BOY WITH HEAD-BINDING
Mural painting. Fourteenth century.
St Stephen's Chapel, House of Commons

CORSETS AND BUMROLL
Boy of seven, 1618.
From a German family portrait in Cassel Museum

form of upbringing, any indulgence being bound to lead to self-destruction in this world and certain hell in the next. Let us consider, for example, the careful upbringing of the most important baby boy in all France, then the most civilized country in Europe, at the beginning of the seventeenth century.

This baby boy was the future King Louis XIII and we know every detail of his nurture from the meticulous journal of his progress entered up daily by his tutor Dr Hérouard, who adored his charge and had most progressive ideas for his time.

First of all the infant prince was suckled by a series of wet-nurses for two years. At this time his staff of servants consisted of two *gouvernantes*, of first and second rank, a doctor, a foster-mother, a dresser, several ladies-in-waiting, a cradle-rocker, two musicians to play him to sleep with flute and viol, a larger number of servants to wait on these servants, together with his own military guard.

Every act of the royal baby's life, his swaddling, eating, stools, and so on, was virtually performed in public, and from birth his *levée* and *couchée* were ceremonies at which many courtiers were present, he of the highest rank being entitled to the honour of handing the baby's shirt to the dresser to be put on the baby. The three bastards of Gabrielle d'Estrées, the six legitimate children of the Queen, as well as Henriette de Balzac d'Entrague's several bastards, were all brought up in the palace together, and from the age of seven quarrelled bitterly every day about this question of precedence, snatching the royal shirt from each other in order to have the coveted honour of handing it to the dresser.

Dressing was from birth a matter of the gravest importance, and the future Louis XIII was always in regalia. Already at the age of one year, a shirt of rich satin fastened over his swaddling bands, a military hat on his head, a sword strapped to his side, and spurred boots on his feet, he had given an audience to the Venetian ambassador. This elegant discomfort was presently added to by severe punishment inflicted for the slightest disobedience. Even before he was weaned he was frequently slapped, and from the age of two whippings of increasing severity were administered by his ladies-in-waiting for the smallest offences, the whippings being promised the day before and punctually delivered the following morning, so that the Dauphin cried all through the night in fearful expectation and was unable to sleep.

These drastic measures were taken, not by sadistic monsters, but by intelligent and adoring parents. King Henry IV, who doted on his heir, wrote to his *gouvernante*: "I am vexed that you have not whipped my son. I command you to whip him every time he is wilful or naughty, knowing by my own experience that nothing else did me so much good."

The King, no doubt owing to his own childhood whippings, unfortunately had as short a temper as the Dauphin, and became even more enraged over trifles. Sometimes he thrashed his heir so mercilessly on the head and all over the body that thereafter "the child could neither eat nor sleep, but nearly burst himself with screaming." When he objected, at the age of three, to his dresser's fastening on to him the painful corset of his dress he was threatened with boiling in the laundry copper, a punishment he had no reason to suppose would not be put into effect, since the other punishments threatened had never failed to be performed.

At the age of six he was promoted from the care of women, a change in his life marked by the commencement of studies in religion, astronomy, and geometry, and by the honour of being held down for his whippings by a lord-in-waiting instead of a lady-in-waiting. He had to learn manners every day from a book on virtue (the *School of Vertue*) wherein every act of dressing had its instructive moral.

> With thy cap fairly brusht thy head cover then,
> Putting it off in speaking to any man.
> Cato doth counsel thee thy elders to reverence....
> Thy shirt collar fast unto thy neck knit,
> Comely thy clothing about thee make fit.

His whippings continued without respite. Such was the rule then in all good homes and schools in France, and so severe were they that some noble children died under the lash. At the age of fourteen other lessons were given up in order that he might concentrate on equitation, fencing, and etiquette. His riding-master[1] ordered his riding-dress thus:

> Hats must not be too high—six inches is ample, and $3\frac{1}{2}$ inches for the brim to keep the sun out of his eyes. The hat riband must be gold or silver or silver thread. A ruff is better than a falling collar. It is well for the doublet to be white, and must always be handsomely embroidered. Trunk hose must be wide and not lower than the middle of the thigh, so that the shapeliness of the legs may be seen, and they must be wide enough to make the waist look slim. Gloves should be long, fringed, and embroidered. The boots of cowhide or wild boar-skin must be higher at the back than the front so as to make the legs look longer.

Display, here as elsewhere, was the occasion for still more discipline. His whippings were continued, even after he became king at the age of ten, when his father was assassinated—and continued to be inflicted right up to the time of his marriage.

"Madame," he observed as the queen-mother curtsied to him on one such occasion, "I could do with less reverence and fewer whippings."

England was no more indulgent to the young, either well-born or of humble birth. By Tudor law a child of fourteen already counted as an adult in the matter of punishment, and a "strolling beggar" of that age, after being soundly whipped through the streets for the sin of being un-employed, was burned through the ear "to the compass of one inch" with a hot iron, a second offence of like nature being punished by death. When more lenient treatment of the young developed two centuries later it was, as we shall see, exclusively an upper-class fashion. It did not last very long, and the more comfortable dress for children that was part of the leniency lasted no longer.

[1] M. de Pluvinal, *Le Manège royale*.

Jean-Jacques Rousseau, whose influence in the education and dress of boys affected for a time much of Europe and also America, was born in 1712. A dreamy and disorganized Swiss theorist, who suffered all his life from persecution mania and bladder trouble, he abandoned all his own bastard children to be brought up in the workhouse, where possibly they were better off, since he was unable to settle down to any one job to earn his living.

LOOSEFEET, CORN-HUSK DOLL
WITH DRIED-APPLE HEAD
Represents a spirit that grants wishes to
children. Cayuga Indian.
Museum of the American Indian, New York

CHILD'S HOME-MADE RATTLE
Straw with dried pea. Berkshire, eigh-
teenth and nineteenth centuries.
Museum of English Rural Life, Reading

A professional amateur, he had tried his hand at everything, from music-scoring and engraving to botany and entomology, before he fell into the role of philosopher by accident. He owes his renown to the fact that he happened to like the countryside better than the town at that moment in French political history when life in the cities was becoming intolerable, and he happened to say so before anyone else in France had the courage to do so.

Rousseau wrote sentimental romances whose erotic nuances were swamped by a flood of uplift—just at the historically psychological moment. He was a precursor of Romanticism. But, it must be pointed out, he was not the precursor of a more humane and sensible attitude to children and their education. William Penn, the English Quaker, more than fifty years earlier, had this to say in criticism of current methods of education, and Penn, unlike Rousseau, took the liveliest interest in his own children:

We press their memory too soon and puzzle, strain and load them with words and rules; to know grammar and rhetoric and a strange tongue or two, that it is ten to one will never be useful to them, leaving their natural genius to mechanical, and physical and natural knowledge uncultivated and neglected, which would be of exceeding use and pleasure to them through the whole course of their life.[1]

Penn added a suggestion that caused him to be regarded as impious, revolutionary, and stark mad, at a time when manual labour was socially degrading:

> Children had rather be making of tools and instruments of play, shaping, drawing, framing and building, than getting by heart some rules of propriety of speech, and those would also follow with more judgment and less trouble and time.[1]

Perhaps William Penn was altogether too reasonable. The world prefers violent jolts to its conscience rather than logical arguments. Rousseau had more success later when he declared roundly that man ought to learn to use his hands; that he was born good and that it was evil society which debased him; and that, since sophisticated society in Europe was vile, primitive society far from Europe must be perfect.

Having thus invented the Noble Savage, whom he never knew at all in the flesh (unlike Penn, who learned Iroquois so that he did not need a translator in his meetings with the American Indians in his colony), Rousseau was immediately hailed by progressive Frenchmen as the arbiter of the noble natural life. He hastily forswore powdered wigs and elegant dress in order to appear in suitably simpler garb in the smart French *salons* of Paris, where he was received with adulation.

Rousseau was the man of the moment. French society was stale. It needed a jolt. When Rousseau presently fled to England for sanctuary, his books having been burned by the French Public Prosecutor, he made England popular with progressive Frenchmen. Was there not, indeed, they thought, something of the noble savage in the Englishman himself?

Émile was Rousseau's attempt to formulate an ideal education which would avoid the pitfalls of fashionable sophistication. It describes the almost clinical experiment in education of one boy (Rousseau did not believe in the education of girls). To save bother, and perhaps also because Rousseau himself was born poor, Émile is a wealthy child, brought up entirely by his tutor. His mother merely makes sufficient entry into Émile's life to breast-feed him, and thereafter disappears. This in itself caused a sensation, for breast-feeding was utterly unfashionable in good French society, where it had long been looked upon as coarse manual labour fit only for peasants and peasant foster-mothers.

Émile is dressed in light, loose garments (indecent at that time) and no

[1] Letter to his first wife.

hat at all (dangerously revolutionary). Free movement of his limbs is encouraged (graceless and demoralizing), and cold baths summer and winter alike (nothing short of insane). His hours of eating and sleeping are carefully regulated to work out irregularly, in order to avoid the formation of regular habits, which Rousseau deplored as "unnatural." Reading, "the scourge of childhood," is totally forbidden until maturity, and then the only book permitted is *Robinson Crusoe*, for the excellent reason that Rousseau happened to have read it himself and liked it very much.

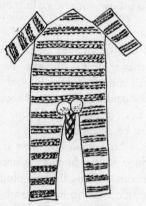

YOUTH'S CIRCUMCISION
DRESS
Woven fibre striped brown and yellow with polished gourds. Angola, Portuguese West Africa. Contemporary.
Musée de l'Homme, Paris

YOUTH'S CONFIRMATION DRESS
Paris. Contemporary.

Émile is taught no manners in order not to make him artificial, and his régime includes late hours, early rising, and often no sleep at all. No ethics and no history are taught him, and, in fact, until the age of fifteen he learns nothing except practical lessons with his hands, spending two days a week in a joiner's workshop to learn how to handle tools.

More startling than all these innovations (which most peasant boys were then brought up on without the privilege of calling them an education) is the sexual education of Émile. Émile is completely secluded from female society and anything in any way even suggesting it (not even a whiff of perfume being allowed) for as long as possible, and violent physical exercise is employed to divert any possible erotic thoughts that might happen to invade his innocence. (This does, indeed, recall the English public-school system, of which, however, Rousseau knew nothing.)

Émile immediately became the Bible of every social reformer, for the well-to-do boy of a good family in the early eighteenth century was wet-nursed, dressed exactly like his mother in *décolleté* bodice and hooped skirts till the age of seven, and then exactly like his father, in brocade and lace, satin breeches and embroidered silk stockings, corsets, powdered wig, and high-heeled shoes. Like his father, he had learned how to take snuff elegantly and to wear patches on his face, and also to show up the whiteness of his hands; and if his father had pretensions to being a beau he also copied his summer fan and winter muff.

Like both his parents, the fashionable well-bred boy regarded the country with distrust and loathing, and looked upon mountains with horror. (Even Rousseau, it must be observed, for all his bias towards Nature, was never altogether happy about mountains, not even in his native Switzerland. They were just too much Nature.)

The publication of *Émile*, therefore, caused a revulsion of sentiment, which affected the wardrobe of fashionable boys no less than it affected their lessons. Rousseau had not specified exactly what kind of loose, light clothing he advocated. No doubt he had something vaguely Greek in mind. So the French dressmakers and man-milliners hurriedly created a species of flimsy boiler-suit to be worn over an airy, ruffled shirt with short, frilled sleeves—to satisfy their smartest customers, who now insisted on a free, natural dress for their boys. Daring *couturiers* even suggested leaving the shirt carelessly open at the throat. Wigmakers in Paris and London presently lost their aristocratic youthful clients, and the most exclusive shoemakers were set to making delicate slippers, without any heels at all, for growing boys.

The lines of this Rousseau-inspired modish boiler-suit were taken from the ordinary peasant dress of France, and thus preceded the *sans-culotte* movement by several decades. By no means all social reformers, however, cared to follow Nature no matter where she wandered, for putting into actual crude practice a theory which made a delightful game of intellectual ping-pong among the perfumed and bewigged *habitués* of the great Paris *salons* of the eighteenth century was quite another matter. Voltaire, it must be noted, although he admired the Hurons, was no uncritical enthusiast for Nature in the raw. "*Mon cul,*" he pointed out to slavish followers of Rousseau, "*est bien dans la nature . . . nevertheless I wear breeches.*"

It was precisely breeches that soon became unfashionable in modish nurseries, where Society, for the first time, began to take some interest in their children. Children became the latest Society pastime, a fascinating new game. Before long it was smart to have portraits painted wherein languishing Society mothers, clad in vaporous 'natural' drapery, were intertwined with their innocent offspring, both as nearly naked as possible, or dressed as peasants, or as simple-hearted beggars.

At the beginning of the eighteenth century well-to-do boys were over-dressed; at the end of the century they were underdressed. The freer use of their limbs and more indulgent parental treatment must certainly have made life pleasanter for them, but there seems to have been no improvement worth mentioning in their health. They died off young in no less numbers, tuberculosis and pneumonia edging out smallpox and scurvy in the new dispensation.

To be natural needed training and discipline, which zealous Society parents did not shrink from exercising. Lady Georgiana Howard reported in a letter how conscientious was a married sister in reading over all her children's books, "scratching out all she disapproves of," so that nothing should interfere with their growing up free and untrammelled. The selection of a suitable governess to nurture this naturalness was no light matter either. "I should describe her state *vis-à-vis* Miss Ashley," reported Lady Georgiana, "as to be one of satisfaction, not elation."

If the genuine noble savage was not so easy to come by in aristocratic English drawing-rooms (for slaves did not count as noble savages either in England or in America, where Rousseau's theories were adopted with even greater zest) there was always Scotland — beautiful, clean, savage, and Presbyterian Scotland. Lady Georgiana triumphantly described the discovery of such a homespun noble savage in another family letter: "We had as guide the most magnificent highlander ever seen or painted, in tartan wove by his mother, beautifully *drapé*; a large sporting knife within the stocking."

Though it was not given to every intellectual Frenchman to renounce Europe and run away to live with the handsome Hurons in Canada, it was possible for a few daring French spirits to brave the Channel and try the English way of life instead; and some actually did, though mostly those obliged to do so by enforced exile. Here on the great Whig estates they would find rosy English children sedately running wild in beautiful gardens, where, in compliment to Rousseau's theories, mazy walks and wildernesses were just beginning to be cultivated. In the Gallic mind the simple savage and the English country gentlemen became allied, and thus the foundations for the ensuing French Anglomania were early laid. English male dress had begun to be copied by French intellectuals, in fact, before English gentlemen had finished going over to France themselves in order to have their clothes made by French tailors.

It was, perhaps, not quite the English as they were that the French so admired, but the English as they expected them to be, as they ought to have been. Rousseau it was who created the prototype of the nature-loving, noble-hearted, wealthy English milord, in the character of Lord Édouard Bompston, whom the French could not but worship and the English gentry hasten to emulate.

Parents who considered themselves truly progressive presently began to look upon any kind of taught education with horror. Even Hannah More thought education unsettling, and complained of the number of tutors who visited aristocratic young ladies, including a military sergeant to teach them how to march. As for the lower classes she considered education positively dangerous. "Our Jack the ploughboy," she complained, "spends half his time going to a shop in our market where they let out books to read."

These advanced ideas on freedom from education, as on the advisability of long, loose trousers for boys instead of tight knee-breeches, did not affect the poorer class of boys, whose parents, after Rousseau as before him, clapped them into decent breeches and heavy shoes and did their utmost to send them to school to learn everything they could, by rote and by rod. Maxims such as these from a Yorkshire dame-school hornbook

> Be courteous to strangers;
> Neglect no means of improvement;
> Emulate virtuous deeds;

were well whacked into farmers' boys lucky enough to get the opportunity to study. There were, it is true, gingerbread letters whereby the alphabet could be taught by the engaging method of allowing the pupil to eat the letter when identified, but such luxurious indulgence was, it appears, reserved for better-off boys.

Tight clothes and tight discipline were thus the lot of the vast majority of lads. Mrs Wesley's famous son John recalled in later life that the Wesley children

> were so constantly used to eat and drink what was given them that when any of them were ill there was no difficulty in making them take the most unpleasant medicine for they durst not refuse it; though presently some of them would throw it up.

Unlike Émile, the Wesley children all had to learn to read at the earliest possible age, one day only being permitted for the mastery of the alphabet. Samuel, who later wrote the hymns, was forward enough to learn his alphabet in less than one day and was therefore at once put on to the study of the first chapter of Genesis. Six hours a day was the regulation time allotted to study right from the beginning, and no talking was permitted. Nor, when punished, were they permitted to make any noise about it, but were obliged "to cry softly so as not to disturb other people."

Rousseau's ideas still clouded one aristocratic horizon when Count Tolstoi (full of religious zeal to justify himself by noble deeds) opened a school for the children of peasants on his estate in the mid-nineteenth century, since he had come to believe that peasants also were human beings, who should not be denied the advantage of classes they need not attend. For naturally it was a school run on 'free' lines. It was, in fact, organized disorganization, such as we to-day know only too well from our own 'progressive' schools. The peasant children were not obliged to attend classes (though the teacher was), and those who did attend were not obliged to listen to the lessons. No discipline of any kind was exercised, nor were there any punishments.

The school was not a success, and after two years of it Count Tolstoi had become so bored with his experiment that he closed it down and attempted to learn to make sandals instead, in the hope of educating himself into understanding the serf mind, since the serf mind appeared incapable of understanding his. Countess Tolstoi, who looked upon her husband's theories with something approaching acerbity, later complained that, though he continually talked of mortifying the flesh, he signally failed to overcome his own weaknesses, which she described as "eating sweets, bicycling, and lust."

In England to-day camp-schools reflect the last ripple of Rousseau. "Skill in woodmanship and the use of tools," offers the brochure of a popular one run by an old Etonian. "Simplicity is our keynote. We enjoy the open air, the sun and stars, the song of birds, the sight of corn waving in the wind, and the smell of the wood fire."

No light achievement in built-up England, where nightingale-haunted woods are apt to shelter atomic experimental laboratories, and it is almost impossible to pitch even the smallest tent on such a site that the camper will not be obliged to look out upon an arterial road bordered by ribbon development.

The spirit of Rousseau, however, has informed the British public school much less than has the spirit of Wesley's mother and not merely the British public school, but the host of pseudo public schools too—the myriad "St Custard's" where public-school trimmings are cheaply copied for the sons of ambitious small traders, and where the radiance of the school cap is in strict ratio to the dimness of the instruction.

Since the real public schools have supplied England and the world with leaders in all spheres for so long, let us see what some of the beneficiaries of the genuine public-school system have thought about it. Thackeray for one was not impressed:

How much ruin has been caused by that accursed system which in England is called "the education of a gentleman" . . . Go, my son, for ten years to a public school. Learn to fight for yourself against the time that your real struggles shall begin. Begin to be selfish at ten years of age. Study for another ten. Get a competent knowledge of boxing, swimming, and cricket, with a pretty knack of Latin hexameters and a decent smattering of Greek plays. Do this and a fond father shall bless you and bless the £2000 he has spent in acquiring all these benefits for you.[1]

Left: BOY'S NANKEEN SUIT,
1820
Victoria and Albert Museum

Right: LAUGHING BOY
Japanese NO mask.
Musée Guimet, Paris

It costs rather more to-day—shall we say, more in the nature of £6000 —and if the money must be found out of income-taxed earnings it will probably be nearer the sum of £12,000.

And besides what else have you not learned? If your father is a grocer you have been beaten for his sake and have learned to be ashamed of him . . . you have learned if you have a kindly heart and open hand to compete with associates much more wealthy than yourself, and consider money as not much, but HONOUR, the honour of dining and wining with your betters, as a great deal. All this does the public school and college boy learn and woe be to his knowledge.[1]

The effects of the Industrial Revolution, with its swift upsurge of toady-ism and snobbery, speak plainly in Thackeray's denunciation, written in the mid-nineteenth century. Certainly the boys at Harrow at the beginning of the nineteenth century were unimpressed by social rank, and when Lord Byron as a schoolboy there insisted on the observation of his nobility they promptly nicknamed him "the old English Baron." As Thackeray makes clear, the worst aspects of the minor public-school spirit grew with

[1] *A Shabby Genteel Story.*

the growing industrialization of England. This mixture of sadism, chauvinism, and arrested development was adored by Rudyard Kipling in his own education, and he wrote in *Stalky & Co.* a faithful account of his own gas-lit schooldays in the eighteen-seventies. These chapters are full of fierce canings, for which the victims politely thank the caning master afterwards, the infliction and reception of punishments of every kind, and a masochistic-sadistic attitude to every incident such as to-day suggests not monitors, but Mau Mau.

The high point of delight in the book is achieved when the three sixteen-year-old heroes kill a cat and hide it beneath the dormitory floorboards to rot and stink. The fags of the Lower Third amuse themselves "with their Saturday evening businesses, cooking sparrows over the gas with rusty nibs, brewing unholy drinks in gallipots, skinning moles with pocket-knives," and the moral lesson that retribution inevitably overtakes the unpopular is driven home by a suitable example of punishment meted out by the three heroes to one such boy. These three sixteen-year-olds "wrapped themselves lovingly about the boy, thrust him to the open window and drew down the sash to the nape of his neck. With equal wittiness they tied his thumbs behind his back with a piece of twine."

If this suggests the horror comic to-day, it won the approval of those lower-middle-class English families who passionately believed in the public-school system, though they could not themselves afford to send their own sons there. The general public loved to think of the product of the British public schools as Ouida, the popular lady novelist and contemporary of Kipling, described him. Ouida's old Etonian hero

> dressed a shade more perfectly than anyone else and with such inimitable carelessness in the perfection too. He had an almost unattainable matchlessness in the sangfroid of his soft, languid insolence and incredibly tough, ever gentle effrontery.[1]

Blood alone, however blue, Ouida was careful to make clear, could not produce such male perfection. Training too was necessary:

> With the strength that lay beneath all the gentle languor of his habits, and with the science of the Eton playing-fields of his boyhood, he wrenched his wrists free ere the steel had closed, and with the single straightening of his left arm felled the detective to earth like a bullock, with a crashing blow that resounded through the stillness like some heavy timber stove in.[1]

Thus did Beauty escape imprisonment for debt.

[1] *Under Two Flags.*

Discarding both Thackeray's darkened glasses and Ouida's rose-tinted ones, let us see what Eton is really like, the most famous English public school, which has lent its name to the most famous English schoolboy dress.

England's greatest public school has long been the subject of fabulous legend and superstitious belief such as attach to no other English school. The facts are simple enough.

ENGLISH SHEPHERD BOY
(THIRTEENTH CENTURY)
Wall-painting.
St Stephen's, House of Commons

ETON SCHOLAR
(FIFTEENTH CENTURY)

Eton was founded by Henry VI, and its charter is dated 1440. The school began modestly with a provision for twenty-five indigent scholars and twenty-five poor and infirm men, whose duty it was, in return for their education, to pray for the health of the King during his lifetime and for his soul after his death, and to pray also for the souls of the King's royal parents. Eton began, in fact, as a charity school for the impoverished.

Within a couple of years it was found possible to extend the provision (by grants from lands confiscated from the French) to include an additional seventy poor scholars and thirteen needy men. The poor and needy scholars were educated chiefly in plainsong, Latin grammar, and reading, from the age of eight years to twelve, and before admittance to the school they were obliged to pass certain tests, one being "No villein or bastard or one suffering from incurable disease nor bodily defect disqualifying from Holy Orders." This dread of deformity, as a manifestation of Divine displeasure, is typical of its period, wherein the cripple, in the eyes of both Church and State, was regarded as already tainted by guilt.

It was a religious foundation, and religion coloured each moment of the scholars' day, from the moment of their rising at five in the morning, when they had to say the matins of the Blessed Virgin as they made their beds (boys under fourteen sleeping two to a bed), until the final prayer before they fell asleep at night.

Dress was important, for by his dress was each person to be kept marked in his rightful place in the social scheme. Each scholar admitted to Eton received a gown and hood, which used up twenty-four yards of cloth and had to last him for three years. The gowns were cut with fashionably pendent sleeves, so that one of the important functions of the servitors was to hold up the hanging sleeves of each Sixth Form boy as he came up to the table at dinner-time to cut his own helping from the meat. This holding up of sleeves continued to be the custom until 1870.

It is clear from the provisions of the founder that he anticipated, as well as pastimes of an ungodly frivolity, a weakness for sartorial finery not in keeping with his plans for the scholars of Eton or the masters either.

"No scholar," states the charter, "fellow, chaplain, or college servant" was permitted to keep "hunting dogs in college, nets for hunting, ferrets, falcons, nor hawk, nor ape, bear, fox, stag, hind, deer, badger, or any other rapacious nor rare beast." Nor were either staff or boys permitted to "grow long hair or wear peaked shoes or moulded hoods nor carry arms unless they walked in the town, nor permitted to wear red, green or white hose."

Within thirty years of its foundation scholars from well-to-do families were being received at Eton. There were no school lists, and it appears that every boy had to fight his own sartorial battle, excessive finery being less of a question than the necessity on the part of the boys to coax an adequate supply of any sort of clothes from their parents or guardians. A letter survives which was written by sixteen-year-old William Paston in 1478, begging his brother to send him something to put on at Eton:

I beseche you to send me a jose clothe one for holy days of sum colore and a nothere for the workyng days how corse it be so ever makyng no matyr, and a stomachere and IJ schyrtes and a paeyer of sclyppers.

In the next century the sons of the nobility were already being sent to Eton to be educated, but there was still no regulation uniform, and even the noblest boys were fobbed off with undistinguished dress, over which as little trouble as possible was taken, perhaps because the gown and hood covered it effectively in school hours.

Thus a school bill dated 1560, for clothes made for Henry Cavendish, later Earl of Devonshire, includes:

4 yards of black cotton at 8*d*. a yard.
20 pence for making a coat.
Canvas to line the "bodys," 8*d*.
3 yards of cotton to line the "dublettes," 14 pence.
Silk for stitching and making buttonhole loops, two shillings.
4 "duss" black silk buttons costing 14 pence.
"Cotton wolle" for the puffing of the sleeves, 4*d*.
Making of the doublet 1 shilling and 4 pence.

This is plain indeed for a nobleman's son, though it admits a brief nod to fashion in the puffings.

Esher Scrummager

The "Esher Scrummager" machine produces tight scrummaging conditions almost identical to the game itself. Makes possible exact and detailed coaching complete with realistic training of the pack in set scrum work, including hooking.

CONTEMPORARY SPORTS EQUIPMENT
By courtesy of Lillywhites, Piccadilly Circus, London

Being under royal patronage, Eton had to step skilfully to keep in with the particular politics of the reigning monarch, and much care was exercised in the manner of compliments offered to the Throne. Thus the accession of Queen Elizabeth was greeted by a collection of fulsome Latin verses composed by the scholars of Eton, asking God to grant her with all speed a husband and children. Later verses addressed to the Queen, however, make no such plea, but single out for particular praise instead whichever of her courtiers the Queen appeared to be favouring at the time. Both the Dudley brothers were thus praised for their beauty when it was not clear which one the Queen preferred.

Eton being most famous in the eyes of the world, perhaps, for its games, it is curious how recently these have found an official place in the curriculum. As late as 1766 sport at Eton was still largely an individual whim. Cricket was played, it is true, and so was fives. More popular, however, were scrambling walls, bally-cally, peg-top, battledore, peg-in-the-ring, hopscotch, hoops, marbles, kites, tops, and a game called chuck, which consisted of throwing and catching a lighted fireball made from tow dipped in spirits of wine. Equally popular was rat-hunting, pursued in the school dormitories with knotted stockings, the rats when caught being banged to death against the beds.

Besides these amusements were those of hunting small birds with loaded sticks, egg-stealing, and run-away knocks on the door of the Dame's House (a pastime which perennially has fascinated British youth of every class). There was no swimming instruction, boys learning to swim by being thrown naked into the Thames and having somehow to scramble themselves ashore. Shelley never did learn to swim all his life.

The arts, however, were not neglected. Painting and drawing at this period was taught by a drawing-master named Alexander Cosens, who was the illegitimate son of Peter the Great, conceived in one of his Greenwich escapades, and who appears to have inherited his royal father's manual aptitude.

There was still in the eighteenth century no formal dress obligatory, no kind of uniform. One boy of eight who went up to Eton as late as 1799 wore a blue coat with a red collar, a white waistcoat, and ruffled shirt. Other boys sported nankeen trousers, or white ducks, or breeches tied with string. On match days the Eton elevens played cricket in short trousers and silk stockings, without, it should be noted, either pads or gloves, which the headmaster considered effeminate.

Dr Keate, whose especial preoccupation it was to ensure the manliness of his pupils, forbade coats and umbrellas as pampering, and it was during his headship that the sixty-round fist-fight was fought out between a boy named Wood and Francis Ashley, Lord Shaftesbury's brother. After fighting for two and a half hours Ashley fell down unconscious and died the same evening. (This event may have had some bearing on his Lordship's later interest in the plight of less well-circumstanced factory children.)

Shelley, who loathed any manifestation of compulsion and brutality, was constantly involved in fist-fights at Eton, stubbornly refusing to submit with good grace to the customary dormitory bullying, such as being jerked out of sleep by means of a cord attached to his great toe, and being thus dragged up and down the room. Nor did he ever hesitate to protest against the bullying of smaller boys by bigger ones, whose custom it was to play battledore and shuttlecock with the little boys as the shuttlecock. Shelley therefore had to fight, and he fought, it was recorded, inexpertly, stalking round his opponent, striking out at him with open palms, and shrilling Homer in Greek.

Yet even Shelley, a strange boy out of this world, fascinated by magic incantation and electricity, given to launching fire-balloons and wandering

off muttering to himself, remembered afterwards his schooldays at Eton
with sweet nostalgia.

> Bottles of warm tea
> Such as we used in summer after six
> To cram in great coat pockets and to mix
> Hard eggs and radishes and rolls at Eton.

he wrote later on. The peaceful green English fields, the beauty of the
great trees and endlessly flowing dark Thames, remained in his imagination all his short life, and (who knows?) perhaps filled his mind at the end
when the stormy breakers of the Ligurian were closing over his head.

Shelley's habitual ill-fitting and unorthodox dress was one relic of his
Eton days. Though the boys adored the dandies, sartorial elegance was
not encouraged, the one exception being "Buck" Brummell, who escaped
the usual penalties of non-enthusiasm for games and was, indeed, not
unpopular, his preoccupation with dress and cleanliness being regarded as
an amusing eccentricity.

Charles James Fox, hauled away from Eton at mid-term by his doting
father, for a Continental introduction into fashionable dissipation, was less
fortunate than Brummell. On his return he was soundly flogged at
school for his luxurious new apparel, to teach him better.

So little attention was expected to be paid to their dress by Eton boys
at this time that those scholars who went up by special invitation to pay
their respects to their patrons, King George III and the Royal family, on
the terrace at Windsor Castle, often were obliged to ink their legs hastily,
where the holes in their black stockings showed the leg through.

Two interesting customs connected with dress at Eton were "Montem"
and "Leaving Money." Montem was the annual procession in gala dress,
which had for object the collection of "salt," or monetary donations from
the spectators. It was, in fact, an early form of the modern "rag," though
the money was kept by the boys themselves and not bestowed on any
other charity. Montem, however, so often ended in a free fight between
Etonians and townspeople and serious rioting that at last it was forbidden
by the authorities.

Leaving Money was another method of raising funds at Eton—not for
the scholars, but for the headmaster from the scholars. Right until 1868
it was the meticulously observed custom for every boy leaving Eton to
deposit a ten-pound note on the table in the headmaster's sitting-room
when he came to say good-bye. This voluntary fine was enacted with
admirable English concern for the proprieties, the headmaster always
observing the ritual of being unaware of what was taking place by making

the excuse that the room was stuffy and turning his back on the pupil by going to the window to open it.

Leaving Money replaced a different practice, more valuable to the historian of dress if less so to the headmaster, by which the leaving pupil was expected to present his portrait to the school. This custom has given us a fascinating series of paintings over a considerable period; the details are indisputably authentic records of contemporary youthful male dress.

BOY STUDENT, RELIGIOUS
SEMINARY, JERUSALEM
The side-curls are a pious observance
of Biblical edict. Contemporary.

SILHOUETTE PORTRAIT OF
ENGLISH BOY
Nineteenth century.
*Museum of English Rural Life,
Reading*

Contrary to popular opinion, the stylized "Eton dress" (short black jacket, top-hat, striped trousers, and stiff round collar) was not instituted as mourning wear for the death of King George III. Like so many other Eton practices, it just happened, and, having happened, it just remained. This Eton uniform, as representative of England's finest and most socially élite school, acquired such immense prestige in the eyes of English people, especially those of the lower-middle class and working class, that it was every mother's dream for well over a century to dress her son in this rig, especially on Sundays.

Eton dress, however, was by no means always worn at Eton at this time. Old Etonians still remember how boys not actually playing for their houses used to wear knee-breeches at Eton, at least until 1921. Baths being then considered pampering, if not actually devitalizing, at Eton as at other schools, the covered knees may have been dictated by prudence in order to hide the dirt.

To-day there is no formal uniform worn at Eton, though the various sporting clubs have their own sartorial insignia, and the score or so members of the élite social club "Pop" reserve for themselves the right to wear sponge-bag trousers, braid on their morning-coats, and coloured waist-coats. Except for the famous Fourth of June, when top-hats are still *de rigueur*, the boys at Eton do not wear hats at all, saluting ladies or their masters merely by lifting the hand.

Why the famous Eton top-hat was abandoned offers an interesting comment on current history. It was found in 1939, during the gas-drill which preceded the Second World War, that the boys at Eton were unable to fit their gasmasks on over their top-hats. The top-hats were thereupon abandoned for the duration of the War, and have never since been resumed for daily wear.

To-day Eton is one of the least dressy schools in the country. "We are, in fact, a secondary grammar school," observed the Headmaster of Eton in January 1957, with traditional careful understatement. Eton tailors keep second-hand "pools" of school clothes, and the typical Etonian wears a tweed jacket and grey flannel trousers, and looks like any boy in any ordinary council school, except that nowadays, the pendulum of fashion having swung the other way, so many boys in contemporary council schools do wear some sort of school uniform, be it only a navy-blue blazer with a makeshift school ensign devised by the headmaster of the school in collaboration with the teacher who takes the boys for "art."

If the boys at Eton are at present enjoying dress which appears easy, comfortable, and classless, this is indeed something quite new in English sartorial history. Untold suffering has been inflicted on English schoolboys for centuries by stiff ruffs, hard collars, waists compressed in rigid corsets busked with wood or iron, high-heeled shoes which were too tight, and heavy hats which ensured headaches. So deep-rooted are our national neuroses (or we may call them sentiments, to be more polite) that dress-reformers have always had to invent moral and religious reasons for advocating the slightest improvement, mere comfort never being acceptable as a reason; and any suggestion of reform has inevitably been opposed by counter-reformers with equally moral reasons for resisting the suggested change.

For instance, the great corset controversy, which began in the eighteen-seventies and rocked not only England, but all Europe and America as well, for over thirty years, enlisted every doctor, priest, scientist, sergeant, and parent in the country, on either one side or the other, the boys themselves, of course, not being consulted in the matter. As late as 1906 Dr James Cantlie published a treatise entitled *Physical Efficiency*, in which he declared that elastic corsets or belts "can only be harmless for boys if worn below the haunch-bones, and in ordinary dress this would bring it below the waistcoat." He therefore urged a return to braces, declaring that the labourer's usual wide belt was causing evils to health which schoolboys should be made to avoid.

This challenge was immediately taken up by other distinguished medical men, who, "after making exhaustive experiments with corsets on men, women, and animals," approved the "beneficial and extensive use of some form or other of the waistbelt by all nations that had passed beyond the verge of absolute barbarity." This pro-corset faction, aided by a mass of

BOY AT PLAY
Dutch Book of Hours, 1500.
Cambridge University Library

CHARM TO CURE
TOOTHACHE
Bosnian gipsy.

statistics and Bible quotations, claimed that corsets actually increased muscular activity. Corsets were in fashion, and discretion suggested the advisability of approving what was modish.

There is no doubt that the taste of the time was definitely for constriction, and Dr Cantlie found himself gravely out of step, though he tried to retrieve his reputation by pointing out (in an overdressed era) that English schoolboys were not wearing enough clothes and that was why they were so puny.

The secret of keeping a schoolboy healthy, declared he, was to keep him warmly clad. Boys' dress weighed only half as much as their sisters' dress instead of double, and, he maintained, the fashionable sailor suits (whose long knickers did, in fact, reach well below the knees) were insufficient protection from the elements. Dr Cantlie, however, again put his foot in it by denouncing "short jackets which do not cover the loins," an unchivalrous attack on Eton which aroused nation-wide resentment, and he totally did for himself in prophesying, "The public school that will introduce the Norfolk jacket in place of the Eton jacket will thrive at the expense of its neighbours." He should have known better. Parents did not dress their sons in Eton jackets to keep them warm, but to make them proud, and Dr Cantlie was preaching, not merely to the unheeding, but to the actively hostile, in attacking the revered Eton collar for clamping "the head at the wrong angle and perpetuating that deformity of jaw which is caused by breathing through the mouth." His final assertion that the Eton collar even "prevented the shoulders from being squared" was regarded as nothing short of insult. What parent would not risk the formation of round shoulders no less than adenoids if the sons of the nobility were submitted to similar risks? Even supposing Dr Cantlie might be right—and it was impossible that so socially obtuse a person could be right in his medical diagnosis—what mother was going to deprive her son of the essential dress of gentility?

The Ladies' Magazines, so popular with the rising and risen middle class, knew their clients much better than the doctors. They wasted no time on reform, but described in luscious detail suitable dress for young gentlemen that pleased purveyors and purchasers alike, such as the following: "Nothing can be better than the Charles the First dress, generally made in dark velveteen or satin. The tight knickerbockers have sashes."

Elegance and the appearance of costliness were important selling points: "No daintiness is too great for this parure. Huge square collars made of the finest silk cambric enhanced by a wide and very delicate lace such as imitation point. Indeed elegance abounds for the youngsters." "A boy's loose jacket in copper velveteen laced by silk cords across a plastron of tinselled brown plush," is singled out for particular commendation.

As with adult male dress in Europe to-day, one of the important influences is the American influence. In the U.S.A. itself, there is an uneasy struggle going on between prestige dress and democratic dress. The looser and more comfortable dress is the democratic dress, based on the garb of engineers, cowboys, and loggers rather than on the business-man's city suit. The tendency, as is to be expected in a country of rapidly increasing wealth, is rather towards the prestige dress, as may be gathered by the banning, in all the schools of Somerville, in Massachusetts, not long ago, of "dungarees for boys and slacks for girls, because boys and girls who are dressed properly in school are much better behaved."

A curious reversal of values, in fact, is taking place, for, just as European youth is beginning to revel in the imported freedom and classlessness of American-styled jeans, dungarees, lumber-jackets, and deliciously soft shoes based on the footwear of the American Indians, some sections of American youth, eager to show that they are getting on socially, are reaching out towards European stiff snob-dress and beginning to cast aside their allegiance to Davy Crockett garb. The more expensive American magazines advertise sweaters made of imported English wool and imported English tweeds, sold at fancy prices under such snob names as "Canterbury" and "Balmoral."

That the comics (not to speak of T.V. and the films, which so often deal with the same themes) are not without effect on the formation of the gangster outlook and gangster dress may be inferred from the fact that during the six months ending in August 1956, a period of the greatest prosperity America has ever known, Stephen Kennedy, New York's Police Commissioner, announced that New York's juvenile crime had increased 41.3 per cent.

Toys too have their influence in the promotion of 'violent' dress. American toys, eagerly copied in other countries since America is so fashionable, tend to be on lethal lines. Such is the climate of our times. Here are two advertisements in the *New Yorker* of Christmas 1956:

Little Smoky, a double-holster set of six-inch pistols with workable triggers, a toy much admired by boys *from 16 months to about three*. (Price two dollars.)

The Automatic Rocket Launcher Truck carries two three-inch plastic rockets which can be loaded, locked in place and fired into space from a special launching platform. (Price 2 dollars 98 cents.)

(It is a pleasure to be able to record also—though their influence is much less strong—that the New York museums sell admirable books for children explaining, with excellent pictures and stick-ons, what the exhibits are about, and written by authorities in clear and simple language.)

English toys for the masses tend towards labour-saving devices. Modern balloons need not—indeed, must not—be blown up by human effort "EESI-PUMP, BLOW UP THE EESI-WAY," does the job for the child, at a mere cost of five shillings.

Pre-digested so-called ART is also all done in advance.

PAINT A 3D FLORAL PICTURE of a bowl of roses moulded in rigid plastic sheeting. Picture can be washed off and painted again, thus providing endless amusement and encouraging any artistic ability the child may have.

Starting thus early, the child of to-day will soon be able to help his father with "do-it-yourself" hobbies, such as the "Leaded Window" outfit offered at a recent exhibition in Olympia, London, which advertised itself thus: "A simple diamond design on the plain glass doors of a bookcase will transform it into a Reproduction-type piece of furniture, adding considerably to its appearance and value." Further, "caravans, garages, garden sheds and summer-houses all offer scope for improvement." "Reproduction-type" means bogus at double remove. And this leads straight to "do-it-yourself Art," which means painting by numbers.

What will be the effect of these perversions of taste and insults on the imagination? It is hard on the children of the machine age. They are the first victims, however well vitamined.

SOVIET TEDDY-BOYS
Cartoon by V. Kashchenko. U.S.S.R.
Contemporary.

The Davy Crockett dress spread like lightning from America all over Europe and into Asia as well. The "beanie" caps, topped by plastic animals or weather-vane whirlers, were never introduced into England, where the tradition in boys' dress has little place for fantasy, but American dress for boys is closely watched nevertheless in England, and there is a strong influence flowing eastward from the United States.

Who can venture to prophesy what the American boy will be wearing next year? It is safe to guess that he will cling to his long trousers, which he puts on almost at birth, and leave the shorts to Pop. Apart from this, he may be wearing the power-conferring cloak and top-boots and tights of Superman, or he may glorify the sack suit of the real American superman of to-day, the wizard of the American Stock Exchange, the Buccaneer of Bulls and Bears. It is reported that Mr Charles S. Mott, a director of General Motors, made eleven and a half million dollars ($11,500,000) between 10 A.M. and 3.30 P.M. one bright day in the summer of 1955, by doing nothing whatever, General Motors stocks having soared $14\frac{3}{8}$ points during those five hours. Such magic power surely supersedes that of any mere pictured Superman.

Or, again, will the American boy influence the dress of the world's youth by preferring to wear a costume which enshrines such favoured science-fiction knick-knacks as inflated synthetic-rubber tyres to ward off supersonic rays from death-ray launching rockets, together with a synthetic glass headdress like a fish-bowl, complete with radar de-atomizing antennæ?

Or, perhaps, will the English Teddy-boy dress (which has actually spread to the U.S.S.R.), make the reverse journey across the Atlantic and influence the American adolescent?

CHAPTER EIGHT

VIRILE MAN

On ne fait plus la cour. You say quite bluntly to a woman that she pleases you and that you are ready to prove it to her where and when she chooses, and this information is communicated, not in the discreet light of a shaded lamp, but in a violent electric glare between dazzling white walls, amongst furniture dry and naked in design from which the bright cushions of yesterday have vanished. Or more likely in a car with the woman at the wheel listening to what you are telling her with only one ear, and attentively watching, not the fugitive expression of passion on your face, but the driving-mirror for the car behind trying to overtake her.

ANDRÉ BILLY, of the Académie Goncourt, 1930

IT is only recently in world history that women have been permitted any choice in selecting a husband, and this is still very far from being a universal practice. It seems, then, that man, in dressing to emphasize his sexual virility, does so, as he has always done in the past, not to impress women with his power and importance, but to impress other men. It is true to say that men dress with their greatest elegance for precisely those functions to which women are not invited. Indeed, it is particularly in the Western world, where women have succeeded in winning more independence and the right to exercise more sexual choice, that men have come to dress with less and less *panache*.

Early man, to whom survival lies at the discretion of gods who must be constantly wooed and propitiated, wears magic charms to invoke and protect his fertility. He does not wear these charms to render himself more pleasing in the eyes of his wives, but to ensure his potency by pleasing his gods.

Thus, by ancient Sanskrit marriage law the bridegroom must wear a particular robe, specially prepared for him by his bride, of which the lower central portion covering the genitals is closely pleated for magic protection against the entry of evil spirits. The dress, in other words, is fertility-insurance.

To primitive man the fertility of his rulers is of even greater importance than his own, for on their fertility depends, he believes, the fertility and survival of all his tribe and of the very land itself. The essence of the

F   161

mystique of kingship is therefore centred on physical fertility, for an impotent king menaces the whole people, and the crops in the fields as well.

African tribes take care to provide elaborate safeguards for their chiefs, lest the slightest injury befalling them bring barrenness upon their fields and disaster upon their own survival. Some African monarchs are never

KHMER STATUE OF
VISHNU

Frontal drapery
symbolizes power.

Musée Guimet, Paris

ENGRAVING ON 8-INCH PEARL-SHELL
PUBIC SHIELD

Niol-Niol tribe, North-west Australia.
Contemporary.

Horniman Museum, London

allowed to set foot on the ground all their lives, but for greater tribal security are carried about everywhere. During periods of tribal warfare at least one king-substitute (dressed and adorned in his likeness) goes into battle to receive the wounds the real king may not receive.

Nor is this custom confined to Africa. During the Crusades and the long Continental wars it was invariable military practice for two or three different nobles to be apparelled and accoutred exactly like their king to safeguard his greater importance. Such occasions, indeed, were the only times these nobles, or any other nobles, were permitted thus to infringe the strict sumptuary laws whereby none might copy royal dress.

James Laver has pointed out that this deep-rooted belief in the potency of kingly power has by no means lost its adherents in our own society to-day, inasmuch as the most popular Western monarchs are precisely those whose legendary sexual prowess is the most spectacular. Thus King Henry VIII, with his train of six wives and many mistresses, remains, despite his ogre disposition, a popular king in the eyes of the people. The fathering of large numbers of offspring, even though born on the wrong side of the blanket, is accounted more of a merit in kingship than barren virtue, and King Charles II is esteemed in the public mind because, though lacking legitimate children, he fathered no less than fifteen bastards. The British public, though always ready to grumble at the large sums they had to provide for allowances and dowries for Queen Victoria's immense family, nevertheless took an immense personal pride in the size of that family.

The *Jus Primæ Noctis*, or "Right of the First Night," whereby a newly married peasant ceded his bed to his lord, derives from this rôle of magic power invested in king and noble. The peasant thereafter could never be sure that his eldest child was his own, and the possibility that it might be his lord's child bound him still more tightly in feudal bondage to his master. This, no doubt, is the reason why the hero of folk-tales is so often not the eldest son of a poor peasant, but the youngest son.

To the early Christians, on the contrary, virility was nothing but a curse and devilish snare, a satanic means of continuing man's existence on this earth when what he should be concentrated on was his hope, not for his future in this world, but in the next. They believed the end of this temporal world was to be not long delayed, and on several occasions even immediately imminent. Therefore they condemned dress which distinguished male from female, as giving possible rise to provocative thoughts.

They approved a common neuter dress which was so long and loose as to suggest a shroud. And this dress women continued to wear long after some men had insisted, against the will of the Church, on wearing something brighter and somewhat more form-revealing.

History proves beyond all doubt that fine clothes originate thus with man, not woman. It is from man that woman subsequently borrowed all her sartorial glamour and finery. It was man who originally wore long hair, corsets, ribbons, lace, high-heeled shoes, feathers and jewels, muffs and fans. Even the original blue-stocking was not female, but male, an eighteenth-century gentleman of culture and learning named Benjamin Stillingfleet. It was only when the fashionably highbrow ladies copied his blue hose that the term became corrupted into a synonym for female cultural pretentiousness.

Once Western man had successfully rebelled against the neutrality of the shroud-garment the way was open to display his power and importance to his fellow-men by means of boastful dress, and that he was ready to risk all in order to do this can be seen by the frantic enactment of sumptuary laws by Church and State for century after century. The history of male dress is the history of virile dress, of man's belief in himself and his desire by means of his dress to command the respect of other men.

Virile dress may be described as dress which endeavours to make the man wearing it look more sexually powerful, taller, broader, slenderer when slimness is considered more noble, and in general more imperious and commanding. The wish to impress his fellow-men may take the form of trains so long that a *cortège* of trainbearers is necessary before he can move, or, in our present age, a motor-car of such greatly extended length that he must extend his garage to contain it.

To make himself look taller man has worn towering headgear, immense wigs, high collars, stilt soles, and high heels. He has commanded retainers to rear high parasols and canopies above his head to lift up the eyes of spectators. A charming old Chinese story in illustration of this relates how the mighty Emperor Chu once made his Court gentlemen learn to walk on stilts, and learned to do so himself, lest face be lost in the reception of tall strangers.

To make himself look wider and heavier man has worn and wears wide-cut robes and cloaks, horizontally pinned necklaces, epaulettes, padding on shoulders, chest, hips, loins, legs, artificial calves, and built-up, duck-toed footwear. He wears hats pushed out east and west instead of only north.

Slimness, when to look slim is aristocratic, because to look stout has become plebeian and socially degrading, is sought by the aid of corsets, tight belts, vertical lines, narrow trousers or tights, narrow, pointed shoes, tight-fitting gloves, and the bearing of slender accessories.

Sexual power has been indicated by such direct boasts as the cod-piece, by embroidery on the garment centring on or near the vital organs, by bows of ribbon, purses, bags, and weapons worn immediately in front, instead of more practically on the left-hand side, by the cut and the line of the dress, leading the eyes of the onlookers directly to this important frontal region. Also by cultivated hairiness of face and body, or by artificial hairiness, or by aristocratic aloofness from hairiness, clean-shaving, pumice-stoning, and hair-plucking.

Sound too plays and has played its part in bolstering male prestige. Though the ambitious youth of to-day can no longer command a flourish of trumpets, a personal musician, bells attached to his garments, or even pleasantly tinkling jewellery to make an agreeable sound when he moves so that other men may hear and admire him, though the impressive *frou-frou* of heavy silks and the susurration of sweeping ostrich feathers are no longer for him, he can and does invest in a noisy motor-bike or a car with a built-in radio to boom and crackle his importance to the world, or if he cannot afford a car or a motor-bike then he refuses to be separated from the noise of his portable radio, which he insists on keeping on loud enough to let everybody know he is there.

ETRUSCAN CERAMIC
Louvre

HEAD OF JOSEPH, THIRTEENTH
CENTURY
Painted wood (Catalan).
*Palacio Nacional, Montjuich,
Barcelona*

In the Western world sumptuary laws have always been regarded rather as a spur to ambitious men than as an insurmountable barrier, and it was the steady battering from below which at last caused their abandonment. There is no reason to-day why a dustman should not wear a Savile Row suit, if he can afford one, and the dustman's Sunday suit does, in fact, attempt, as far as his means permit, to copy the Savile Row suit. This is precisely the reason why the ideal Savile Row English gentleman to-day is tall and slender to the point of emaciation. He must try to distinguish himself by aristocratic slimness from the muscular dustman. His virility boast must take the only form left to him, which is to appear the opposite of virile. Thus far has man evolved in his dress from the original meaning and purpose of his dress, which began in the Garden of Eden with the symbolic placing of the life-giving fig-leaf (the fig, with its many seeds, representing fertility) over that part of his body which was designed to give life.

Now let us look closer at man's various attempts to impress.

The Head

What man wears upon his head proclaims to the world not necessarily what manner of man he is, but, as far as sumptuary laws overt or unwritten permit or as far as he dare defy them, what manner of man he wishes to appear. Bareheaded he simultaneously attains anonymity and loses caste, as we find in the youth of to-day desperately (and with many backward glances) groping towards some form of classlessness.

The Orient grades headdresses with the utmost precision, even to the Civil Service cap-button of old China. The turban and tarboosh assume a thousand different shapes to indicate precise social and professional gradations. It is still accounted an infringement of the law in India for a

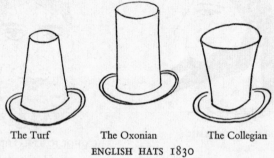

The Turf   The Oxonian   The Collegian
ENGLISH HATS 1830

craftsman to wear the turban sacred to a different craft. When this happens, as for reasons of social ambition it sometimes does happen, the offender is summoned before a special religious council to be punished.

In Tudor England the social distinction attached to a tall black hat offered a chance for unscrupulous hatters to practise a cheap form of renovation. Robert Greene complained of this "Cozenage, used in selling old hattes found upon dunghilles, instead of newe, blackt over with the smoak of an olde linke."

The Puritan form of this tall black hat was a stern declaration of manhood as distinct from mere gallantry, and it is perhaps a measure of our present assumption of decadence that we have found no more grandiose headdress for commandos, singled out of all army units for duties of particular daring and dash, than the dingy and dowdy beret.

The crash-helmet for fox-hunting English squires gave Western civilization its original top-hat, a form it still retains, not only for hunting the fox, but for the bigger game of high society. The tall hat remains a strong assertion of power and pride. The American slang expression "high-hat" is indeed precise. The top-hat played its part in impressing Africa in the nineteenth century, and Sir Harry Johnson has reported how the native King of the Cameroons (King Duke Ephraim IX), a stickler for etiquette, once paid him a social call dressed in nothing whatever except a top-hat.

Havelock Ellis has related how he journeyed far into the interior of Australia in the eighteen-seventies in order to start a rudimentary school in a primitive log hut for the two or three settlers' children he had been engaged to teach, and how, in order to uphold the dignity of his profession of teacher, he was obliged to wear a frock-coat and tall black hat every day for the edification of the kangaroos.

"Is the silk hat doomed?" demanded an English newspaper, early in the twentieth century. "Don't give it away yet. No dress hat has yet been recognized in its place." This is, indeed, still the case. Weddings still demand the top-hat. So do Ascot and royal garden parties and important funerals. "The Lancashire operative usually has a 'buryin' 'at' for funerals and State occasions," said H. G. Wells in 1932, which shows that the practice has not been confined to the upper classes.

A form of hat that has fascinated men for many centuries is the *chapeau melon*. It was first worn in Europe in the early Middle Ages, and has been worn ever since, in one form or another, and it pops up throughout history in different continents and at different times with undiminished vigour. It appears to-day in such distant countries as Bolivia, where the natives call it a *chola*, and perhaps they copied it long ago from the *conquistadores*.

The assumption of the true *chapeau melon*, or bowler hat, called after Mr Bowler, who certainly did not originate it, ranks in present-day England with the mystic attainment of adult prestige in a primitive society. The bowler hat and rolled umbrella, sacred rig of the Stock Exchange and City and dream of every petty-cash clerk, instantly mark out their wearer as a man who does not earn his living by working with his hands, and the social prestige conferred thereby has caused this particular hat to become the favourite gala wear of dockers, who do thus earn their living. The bowler hat is hard, heavy, airless, uncomfortable to wear, and likely to cause a nasty red line round the forehead. All these are further points in its favour as prestige wear, for comfortable clothes are "lazy," therefore without effort, and consequently socially downgrading.

Dunn's of London to-day stock bowler hats in bright yellow with an emerald-green band, in scarlet with a black-ribbon band, and in bright blue with a brown band. These coloured bowlers are, however, sold exclusively to Americans or Continental customers. No Englishman has ever been known to ask for one, for the Englishman wears bowlers in no other colour than plain black, except in grey for excessively audacious and horsy sportsmen at race-meetings, and then only sometimes.

Smart London outfitters also stock Sherlock Holmes deerstalkers in vivid plaids and loud tweeds, which also command a lively sale to non-British and never to British clients. Beau Brummell's neurotic preoccupation with gentlemanly discretion has left its mark on our national headgear.

It is therefore difficult to realize in our present deprived condition how passionately Englishmen felt about their hats not so very long ago. Before Brummell was dead a *nouveau riche* generation was clamouring at the gates of Society, trying to learn to be gentlemen according to the advice of dubious etiquette books, and with an enthusiasm in itself un-gentlemanly. What they put upon their heads, the guide-books warned, might make or mar them for life.

"It is impossible to be conceived by a person inexperienced in dress the immense influence exclusively this department of dress has over the countenance and figure," observed the author of *The Whole Art of Dress*, a not very coherent cavalryman, whose object in writing the manual was to enable the less wealthy young men of 1830 to cut a coveted dash in Society.

It affects both the appearance of age and stature, sobriety and rakishness in the individual [he assured his readers]. A very high and small crowned hat with a narrow round brim (as the Tilbury), contrasted with a broad wide crown and brim (as the Turf), will make a man, if about 40, look about 10 or 11 years younger and an inch or so taller.

Since he was writing for those with pretensions to gentility the author was careful to warn them how not to appear vulgar:

Beaver until latterly has been almost solely worn amongst the nobility and gentry. A silk hat (if known) only recalling a low mechanic to the ideas of the former on the subject.

An impasse which the author skilfully indicates has been dodged without too much loss of face.

This however has been remedied I am happy to say and to such perfection are silk hats now manufactured at half the price of Beaver.

Among the superiorities of beaver, however, he regrets that silk hats show more facility for "getting bent or broken." He also warns against the wearing of "Copper hats" as very pernicious from their poisonous dye during a hot summer season. I think the probable chance should be greatly in favour of getting a brain-fever.

He advocates breadth of brim as a perfect method of adding importance:

> In the present state of fashion broad brims for a handsome shape with a new hat is quite indispensable, and which, by giving orders to the shopman, may always be obtained.

That the reader's social ascent is not going to be too easy the author endeavours to explain at almost every step. If it were where would be the advantage? Cads must be kept in their place, for where is the prestige if the top storey is not to be exclusive?

"We have but to take a short walk either west or east to have our risibility provoked," declares the cavalryman grandly,

> [at the] crude and undigested shapes one is fated to meet with, in those perhaps too [not, we must suppose, however, readers of his manual] who would fain be thought mashers in the most noble art of dress, an art be it said and heard with veneration that gradually in its various degrees of civilization throughout the world is one of the grand outward distinctions between the untaught savage and the European.

In the changing Orient of to-day the headdress is the item of dress which changes least and slowest, for it is by his hat that a man is recognized. The Arab world wraps a coloured scarf round the fez to indicate religions.

THE "TEMBL," COTTON
HAT OF ISRAEL
Contemporary.

CIVILIAN HEADDRESS (BOWLER-
HAT SHAPE), 1350
Wall-painting, St Stephen's, House of
Commons.
"The bowler is man's smartest hat and
his best business-winner. It sits suavely,
inspires respect, engenders confidence."
Evening Standard, 1957

Thus a Muslim wears white, a Jew yellow, and a Christian blue. Since 1377 only descendants of Mohammed may wear green, and for centuries there has been a special office ("Inspector of Descendants of the Prophet") to control the wearing of this privileged headdress.

All male Bedouin wear skull-caps underneath their *keffiyehs*—their heads being shaved. This suggests the origin of the medieval female *bon-grâce*—worn under the veiled headdress.

The most popular and significant headdress in Israel to-day is the *tembl*, a cotton khaki hat stitched like a child's sun-hat. It is worn by both sexes, and there is no age-limit. It is worn at every angle and twisted into all manner of shapes—according to the mood of the wearer. Most popular of all is to wear it perching on top of the head as though by a miracle. It expresses jauntiness, lack of formality, grim determination beneath a gay exterior, and is the particular mark of the "Sabre," or Israel-born Jew.

The origin of the word *tembl* is significant of Israel's East-West attitude. The word means "silly, clownish," and derives from the American slang word "dumb-bell."

Artificial Hair

Artificial hair, with its fascinating power to disguise, has always been a human frailty, which is why the early Christian Church denounced it so vehemently. St Jerome forbade wigs as demeaning to Christians, and St Clement warned his congregation that the Benediction could never pass through a wig to its wearer. The idea that a Christian might be wearing a wig made from hair from an infidel even then burning in hell haunted the clergy, if not their flock, and they pointed out that Hannibal, the wicked pagan, displayed both his earthly vanity and sinful cunning in his habitual use of two wigs, one for beautification and the other for military disguise. Nevertheless the last official clerical wig to be worn in England was worn by a bishop of the Church of England at the wedding of Queen Victoria.

It was King Louis XIV, who was no less than 6 feet 2 inches tall and an imposing figure anyway, who raised the peruke to a fine art and made it essential gentlemanly wear in Europe for more than 150 years. In his time the Court of Versailles employed no less than forty perruquiers entitled by Order in Council to style themselves "Artists."

The Egyptians, the Greeks, the Romans, the Tudors, had all worn coloured wigs. It was left to Louis XIV in his old age to introduce white wigs into fashion, and since every man and woman in his Court copied him, and every European and colonist of distinction copied his courtiers, snowy hair rapidly spread all over the world.

The putting on of the huge full-bottomed wig was an art in itself and a critical moment in every gentlemanly *levée*, though Louis, who had been vain of his long fair hair in youth and would never consent to face daylight bald, insisted on having his wig passed to him by his perruquier through the curtains of his bed and emerged only when he had got it on.

Public combing of the wig with a small ivory comb set with jewels became a modish London pastime well suited to the Mall, the theatre box, or a ladies' drawing-room, as Congreve mentions in *The Way of the World*. "The gentlemen stay but to comb, Madame, and will wait upon you." The size of the wig was of the utmost importance. It could not be too big. Lord Foppington, in Vanbrugh's Restoration comedy *The Relapse*, demands that his perruquier cram more than twenty ounces of hair into his new wig, declaring, "A wig to a man should be like a mask to a woman. Nothing should be seen but his eyes." A colossal wig was the hallmark of the socially élite, and Thomas Brown in his description of a beau at the beginning of the eighteenth century describes his periwig as "large enough to have loaded a camel, and he bestowed upon it at least a bushel of powder."

Even Dr Johnson, who, according to Fanny Burney, went into Society unwashed and in black worsted stockings, would not have thought of appearing without a large wig.

Wigs were expensive and large wigs very expensive. In Dean Swift's time the cult of the wig was such as to make it a perfect prize for thieves, being light, accessible, and anonymous and worth at least thirty or forty pounds. Wig-snatching became a profitable crime, and professional thieves trained up likely young boys as apprentices in the art.

A favourite device was to carry a young boy on a covered butcher's tray on the shoulders of a tall butcher passing in the opposite direction to the intended victim. At the moment of encounter the boy would pop up from the tray and snatch off the wig, while a third party to the plot, arriving precisely then upon the scene, would adroitly detain the victim while the thief made his getaway with the boy, the tray, and the wig. John Gay made merry on this theme:

> Nor is the flaxen wig with safety worn.
> High on the shoulder in a basket borne
> Lurks the sly boy, who hand to rapine bred
> Plucks off the curling honours of thy head.

Hair-dyeing, a venerable practice, must have been child's-play compared to the difficulties of powdering. It was a time-consuming and difficult ritual and one which caused vital changes to be made, moreover, in the

Campaign wig. "Hath knobs or bobs or dildo on each side with curled forehead" (1684).

Popular military pigtail wig—length reduced to seven inches in 1804.

Ramillie wig. Officers of Horse and Foot Guards. Worn by King's Order (1736).

WIGS: SEVENTEENTH, EIGHTEENTH, AND NINETEENTH CENTURIES

architecture of the period. At a time when scent was a substitute for bathing no gentleman would have dreamed of scamping his daily, or twice-daily (beaux made a point of thrice-daily), rendezvous with the dredging-box. There were various methods of applying the powder. Some gentlemen preferred to stick their heads through a curtain during the operation to spare their laced coats. Another method was to bury the face in a glass funnel during the powdering. But, whatever the method, it was essential that there should be a special room to do it in, and houses built at this period are notable for special "powder-closets," small, windowless rooms used only for this one purpose. It was, however, always a messy process, and once on the wig the powder by no means always adhered there.

> Him like the miller pass with caution by
> Lest from his shoulders clouds of powder fly,

jeered John Gay at a passing beau.

Hair-powder was supposed to be made of fine-ground porcelain clay, which, delicately perfumed, sold at exorbitant prices, but flour was much oftener used instead. In a competitive society no fashion that can be copied is for ever entrenched. By 1765 so many gentlemen were choosing to wear short rather than long wigs, and even their own hair—since powdering was by now more important than tossing curls—that the wig-makers, who were losing trade and made less on short wigs than on long wigs, marched in procession to beseech George II to help them in their plight. They were one and all wigless in order to draw attention to their deprivation, and thus were gleefully seized upon by the London mob, who cut off their individual locks forcibly. Commented Horace Walpole on this episode: "Should we wonder if carpenters were to remonstrate that since the peace there is no demand for wooden legs?"

In 1795 Pitt, trying to raise funds to prosecute the war against Napoleon, introduced a Bill taxing hair-powder users one guinea each per annum. So much powder was then in use that he expected this tax to produce at least £200,000 annually. This measure Charles James Fox promptly and vigorously opposed, giving up hair-powder himself and inciting all his Whig friends to do likewise, though he himself had sported modish blue hair-powder in his younger days.

Crop clubs became the rage, members of which, to show their Whig sympathies and embarrass the Government, wore their hair short and un-powdered. Unfortunately for Pitt's Bill, however, a series of disastrously bad harvests began in 1795, which caused the price of grain all over

Europe to rocket upward. Hungry mobs threatened the stability of more thrones than one, and there was a bitter outcry against the wasting of flour on hair-powder at a time of famine. It was an old grievance, sharpened now by hunger.

> Their hoarded grain contractors spare
> And starve the poor to beautify their hair.

Those Tory supporters who continued to use hair-powder and paid up their annual guinea for the privilege were derided and threatened as "guinea-pigs" in street ballads, and when Pitt raised the tax on hair-powder to a guinea and a half his supporters vowed it was a loyal measure and paid up patriotically.

There were certain exemptions from the powder tax. Such were the Royal family and their retainers, those of the clergy whose income was less than £100 per annum, subalterns, N.C.O.'s and privates of the Yeomanry, and fathers of more than two daughters. The rest had to pay up.

Meanwhile there was a panic of hasty legislation to counter the phenomenally high price of bread. Bakers were heavily fined for giving short weight, and at the same time the Privy Council urged that no more puddings or pies should be made with flour. King George III set a public-spirited example in ordering rye and meal to be mixed with the flour used in the Royal household, and the Mayor of Yarmouth issued a special proclamation exorting the gentry to

> Leave off for a time the custom of wearing powder for the hair; by which means a great quantity of wheat must infallibly be saved to the nation, and if the price be not reduced it may at least be prevented from increasing. Appearances are at all times to be sacrificed to the public weal because of the present enormous price of corn and the alarming approach of a scarcity.

It was a nice problem whether it was more patriotic to continue to use hair powder, and by paying the powder tax help the country win the war, or to abandon hair-powder so that the country could be helped directly to the amount of flour thus saved. While this was briskly debated in all the West End clubs the price of flour continued to rise steadily. In 1800 Parliament brought in a Bill fining bakers very heavily for selling new bread, because it could be consumed more rapidly than old bread.

Flour versus hair-powder was an issue which cut deep into the roots of English social life. Hair-powder was aristocratic, a noble gesture against Whigs and Radicals, and, though England was near starvation, patriotic

Tories continued to demonstrate their political principles by continuing to use hair-powder, and even had their dogs and their horses powdered as well. Tories of the old school upheld the use of hair-powder even as late as 1820, long after Napoleon had been vanquished and harvests had improved and the fashion was really dead anyway, and it was in this year that a certain Tory gentleman named Major Cox forbade his son Edward to study under a famous clerical tutor for no other reason than that the tutor wore his hair short and unpowdered, like most other people.

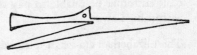

BRONZE WIG-CURLER
Egyptian, Eighteenth Dynasty.
Fitzwilliam Museum, Cambridge

The hair-powder tax was not finally repealed until 1869, and in that final year of its existence there still remained enough stiff-necked Tory users of it to furnish the Exchequer with about £1000, a choice example of the triumph of prejudice over fashion.

Facial Hair

Considering how simple it would have been to trick the tax-collector by a mere flourish of the razor, it is curious that beards should have been so frequently a subject of taxation. When young King Edward VI, in the second year of his brief reign, attempted to raise money by clapping a tax on beards feeling rose high all over the country. For England has enjoyed her hairiness, and the stout descendants of Britons who had refused to let the conquering Romans persuade them to shave off their facial hair were certainly not going to let an English monarch make them pay for the privilege of growing their own hair on their own chins if they had a mind to. The Sheriff of Canterbury, who was fined 3s. 4d. for non-payment of the tax, instantly became a popular martyr.

Nevertheless Queen Elizabeth in due course also tried to raise revenue by taxing all beards of more than fourteen days' growth, but beards were so fashionable that the law could never be enforced. Barbers' shops had become fashion-

HEAD OF THE GOD SIVA
Stone. Cambodia, Tenth century.
Musée Guimet, Paris

able clubs for young gallants, who spent most of the day hanging about there, strumming lutes, scribbling odes, or idly picking quarrels with one another while waiting for their turn in the chair.

Prominently hung on the wall was this set of rules:

1. First come first served.
2. Boots and spurs if worn are not to be used to hurt anyone.
3. Cursing and swearing to be fined seven farthings.
4. Fine of 1 pint of ale for interrupting the barber's discourse.
5. Fine of 1 pint of ale for losing the hat.
6. If customer be unable to pay the barber's fee he shall be sent half-trimmed away.

The Elizabethan era was a splendid period for virility-boasting, and the beard was a splendid means of so doing. There was no end to the different fancies it could be made to take.

> Some seem as they were starched stiff and fine
> Like to the bristles of some angry swine
> And some to set their love's desire on edge
> Are cut and pruned like to a quick-set hedge.
> Some like a spade, some like a fork, some square,
> Some round, some mowed like stubble, some stark bare,
> Some sharp, stiletto-fashion, dagger-like
> That may with whispering a man's eyes outpike.
> Some with the quadrate, some triangle-fashion,
> Some circular, some oval in translation.

So sang John Taylor of the multitudinous arrangements in which a gallant's chin could be embellished. The very utmost height of fashion was to be cut and arranged in Continental style, for an English trim was regarded as parochial by these world adventurers.

"Sir," Robert Greene has a barber demand of his client in 1592,

> Sir, will you have your Worship's hair cut after the Italian manner, short and round, and then frounct with the curling tongs to make it look like a half-moon in a mist; or like a Spaniard, long at the ears and curled like to the two ends of an old cast periwig; or will you be Frenchified with a lovelock down to your shoulders, whereon you may wear your mistress' favour? . . . The English cut is base and gentlemen scorn it. Novelty is dainty. Speak the word, sir. My scissors are ready to execute your Worship's will.

Every one was agreed that the beard itself was both manly and patriotic. It was, declared the reformers and moralists, these imported fashions of wearing it that were unmanly and unpatriotic. (As happens in all countries and at all periods when they blame what they disapprove on another race . . . Italian plague, French disease, Spanish flu.)

The Puritan Stubbes was particularly irate at the new-fangled niceties of *toilette* he believed were undermining British manhood.

> It is a world to consider, when they have done all their feats, how their mowchatows must be preserved and laid from one cheek to the other; yea almost from one ear to another and turned up like two horns toward the forehead: the hair of the nostrils cut away, ears picked, washing in sweet balls and everything in order comely to behold.

MOUSTACHE–LIFTER
Lacquer. Ainu.
Musée de l'Homme, Paris

BEARD TAX: METAL RECEIPT
Russian. First part of eighteenth
       century.

The beard flourished boldly in periods of intense national pride, such as the Elizabethan and the Victorian periods in England. Such was its manly appeal that even after adoption of the full-bottomed peruke in the seventeenth century drove it out of fashion not a few English gentlemen still refused to give it up, and portraits have come down to us in which both full-bottomed wig and sizeable beard are being worn at the same time, a style which hides practically the entire face.

Peter the Great, determined to break down the old Russian order and at the same time build up his exchequer, introduced an anti-beard law into Russia in 1705, whereby the fines for non-shaving were carefully graduated, starting with one kopek for peasants who clung to their beards and rising steeply with each social class, so that the rich boyars had to pay heavily for their reluctance to change their style. Tax-collectors were stationed at the gates of every Russian city (except St Petersburg, and even St Petersburg was obliged to capitulate after nine years' defiance).

By 1722 every beard in Russia not ransomed for fifty roubles had to be shaved off or its owner work off his intransigence by hard labour. A special metal token was cast as receipt for the beard fine, which had to be produced on demand. The beard tax, despite bitter outcry (and not a few outraged citizens preferred to flee their country with their beards than remain there without them), remained on the statute books till Catherine the Great consented to remove the tax in 1762, when fervent prayers of thanksgiving were offered up in every church throughout the land, bells pealed, and there was rejoicing among all classes from peasant to boyar.

It is worth remembering in this connexion that St Modeste is a saint particularly venerated by the Slavs, who attach a mystic significance to the beard, apart from its virility boast. St Modeste, it will be recalled, was an early Christian lady betrothed against her will by her tyrannical and impious father to a heathen lord. Not wishing to incur either the sin of unfilial behaviour by disobedience to her father or the sin of betraying her faith by acceding to his choice of a pagan husband, she prayed desperately for Divine help. Heaven duly heard her prayers, and on the morning of her wedding-day she woke to find she had grown a fine bushy beard during the night.

The long reign of the wig was, generally speaking, a clean-shaven era, though some soldiers sported fierce moustaches. Lord Byron's delicate Oriental moustache, slight as an eyebrow line, which he had briefly cultivated on his Near East travels, certainly helped to reintroduce facial hair, and before the third decade of the nineteenth century men of fashion had once again discovered that beards were irresistibly dashing. A French *Manuel de la Toilette* published in 1828 insists that "La barbe est l'attribut de la virilité," and makes it quite clear that its cultivation is an essential part of every gentleman's social assets. The beard, however, was to be sternly separated from the socially degrading moustache, fit, in the editor's opinion, only for such *canaille* as soldiers. He also cautions his readers against the use of pomade for the hair, "exceedingly vulgar, fit only for masons and fruiterers," recommending instead the use of egg-yolk in warm water to "give the hair a brilliant gloss without nits."

The beard without the moustache led to the flue-brush effect, whereby the gentlemanly face was naked, but encircled by beard like Saturn by its ring. But before the 'fifties gentlemanly faces were growing hairier season by season, so that by the middle of the century every adult male looked like a patriarch.

Beards, as has already been noted, can be powerfully disguising, and many a weak-chinned man with a skinny throat, thus aided, was able to present to the world an erroneous impression of indomitable strength and determination, and perhaps, better still, make himself feel stronger and more determined. Along with the wide and bushy beard were cultivated bushy eyebrows and shoulder-length hair, and most of the family photographs taken in the eighteen-sixties and -seventies show the visage of paterfamilias as nothing but eyes, nose, and cheekbones glimpsed through a jungle of hair.

It was not merely a question of Victorian gentlemen liking their beards. True to their epoch, they had to find religious justification as well, and beards became the subject of the most earnest debate. The animal-painter James Ward laid aside his canvases to write a scriptural volume entitled *In Defence of the Beard*, in which he cited no less than eighteen incontrovertible reasons why men must grow beards in order not to offend their Creator.

MAHARAJAH RANI SINGH OF BUNDI
Udaipur, 1884.
Journal of Indian Art, 1909

In 1859 the public-spirited electors of Hull passed a resolution ordering all their local police to wear both beards and moustaches, one member of the Watch Committee gravely pointing out that "It would be helpful and give a fierce appearance."

It took the Crimean War, however, to win British soldiers the right to grow beards, at least in some regiments, the reason given being to protect the troops against colds and neuralgia. Leaders of political parties, how-ever, warned candidates for older-fashioned rural constituencies that the electorate would not tolerate a bearded politician, and daring aspirants to Westminster who actually ventured bearded on to the hustings were, indeed, pelted with stones and jeered at as "Frenchies." In England the beard depended for its acceptance upon the social *milieu* where it was dis-played, and beards were already going out of fashion in aristocratic sections of British life before they had even come to be accepted at all in poorer districts. Professional prejudices too exercised some control, and the British Bar, for instance, never really approved of beards at all, and there were cases of bearded barristers being chased out of court by the non-bearded.

By 1887 beards had fallen out of fashion so generally in England that the painter Frith searched London in vain for a bearded model, until he came by chance in Soho Square upon a decrepit old man being set upon by a crowd of young hooligans on account of his beard. What by this time had caused the beard to become *passé* was the increasing popularity of moustaches worn alone, a mode viewed by the older generation, who themselves had spent their lives handsomely bearded, with the utmost alarm and disapproval. They denounced moustaches worn alone as worse than martial, as "frivolous," dread epithet in those serious days. When cultivated by men of inferior rank the moustache was looked upon as nothing short of criminal.

The Times of September 21, 1837, reported the case of a carpenter who applied for an assault warrant to protect his moustaches from attack. The sitting magistrate, Mr Rawlinson, asked him indignantly what business a carpenter had "with a long quantity of hair hanging from his lips," adding, "It is disgusting to see *persons* strutting through the streets with moustaches."

Flouted parents, whose rebellious sons defiantly grew moustaches, had their own methods of revenge. A Mr Henry Budd, in his will drawn up in 1862, directed:

> In case my son Edward shall wear moustaches the devise hitherto contained in favour of him, his appointees, heirs and assigns of my said estate, Pepper Park, shall be void [the property being willed to another son instead]. And if my said son William shall wear moustaches he is to forfeit my other estate, Twickenham Park.

Shop-owners, fearful of losing customers, tried their best to prevent their salesmen growing the odious moustaches. One such upholsterer, a tradesman named Fleming, who kept his store in Pimlico, left a will proved in 1869 wherein ten pounds each were to be given to his employees "if no moustaches." As late as 1911 the conviction that moustaches were presumptuous for servants to wear drove French car-owners to form themselves into an employers' federation in an effort to enforce clean-shaving for chauffeurs. The chauffeurs immediately tried to form a counter-union in defence of their moustaches, which they declared to be necessary for "sanitary protection," following the gallant lead of the waiters of Paris, who had already gone on strike to win the right to wear moustaches.

England was less disposed to stand such dangerous nonsense from her employees. In 1904 the Regent Street drapers firmly refused to employ any shop assistants who wore moustaches or dared to part their hair in the middle, and a Bank of England edict somewhat ambiguously forbade its employees to wear moustaches "during business hours."

The grooming of the moustaches required much time, patience, and pomatum, and moustache-fanciers had reason to be grateful to the Spaniards for their invention of the *bigotera*, a metal contrivance in use there for centuries, and which, worn all night like a curling-pin, gave the moustaches a crisp, cockleshell twist next day. Even with the aid of the *bigotera*, however, the glory of facial hair was utterly dependent upon incessant grooming, and English gentlemen of fashion and substance kept their own private hairdressers. Mrs Beeton in her list of essential qualifications for a valet in the eighteen-seventies includes the following: "He should be a good hairdresser. He has to brush the hair, beard and moustaches, arranging the whole simply and gracefully according to the style preferred."

For lesser men there were the barbers' shops, which had never ceased to be an excellent place for relaxation and gossip. London was full of them in the nineteenth century, and an added pleasure was the choice of women barbers, five of whom practised at different shops in Drury Lane, while among the barbers of Fleet Street in the days of Sweeney Todd was a popular Negress barber.

Every European war, with its instant resurgence of male swagger, introduces new styles in facial hair, always with the transparent excuse that it is essential as a hygienic measure, chest-protector, or germ-filter. The heavy beard of the Crimean War soldier changed into the heavy Rudyard Kipling moustache of the South African War, and that changed into the toothbrush moustache of the 1914 War, and we have seen how that moustache grew into the Eighth Army extravaganzas (nearer the Elizabethan models than any other) of the 1939 War. The cult of pogonotrophy has by no means died out. Nor is it ever likely to. It is one of the few male styles that women cannot imitate, and as such means much to men. In present-day England a beard usually indicates a literary man or painter, more likely a naval man, for many sailors like to take advantage of H.M. Regulations permitting a "full set." Hair in the minds of most people still symbolizes virility, and the Sampson legend grips popular imagination no less to-day than thousands of years ago.

The Times, in November 1955, reported the curious case of the English doctor who inadvertently discovered a cure for baldness, when tablets he had prescribed for a different complaint altogether caused hair to start growing on his patient's bald head. The embarrassed doctor "became involved in a blaze of publicity almost throughout the world," and was immediately offered the directorship of an American scalp clinic at a salary of 10,000 dollars per annum.

To bring this section on man's hirsute attractions up to our own period, an article in the *Manchester Guardian* in March 1954 which reports on the revival of interest in male hairdressing states: "The male interest in hair styles is now quite as feverish as any woman's," Mr L. M. Lawrence, secretary to the Committee of National Hair and Beauty Week, is quoted:

> Some men are even keener than women. Youths in their teens and early twenties are keenest on the styles of Tony Curtis, "one curl at the front and occasionally a bunch of curls"—subtle variations on that of the Duck's Anatomy (which had to be renamed because some critics called it by slang expressions, as the District Attorney).
>
> Hair is fashioned to suit the client's type of face and personality. The crew cut (from the lumberjacks of Canada) can be rendered round, square, British or American. . . . The younger men are going in for more elaborate hairdo's partly as a revolt against the standardization they have to submit to in the forces, but the mass of men are simply becoming "more hair-conscious".

A notable aspect of this revival is the interest shown by older men.

> Some of the older men in the suburbs no longer seek a "simple back and sides," but sit back for such improvements as permanent waving, silver and gilt threads, tipped gilt ends, and give the most complicated directions to enhance their masculine features

Dyeing is making a male come-back "unknown for generations and not at all surreptitious."

> Many middle-aged men prematurely going grey, particularly the commercial-traveller type, are erasing the signs of age at the roots and going home a different colour—blond, red, brown, or whatever they fancy.

Prices for male hairdressing are not cheap. A "Dale Robertson" cut costs fifteen shillings, for instance, but this, far from discouraging clients, acts, it appears, as a positive stimulant.

Among other favoured styles are "the Director" (slight wave on crown), "the Academician" (high side part), the "Author," "the Olympic," "the Continental," and "the Editor" (high side part, both sides swept up, with part immediately above the ears going back fully). The social-snob names of these new hair styles, it should be noted, are in the worthiest tradition of sartorial social climbing.

The *Daily Mirror* (April 28, 1956) reports a different trend in male hair-dressing in the Cricklewood adoption of such American styles as "the Flying Saucer" and "the Droop Snoot," both of which feature a horizontal parting across the head from ear to ear.

GENTLEMAN'S EMBROIDERED
NIGHTCAP
Silver-gilt thread on linen.
Late sixteenth century.
Victoria and Albert Museum

VOLTAIRE'S INDOOR CAP
Pink silk. Eighteenth century.
Musée Carnavalet, Paris

It is, it should not be forgotten, less than fifty years since men gave up covering their heads indoors as well as outdoors and wearing nightcaps in bed. During the long reign of the wig, turbans were often worn indoors when the wig was removed. The head was never for a moment left un-covered, especially at night. All men wore nightcaps of a richness accord-ing to their purses and social position, from the finest damask, embroidered heavily with bullion and inset with precious stones, of the wealthy and noble, down to the clumsy "Biggin" of plain, unbleached homespun of the poorest journeymen. Lord Byron's poetically disordered tresses must have had a lot to do with the temporary decline of the nightcap early in the nineteenth century, for we know that the Duke of Wellington (an equal if not greater figure in the public mind) clung stubbornly to his nightcap and invariably wore on all his campaigns an unromantic one knitted in white wool with a prim tassel. Four years only after Lord Byron's death a French manual on the art of dress issued a solemn warning against the anti-aphrodisiac properties of the nightcap.

Grand Dieu! What would a young and pretty woman say now if she should see, lying beside her, her husband, or, what would be still worse, her lover, tricked up in a well-starched cotton nightcap. The poor little woman would be paralysed.

Rubbing in the moral, that his reader's chances of securing a rich wife or a strategically placed mistress to assist his way into the world of rank and wealth are utterly dependent upon his powers to impress, the author insists that a nightcap would be fatal to such plans. "We should not need to declare that the sight of a cotton nightcap is to love what the sight of the rope is to some one about to be hanged."

Definitely no nightcaps. But the head could not be left bare either, for that would not only be gauche, but also decidedly imprudent. The fool-hardy British might like to court their death from draughts, but such was not the French way of life. The author recommends a silk foulard tied up like a turban, as both romantic and draught-excluding.

The nightcap, nevertheless, remained essential wear for respectable men for many decades, and is still worn even to-day by a few old men who cling to the customs of their working-class youth—no longer wearing it tied round the chin like Mr Pickwick's unfortunate nightcap, but cut round and flat on the top like the national headdress of India.

The Neck

The neck in all countries and at all times has been a most important object of male self-assertion, whether left dramatically bare, as with the Romans or modern sportsmen, or, more usually, encircled by rich jewels, majestic ruff, seductive lace cravat or dignified collar of a height and stiffness calculated to add considerable authority to the wearer.

The very word "cravat" comes to us from Louis XIV's special guard of Croatian mercenaries, who refused to be deprived of their military neck-cloth, believing that it had magic properties which protected the heart from damage in battle. Louis himself kept his own private *cravatier*, M. Miramond, whose duty it was to present to his sovereign each morning, at the given moment during the *levée* a basket full of exquisite confections, and then, rising from his knees, place the selected cravat round the royal neck. With extraordinary independence, for his era and his rank, Louis actually tied his own knot.

Since the sixteenth century lace had been becoming increasingly popular, and in France kept no less than 10,000 families busy making it. Equally flourishing were the lace industries of Italy and Holland, for lace proved a most satisfactory method of displaying wealth and self-importance, since in those days it could not be easily nor cheaply faked. At the Parliament of Blois King Henry III of France had managed to display 4000 yards of costly gold lace on one suit alone. King James I of England, for his part, contrived to cram twenty-five yards of expensive lace into each of his ruffs.

England too had her own lacemaking industry, which the Government tried to encourage by forbidding the import of foreign-made lace, the only result of which was to stimulate lace-smuggling, obviously Brussels-made lace being openly sold in London labelled "British-made."

Lace was so important an item of dress for men of quality in France before the Revolution that Mercier reported that a man of fashion might wear a soiled shirt, or, indeed, no shirt at all, but his jabot and wrist-ruffles had to be of lace and that lace of the finest quality. No less than their masters lackeys flaunted lace at throat and wrists, and even during the Revolution the very executioners at the guillotine wore lace.

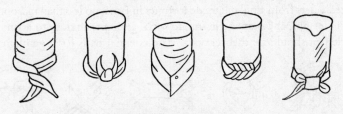

PARIS CRAVATS, 1830

From left: Populaire, Orientale, Paresseuse, Coquille de Pucellage, Trône d'Amour.

Of the two ways of overcoming social rank in dress—that is, by every one dressing up or by every one dressing down—the first is the one that in the past has most tempted humanity. Rich commoners eagerly bedecked themselves in fine lace, and the not-so-rich bedecked themselves in imitation lace as soon as imitation lace had been invented. The gentleman therefore had to distinguish himself in other ways from the less well-born. One way, and an immensely important way, was to understand how to knot a cravat properly. It was this which explains Beau Brummell's absorption in the putting on of his cravat, and the awed reverence with which this process was regarded by aspirants to fashion.

It was absolutely essential for the Regency gentleman to present an inflexibly rigid neck, and to elongate his neck further the cravat was tightly swathed until it reached as high as the ears at least. Gentlemen, the mode demonstrated, held their heads up. They had to. One form of cravat at this period was made of leather beaten on a block to iron-hardness, so that it held the neck like a slave-halter. The aristocratically stiff neck was England's psychological reply to the disturbingly democratic ideas launched by the French Revolution. Observe how the manual of dress (1830) describes the *"Plain beau or bow* . . . very pliant and with a common bow in front. Of humble aspect beside its more haughty and aristocratical contemporaries, it is unassuming and businesslike."

On the other hand blue blood demanded ostentation of a special kind, length of neck particularly:

> The *ROYAL GEORGE CRAVAT or FULL DRESS* is composed of richest black Genoa velvet and satin (particularly becoming to dark complexions). His Majesty and his Royal Brothers were always remarkable for wearing them extremely high on the cheek, so that the sides came close under the ears, extending to the utmost verge of the chin.

In France the cravat quickly became not merely a clue to a man's profession, but a guide to his social and political convictions. Superannuated valets from England made fortunes in Paris, no less than in London, giving lessons, at a guinea a lesson, to social aspirants anxious to learn how gentlemen should tie their cravats. The essential basis for a gentlemanly

PARIS CRAVATS, 1830
From left: Byron, Anglaise, Gastronome, Bergami, Colin.

cravat, Brummell had maintained, was starch, "used in such proportions as to stiffen the cloth to the consistency of fine writing-paper," and ironed well in with the smoothing-iron until it "effectually prevents the admission of the least portion of cold air," according to the manual.

This covering up was the answer to the French peasants, who had worn a mere rag tied with string round their necks, or nothing at all. The Revolutionary bare necks *à la Spartiate* or *à la Brutus* had quickly been replaced by high shirt-collars and increasingly stiff cravats, buckling at the back and so tight as to endanger health and make it totally impossible for a modish man to see his feet. The sartorial class-structure that the French Revolution broke down revived and flourished more wildly than ever in the cravat, and more excessively in France than in England.

Neckwear in France was presently so heavily starched and so bloated out by cushions worn under the chin that aspiring gentlemen resembled pouter pigeons, and secrets which Brummell did not initiate and would vehemently have disapproved began to creep into the guide-books—how, for instance, to cheat on methods of knotting the cravat.

> After the knot is made take a piece of white tape and tie one end of it tight to the end of your neckcloth, then carry the tape under your arm behind your back under the other arm and fasten it tightly to the other end of your neckcloth. The tape must not be visible. This way prevents the knot from flying up.

Such quick tricks for social success are interlarded in the manuals between lofty dissertations on the folly of just such behaviour, for the author's claim to knowledge of the *beau monde* was what sold the books. "Undue assumption in dress, it may be relied on, never fails to meet with contempt in society, where, in fact, it can only expose a party to a very just and proper censure."

Time was not long in revenging itself upon Brummell and on his innovations. By 1820 paper collars were already being sold in the stationers' shops for those who wanted to ape the gentleman on the cheap, and there were even zinc collars for sale.

Footwear

Tall hats and high collars add height. Footwear too can be used to add stature. The cavalryman Editor of the dress manual has much to say on this subject:

> In undress it is impossible to dress a fine leg, more especially for a short person, to greater advantage than in a *Hessian*. It adds a great deal of command and dignity to the person, setting off the figure to considerable advantage. The shape most admired when pulled on the leg should be high enough to let the tassel touch the knee-pan.

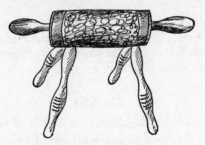

AMERICAN CYLINDER FOOTSTOOL
UPHOLSTERED WITH CARPET
Wet shoes were hung over the two ends to dry.
New England, nineteenth century.
By courtesy of Mrs Herbert Wechsler

He cautions severely against the degrading effect of top-boots:

> They are in general use amongst the lowest orders, such as jockeys, grooms, butchers, etc. We are apt in London to connect something very low with their appearance.

For evening wear pumps "are absolutely indispensable for etiquette."

They show off the feet very nicely, he explains, and offer a gentlemanly opportunity to wear buckles set with brilliants on the toes.

"As in China," insists the author,

> the greatest attention is displayed to the feet in the fashionable world, their importance vying with any other portion of the figure. Frequently in company I have heard the chief beauties singled out amongst good-looking individuals were their feet . . . small and encased in a neat pump.

Neat feet in elegant boots could also artfully contrive to add inches to height, and he recommends the "dress-boot-shoe" so warmly that it is impossible not to wonder whether he himself did not stand to gain something by their sale, particularly as he indicates where they may be purchased.

> The dress-boot-shoe is a new invention for dinner-dress, in the shape of a Wellington boot; the stocking is affected by black cloth indiarubber in appearance. Recommended for those who wish to heighten themselves, having a high heel (2 or even 3 inches is required). When they are very high they should be tipped with cork at least ½ an inch thick to avoid reverberation.

He details the best methods of concealing the trick:

> The trousers should be made very long, even to touching the ground, and tightly strapped. If followed in the manner my instructions have pointed out, you cannot give the slightest cause to suspect that you are actually walking upon raisers.

The Stick

Walking-sticks, another heightener rarely out of fashion, came into their own when swords for normal wear were forbidden in England by Act of Parliament, and the early sticks following this were swordsticks. Henry VIII had owned a handsome collection of sticks, some entirely covered in gold, and one containing a little astronomical clock in the handle. Louis XIV preferred richly jewelled sticks. The Emperor Ferdinand III ordered himself a marshal's baton in ivory on which ninety-three rubies were spirally mounted, and which inside contained a pair of field-glasses. Here we see sticks used in their original sense—that is, to exemplify power.

In the eighteenth century most gentlemen owned dozens of sticks as they owned quantities of snuff boxes. Voltaire, who was no beau, nevertheless had a collection of over eighty sticks, and even Rousseau, who, in accordance with what his admirers expected of him, prided himself on his extreme sartorial simplicity, owned no less than forty walking-sticks.

Tough sticks for country walks (or for giving the impression that the bearer is devoted to country pursuits) were a fashion set up by Rousseau, and these have never since gone out of fashion, particularly for city-dwellers. But in general walking-sticks were and remain fashionable playthings, suggesting height if they are slenderly elegant, and importance by their rich mounting. They were once frequently given as presents by

Top: CEREMONIAL UMBRELLA HELD OVER CHIEFTAIN ON SAFARI
Four-inch brass figure. Togoland, nineteenth century.
Smithsonian Museum, Washington

HEAD OF STAFF REPRESENTING EUROPEAN
West Africa. Contemporary.

Bottom: JADE STICK HANDLE IN FORM OF BIRD
Chinese.
Musée Guimet, Paris

admirers or relatives. Benjamin Franklin was thus given a gift of a walking-stick which, with charming confusion of noble sentiments, was carved from the wood of a wild apple-tree and sported a costly gold knob wrought in the shape of the cap of liberty. He passed it on to George Washington.

Mercier reported an enormous multiplicity of sticks in 1782, of all patterns, shapes, and sizes, different weights for different times of the day and night, month and year, and equally carried by both sexes. Many of these sticks contained toilet mirrors or amorous pictures in the handle, or two different kinds of perfume, and dandies had a walking-stick as well as a snuffbox to match each suit. Even Napoleon succumbed to the fashion and carried a fancy tortoiseshell walking-stick, in the handle of which was a tiny music-box.

"Our elegants are carrying walking-sticks," reported a French fashion-book of 1828, "but only to give the impression of being occupied with something, not knowing otherwise what to do with their arms." Though both swords and swordsticks were then equally illegal, it openly lists nine shops where they were for sale. Disraeli on his Grand Tour in 1830 wrote home:

> I have also the fame of being the first who ever crossed the straits with two canes, a morning and an evening cane. I changed my cane as the gun fired 6. It is wonderful the effect these magic wands produce.

Into the late nineteenth century, and, indeed, right up to the 1914 War, a silver-mounted stick was an essential item of gentlemanly dress, even for a visit to the theatre, and Messrs Moss Bros are careful to keep a fine stock of elegant silver-mounted sticks to-day as part of their hiring service.

Umbrellas

Umbrellas, which no gentleman would have dreamed of being seen with in the middle of the eighteenth century, were quite modish by 1800, especially as it was known that the Duke of Wellington and the Guards Regiment were partial to them. The frames, far from that elegance we have attained to-day, were heavy, even clumsy, but handsomely covered with fancy silk, and the handles were carved in ivory or staghorn or beautifully wrought in silver and gold. Since the less well-bred could also carry umbrellas it was essential for gentlemen to learn the correct gentlemanly deportment for this accessory.

It was regarded as intolerably vulgar, for instance, to carry the umbrella under the arm or like a walking-stick. The aristocratic method was to hold the umbrella by its middle with the handle turned towards the ground. The umbrella, moreover, was only to be made of blue or green silk, with a frame of polished steel or silver. No other colour, no other material, and no other way of carrying it were *bon ton*. Unfortunately, however, the vulgar soon tumbled to the trick of carrying the umbrella upside-down, and the gentleman had to seek other means of putting a rightful distance between them.

How popular the umbrella had become is revealed by this comment in the French Press in the middle of the nineteenth century:

In the South of France, when the sky remains for months at a time
without presenting to the earth a single drop of rain, every individual
carries his umbrella. Folly, but no greater folly than that of the Paris
dandy who carries his umbrella during a hard frost with the temperature
10 degrees below freezing-point.

It is unreasonable to expect the exercise of reason in such manly
accessories as the umbrella, which is to-day still carried more for prestige
than purpose—in fact, exclusively for prestige, for the London man-
about-town would not feel properly dressed without his neatly rolled
umbrella, never unfurled, for to unfurl it would be an act of grossest
vulgarity. If it should happen to rain the gentleman hails a taxi and
jumps into it with his umbrella still furled. It must not get wet any more
than he.

Perhaps the nearest modern approach to a virility accessory is the favourite swagger 'pestle' stick used by British officers in North Africa during
the Second World War. It was made from a bull's genitalia, and was
supplied to British officers by the Arabs for twenty cigarettes.

The Waist

A narrow waist has always been looked upon with approval as a sign of
manly virility, and waist-suppression was familiar to the ancient Egyptians no less than to the warriors of Crete, while Romans, whose waistlines
suffered from the luxury of their banquets, were accustomed to wear
corrective corsets of wooden discs. In history corsets are by no means
always called by their rightful name, any more than they are to-day. But
corsets they are nevertheless, whenever they are worn for the purpose of
waist-suppression, and as such we must recognize them.

They are first mentioned by name in European literature in a song of
1350 composed by the trouvère Guillaume de Machault, describing how
the lords and ladies, retiring to their rooms after the evening's festivities,
removed their corsets for the night.

> Quant on ot chante tout a trait
> Chascun ala a son retrait
> Qui dut son corset devestir.

By 1371 the Chevalier de la Tour Landry was blaming the introduction of
the corset into decent French life on the riff-raff who followed the English
armies into France.

At this time corsets were common to both sexes, and were worn either inside or outside the dress, or else the upper part of the dress itself was stiffened and laced up like a corset. When the ladies in due course changed the fastening round so that their corsets laced up the back instead of the front the jovial prelate Rabelais was vexed because "L'on n'y pouvoit plus mettre la main par dessoiltz car la fente d'iceultz avoyent mise par derrière et estoyent tous cloz par devant."

The amorously named colours in which corsets were created were common to both male and female corsets (such as *désirs amoureux*) or more specifically for gentleman (*baise-moi, ma mignonne*), and one or two were intended for ladies alone (*veuve réjouie*).

In the Renaissance pourpoints were so heavily busked that they served admirably as corsets themselves, but Montaigne registered his disapproval of busks which were so long as to encase the thighs as well as the torso, describing them as "inepte et insupportable." These busks were made from wood, ivory, whalebone, iron, or any available kind of bone, and it was an elegant pastime for a gallant to pull out one of his busks and play with it in company, just as a pretty woman was later expected to play with her fan. Italian busks sometimes were made hollow to contain a small dagger. In the sixteenth century it was not the English who were blamed for sending corsets into France, but the Spanish for sending them into England. The *corps espagnol* was so stiff and heavy as to approach to armour, and was used as much to give smoothness to the pourpoint as to compress the waist into as small a compass as possible.

It was not only European men who were squeezing their middles in Napoleon's day, for the traveller Edward Harding reported in 1811:

> It is the practice among the Circassians to compress the waist from early infancy as much as possible by means of the straps on which the sabre is suspended; hence they are generally extremely thin between the loins and the breast.

Corsets were never out of male fashion in the fifteenth, sixteenth, seventeenth, and eighteenth centuries, and there was a fresh outburst of masculine waist-squeezing in the nineteenth. "Sent for tailor and stay-maker," recorded an English officer in his diary, soon after Waterloo. His orders included "Cumberland corset with a whalebone back. The last pair gave way in stooping to pick up Lady B.'s glove."

There was no embarrassment or coyness displayed in the use of corsets to improve the male figure throughout the nineteenth century. Rather was the practice looked upon with approval, as many references make clear, and though a small section of medical opinion, as we have seen in the matter of corsets for growing boys, ventured to doubt whether corsets were actually beneficial to health, no one dreamed of suggesting that they were not a manly and virile article of dress. They were never out of fashion, and from time to time the fashion grew into a passion.

The *Tailor and Cutter* in 1892 reported:

> For many years there has been a certain demand by gentlemen for an article of support round the ribs or hips; owing undoubtedly to the growing fancy for a defined waist the demand for some undergarment that would give a proper shape and retain it in wear on the outer garment has been the reason for a more general use of the GENTLEMEN'S CORSET, and the present unusual demand.

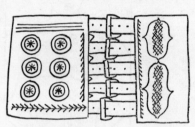

LEATHER CORSET BELT WORN BY
SHEPHERDS IN POLISH MOUNTAIN
DISTRICTS
Contemporary.

GENTLEMEN'S CORSET,
1895
Tailor and Cutter

A West End firm of corset specialists claimed to supply gentlemen all over the country, not only young military officers, but also university professors, country squires, and clergymen of mature age.

> Any gentleman who feels proud of his figure and wishes to improve it can be supplied with a most comfortable-fitting corset at from 2 to 6 guineas. 36 in. breast and 26 in. waist is the extreme. 34 in. breast and 26 in. more usual.

The accompanying idealized illustration, as we see, shows a waist very much smaller than 26 inches.

It seems that only to-day, half-way through the twentieth century, have

G

Western men grown ashamed to have the matter of corsets mentioned. They are still worn, but always described ambiguously as "belts" or "supports," like alcoholic drinks purporting sanctimoniously to be medicines. But their true objective is waist-suppression, and waist-suppression not in the interest of health but of elegance.

West End tailors to-day deny vehemently that their clients wear anything in the nature of corsets, but the corsetiers tell a different story. American and Canadian men are less sensitive in this matter, and in North America male corsets are openly advertised and sold over the counter with much less embarrassment, a frequent reason advanced being that they buy them because their wives insist upon their retaining their youthful figures.

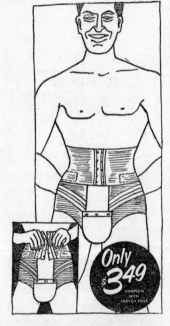

Above: "LINIA" BELT
English. Contemporary.

Right: MALE CORSET
American. Contemporary.

"When I began wearing corsets, nearly fifty years ago," writes an elderly Canadian businessman, "a man had to keep his corsets as carefully concealed as any other family skeleton. Now I do not worry at all about disclosures to tailors or fitters."

Under the title "Girdles are no Longer Strictly Feminine" the *Canadian Expositor* (March 11, 1948) remarks:

Gone are the days when men could poke fun at the fair sex for pouring itself into unmentionables known politely as "foundation garments." According to the records of girdle makers and retailers a goodly number of Brantford males owe their figures, not to plenty of exercise and sensible diet, but to the efforts of manufacturers to turn the Canadian man into a combination of Adonis and Adolphe Menjou. Girdles (or rather supporters) range from 3 dollars to 15 dollars. . . . They also come in several sizes—small, medium, large and extra large—and the claim is that the average waist-whittler will haul the wearer in 2 or 3 inches right away.

America, with her passion for improving on nature, is still less restrained on this subject. "Girdles may soon be more popular with men than face-lifting is with actresses," reports *Corsets and Brassieres*, an American trade publication (January 2, 1952).

I have noticed many men who looked as if they were wearing girdles. The number of girdles sold to men has been booming upwards in the last five years . . . and 1952 is expected to be a bumper year. Male girdles in the U.S.A. will cover more than 20,000 miles stretched end to end. Corset-makers are spending millions to make the contraptions as painless as possible. Eventually you'll be able to buy them in any shade you want. The coming thing in girdles is co-ordination between underwear and outerwear.

Boxers and sportsmen, it is pointed out, are among the most regular customers.

If the smart tailors in London are sensitive on the subject of male corsets other sections of the English community may think differently—such as the writer of the following letter (from E. S., Upton Park, London, E.12), published in *Reynolds News* of November 22, 1953:

Your illustration of a man's corset of Victorian days may look ridiculous to us now, but not more so than women's corsets of the same period. Many men to-day are glad to wear a corset to improve their figure. Surely this is better than the sagging pot-bellies we see too often.

My husband has worn a corset ever since he was a lad, and at 45 his figure is as good as most men 20 years younger. My two sons aged 14 and 11 had their first corsets when they were 10. I would advise other mothers to try this out. Start young and the results are worth while.

Next to the corset, in manly concentration on the possible elegance to be bestowed on this part of his anatomy, comes the waistcoat itself, a garment which has been particularly dear to men throughout recorded history. So fascinated have they been by this one article of dress that whole libraries have been compiled from the literature devoted to its cult.

A simple, sleeveless short garment open in front was probably one of the very first garments worn by early man. Since then men of all classes have clung to the waistcoat, from the ploughman who stubbornly refuses to dispense with it, even on the hottest summer day, to the well-bred dandy who is careful to observe his particular public-school ritual of keeping the bottom button done up—or undone.

The waistcoats of the eighteenth century reached a high point of gorgeousness, and offered a splendid opportunity for sweethearts and wives to display their skill with the embroidery needle. "I work very hard with my needle upon his linen," writes Samuel Richardson's Pamela in 1740, "and am besides about flowering him a waistcoat."

Such waistcoats were garments of show in their own right, and, though without sleeves, were, in fact, entire coats and intended to look such, the sleeved coats worn over them not fastening in front at all, their buttons being purely decorative.

The extreme richness and delicate sumptuousness of these waistcoats owed much to the vogue for Oriental, especially Chinese, embroidery, tiny mirrors sometimes being worked into the borders and held in place by minute buttonhole stitches in the Indian style, and entire waistcoats being sent off to Pekin to be embroidered by Chinese craftsmen with designs of flowers and birds in rare silks. One such waistcoat, dating from 1775, is quilted and adorned by several rows of tiny silk buttons, each button exquisitely worked with a different flower. A gamester's waistcoat of the same period is embroidered not only with elegant sprays of flowers, but also with pairs of fighting cocks in action.

Even so Puritan a man as Beethoven could not resist the lure of the elegant waistcoat, and in 1793 we find him writing to Fräulein Eleonore Breuning, begging her services, "that I may be lucky enough to possess a waistcoat worked by you in goat's wool. Forgive this indiscreet request from your friend."

Such was the vogue for waistcoats that sometimes two were worn at the same time. Fulwar Creven, a popular Regency dandy, habitually wore two waistcoats together, a scarlet one beneath and a canary-yellow one on top. By leaving buttons carelessly open both could be made visible beneath the unbuttoned coat.

As the nineteenth century progressed waistcoats grew shorter, tighter, and more richly sombre, and in the eighteen-thirties there was a craze for Paisley waistcoats of fine wool, woven and printed in Scotland with the ancient Persian *motif* of interlacing ears. Long after male dress in England had lost its vitality it was still possible for an individual man to express something of himself in his choice of waistcoat. One such worn in the eighteen-forties was made of rich crimson velvet lavishly embroidered all over the front with bullion-edged silk flowers and twining tendrils. The French were especially loath to let the waistcoat, this last possibility of fantasy, slip from their grasp, and a dress manual of the time pleads for its retention, if but "to protect breast and stomach from the air and encourage a healthy tendency to sweat in the summer," pointing out artfully that there was wide choice of material to tempt the hesitant, "woollen with

WOODEN GINGERBREAD
MOULD
English, eighteenth century.
Museum of English Rural Life,
Reading

SIOUX DEERSKIN WAISTCOAT
Worked in traditional porcupine quills,
but showing White influence in design.

fancy cashmere front, taffeta, merino or satin," and denouncing renegades who "prefer to wear no waistcoat at all and keep their coat buttoned up in front," a barbarous solecism "fit only for soldiers. Better two waistcoats than none at all," especially for a "jeune homme jaloux de se faire remarquer par sa mise."

Hands and Feet

In the industrial nineteenth century in England there were many sons of wealthy tradesmen climbing their way up into a society which they could hardly have hoped to attain in former periods. Such young men were anxious above all to make it clear that they did not have to work for a living, just as their sisters were preoccupied with the necessity to look fragile and therefore unlike the offspring of sturdy commoners. These heirs to industrial fortunes concentrated fanatically on acquiring aristocratically small and useless hands and feet, and the manuals of etiquette they studied are full of advice on how this might be done. However cleverly an upstart might contrive to slip in beside his betters, the manuals warned, it was always by his gloves and shoes that he could be detected, especially his gloves. Gentlemanly and ladylike hands must be very small and very white, and, though the lavish use of lotions and unguents could be of service, most important of all was the aid of large quantities of tight, expensive gloves, worn by day and by night, each occasion demanding gentlemanly familiarity with exactly the right kind, "light cotton or lawn for the young gentlemen" during summer social occasions, white gloves for weddings and baptisms, *glacé* kid gloves "d'un couleur tendre" for a ball.

It was absolutely essential for a young man with any pretence to *savoir-faire* (the English etiquette manual's addiction to French phrases at this time is only equalled by the French etiquette manual's addiction to English phrases) to take a large supply of such *glacé* kid gloves with him to the ball, changing into fresh ones for every dance. It was the acme of refinement to keep gloves on during supper, and ladies of the acutest social sensibilities did not remove their gloves in company even when playing the harp.

Gentlemanly stockings and socks needed equal thought and care. No less than five different weights were essential—silk, wool, thread, cotton, and a mixture. It was proper to wear two pairs at a time, one on top of the other (not like poor Malherbe—who in his day had worn eleven pairs one on top of the other to keep out draughts—but to conceal the flesh). Socks were advised for those with handsome legs "to render nugatory that horror of horrors to persons possessing good legs, a garter. This is an order the knights of fashion have universally forsworn." White socks were correct only with uniform and white or yellow kerseymere small-clothes. Otherwise nothing but grey and white shotted or sombre black. Here the author throws in a sly tip for those young men whose social aspirations were unsupported by great riches: "It is at the option of the individual to make a great saving by having the tops, toes and soles of cotton and the rest, where they are seen, of silk."

Besides the smallness, neatness, and height-conferring qualities of properly selected footwear (and the author claimed that a man of five foot four would appear at least five foot six at a distance of three yards by wearing heels one and a half inches high, and no less than five foot eight tall at twenty yards), the varnishing of the footwear was of the utmost moment. Dandies devoted themselves to chemical experiments to produce more gleaming polishes than their rivals, and not a few took quite seriously Brummell's recipe for his own boot-polish, which he vowed owed its brilliance to the vintage champagne with which it was mixed.

A hero of the time was Lieutenant-Colonel Kelly, of the First Foot Guards, a famous dandy especially renowned for his brilliant top-boots, who met an untimely death endeavouring to rescue these boots during a fire at the Customs House, where he happened to be visiting his sister, who was a housekeeper there. After his funeral all the dandies in London tried to secure the services of his valet in order to learn the formula of his boot-polish. Even Brummell put in his bid. But the valet was eventually bribed into the service of the Earl of Plymouth.

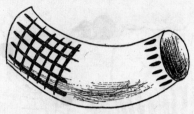

COD-PIECE OF ENGRAVED IVORY
Pigmy. Central Africa. Contemporary.
Musée de l'Homme, Paris

It must be remarked that only in young and vigorous new societies is rude health and physical vigour regarded with approval and a man not despised for making use of his muscles instead of his money to move himself from one place to another. In older societies, where social classes have had a long time to solidify, the more socially important a man is the less he uses his feet for locomotion, and the less he uses his hands for helping himself. This is why in ancient cultures even the fan is wielded by a retainer, the mere act of waving it being regarded as manual labour fit only for inferiors. The point about small feet is that they do not walk. They are carried. Litters and sedan chairs, true to this code, were not invented either for speed or for safe transport, since they were slow and an attractive target for highwaymen, but for aristocratic prestige.

Their introduction into England from Spain caused considerable rioting in the days of Charles I, coachmen bristling with indignation, and for understandable reasons swearing that such work degraded Englishmen into slaves and beasts. But the demand was keen, and by 1634 Sir Francis Duncombe had obtained a highly profitable patent from the King "for carrying people up and down in close chairs," so that from his fleet of fifty he made a handsome fortune.

Perhaps the most successful effort in such prestige travelling was the journey from London to Bath by sedan chair, undertaken by Princess Amelia in the spring of 1728. It took eight chairmen seven days and nights to cover the distance, working in continual relays supplied from the accompanying coach pulled by six horses.

The Cod-piece

The one area of male dress upon which fashion most truly demonstrates its interest in virility is that which to-day we have grown too prudish to mention at all. A modest reticence would be understandable, but our present agonized shame surely merits the particular attention of psychologists. Such is its resolute blindness to this subject that the Western world to-day appears to wish to give the impression that its men have no

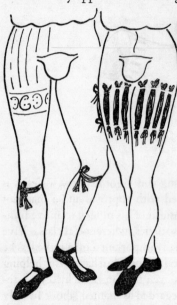

COD-PIECES AND POINTS USED AS
DECORATION

From *La Prova del Fuoco di Mosé*,
Giorgione. Uffizi Gallery, Florence.

MANNER OF WEARING A
WEAPON

Votive tablet of Jan Očko of Vlašim.
Late fourteenth century.
National Gallery, Prague

genitalia at all. This aspect of our brave new world is a far cry, indeed, from the practice of the sixteenth century, when the cod-piece was an esteemed, honoured, and, indeed, essential part of every male dress, peasant and noble alike.

Instigated in the first place by the Church, in a mistaken effort towards decency because the abbreviated tunics were exposing too much, cod-pieces soon became formal wear in every Christian country where the long Oriental gown was not worn. Ploughmen, peers, tottering old men, emperors, sailors, servants, soldiers, and young lads emerging from the nursery, all wore cod-pieces, and in the paintings and statues of the time we find even angels wearing cod-pieces.

Fastened on separately with ribbons or strings or jewelled buttons, the cod-piece did not have to match the rest of the dress, and every country developed its own national shapes and its own individual manner of wearing the cod-piece. Here at last, in this direct male vaunt, man had invented a garment which women simply could not copy (though Stubbes indignantly accuses the tradsmen's wives of his time of trying to do so by wearing imitation cod-pieces "hanging down before").

Richly embroidered, stuffed heavily with bombast for a sturdy appearance, lavishly set with jewels, and glorified with expensive bullion, the cod-piece made a fine accessory for the rich and noble and added swagger to the simple dress of the poorest labourer. The wearing of the cod-piece necessitated an aggressively straddled stance, in itself giving a look of insolent self-importance, and every step taken by its wearer became an assertive stride. All of a piece with the boastful cod-piece were the built-out shoulders, the swollen sleeves, and the duck-billed heel-less footwear. Weight and power shout out in every item of this Renaissance male dress. It was not a mode intended for the thin and timid undersized man with bent shoulders, and, logically enough, it was in the end the military, in whose dress the cod-piece attained its most grandiose forms, who were most reluctant to give it up when the mode changed, and who went on wearing it very long after its day was officially over.

Besides the cod-piece proper there were other possibilities of virility-assertion, little less direct. Sashes tied low on the hips with bows and ends carried to the front were popular in Italy, and the low-slung belt whereon the dependent sheath and dagger were dangled between the legs was a popular mode all over Europe. The survival of the sporran in Scottish dress is an excellent example of the virility-boast masquerading as something else. As a purse there is no logical reason why the sporran should not be worn on the left-hand side to avoid interference with the sword arm. But there is an excellent human reason why it should be worn where it is.

Though the cod-piece proper has long quitted the dress of European men, curious survivals still haunt some corners of Europe, such as the elaborate frontal embroideries which embellish the skintight trousers of certain Central European regiments, especially those of the old Austro-Hungarian Empire and the shorts worn in the Tyrol, with their ancient squared front-flap fastenings.

More primitive peoples are less circumspect in the matter of the cod-piece, and we find to-day that the tribesmen of the Kejana region, in Brazil, on gala occasions and days of ceremony wear true cod-pieces in the form of penis-wrappers made of palm-leaf fibre, on which are painted the decorative patterns sacred to each man's particular tribe, like an old school tie.

Since men in the Christian world first defied their religious leaders by shortening their garments manly legs have been a favourite subject for sartorial display, and in the Middle Ages the whole attention was focused on the handsomely long, elegant legs by such means as particoloured hose, extending the apparent length of leg upward even beyond the waist and down to the drawn-out toes. Such hose was cleverly sewn together from bias-cut woollen stuff, and at first each leg had to be put on and fastened separately, with laced points. That there were mishaps and revelations is testified by many witnesses of the time, but such was the worship of long legs that tights were in general use and worn even by old men who could have worn long gowns more suited to their years, but instead frequently dressed in the same sort of hose as their pages.

The square-built Renaissance male shape retained its slender legs, balancing the danger of a spindle-shank appearance by duck-billed shoes, and the male leg, of which the thigh was concealed to some extent during the sixteenth and seventeenth centuries, concentrated for its appeal on the beauty of the calf, which could be faked. It was the pantaloons which came into fashion towards the end of the eighteenth century which gave men the chance once more, a chance they seized with understandable eagerness, to display the whole length of the leg.

Dress manuals suggest that they were worn so tight that there was constant danger of the material tearing. There were also other possibilities of embarrassment.

> Our young men of *soi-disant bon ton* apparently think that nothing shows them off to greater advantage than exposing to the view of honest women that part of themselves which we have more than once observed causes them to blush.

The pantaloons were worn in extremely pale colours—if not actually white, then delicate grey or faintly heliotrope or palest mushroom, to look like the flesh itself, and there was a belief that the dandies were thus enabled to look like the heroic and beautiful youths of ancient Greece. Not merely were the well-defined legs now on view — and the cutaway coat displayed them and the torso almost up to the armpits—but the pouter-pigeon breast above, puffed out by frilled shirt and padded cravat, intensified by contrast the long, slender line below.

Slimness was worshipped. But not thinness. The desired silhouette included a very broad chest, very narrow waist, very long, straight legs with suddenly swelling calves, and very small, narrow feet. Muscles had to appear only where required, and many gentlemen found it easiest to buy them ready-made from an outfitters. "Heavy padding under arms, down side, tapering off at the waist" was urged by the manuals "to avoid a very imbecile appearance," and to set off the glory of the long legs in their skintight sheath. Pantaloons could be, and usually were, made too tight for comfort and too tight even to sit down, let alone bend, in, but they could not be too tight for fashion. A dandy writing about his new pantaloons to his tailor early in the nineteenth century warns "and if I can

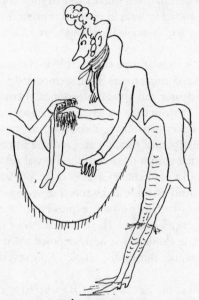

FAUX-MOLLETS
PARIS, 1840
White-thread false calves padded with hanks of wool.
By courtesy of Professor François Boucher

A NEW YEAR'S GIFT OF FALSE CALVES
French caricature, 1799.

get into them I won't have them." One difficulty with such tight garments was the problem of keeping them moored at the ankles. Steel chains sewn into the bottom hems of the pantaloons proved insufficient, and so straps were used instead, the pantaloons being buckled on to the feet by a thong passing under the instep.

The manual suggests the exercise of the utmost care in choosing the most suitable form of "trowsers." Hopelessly thin or otherwise unsatisfactory legs could be concealed in very wide trousers if it was found impossible to fake them sufficiently by padding. This is how Lord Byron usually hid his crippled leg.

Cossack-trowsers are more indispensably requisite when the legs are crooked or ill-formed. Regarding pantaloons in full dress, though certainly the most proper and becoming in every point of view, yet I would by no means advise any of my readers to assume these without having at least tolerably good legs. Unless indeed they choose to have recourse to art to supply the defects of a crooked or thin leg; in which case a slight degree of stuffing is absolutely requisite.

There were various types of false calves on sale. Particularly popular were special inner stockings to which false calves were attached in the form of wads of yarn sewn on by neat darning stitches so that they could not slip down, though care was required in wear in order to prevent them working round to the front of the leg. *Faux-mollets* they were called in Paris.

It is interesting that plus-fours, which became fashionable in the nine-teen-twenties when the boy-girl was coming to the front, seemed designed to dodge the issue of whether the wearer had good calves or not. Perhaps it was intentional, a snook cocked at woman, who seemed to be usurping all his privileges. To-day none can guess what shape a man's legs are inside his elephant-leg trousers. He himself hardly knows any more, and only the Teddy-boys seem to care. What pathos there is in the avowal of Mr H. T. Price, who declares, writing in 1936 about trousers in his book on dress, "The crease has given us a thrill of pride and a touch of swagger."

The authentic Arab male dress is the long gown, expressive of male dignity and appropriate wear for camel-riding. The introduction of the *shalwar* (trousers) by the horse-riding Persians was hotly opposed by Arab religious leaders, the controversy raging during the whole of the seventh and eighth centuries.

The *shalwar* fits the calves, and in contemporary wear is gathered at the waist to form a very loose pouch front and back. The amount of material lavished on this pouch increases with the owner's wealth.

The most virile—indeed, the only virile—dress left in Europe to-day is undoubtedly that of the Spanish bull-fighter. Daring and effrontery are implicit in its every detail, and such is its authority that even a small matador who has already put on weight is given pride by it. The padded and heavily epauletted short wide jacket gives manly breadth to the chest and manly width to the shoulders, and at the same time, by contrast, slims the tightly belted waist. Skintight satin breeches and tightly drawn silk stockings reveal every movement and muscle of abdomen, buttocks, and legs, which themselves are further slimmed and thrown into import-ance by the line of glittering embroidery sewn down the sides of the breeches. The dark hat, curled under at each side like the volutes of an Ionic column, is fastened over a *chignon* (for Samson must not be deprived of his force), and the simple austerity of plain shirt and simple tie contrast splendidly with the brilliant colour and rich material of the whole dress.

The capes, for the parade and the baiting, are the high point of colour and simplicity of line. The classical toreador stance, with arms raised, head up, and chin down, and the whole body proudly arched backward to present every vital organ to the bull's horns, expresses in the uttermost degree a swaggering male contempt for danger.

CHAPTER NINE

ADAM'S RIB

*We keep mistresses for our pleasures, concubines for constant attendance,
and wives to bear us legitimate children and to be our faithful housekeepers.*
Ascribed to DEMOSTHENES

To understand what has happened to Western men we must also find
out what has been happening to Western women, for woman, whose
deepest instinct is to continue the human species, must always seek to
please man by reflecting in herself as in a mirror that aspect of woman her
instinct tells her man desires to see—whether it be slave, business partner,
boy-girl, courtesan, immature girl or plain housekeeper, mother or lion-
tamer, all of which have at one time or another been what he has wanted.
It has happened, and it may be happening to-day, that man may feel himself so oppressed by the responsibilities of being a man that he wants a wife
who will, in fact, be a husband, while he takes on the rôle of wife himself.

BANTEAU SREI FRONTON: SUNDRA AND UPSANUDA FIGHTING
OVER A LADY
Khmer. A.D. 1050.
Musée Guimet, Paris

Until recently, and in not a few countries to-day, too, a wife was something that happened to a man, like birth or death. Just who she would be was entirely a family matter dependent upon estates, size of dowry, intricate family relationships, and delicate balances and adjustments of property. The natural inclinations of the man and woman concerned did not count, both bridegroom and bride being expected to obey their parents' choice of partner.

If he was in luck a man might find his chosen wife to his taste, and might even fall in love with her. At all events he would grow used to her and, after many years of marriage and numerous children, even fond of her, for habit is a powerful force, and serenity often the supreme compensation for lack of choice. Love, in its current romantic sense, simply did not enter the business of giving and being given in marriage.

Right from the Middle Ages in noble circles, which were quite specific on this point, love and marriage were, indeed, regarded as utterly incompatible. The mistress, or lady to whom the lover paid his court and wrote his odes, was expected to be the wife of another, never his own betrothed, never in any circumstances his own wife. Such was the familiar amorous pattern in English noble society for many centuries. In looser eras extramarital mating was permitted, in stricter eras only romantic sighs, stiff upper lips, and dramatic farewells, after which the broken-hearted lover was expected to take himself off to the Crusades or to extend the Empire or to shoot big game and try to forget. But the lady in question could never be his wife, for it was no fun to have no barriers. Lord Byron truly observed:

> Think you, if Laura had been Petrarch's wife,
> He would have written sonnets all his life?

It was therefore only in the very poorest strata of society, where there was neither money nor property for dowries, that young people had much of a chance of marrying whom they fancied. And even there, if folk-songs are to be trusted, the possession of a pig or a few chickens made the plainest village wench much more desirable than the village beauty, if she had no such wealth, in the eyes of peasant parents seeking a wife for their son. Father Benedict Kiely, in confirmation of the matrimonial lure of property, has recorded that "Daughters of strong Irish farmers going in former years to country dances used to rub cow-dung on their aprons to show that their fathers owned cattle."

The conception of sex as a matrimonial duty was already an advance on the extreme early Christian attitude, which looked upon sex entirely in the light of a sin, and upon woman, unless vowed to virginity, as the

Devil's chief ambassador. Thus St Jerome approved of the lady Blesilla, who became a nun at the age of twenty, after having been married and widowed, because "she was more sorry for the loss of her virginity than for the decease of her husband," and in expiation of the loss of her virginity (though decently and in lawful wedlock), inflicted on herself such atrocious penances that her early death was considerably hastened thereby.

It is understandable that the wild excesses of luxury-sodden Rome so disgusted the early Christians that the life of a hermit, with the debarrassment of possessions and social duties thus offered, proved more congenial to them, and, since they believed the Day of Judgment was at hand anyway, there was no real point in performing the essential act to increase the population. Nevertheless the association of sex with sin (something the Greeks happily never knew) has poisoned relations between Christian men and women for two thousand years, especially in puritanical countries, and given an extra problem to the always delicate adjustment between the sexes.

Puritans and reformers in all ages always try to close the brothels, only to find themselves up against a horde of economic problems and vested interests. In the Middle Ages London, like other big European cities, made its brothels pay. In 1383, for instance, London Bridge was crowded with municipal stews which belonged to the Lord Mayor, Sir William Walworth, who farmed them out profitably on behalf of the London Corporation. During the Commonwealth prostitution was very severely dealt with. Pillory and branding for a first offence, besides whipping and three months in gaol. A second offence carried the death sentence. All brothels were closed down. These measures, however, do not seem to have solved the problem completely, for from time to time shiploads of prostitutes were transported to the New World.

Sin or no, it needs leisure to develop sex into either a romantic or a carnal pastime, and of all amateurs of this hobby it was Louis XIV of France, perhaps, who did most to turn it into an art. His motives were not unmixed, for he was anxious to keep the reins of power and government in his own hands, and therefore he encouraged his courtiers to turn their attention to the bedroom instead of the council chamber. This mighty monarch exacted from his nobility an endless amount of petty attendance at Court, where they had nothing to do but hang about, quarrel about precedence, try to catch his royal eye with a view to the soliciting of some trifling advantage, bicker, gamble, and, most of all, fall interminably in and out of love with each other's mistresses and wives.

Hunting and love, chasing the deer and chasing the ladies, were the Court specific for getting through every twenty-four hours. The conversation centred on the endless discussion and evaluation of every male and female attribute of every one at Court, as at a livestock sale, to the total exclusion of matters outside the Court. This suited the King very well. It kept the nobles from interfering with politics, and effectively prevented them from combining against him.

Prestige depended upon the lifting of the King's eyebrow, and the most intelligent and brilliant courtiers played the game according to the King's rules. That the proudest nobles of France, in the greatest period of France's glory, should have disputed bitterly among themselves, for instance, for the privilege of attendance at the King's post-luncheon session on his *chaise percée* (a grandiose *nécessaire* of Japanese aventurine ornamented with Chinese landscapes and gilt birds, precious stones, and mosaics in mother-of-pearl), and been eager to pay handsomely for the honour of such attendance, is difficult for us to understand to-day. But it was statesmanship of a high order on the part of the King, in that it kept the nobility divided and ineffective, and at a time when England was in revolution and about to cut her own king's head off.

Tall and well built as he was, Louis XIV, aggrandized by large wig and huge plumed hat, swathed sashes, capacious petticoat breeches, yards of richly flounced lace at throat, wrists, and boot-tops, looked larger than life, as he intended.

The prize of attaining Royal favour was so esteemed that noble ladies were prepared to go to any lengths to attain it, even, as in the case of Mme de Montespan, witchcraft and pacts with the Devil. And the Court

"VIRTUE" (IN ARMOUR)
English mural painting, 1270.
St Stephen's, House of Commons

"VICE"
After Hieronymus Bosch.

put its heart and soul into the pursuit of illicit love. "Married love is the one thing that will not be tolerated here," an old priest warned a noble young lady, newly arrived at Court with her husband, to whom she was, unfortunately, devoted. Married love was accounted utterly vulgar and in extremely bad taste.

Nor was marriage any more popular at the Court of Charles II in England, for he had served a brief apprenticeship at Versailles, and did not delay on his return to England and the throne to put these ideas into practice. The dress, so *négligé* as to suggest undress, the furniture, of which the *péché mortel* is a notable example, all the arts of the time served but to one end, and poor Dryden was hard put to it to write the scabrous comedies the Court preferred to his serious poems. He soon learned that he must denigrate married love if he were to hope for success in the Restoration theatre.

"A married man is the creature of the world most out of fashion," declares Doralice, in his *Marriage à la Mode*, written in 1673.

> His behaviour is dumpish, his discourse his wife and family, his habit so much neglected it looks as if that were married too. His hat is married. His peruke is married. His breeches are married and if we could look within his breeches, we should find him married there too.

The memoirs of the Comte de Gramont, one of the notable foreign figures at the Court of Charles II, give us a vivid picture of Restoration Society. The lines of Restoration Court dress are so loose and slippery that the ladies looked as though their dresses were falling off, and the courtiers looked as though they had not yet dressed at all. "Everywhere one looked," he remarked of the English Court, "there were beauties. Hamilton and Stewart were the handsomest." The disastrous Queen clearly added no lustre, and her Spanish *entourage* he dismissed briefly as "*monstres*." Beauty was essential and sufficient, stupidity an added attraction. He declares approvingly that Stewart was so silly that no one could possibly have had less intelligence, that she spent all her time giggling and building card castles and persuading all the Court to do likewise. He describes in admiring detail how she made a bet with the Russian Ambassador that she had a prettier leg than his own countrywomen, and how, applauded by the King, who had taken on her bet, she exposed her leg to the thigh and won the wager.

But chasing even married noblewomen was apt to pall unless some obstacles could be introduced to add a little interest and excitement. The best sport of all was to trick a jealous lover, and Gramont's memoirs are so filled with such amorous double-crossing, boasting, bribery, and plain poltroonery that they read more like the log of a badly run brothel than an English Court.

Here you are [expostulated his friend Saint-Évrémond] in the most agreeable circumstances that a man of your kind can hope for. You have for your enjoyment all the pleasures of a Court which is young, lively and gallant. The King never leaves you out of any party of pleasure. ... Don't go and spoil it all with your old sinful practices. Leave the pursuit of love alone and seek other pleasures. You know that the moment a woman pleases you your first thought is to discover whether she is loved by another and your second thought is to make him jealous. A mistress with no admirers would have no attraction for you. You only enjoy stealing other men's mistresses and making mischief ... it pleases you to be discovered in the bedroom of another man's mistress, as you were with your friend the Duke of Buckingham.

The Comte de Gramont, heedless of his friend's prudent counsel, continued to pursue the most popular Court beauties with costly little presents of perfumed gloves, pocket-mirrors, and packets of apricot marzipan brought to him every week from Paris by his special courier, a valet named Ternes. Gramont had but a poor opinion of English tailoring, and all his own clothes were made for him in Paris, where Ternes was regularly sent to command and supervise the orders and return with the finished suits, for Gramont himself dared not be seen in France, whence he had been exiled on account of misbehaviour.

Ternes spent all his time continually crossing over to France for *bonbons* and finery for his master, returning with them to London and crossing over again for more. On one occasion, when the Queen proposed to give a masquerade, Gramont vowed to the King that he would eclipse all the other guests by the brilliance of his attire. On this occasion, however, Ternes, after working twelve *couturiers* and twelve embroiderers in relays day and night for weeks to get his master's dress ready in time, was caught in a quicksand near the French coast on his return journey, and the precious parcel was lost. Gramont was obliged to appear at the masquerade in ordinary dress, where, making the best of a bad job, he hugely entertained the Court by recounting the sound beating he had given Ternes for his misfortune. It was, it appears, not a difficult Court to amuse, nor was the standard of wit on a level with that of the King or Eleanor Gwyn.

After a lifetime of such unfaltering devotion to gambling and amorous entanglements Gramont in his old age was described by Saint Simon as having "the countenance of a withered old monkey."

Naturally, women were also pursued in less aristocratic circles, and to balance this picture of English Court life during the Restoration we need only a glimpse of another kind of amorous approach during the same period. Here is an entry from the *Journal* of George Fox, founder of the Quaker movement. It relates how, on a preaching tour in 1669, he proposed to his future wife, Margaret Fell, widow of the judge.

> After this meeting in Gloucester was over, we travelled till we came to Bristol where I met with Margaret Fell, who was come to visit her daughter Yeomans. I had seen from the Lord a considerable time before that I should take Margaret Fell to my wife. And when I first mentioned it to her, she felt the answer of Life from God thereunto.

The emotional life of fashionable gentlemen of the upper circles of English society in the eighteenth century was lived on two levels, according to such witnesses as James Boswell and Hogarth—fine words and graces in the smart *salons* and brutal reality in the stews. The game of love had its own code of honour within the aristocratic circles themselves, where it was considered perfectly all right to play with fire, providing the dignity of rank was respected.

Thus bastards were of no account, and everybody had them, like measles, provided they were begot on the lower orders. If a gentleman of rank, however, hopelessly compromised a lady of his own social status he was expected to marry her. If she happened to be already married, which was usually the case, then a duel or a divorce (more difficult to arrange) was expected—was, indeed, essential. If the lady were of lesser rank she could be discarded without any serious trouble, though she might, like Harriette Wilson, try to make good her loss by publishing or threatening to publish her memoirs.

Maidservants in all the great houses were, by all accounts, easy and often not unwilling of access. Some lords even became fond of their bastards, and it was not unusual for them to fling a purse of money for maintenance to pregnant parlourmaids, if there happened to be a purse to fling. But it was also a period of heavy gambling, and most of the great houses were more likely to have duns in the drawing-room than money in the bank.

Sometimes the social vetoes cutting into honest affection caused real anguish, as with Charles James Fox, who deeply loved and respected his mistress, who was an actress and therefore socially unacceptable. He never could bring his friends to meet her socially without putting both to acute shame and loss of face, and so never did, till the very end of his life, when at last he brought himself to marry her. Conversely, Lord Byron, in his frantic and brutal struggles to break off his liaison with Lady Caroline Lamb, whom at first he had been flattered to win and who was, in her

neurotic fashion, determined to keep him or break him, was haunted by
fear lest he should have to marry her. This, indeed, he would have had to
do if, as she tried, she had succeeded in leaving her husband and publicly
throwing herself on his honour, thus obliging him to demand that her
husband divorce her. It was to a considerable degree his anxiety to
escape from this situation which thrust him into his disastrous marriage
with her prudish bluestocking cousin Annabella Milbanke.

SOLOMON AND SHEBA
Picture-story (detail) in earth colour on coarse canvas. Ethiopian.
Contemporary.
Author's collection

The game of love is, of all lotteries, the one with the most tempting
prizes and bleakest hangovers. Not only attractive young women but
also comely young men have risen, through the right bedrooms, to dizzy
heights of social eminence, and, granted intelligence and opportunity,
made a great career, like young John Churchill.

The French Court in particular offered glittering rewards for a beautiful
girl who could learn when to say yes and when to say no. Sometimes no
more than that. It is true that Mme de Pompadour had brains as well as

beauty, but Du Barry, on the other hand, was an insignificant and signally stupid little milliner's apprentice who, before her elevation, had been thankful to earn eighteen francs a night by prostitution. As mistress of Louis XV of France her pin-money amounted to 300,000 francs a month (apart from lavish if irregular royal gifts), this allowance being paid to her punctually wherever she happened to be staying, by special delivery in a cart kept for this purpose, in silver six-franc pieces.

All these details were pitilessly laid bare at her trial when the French Revolution caught her in its whirlpool, in the evidence of her little Negro page, Zamore. It was recorded how she sobbed all the way to the scaffold, screaming from the tumbril, "Life! Life! If my life is spared me I will give the people all I possess!" To which the contemptuous reply was, "You are only offering the people what belongs to it."

As the gorgeous velvet coats, the richly embroidered satin waistcoats, the scarlet heels, the wigs caked with perfumed blue powder, and gallooned tricornes of the eighteenth century dwindled into George Brummell's severe uniform of the nineteenth century a new attitude towards love began to show itself. The unsavoury and insolvent Regency Court was presently replaced by the sentimental and solvent respectability of Queen Victoria and her painstaking Consort. England became, faithfully following the example of the Throne, which itself exactly reflected the social climate, first respectable and then prudish. As befitted the mother of a nation of shopkeepers, she began locking everything up, especially wives and daughters. Outside an Oriental seraglio it is doubtful if women in any country led a more blinkered and confined life than respectable women in the middle of the nineteenth century in England. Even when they went outside their homes, which they never could do unescorted by maid, mother, or chaperon, their very bonnets were designed to prevent them seeing anything on either side of them. Lady Teazle's complaint about the tedium of her country home, where she had nothing to do but a little needlework and music, might well have been echoed throughout most of the nineteenth century by young ladies all over England, who did not dare complain, however, filial duty and obedience forbidding. There was no alternative. Marriage was their one hope, save for that daughter marked down for long spinsterhood in order to look after her mother. The fate of respectable young ladies without money and without male relations with the obligation to maintain them was terrible indeed. They had to become governesses. Charlotte Brontë has well portrayed their tragic lot, for learning was accounted positively detrimental to ladies, and to be poor invited contempt. That Jane Eyre, a mere governess, should actually have married her employer in the story was regarded as so scandalous that mothers locked the book away from their daughters, though the heroine comes from a respectable family, resists all threats to her virtue, and even achieves money of her own by rightful inheritance.

In such a climate of real inhibition and false refinement the game of love faltered in England. There were no longer ladies who were accessible and other ladies who were less accessible. Now there were good women and bad women, and even bad women had to be set up in a house, provided with maids and a carriage and all the stuffy appurtenances of domesticity, like another wife. Making money and churchgoing were the major preoccupations of the typical middle-class Englishman of the nineteenth century. He regarded the carnal appetites as sinful. There is something pathetic in the way his mistress took on the refinements and conventionalities of his wife. This was protective colouring, for she was not supposed to be there at all—just as his bastards, pushed into cheap boarding-schools in the outer suburbs, were not supposed to be there at all. Perhaps the greatest art of the nineteenth century was the art of hypocrisy, for commerce, which was making England rich and heavy-handed, set its mark on the bedroom no less than the drawing-room.

A fog of weighty respectability pervaded England, a fog produced by her profitably belching factory chimneys. Mediocrity was esteemed. Dullness was no longer a social disaster. On the contrary, vivacity and wit in a woman were regarded as not quite good form in the plush drawing-rooms, where wives and daughters were as upholstered as the furniture. Young ladies kept their gloves on, kept their eyes down, kept their ankles hidden, and relied on their parents for moral directives, sustenance, and choice of husband.

Byronic heroes, "wild, melancholy and elevating," in Charlotte Brontë's words, were all very well bound between the gilt-edged pages of delicate little books of romantic verse, but they were not at all the kind of men English mammas permitted their daughters to meet, or, as might have happened a generation or two earlier, ran away with themselves. The game of love was no longer a game. Marriage, overshadowed by the all-important counting-house and dedicated to the raising on severe principles of a large brood of offspring, was a serious matter indeed. The obedient, artless maiden was expected to transfer her dependency, oh marriage, from her papa to her husband, who had to take over the task of making up her mind, taking all responsibility from her shoulders, and making himself her life's master as papa had been before. Humility and obedience were her duties to her husband as they had been to her father.

At least such was the theory, bolstered up in every possible way by Church and State, in fiction, art, the courts of law, and by the iron tyranny of social custom. The practice, we may well believe, was something rather different.

The very fact that intelligent and forceful women (and how many of them the Victorian age produced) were obliged to use their wits underhandedly made the Victorian home a web of intrigue and double-crossing. Flattered and cosseted into believing it was his own way he was getting, the head of the family and master of the house, so outwardly imposing in his heavy and numerous garments, was no doubt often led when he believed himself to be driving.

The nuptial bedroom, with its dark wallpaper and merciless, brass-knobbed double bed, its cold, marble-topped washstand and gloomy pier-glass, could hold humiliating secrets, not only to do with false female ringlets, but also false male calves, padded male shoulders, male corsets, and "raisers." Divested of his many heavy layers of outer clothing, perhaps the awesome head of the house did not present so overwhelming a figure in his nightgown and nightcap, though he was still able to conceal most of his facial weaknesses behind his heavy beard and moustaches.

One curious feature of Victorian fashion-plates of male dress is the extraordinarily doll-like, even girlish, appearance of the idealized men engraved thereon, in their pompous frock-coats and tall hats. The smooth, weak faces look as though their beards could not possibly have grown there, and the small soft hands and tiny feet suggest the exact opposite of overbearing masculinity. Clearly the men were as anxious as the women to look genteel.

The reason is, of course, that the self-made man, no less than his wife, was above all desirous of climbing socially. His goal was to haul himself up into the ranks of the gentry. Gradgrind wanted to become Lord Gradgrind. To achieve this, he well knew, it was useless being a little tradesman. He would have to make a great deal of money, enough money to qualify for admission into good society as a "prince of commerce."

Thus the double standards. Gradgrind wanted to look like a gentleman, though by ethical standards he did not behave like one. He overworked and underpaid his factory hands at the same time as he was subscribing handsome donations to the sort of charity which might do him good socially, and his wife, who was no less eager to become Lady Gradgrind, half starved her own servants and kept the pantry door tightly locked at the same time as she was presiding over the "Poor Soup Distribution," where she might mingle with pukka Society ladies who engaged in such largesse.

Industrialization had increased the numbers of the poor, and they were a greater problem than ever. Sunday schools, soup-kitchens, the bestowal of a flannel blanket at Christmas on carefully chosen aged, needy, and properly grateful recipients—such were the legitimate social activities of middle-class married women. Even here they were careful not to let their hearts carry them away. New blankets might be pawned and the money spent on gin. Some ladies' books of domestic economy advised patching beforehand, so as to render the blanket less pledgeable.

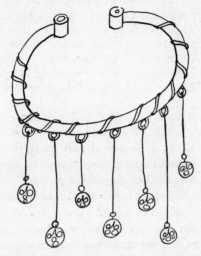

HEBREW SILVER BRIDAL TORQUE ENGRAVED
IN HEBREW WITH PRECEPTS CONCERNING
MARRIED LIFE
Jerusalem.
Smithsonian Museum, Washington

The Misses Gradgrind were less active in charitable enterprises than their mother. They were kept at home in the closest confinement, to retain their innocence and malleability, and were dedicated to the one objective of an early marriage.

"To be the sweet refuge of a husband fatigued by the jarring world, to be his enlightened companion and the chosen friend of his heart. These, these are a woman's duties," says the same book of domestic economy, suggesting that the best method of becoming an enlightened companion was to acquire "ductility of mind and a great readiness at figures." Girls were married in their teens, and often mothers of a brood of children before they were thirty, and grandmothers at forty. One wedding-dress in Dr Cunnington's famous collection is made of grey silk because the Victorian bride who wore it was an elderly lady of twenty-six, for whom white was felt to be hardly suitable.

The historian William Lecky (in his *History of European Morals*) suggested in 1869 that, though early marriage suited the middle-class young lady perfectly, it was unfortunately quite otherwise for young gentlemen, and even went so far as to advocate proper recognition of bastards in order to stabilize English society:

> It is extremely important both for the happiness and for the moral well-being of men that life-long unions should not be effected under the imperious prompting of a blind appetite. There are always multitudes who, in the period of their lives when their passions are most strong, are incapable of supporting children in their own social rank, and who would therefore injure society by marrying in it, but are nevertheless perfectly capable of securing an honourable career for their illegitimate children in the lower social sphere to which these would naturally belong.

This, Lecky argues, would be of great value to their future wives, who would be chosen (all unruly passion already spent) from their own social sphere. "Under the conditions I have mentioned these connexions are not injurious, but beneficial to the weaker partner."

The Right Hon. William Lecky, who refers to women as "the sex" and to sex as "the vice," ends his great *œuvre* worried about the position of women altogether. For such ladies as were unmarried he regretted the absence of convents, and for unmarried women who were not ladies he feared "the most extreme and agonizing poverty," leading all too frequently "to the paths of vice," because machinery was replacing women in the sewing trades. "The distaff," he warns,

> has fallen from the hand. The needle is being rapidly superseded and the work which, from the days of Homer to the present century, was accomplished in the centre of the family, has been transferred to the crowded manufactory.

He fears this may cause a convulsion in prevailing moral notions. Certainly the gentility and refinement so carefully cultivated by the wives and daughters of the English middle class during the middle part of the nineteenth century was a positive disadvantage to them when, as sometimes happened, they were obliged to earn their own bread, papa having died poorer than was expected, or having gone bankrupt while still alive. Many Victorian novels centre on this particular predicament. Something has gone awry in the city or the counting-house, and mamma, on her invalid sofa, wrings her impotent hands while her bewildered and horror-struck daughters burst into tears, faint, and share round the smelling-salts. The usual solution is for mamma to die, as in *The Wide, Wide World*, and for the daughters to brave the ignominy of the world as

governesses or companions, as in *Vanity Fair* and *Bleak House*—since
without dowries their chances of marriage had dwindled to nil. The
saddest lot of all, perhaps, was that of the vestal daughter dedicated to the
care of one or both ageing parents, and always left alone, high and dry
in an enormous entailed and unmanageable house, when death finally
claimed the object of her sacrifice.

That it was humiliating and socially degrading for ladies to earn their
living was a belief that persisted blindly, despite the real necessity for
giving them an education to allow them to do so honourably. Even to-day
The Times agony column is filled with appeals for a home from "ladies"
who have no qualification whatever to offer except "refinement."
The best they can hope for is to become unpaid companions to other
elderly ladies in less harrowing circumstances, where, in return for the
privilege of eating in the dining-room, they often have to put up with
endless petty oppression.

Gentility and refinement were regarded as so essential that it was these
very families who, with many daughters to provide for and a rising cost
of living to contend with, set their faces most stubbornly against higher
education for women when at last it was introduced. For they felt that
such education might make their daughters definitely unmarriageable and
nail them to the shelf, whereas if they remained at home in ignorance and
refurbished last year's frocks, perhaps Mr Right, or at least Mr Somebody,
might come along and carry one off.

So the quantities of daughters stayed at home, mooned about, read
romances from the circulating library, and fell in love with the curate,
for he was almost the only man they ever met. They sank into declines,
became unpaid maids-of-all-work (except for the actual scrubbing), at
the beck and call of married sisters, and produced an enormous amount of
excruciatingly tasteless handwork, such as plush umbrella-stand covers
painted with ivy and moss roses, for none of these needless domestic
occupations was unsexing or socially degrading, as was an education.

The effort to burst through this middle-class bondage tempered to steel
the will and moral strength of such women as did so, as we may see
by the life-stories of such Victorian women as Florence Nightingale, and
it is impossible not to feel that among the numerous Victorian lady
novelists, both the published and the unpublished, were not a few energetic
intelligent spirits which might have contributed much of a different and
better nature to English life had there been any way available for them to
do so.

Undoubtedly the Church absorbed much of this unused feminine
energy and zeal. It was possible and respectable for ladies to become

missionaries, and thus to extend their narrow confines by travelling. Appetites for Oriental glamour, nourished on Lord Byron and whetted by Burton, could be sated by donning a topee and sailing off to China or India to be a lady missionary, one of the very few professions a single lady might undertake without loss of face.

Lord Byron's popularity had by no means ebbed as portrayer of the glamorous Orient when a fresh wave of enthusiasm was provoked in the eighteen-seventies by the publication of Sir Richard Burton's translation

ORIENTAL ROMANTICISM

Djibbah (worn for sports) at Coombe Hill Girls' School, 1905. No fastenings. "The girls are very proud of it."

ISRAELI GIRL FARM-HAND IN NEGEV

Shirt and shorts have become uniform wear for both sexes. The *keffiyeh* serves as a sweat rag. The heavy boots are suitable for farm-work and a protection against snake-bite. Beersheba. Contemporary.

of the *Thousand Nights and a Night*. It was an immediate and overwhelming success, to the somewhat cynical surprise of Sir Richard. "I have struggled for forty-seven years," he commented,

distinguished myself honourably in every way that I could. I never had a compliment nor a thank you nor a single farthing. I translate a doubtful book in my old age and immediately make 16,000 guineas. Now that I know the tastes of England we need never be without money.

Lady Burton, on the continuing royalties from this one work, was able to afford a splendid Arab tent done in white marble to his memory in Mortlake churchyard.

The truth of the matter was that the Industrial Revolution, the dirty factories, the respectable, pinch-penny outlook and way of life had made England intolerably dull to live in, and the glamorous East, between the pages of a handsomely bound book, was a welcome opportunity for escapism. Burton had found, as so many others were to find, that the prudish English are only embarrassed by reference to sex when they have not the excuse that it is a translation from the classics.

There was in nineteenth-century England a delightedly scandalized interest in harem *mœurs* (which in truth are considerably duller than life in an English rectory), which has ever since afforded a lucrative English market for paintings, songs, romances, and musical plays; and such ladies as could possibly contrive to move themselves out East rushed to do so— as missionaries, officers' wives, governesses to Asiatic princelings, and so on.

In 1880 a sumptuously gilded and splendidly engraved travel book very much in the fashionable mode was published in Paris, the author being a middle-aged French lady named Mme de Falvy-Bourdon, who recounted her impressions of a journey to Samarkand and back which she had undertaken with her commercial-attaché husband. Complacent and unshakeable in her French travelling dolman and elegant toque trimmed with ducks' wings, she proved an indiscriminate and indefatigable note-taker, her chiefest comment being disapproval at the lack of gallantry towards women she had discovered in the older civilizations.

Scarcely was Paris left behind her than she found it necessary to state her firm conviction that, whatever lay before her, the rôle of the female sex should not be a passive one. "Il ne faut pas douter, c'est à l'influence de la femme que la civilisation doit son existence." The condition of Asiatic women shocked Mme de Falvy-Bourdon no less than her appearance with her face unveiled shocked her Asiatic hosts. "The condition of women in the Orient is truly lamentable," she scribbled, balancing on the back of a camel in the Kirghiz desert, "condemned by polygamy to be nothing but an instrument of pleasure for the men, by whom she is often valued even less than a horse." Their acceptance of this sad lot aroused her particular ire. "No quarrels or arguments," she commented acidly.

Mme de Falvy-Bourdon, nurtured on Byron, had hoped to find gilded splendour in the Orient. Instead she found filth and destitution. She had hoped to find women of surpassing beauty and unimpaired wit adorned with a studied splendour that might even offer a hint or two to ladies dressed by Paris *couturiers*. Instead she found emaciated lepers, and fat women in paralysing purdah, dull, dirty, and inexpressibly boring.

The common people she encountered were far too poor to sport fine clothes, and she noted that the Bashkir peasants, no longer able to afford their traditional jerkin decoration of gold coins (from the reign of Catherine the Great), were despondently making do by embroidering the jerkins with old trouser buttons instead.

Indeed, the golden opulence of the Orient, artfully suggested by the rich gilt edges of her handsome book, was so painfully lacking that English lady readers were sadly disappointed, the truth about Asia being the last thing they wished to learn. What they had hoped for, as Burton had profitably discovered, was another *Arabian Nights*. There was plenty of destitution in England without going all the way to Samarkand to find it.

Lady readers, nevertheless, for private emotional reasons, were certainly interested in the rôle of Asiatic women. Serving as mere "instruments of pleasure" (providing the Eastern potentate were wealthy enough) may not have appeared such a terrible fate to English spinsters doomed to celibacy as it did to Mme de Falvy-Bourdon, and even married English ladies immersed in thankless, endless chores and petty domestic economies were not disinclined to daydream of harems which were provided with hordes of obedient slaves, priceless jewels, and unlimited supplies of Turkish delight, and where, moreover, coal fires were unnecessary.

The fantasy East has played and still plays a most important part in the imaginations of Western men and women, and the more depressing and disturbing the reality the more richly glows the fantasy. Englishmen and American men, no less than their wives and daughters, packed the theatres playing *Kismet* throughout a run of more than two years, just as their parents packed the theatre to see *Chu Chin Chow* and the early cinema to see *The Sheikh*. This is the Orient as they would like it to be, not a sun-devoured desert likely to spout oil and cause still more political tension, or, worse still, refuse to spout oil because of political trouble. The desire for colour and glamour and fantasy is a deeply felt human yearning for which there is no intrinsic provision in our machine-dominated culture. The width of the gap between the real Asia and the fantasy Asia may be judged by the fact that when the American film *The Thief of Baghdad* was shown, just after the 1939 War, to a native audience in Baghdad they received it rapturously as a documentary of contemporary American urban life, not one of the audience having the slightest inkling that it was intended to depict their own fairy-tale in their native city.

The Eastern fantasy has offered an invaluable outlet to the pent-up emotions of generations of frustrated English middle-class women, and the impact of Miss Amy Woodforde-Finden has yet to be assessed. It has certainly been enormous. What young, and not-so-young, English female in the nineteen-twenties did not spend countless afternoons sitting on a piano stool practising *Pale hands I loved beside the Shalimar*, without having the least idea or concern as to where or what the Shalimar was. Even more popular was *Temple Bells*, with its ecstatic nuptial assurance. The combination of lack of men, lack of opportunity of meeting such men as there were, increasing impoverishment, lack of useful education, and stubborn gentility had created so hopeless an emotional impasse for thousands of Englishwomen that Miss Woodforde-Finden's *Indian Love Lyrics* provided no less essential an emotional release than Mr Liberace's musical titivation does to-day to a new generation.

Not for such women had Lady Mary Wortley Montagu pleaded that "The use of knowledge in our sex besides the amusement of solitude is to moderate the passions and learn to be contented with a small expense." Those women who determined to be educated had to be possessed of the zeal and discipline of martyrs, for, whereas unmarried and unendowed women were treated with amused contempt in English society in the nineteenth century, those women who sought to make themselves useful by acquiring professional status met with active hostility.

One or two dangerously progressive parents, in the teeth of the most violent opposition from all classes and both sexes, did set out to educate their daughters to university level. They had, above all, to be extremely careful to avoid any possibility of 'unsexing' them, and Newnham, whose portals at last opened in 1873, was designed by Basil Champneys in modest Dutch red brick as being "of a more domestic appeal than the Gothic and Tudor favoured by the men's colleges," since red brick suggested "a certain feminine daintiness and an atmosphere almost of Pieter de Hooch." It was a college for girls, and therefore it had to look like a kitchen.

Even more important than not becoming unsexed by education was to remain a perfect lady. Refinement and gentility were regarded as even

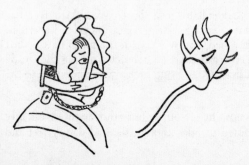

Left: BRANK IN ACTION
England, fifteenth and sixteenth
centuries.

Right: 'STOCKPORT BRANK'
Barbed gag to pierce tongue.

more important to these venturesome young ladies who wished to use their brains than to their stay-at-home sisters. Ladies first, bluestockings afterwards. Students at Newnham were encouraged to cultivate, within suitable bounds, both sports and æsthetic sensibility. Tennis was the approved sport, for on the grass courts students could decorously meet the opposite sex, with a college chaperon watchfully brooding on the sidelines.

The *Queen*, as eagerly devoured in Newnham as outside Newnham, obligingly catered for both sporting and æsthetic students at the same time by giving away (in 1881) a free pattern for "embroidering a tennis apron of peacock-coloured plush" with a grandiose design of "cobwebs and spiders' webs with dainty twigs on the pockets."

Parents and moralists alike raised few objections to tennis, which was considered a perfectly ladylike pursuit, and much less strenuous than the other popular society sport of archery. But even a small taste of freedom may lead to revolution. It was in her addiction to sport that the alarming phenomenon of the "new woman" made her appearance. The "sporting type" established herself with the advent of the bicycle. No chaperon for her, though she went for rides with young gentlemen, because what chaperon could be induced to mount a wheel herself?

Even though it was Society who launched the bicycle, it frightened the nation's moralists, among whom were the lady novelists. Society ladies knew better than to use the bicycle for transport. They would have their "wheel" brought to them by carriage to the park, where they rode round and round for an hour (as a change from equestrianship), after which they would be driven home in their carriage, a footman bringing back the wheel in a separate cab. That was all right. But to use the bicycle to go somewhere, to use it instead of a carriage, was far from all right. It was dreadfully wrong, and could be copied by common people who could never afford a carriage. As, indeed, it quickly was. The new woman thus not only unsexed herself, but also declassed herself. Marie Corelli, for one, had no mercy on such renegades. She wrote in 1897:

> The honourable Mrs Maddenham, in a short tweed skirt over her knickers appearing beneath, sitting astride of a bicycle, her thick ankles and flat feet well exposed, and working at the machine she thus bestrode with the measured regularity of a convict working the tread-mill, was certainly a girl calculated to bring such a woman as Jane to the brink of the grave.

For Jane, the heroine, was not a new woman, but a thoroughly womanly woman, who resolutely refused to bike, though she had dainty feet and unexceptionable ankles.

... all the best set bike [Mrs Maddenham declared]; a woman's legs have never had fair play till now. What are legs for I should like to know? We've had to hide them under long skirts for ages except on the stage. It's time they should see daylight.

This, naturally, was too much for Jane.

Jane shivered as though a douche of cold water had been poured down her back, then blushed as deeply as though scalding wine had been poured down her throat.

But Mrs Maddenham was on the winning side, the awkward grand-mother of the blithe and shapely young women who skim by, with their boy friends, in such gay cycle-flights every Sunday on the Great West Road. They don't blush like Jane. They wear the briefest shorts, which expose legs and thighs to the torso, and sweaters which leave nothing to be divined as to the shape of that as well. Have they lost their femininity? Not at all. They wear filmy long dresses and flowers in their hair at club dances, and would regard Jane not so much with amusement as pity, as one in need of psychiatric treatment for her blushing and inhibitions.

To contemporary young women both sport and education are no longer battles to be won, and, if the economic prospects permit, all they wish for (it seems) is to be married early and be good housewives. They are not interested in politics or causes, but only domesticity and immediate security. But they are deeply interested in being beautiful and getting a husband, neither objective offering much difficulty to-day because diet is understood, cosmetics are respectable, and at last (because modern wars kill off both sexes) the sex ratio has righted itself and there are enough boys to go round, rather more than enough in fact, which gives the girls their first such break for generations.

Standards of beauty have changed as frequently as fashions in dress, but the pursuit of beauty, or what is currently regarded as beauty, never slackens. In fact, almost the only profession that knows no hard times has been and is that of the beautifier. Cosmetics, exercises, dieting instructors, hair-fixers, masseurs, skin-embellishers, all mean lucrative trades, and both sexes and all classes seek their assistance, for men and women alike desire to be more beautiful than they are.

To-day beauty magazines prove a fantastically profitable business, with their endless pages of lucrative advertisements. Chief among the remedies sought by their readers are methods of growing hair where there is none or not sufficient, restoring faded hair to its original or some other colour, removing hair from where it is not desired, and getting rid of wrinkles and superfluous fat. All these remedies are earnestly sought by men as well as by women, and American television features special popular slimming courses for twelve- and thirteen-year-old schoolgirls, including the use of Turkish baths.

Let us take a look at a popular French magazine *Votre Beauté*. Here, in page after page of advertisement, eminent specialists guarantee to remodel the female bust to a new shape in a new manner:

> Thanks to the preparatory work of French savants who have studied the exotic extracts distilled in Guinea, which exert a powerful regenerative effect on the mammary cellules. *Confiez votre poitrine à* . . .

Equally eminent specialists warn gentlemen of a certain age against apathy in dealing with excessive fat. "Watch out for *bourrelets!*" urges the typical blurb, guaranteeing to debarrass the sufferer in a few weeks' time by the simple use of a completely new kind of apparatus. One such is called *Amaigrisseur Névade* (self-mass). The American touch, combined with the manly independence of dispensing with a professional masseur, is cunningly calculated to appeal to the tenderest susceptibilities of the contemporary Frenchman.

A popular feature of this magazine (as of all other such magazines) is the readers' inquiries, answered by staff experts, which fill several highly useful pages with excellent product-boosting answers. The most persistent inquiry (to-day as since the dawn of history) is how to hold a husband's love.

> I am still young [writes prudent but worried Michou, thirty-five years old and well preserved]. I am devoted to my husband, who is, alas! somewhat flighty. Nothing serious, but he likes to flirt. He loves to be noticed by women. *Toutes ses batteries sont dressées dans ce but.* Nevertheless I think, on the whole, he is still faithful to me.

Michou demands counsel on how to make herself so magnetic to him that he will never look at any other woman.

> You don't offer enough practical little hints [she writes reproachfully]. You never give recipes for infusions, simple decoctions, face-masks made with the white or the yoke of an egg, vinegar poultices, and such inexpensive little treatments. On the contrary, all the things you suggest are costly, and, though my circumstances are well enough, I don't wish to throw money away.

Such a letter requires firm handling, and the beauty expert pulls no punches, advising her to concentrate on minute and unremitting care of the face and body, fantasy in make-up, continual and dazzling changes of coiffure. She reminds Michou, somewhat tartly, that Ninon de Lenclos was reputed to have used fresh *escalopes* on her face, which to-day would cost considerably more than a pot of beauty cream.

American girls too write to their magazines asking for help, not only with their complexions and complexes, but with the problem of how to make themselves loved, or at least invited out. Sometimes the experts are brutally frank in their answers. Thus: "When you do not get invitations to parties," declares one male counsellor, answering a worried query from a teen-ager in an American girls' magazine, "accept one thing as a fact. *They dont want you.*" And he proceeds to list the most likely reasons for this painful social rejection. "Perhaps you cannot carry your liquor properly."

At the other extreme, and dealt with more affably because their trouble is not one of failure, but rather of too precipitate success, comes the ticklish problem of how to keep ardent admirers within the bounds of physical prudence. Miss Dorothy Dix writing in *Success* (price 25 cents) advises, as the first step to success:

> It is really quite simple. Nothing succeeds with a man like success. The more cut-ins a girl has the better the boys like to dance with her. The harder it is to get a date with her the more eager they are to make one.

Hectic competition is her specific. "So put up a bluff of popularity and make them feel it is a favour when you step out with them." This, however, in itself needs application. Besides beauty creams, hair-restyling, dieting, slinky clothes, and making yourself difficult to get, you must know how to behave like an assured success. "Study movie stars' hand motions," advises Margery Wilson, author of *Charm*, and "practise gestures before a mirror."

The practical difficulties of finding men to attract is a problem briskly dealt with by Hildegarde Dolson, another brilliantly successful dispenser of clues to social success leading to marriage. In *How about a Man* she advises her female readers to inscribe themselves in university courses, the expense being well rewarded because that is where unattached professors and guest speakers of the male sex may be expected to be found. Miss Dolson takes a strong moral tone. "Try," she urges, "to concentrate on single men, though there are bound to be exceptions to the rule since married men are more susceptible than wily bachelors. Nevertheless somebody else's husband will generally give you more headaches than happiness."

Her technique is commendably pointed. "Learn enough of a man's job to ask intelligent questions," and then, when things begin to move, press hard on the soft pedal. "Men like soft feminine blouses. They love big-brimmed hats. They go for romantic fragility by night provided you are the type to swing it." Learn also, she urges, to recognize signs of

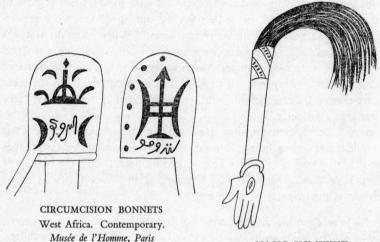

CIRCUMCISION BONNETS
West Africa. Contemporary.
Musée de l'Homme, Paris

MAGIC FLY-WHISK
Used for ceremonial purification of violated girl. Wood and monkey hair. Congo. Contemporary.
Musée de l'Homme, Paris

coming success. "When he asks you out a second time you have scored the first point towards a touch-down." This is a moment which needs masterly handling. "Watch your inferiority complex. Don't become too exclusive and seclusive. You need not shun necking and petting provided, however, you keep them within decent bounds."

Just what are the precise limits of decent bounds thousands of anguished teen-agers regularly write in to inquire, usually when they fear they have already exceeded them. This ticklish problem of how to keep ardent admirers just above the Plimsoll line of physical prudence needs the expert advice of a whole battery of highly paid specialists.

"As to how to say good-night, Be Brief but not curt about it with new beaux. Never let a man come in with you very late unless you know him rather well... or WANT THINGS TO HAPPEN." Case-histories of what happened to unwise virgins who failed to see the red light in time express in contemporary phrases the same gloomy situation that abounds in Victorian cautionary novels. Here too the good and successful virgin is singled out for commendation. Sylvia gets A-plus for knowing just how to manage everything, and is quoted with approval.

"I seldom turn down a date," says Sylvia briefly, "unless I think a fellow is a bum."

In all this welter of advice, both in America and in our own country, the influence of the cinema is paramount. Girls consciously model themselves, their face, voice, dress, and behaviour on the female film-stars they adore, with an almost religious attachment. Moreover, they urge their boy-friends to resemble, in face, voice, dress, and behaviour, the male film stars of their choice, and there is every reason to believe that they are being successful in this. The streets of Western cities are full of imitation Bogarts, Brandos, and latterly James Deans, this last model being much easier to copy, as being in the general contemporary pattern of crazy mixed-up adolescent male.

Hollywood, more than ever on the prowl for types of female beauty which embody the ordinary man's dreams, has concentrated on women with overdeveloped mammary attributes, to the exclusion of almost all other attributes. The student of social history needs to study this phenomenon very carefully, for the rest of the fashionable Hollywood female body is not developed in proportion. The ideal seems to be a childish body, baby face, and little-girl voice, small waist and narrow hips—with the addition of an astonishingly large bust.

The parallel development is the American insistence on artificial feeding of babies as against breast-feeding (reported recently from every state in America except those Southern states where the Negroes predominate). The conclusion to be drawn is that the overdeveloped female breast is not meant for use, but ornament, not meant to feed babies, but to symbolize "Mom" for present-day American males who can only feel virile thus confronted. In this atom-bomb age it is not surprising, perhaps, that men should seek emotional security by thus returning to the comforting symbols of their babyhood, when they did not have to be responsible for the control of something too difficult and frightening. Mom would protect them. Marilyn Monroe, Anita Ekberg, and their sister satellites are notably wider round the bust than the hips, and a notice on the wall of a Southsea café, where the buxom waitress attracts growing numbers of male customers, reads:

PATRONS ARE REQUESTED NOT TO WASTE THE WAITRESS'S TIME BY ASKING FOR HER VITAL STATISTICS. THEY ARE $41\frac{1}{2}$, 26, 37.

Dior tried for years to bring the female bust within manageable proportions, but this current male fixation defeated him. However artfully he created a charmingly immature teen-ager figure with a small, high bust, the wearers of his models and the copiers of his models immediately inflated the bust to VistaVision proportions which ruined his line but is what the men want. This stupendous bust is, in fact, more than

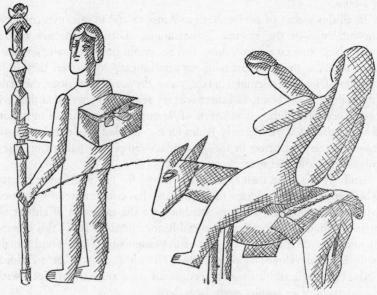

WOOD-CARVING OF THE HOLY FAMILY
Mexican. Contemporary.
By courtesy of Miss Gertrude Ely

a fashion, for what other recent fashion has lasted unchanged for over ten years? It is, alas, a fixation, and all the efforts of all the Western psychologists and psychiatrists are unable to shake it. Indeed, their very efforts may be tightening the bonds. The kind of girl the men want may have the mask of a girl, but it is Mom they really require.

Perhaps it will be the women who will have to make the giant effort to oblige their cavaliers to grow up, for the charms of Peter Pan and James Dean are strictly limited and women still want to have babies and nourish them. They are well aware of the difficulty of their task. They realize, for instance, that it is not because of stomach ulcers alone that men drink milk so desperately in America, as though fearing, in this eroded age, that the great national breast might prematurely run dry. It is certainly not the arduously dieting New York women who imbibe the more than 3,500,000 quarts of milk daily consumed in that great metropolis.

A generation ago young women were enthralled when Rudolf Valentino, wearing different national dress in every film—Spanish,

Russian, Arab (his greatest hit)—romantically kissed the palm (instead of the customary back of the hand) of his leading lady, as Elinor Glyn, that great and ladylike expert, had advised him to do. Nowadays they become hysterical and fling off their brassières at Liberace concerts. It is not the present generation of women who steal museum copies of Valentino's poems and his photographs from the Exhibition in the Film Department of the American Museum of Modern Art. Young women of to-day tattoo their forearms with "Liberace" and join well-organized fan clubs to root for him—and his brocade blazers—though they realize well enough that whom they are really rooting for is his Mom. And it may well be that that is what they are so hysterical about.

Perhaps Disney has given Hollywood its clue, and the enterprising film producers, instead of sending out their talent scouts to bigger and brassier night-clubs, ought to send them out into the deserts and the jungles, where complexes are more closely related to survival. Or even into the back garden, where they could profitably study the mating habits of the lesser creatures. Here they would find variety and originality of attack in love-making enough to give the cinema a salutary fresh lease of life. What wealth of new possibilities here awaits the enterprising Hollywood director who cares to apply the knowledge he will learn, for instance from spiders.

> The male walks towards the female in a groping fashion with front legs spread out before him. On touching her he proceeds to caress her with his legs, almost as though soothing her ... then he seizes her perhaps by a leg or some other part of the body, and in one case at least he fastens her to the ground by threads attached to her legs and body.

What a perfect set-up for a modern thriller.

"In a strongly carnivorous species such as the average spider the result, for the male, could be fatal."

The seashore, no less, has everything to offer to the bash-and-grab Hollywood school of amorous dalliance. Consider the tactics of the bull elephant seal.

"He fights intruders on his cow harem, trampling down his cows as he attacks," pressing his suit, having beaten off his male rivals, by "embracing the cow with one of his foreflippers and drawing her to him. Then he takes hold of her neck in his mouth."

Armed with such a technique Yul Brynner surely would succeed in bringing back into the cinema theatres the fickle women who have deserted them to stay at home and watch television.

It may be, however, that America, whose techniques are so closely watched and followed by Europe, might prefer to tackle its romantic difficulties in a different way, in a way it understands so much better—that is, by machinery. Vast wealth and honour might be awaiting the enterprising businessman who first sets up a chain of Romance Parlours on the self-service principle.

Herein, by simple cash payment (or on deferred terms if so wished), the desired courtesies would be efficiently administered entirely by machinery. Soft-carpeted saloons, opulent and imposing as the most important banks, would be lavishly equipped with rows of gaily coloured and sweetly perfumed machines (perhaps blue for gentlemen and pink for ladies, or, perhaps, vice versa). At the touch of the appropriate levers these machines would produce, with a calm expertise no mere human could ever hope to emulate, the required number of little compliments, big compliments, light and heavy datings, gifts, and gardenias. All the intricate romantic human longings could in these Romance Parlours easily be satisfied by preset mechanical devices, and no doubt at an astonishingly moderate cost, for, of course, every machine would be fully automated.

TREE OF LIFE
Chinese papercut. Contemporary.

CHAPTER TEN

MANLY SPORT

Must we have the synthetic conker? In case some of your older readers have not heard of it, I am told that it is sold stringed for use and is made so that when it breaks in play it can be put together again. I need not enlarge on the horror of a monstrous innovation which threatens to destroy an ancient and typically British pastime. Gone is the initiative and skill in acquiring one's weapons and preparing them for action. The logical conclusion is, I suppose, an all-the-year-round conker season. All that can be said for the new conker is that it saves labour. I have enough faith in our youth to believe that they will not be seduced by artificial advantages of ease and convenience. I appeal to you to use your great influence to save a national institution.

J. A. R. PIMLETT, Wimbledon, in a letter to
The Times, October 28, 1955

EASY sport, as the writer of the above letter suggests, is no sport at all. It always ends in spectator sport, in which the onlookers merely observe and the performers, having lost amateur status, do it for a living and are expected to display professional standards of skill. It has, then, like so many former pleasures in life, ceased to be fun all round, and has developed into a hard-headed business.

The reason why sport has always been popular with all classes of all communities is because it furnishes an admirable medium for showing off, both showing off social rank and showing off in front of the ladies or the gentlemen, the former being much the more powerful urge of the two.

By legal veto, no less than by prohibitive cost, people of rank and power in the past have been singularly successful in preserving for themselves certain sports. In our present state of class flux, wherein lines of strict demarkation are undoubtedly slipping, money no longer is the criterion either of birth or of breeding—often, indeed, quite the contrary, and certain traditionally upper-class sports are therefore now practised in such esoteric jargon, and with the addition of so many sly inessential "U" rules of etiquette, that the non- "U" exponent, no matter how wealthy, is deliberately made to feel an outsider. And, of course, vice versa. Darts and shove-halfpenny, no less than polo and steeplechasing, have their own peculiar *mystiques*, and it does not do for the rich outsider to think that by stripping off his jacket he makes himself welcome in the village-pub darts game, any more than it would be thinkable for the chap from the village pub to acquire the right sort of tweeds and waders and tackle and think he had thereby won himself an *entrée* into the jealous ranks of the dry-fly fishers.

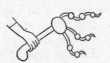

SCOURGING FOR WRONG-
DOING
Wall-painting, thirteenth century.
St Stephen's, House of Commons

EMBROIDERED HOOD FOR
HAWK
Silk and silver thread on linen stretched
over leather. Two inches high. English,
seventeenth century.
Victoria and Albert Museum

The world's oldest sport is certainly hunting, which is even older than waging war, which was long regarded as a noble—in fact, the only truly noble—aristocratic diversion. It is thought that the game of chess was actually invented by the Buddhist priests thousands of years ago in a pious attempt to save human life by replacing the savagery of armed human conflict by this peaceful diversion, which nevertheless sufficiently embodies the military principles to be attractive to the military-minded, and in which the equipment can be made so costly as to flatter aristocratic privilege.

We find that war and hunting are frequently combined, the one proving the excuse for or providing the means for the other. Thus the English Crusaders hunted their way to the Holy Land and hunted their way back again, and every other war expedition which has taken the English soldier overseas has also proved an admirable excuse for sport as well. The Duke of Wellington, for instance, hunted throughout the whole of the Peninsular War and right up to the defeat of Napoleon. In the year 1813 he was keeping a pack of hounds at St Jean-de-Luz, whence he hunted all over the neighbouring districts; correctly attired in the light-blue frock-coat and accessories of the Hatfield Hunt, a rig presented to him by his admirer the fashionable Lady Salisbury.

In Hunting with a capital 'H,' as distinct from hunting, with a small 'h,' size, ferocity, and inedibility form the criterion as to who may hunt what. Tiger-hunting is for rajahs. Rabbit-hunting is for peasants. *Shikar* in India. *Safari* in Africa. These big-game-hunting terrains have supplied one of the high privileges of Empire for the British aristocracy in the last two centuries.

If the death of what is hunted is useful to the community, especially if it means food, something of the essential glamour of the aristocratic hunt is thereby diminished. The game should serve absolutely no other purpose than a lordly trophy. A book of sporting reminiscences of hunting adventures in South America, written not long since by an English gentleman, recounts how, within a period of twenty-two months beginning in 1919, he successfully dispatched no less than 23,470 creatures single-handed, including deer, peccary, ant-bear, alligator, racoon, rheas, ibis, and doves. The author recorded his poor opinion of the natives of these parts for their lack of desire and equipment to do likewise:

> They are very poor specimens, rapidly dying out. Almost naked, dirty and with shocks of matted hair, they represent a very sorry spectacle. They have no weapons with which to hunt animals and birds, and if they had would be too lazy to go after them.

Nevertheless, alongside the grand Hunting of the gentry (and not only in England) has always flourished the surreptitious hunting of their social inferiors, no less keen to kill, if only for the pot. Poaching is certainly as venerable a sport as Hunting. Despite most vindictive game laws, trapping, snaring, 'knocking off' small and even large game by every cunning illegal device contrivable, has always been a deeply rooted English pursuit; and what English village is complete without its poacher?

The poacher wears his camouflage sports dress (ragged jacket with concealed capacious pockets, and muffler to hide his face) no less meticulously than the owner of the land he poaches from wears his meticulous Hunting kit on the prescribed occasions. Nor, it must be confessed, though English people are perhaps the most law-abiding in the world, is the village poacher regarded by the other villagers as an offender, for in rural districts there persists the stubborn sentiment that game laws are unjust and that the local landowner has no right in the eyes of God or man to keep the game all for himself.

Largeness and ferocity cannot in themselves confer social distinction on the hunted animal. The whale, for instance, hunted in frail rowing-boats a century ago, is the largest creature in the world, and can be one of the most dangerous. Yet, because its oil was so useful when it was caught, whale-hunting never became the sport of gentlemen, though Herman Melville mentions that in his day whale-hunting was a notable refuge for romantic young near-gentlemen suffering from broken hearts.

To-day, when wealth can buy practically everything, rich amateurs can hire professional hunters who will supply and organize everything for Indian *shikar* or African *safari*, including porters, guides, equipment, food, tents, guns, cars, and so on, and guarantee the bagging of so many head of game, which they often enough have to shoot themselves, standing respectfully by their employers in order to deliver the vital shot that the wealthy novice may well fumble.

That something of the excitement formerly experienced seems to be lacking from present-day big-game hunting may be guessed from the following item of news reported by the French special correspondent of the *Daily Telegraph* (April 23, 1956):

> Equipped with a bow and three dozen arrows each, a party of American archers have just flown to French Africa "to hunt big game," as they said. A similar expedition last year bagged antelope and gazelles. The party also killed 2 elephants and a lion. Asked how many arrows it needed to kill an elephant, they kept a dignified silence. It appears that the archers are accompanied by professional hunters with less primitive weapons.

The 12th of August still stirs many British hearts, and the traditional English fox-hunt still splashes the English countryside with its pink coats and tears down the farmers' crops and fences. Both these sports, however, are becoming too costly for many of their former followers.

Fifty years ago the daily bag of game for one shooting party on one of the jealously guarded moors would run into four figures. Such shoots were very highly organized, involving the costly rearing of the pheasants and the attendance of such retinues of salaried assistants that all the sportsman was required to do was to shoot accurately with the gun which his personal loader had already charged for him and put into his hands. The development of the syndicate shoot (to-day's curious version), whose members are rarely country people—in fact, are often unable to identify the birds, and who join the syndicate because they consider it socially elevating—has turned the sport into something of a farce.

The great period of hunting was that of the Court of Louis XIV, so passionate a devotee of the sport that he kept no less than 2000 fine hunters in his Grand Stables and had miles of paths and *allées* specially cut and widened in his game forest. The uniform of his Royal Hunt was sumptuous, a richly embroidered, gold-laced blue coat with red velvet cuffs and collar, embossed silver buttons, and scarlet waistcoat and breeches.

Adding to the glory of the total spectacle, each of the princes of the blood designed his own particular liveries, vying with one another to achieve the most gorgeous effect. The Duc d'Orléans and his retinue wore scarlet combined with blue and silver, the Prince de Condé fawn and amaranth, and the Comte de Toulouse red and gold.

ENGLISH SOLDIERS AT CRÉCY
Illuminated manuscript.
Bibliothèque Nationale, Paris

By the time Louis XV, another passionate hunter, had grown to maturity, the fashion for large-brimmed hats created difficulties during the hunt because they interfered with the blowing of the hunting-horn. The design of the hunting-horn was thereupon altered to accommodate the headgear, the great curled hunting-horn *à la Dampière* being invented for this purpose. The King amused himself composing special fanfares for this improved instrument, fanfares which are still used in French hunting to-day.

Both Louis XIV and Louis XV found no difficulty in combining the sport of hunting with the sport of gallantry, unlike most of the English gentry, who, Voltaire remarked, unkindly if truthfully, after his visit to England, hunted all day long until they were weary and covered with mud and then fell fast asleep straight after dinner, so that, according to his Gallic standards, their wives were piteously neglected. Captain Gronow, a century later, observed that nothing had changed. Cards, the bottle, and the fox still ousted the ladies.

Indeed female society amongst the upper classes was most notoriously neglected for gambling and drinking, except perhaps by romantic foreigners. How could it be otherwise when husbands spent their days on the hunting-field?

As in military uniform, prestige has frequently preferred the discomfort and even danger of the splendid to the ease and safety of the practical, in hunting dress. The striking pink coat and white breeches of the English hunt might, by rendering their wearer visible after a fall on the hunting-field, be instrumental in preventing further damage from over-riding. But this point is not the point that matters. Safety, in the scale of values of aristocratic sports dress, must always take second place to social distinction, and the courting of danger in itself adds to prestige. Therefore hunting dress is sometimes worn which not only fails to afford protection from danger to its wearer, but definitely adds to the danger.

In hunting the chief danger lies in being thrown and thereby fracturing the skull. In fact, the hunting top-hat was originally invented as a crash helmet for just such an emergency. But it is no longer worn for this purpose, and youthful followers of the hunt, whose skulls may be expected to be more fragile than adult skulls, are often protected by nothing stronger than a peaked velvet skull-cap. The *chignon, de rigueur* with female hunting dress, was certainly originally useful to moor the veiled top-hot on to. But in a period of short hair (such as has been in vogue now for nearly thirty years) this involves the introduction of an artificial *chignon*, practically impossible to secure to the head, and therefore far from affording a safe mooring for the top-hat and likely to do more harm than good from the point of view of safety. But from the point of view of adding distinction to the wearer and giving an appearance of superiority the *chignon* is definitely "U."

Similarly the long riding-skirt worn with the side-saddle. It looked picturesque and required arduous training to wear properly. That its yards of heavy drapery also rendered it a positive menace to life on the hunting-field was undoubtedly an important aspect of its appeal.

Of all sports dress hunting dress clings the most ardently to its former glories. So anxious was Field-Marshal Hermann Goering that hunting in Germany should not lose prestige by lack of showy dress that he designed his own romantic hunting costume, together with a somewhat Wardour Street livery for his retainers. In 1935 the *Berlinske Tidende* reported his dress at a hunting dinner as

Dark green suède boots reaching over his knees in front. A dark green sleeveless leather jerkin with silver-mounted buttons made from the teeth of an elk he had shot himself. Riding-breeches of fawn-coloured serge. A wide shirt with an extremely high collar and large sleeves ending in tight cuffs [like the hero of the ballet *Sylphides*]. A

Scottish tartan tie with an enormous gold pin. A gold-embroidered belt complete with a gold hunting-knife in a gold sheath, and on his left breast was pinned a large hunting-medal of a golden stag bearing between its antlers a diamond swastika. During the service of the dinner the waiters wore green velvet suits embellished with lace ruffles and jabots—and white top-boots.

If true sport consists in killing something large in a manner involving danger to the killer, then war must count as a top-ranking sport, and there is no doubt that earlier and less mechanized wars than those of to-day did so count as sport—at least to the commanders and to the higher officers who engaged in them.

On a more individual plane, duelling was the passionate preoccupation of European gentlemen. Social snobbery, physical adroitness, and individual courage combined to make duelling a major sport for those socially eligible. Other ranks merely fought. It was only gentlemen who duelled. Carrying a sword, a gentlemanly privilege, implied knowing how to use it, and, though duelling was illegal, no gentleman's education was considered complete without a careful training in the art.

To be "sudden and quick in quarrel" became in itself a point of honour, for the issue at stake was often enough pointless or worse. At the Court of Marie-Antoinette, to give one famous example, Comte Montrond was on one occasion playing cards with a certain M. de Champagne, when the latter truthfully but imprudently observed, "Monsieur, vous trichez!" Cheating was customary at that Court, but it was not etiquette to appear to notice it. (Voltaire had been obliged to flee into exile for a similar comment not long before, though he had whispered it in English, mis-takenly supposing that the guilty player understood nothing but French.)

On this occasion Comte Montrond replied that he may well have been cheating, but that he did not propose to permit anyone to tell him so, and threw his cards into M. de Champagne's face. The following morning the two men fought a duel. Montrond was run through the body and lay at death's door for two months. When he had recovered he again called out Champagne and was again wounded, though this time he succeeded in killing M. de Champagne.

After this people tried not to quarrel with Comte Montrond, but let him cheat as much as he desired. Talleyrand's comment on the affair was that the Comte "vit sur son mort."

In the eighteenth and nineteenth centuries, wherever gentlemen gathered together, valuable young lives were liable to be cut down in duels provoked and fought on the paltriest excuses, often enough out of sheer boredom. Duelling was fashionable among Army officers who had much time on their hands, and more especially among officers of armies of occupation, who had even more time for ennui than the others.

The height of duelling mania seems to have been reached in Paris among the various nationalities of officers in occupation after Waterloo. Captain Gronow, who was one such officer, reported an endless series of

REFEREE CONDUCTING
A DUEL
From *Les Droits d'Armes*, chivalry manual of Charles the Bold, Duke of Burgundy, 1450.
Yale University Library

PEASANT BOY
English, fourteenth century.

duels fought between English and French officers, English and German officers, French and German officers, English and English, French and French, German and German, not to speak of Irish officers fighting every other nationality, and themselves as well. One inflammable Irish officer killed nine opponents within a year in duels. At Silvé's, the fashionable café for the military, two officers kept their cards perpetually pinned up above the mantelshelf, in a permanent challenge to fight any Bonapartist officer or group of officers who cared to present themselves.

Frequently the second of an officer slain in a duel immediately challenged the victor to a further duel, and there were also vendetta duels. The favourite duelling weapons at this time were the sabre and small sword, and the favourite rendezvous the Bois de Boulogne, then a marshy and unfrequented district. The law set its face sternly against duelling, but it was considered bad taste to invoke the law.

It was etiquette to dress immaculately for the duel, seconds and attendant surgeons being equally costumed with care and distinction, the casting off of the long cape, in many cases never to be put on again, playing a dramatic part in the elaborate ritual.

In duelling the niceties of rank were always meticulously observed, no gentleman ever lowering himself to fight a social inferior. In Pisa in 1822 Lord Byron, in a *mêlée* of confused hustling with the Italian secret police, and putting the wrong interpretation on the lavish gold braid, array of medals, and splendid mount of his chief annoyer, on one occasion actually challenged a mere sergeant-major of Dragoons to a duel. His lordship's extreme subsequent chagrin and embarrassment testify to the extent of his mortification at this major social gaffe, and he wrote at the greatest length to all his friends to explain just how such a dreadful slip could possibly have happened.

Between gentlemen, however, anything served to start the necessary quarrel. A look was enough. Once involved, no gentleman, if he withdrew, could ever hope to hold his head up again. There had also to be no evasion of danger during the actual duel. A certain German officer among the occupation forces of Paris in 1815, who was wounded in a duel and whose miraculous escape from death was discovered by the surgeon to be due to the generous protective wadding of brown paper with which he had prudently lined his duelling-jacket, was kicked soundly on the posterior then and there by his own disgusted second.

Duelling continued in America, where the laws were less regarded, much later than in Europe. No democrat could honourably refuse any duel provoked on any excuse, and an etiquette book published in 1855 in New York reminded its male readers in this regard that "the name of every woman is sacred."

Sports involving cruelty have unhappily always been the most popular kind of spectator sports in all parts of the world. A man risking his life in combat with a dangerous animal (or two dangerous animals goaded to destroy each other) has never failed to appeal to the mob. And not only to the mob. Imperial combats between gladiators and savage beasts excited aristocratic Romans in the seats of honour in ancient Rome no less than the brutalized plebeians up in the cheap seats. Bull-fighting, with its infallible stimulants of danger, pageantry, and cruelty, and its ballet of sternly controlled movements, still thrills all of Spain, much of Southern France, Mexico, and the whole of Latin America. It is almost the only entertainment young ladies in Spain can go to without some sort of chaperon, and mothers attend with infants of the tenderest age.

Bull-fighting is no new sport. It was practised in Crete, in a particularly dangerous and difficult version involving jumping on to the bull's back from behind and somersaulting over its horns, and this was performed by young women specially trained for the feat. It was practised in Thessaly by chasing the bull on horseback, whence the fighter had to leap upon the bull's back and break its neck by flinging it to earth by its horns. Up to the end of the eighteenth century bulls were fought on horseback in Spain, as may be seen in Goya's pictures, and some bull-fighters practise this to-day too, though mostly women bull-fighters.

It is perhaps worth examining the sport of bull-fighting in some detail, since its appeal has not diminished for over two thousand years, and it is nowadays embellished by the most masculine and gorgeous of contemporary dress, a dress, moreover, which owes nothing to class snobbery, nor is intended to, but owes its beauty entirely to masculine pride and physical display. That is to say, the bull-fighter's dress is not an aristocratic or plutocratic dress, though it is gorgeously embroidered and very expensive, for most of the famous bull-fighters have been of peasant origin and usually illiterate. It is a dress that has won the right to gorgeousness.

Though the sanded arenas of Barcelona and Madrid to-day display garish advertisements for Pepsi-Cola, there is little else about the actual performance of the sport that echoes the commercial values of to-day. It has always been and remains one of the most dangerous of all sports. Few bull-fighters live out their natural days, and all of them suffer injuries from the bull's horns at one time or another. There is an infirmary attached to every bull-ring by law, with a surgeon, two doctors and assistants, and a priest in constant attendance during every fight.

There are flourishing schools for training bull-fighters in Madrid, Valladolid, and Seville to-day. A successful bull-fighter carries the prestige of the greatest of artists, and there is no lack of eager candidates. Each year at least three thousand young Spaniards in their early teens, and almost always of humble origin, enter the ranks of these apprentices, but only half a dozen or so make the grade. The rest become discouraged, maimed, or killed during the course of their training, or content themselves with staffing the subsidiary rôles in the organization and performance of the bull-fights.

A successful bull-fighter can earn about two million pesetas during the six-month annual season. This is about £20,000, and is a powerful incentive in a country where the poor are so miserably poor and the pay for an hour's work may be as low as five pesetas or less. But the remuneration is only a small part of the inducement. After all, successful businessmen and rich landowners gain more than £20,000 a year. The glamour and prestige of the bull-fighter enthral the youth of Spain, but it is, above all, the challenge to sheer daring and physical courage that counts most. Sheer courage and recklessness do not make the best bull-fighters, however, nor do the audiences applaud suicidal passes in the ring, such as the youngest bull-fighters invariably try. What counts is absolute courage controlled to within fractions of an inch of death by experienced skill and coolness—and the clean and graceful killing of the bull—and it is this which evokes the deafening applause, the hats and the flowers hurled on to the bloodstained sand at the end of the *corrida*.

To risk one's life repeatedly in the shortest space of time, in movements and poses of the extremest tragic beauty, wearing magnificent costume, and in the presence of applauding multitudes, is an ideal which sets Spanish youth so ablaze that at almost every *corrida* ragged young lads of thirteen leap the wooden barriers and fling themselves before the bull to try daring passes themselves. These *spontaneos*, who dangerously upset the bull, the performers, and the performance, have to be quickly removed, and are usually goodnaturedly locked up in every one's interest for the rest of the afternoon.

It is well to remember this idealization of physical bravery when we come to consider why, of all countries, Spain and Spanish-influenced countries to-day wear the most manly dress left in the world.

Such is the passion for the *corrida* that the glossary of the bull-ring is enormous and extremely detailed. There are, for instance, no less than twenty-two different words to define the exact markings of a bull, and nine different words for the various formations of its horns.

Religion plays a notable part in the drama of the *corrida*, some of the passes being named after Christian symbols. Thus the Veronica is named in honour of the traditional aspect of the body of Christ being received by Mary Magdalene. The bull-fighter's embroidered short cloak is often embellished with religious *motifs*, and perhaps the head of the Virgin and the fighter's patron saint as well. It is customary for the bull-fighter's mother and wife or fiancée to pray in church for his safety during his performance.

As to the bull-fighter's costume itself, though mostly dating from the eighteenth century, it embodies certain modern modifications and also certain items which belong to far older civilizations. The flat, wide black hat has curled-under projections at each side which suggest the ram's horn volutes of Ionic columns. Beneath this hat is worn a small *chignon* pinned on to the bull-fighter's hair. This *chignon* is the vestige of the former pigtail, and is such an essential part of the costume that when a bull-fighter retires from active life in the ring he is said to "cut off his *chignon*."

The shirt of pure silk is cut in a traditional shape and worn with a narrow coloured tie to match the costume. Beneath the shirt a long silk bandage is tightly bound round the body to act as corset and afford some slight protection to the stomach from the murderous horns. Two pairs of tightly fitting stockings are worn, linen thread for the under pair and rose-pink or crimson or white silk for the top pair. The soft slippers, of an elegance only otherwise seen in ballet, are made of the finest, softest Spanish leather. The padded, epauletted short open jacket and skintight breeches are made of brilliantly hued satin or velvet, thickly embroidered with a

COSTUME OF THE BULL–FIGHTER
JOAQUIN BERNADÓ
Spain. Contemporary.

rich design in gold bullion and ducat *paillettes*, the design always forming a wide stripe from shoulder to wrist of the sleeves and on the outer edges of the breeches. Thus, while not interfering with freedom of movement in any way, the utmost magnificence embellishes the actual shape and line of the body. For the preliminary parade a short wide cloak swings from the shoulders, and upon this cloak all the resources and richness of the embroiderer's art are massed, and it is handsomely lined with con-trasting silk.

Bull-fighters are not only very religious, but also highly superstitious, preferring to restrict themselves to certain colours of dress, certain num-bers, and certain hotel rooms, and so on, which they believe to be lucky for them. Their dress is extremely costly, the short exhibition cloak alone costing more than £100, and they must have a whole wardrobe of dresses for their prestige, and also for the practical reason that the hazards of their profession entail the ruin of their costume by bloodstains at almost every *corrida*. Whether it is their own blood or the blood of the bull, once stained their costume is ruined for good.

Such is the most dazzling male dress worn to-day, of so arrogant a masculinity that it gives dignity even to the short, stout secondary toreadors in the *corrida*. It combines tightness and looseness, austerity and luxury, the ancient and the modern, and even without the ducat embroidery and the sequins is still overwhelmingly impressive. Indeed, one of the most beautiful of all bull-fighting costumes was Belmonte's dark claret velvet trimmed with black bobbled braid.

Few Englishmen to-day venture to watch a *corrida*, the goring of the bull by the picador and of the wretched padded horses by the enraged bull upsetting their strongest R.S.P.C.A. instincts. This tenderness towards the suffering of animals, it must be stated, is something quite new in English life, for no people in the world have enjoyed animal-baiting more than the English, and this until quite recently.

Bulls, bears, badgers, dogs, cocks, have all been brutally baited in England to provide amusement for all classes of the community, as the names of some of our city and village streets and alleys reveal, and bull-*baiting* (not bull-*fighting*) was so popular a spectator sport in England that a special breed of savagely tenacious dog was bred for this purpose, still known to-day by the name of bulldog and still affectionately regarded as a symbol of England.

It was believed that the flesh of bulls was dangerous to eat until it had been "thinned by baiting," and a law was passed early in the seventeenth century forbidding butchers to kill a bull for human consumption until it had been first so baited, infringement of which law was punished by heavy fines. Bull-baiting and dog-fighting were so popular as sports that even after they were banned by law in 1835 opposition to the law proved so strong that the law could not be enforced for years afterwards.

The baiting of bears by savage dogs rendered wild by goading and starvation was, up to the end of the seventeenth century, the particular sport of royalty, the bear-pit forming as essential an amenity in the ducal grounds as the tennis-court does to-day in middle-class English country families. Badger-baiting, in which half-starved badgers were set upon by hungry dogs, was a favourite rural sport enjoyed in English villages, where enthusiasts described it delightedly as "most barbarous."

Cock-fighting has probably been, of all English spectator sports, the most beloved. It has a very ancient pedigree indeed, and was not new when practised in ancient Greece—to inspire Greek warriors, it was believed, with examples of courage. In the days of Themistocles certainly it was the preferred Athenian pastime, likely fighting cocks being carefully reared on a diet of leeks and onions to make them more aggressive. In Rome tremendous stakes were laid on cock-fights, to the usual accompaniment of graft, doping, and the artificial stimulation of prize birds. It is from Rome, via the Roman army of occupation in Britain, that cock-fighting was introduced to these shores, and, although in the course of two thousand years quail-fighting and partridge combats developed their own *aficionados*, it was undoubtedly cock-fighting that proved the most popular sport of all.

Perhaps the limited size of the combatants made the ownership of them and organization of their combats more easy, but certain it is that all classes of the community shared the passion. In Henry II's reign schoolboys of good families were always given a special allowance of money for the purchase of their own fighting cocks, so essential to the English way of life had the sport become, and we know that Wellington's officers took their favourite fighting cocks with them on their Spanish campaign. At a period when class distinctions were never more absolute nobility and commoners mingled in the cockpit. James Boswell has left us a vivid account of one such combat he attended in 1763:

> The pit and seat are covered with mat ... the cocks nicely cut and dressed and armed with silver heels are set down to fight with amazing courage and resolution. One pair fought for three-quarters of an hour. The uproar and noise of betting is prodigious.

Enormous sums of money changed hands at such cock-fights, stakes of five thousand guineas being regarded as nothing out of the ordinary.

Here we must consider the question of dress in relation to spectator sports, a question that the passing of time has only rendered more acute, since to-day the numbers of spectators of sports as against performers has enormously increased.

The spectators derive their excitement at second hand, and the betting is part of the excitement, for no man can feel his own manhood enhanced by merely watching other men or other creatures displaying a reckless bravery he is not himself called upon to display. That is why spectator-sports dress has always been uncertain and essentially bogus, usually the imitation tough. Eccentric Regency dandies sometimes had their upper waistcoat embroidered with fighting cocks, or secured their sporting kerchief with a gold pin wrought in the shape of two pugilists, as did Fulwar Creven. But such is not authentic sports dress, and the Regency aristocratic passion for driving four-in-hands indicates a deep-seated desire to justify themselves by winning the right to dress like stagecoach drivers—treble-caped coats, mufflers, swaggering top-boots, and all.

This psychological necessity was never understood in France. If Count d'Orsay was an intrepid horseman, Beau Brummell, they knew for a fact, had loathed horses as much as they did themselves, and it was Brummell who was their god. The Paris dandy of 1834 clanked about in spurs, to look as though he had just got off a horse or was just about to get on one, but the horse itself was never there, and his yellow gloves and riding-whip were purely decorative.

PUNISHMENT: LOSS OF HAND
From *Coutumes de Toulouse* (1296).
Bibliothèque Nationale, Paris

Few Paris dandies cared even to ride the creatures, still less to risk their necks in a steeplechase. "En France la course de haies n'a jusqu'à présent trouvé que peu de *riders*," reports *La Mode* in 1843, adding prudently, "Why should one expose oneself to needless dangers?"

It may be that the French, unlike the English, are essentially volatile and sociable, therefore less likely to be bored without the stimulus of sports to absorb them, either as participators or onlookers. Certainly it was English soldiers, not French, who used to get up scorpion-fights in South India in the years before the Second World War, because they were utterly bored and could contrive no other kind of fight. Their technique was to catch the scorpions and cut off their stings (lest they kill each other too quickly and spoil the sport), supplying them instead with a splinter of wood each with which to attack. A lot of Army pay dribbled away in bets on these scorpion-matches.

If boredom accounts in some measure for spectator blood-sports it cannot be denied that cruelty is a human appetite easily whetted and hard to subdue once whetted. Periods of religious exaltation, sadly enough, are peculiarly liable to outbreaks of ferocity and the enjoyment of deliberately inflicted pain, especially human pain. The spectacle of degrading cruel punishment inflicted on wrongdoers, or supposed wrongdoers, has been relished in many pious countries at different times as public entertainment, England coming high on the list—so high that we must include it in the term sport.

That these cruelties were inflicted in the name of Christian mercy shows how contradictory man can be and how persistent his least noble instincts. Thus William the Conqueror, in an access of Christian magnanimity, actually abolished capital punishment from his English realm. His law runs: "I forbid that anyone be killed or hanged for any crime, but instead his eyes are to be torn out and his testicles cut off."

While there was a steady history of domestic and State torture from then onward, the sixteenth and seventeenth centuries, which were notable for deep religious ferment in the Western world, were especially pitiless in their unbridled enjoyment of cruel punishment. The rack, the pillory, the whipping-post, the stang, and the brank had already been in use for five hundred years or so, but under the Commonwealth this appetite intensified, because other emotional outlets were stopped, just as witch-hunting became a national hysteria because people were not allowed to wear fine clothes or dance or sing or ring bells or even play tipcat.

John Taylor, the poet, noted in 1630:

> In London and within a mile I ween
> There are jails and prisons full eighteen,
> And stocks and cages.

Parish records are filled with entries of punishments of suspected wrong-doers, or even mere wanderers, often enough of the most tender ages, for it was believed that the Devil could not too early be whipped out of the human body. Every parish maintained a paid employee to administer the whippings, which were publicly performed. Here are a few random entries from various English parish registers. Constable Barnsley parish register in the year 1636:

To Edward Wood for whipping of three wanderers to their
dwelling-place   ...   .   1 *shilling*.

From the parish register of Great Staughton, in Huntingdon, in 1691
(one among many such entries, lunacy being then regarded and punished
as an offence):

> Paid in charges for taking up a distracted woman, watching
> her and whipping her the next day ...   ...   3 *shillings*, 6 *pence*.

Another entry from 1714:

> Spent on Nurse for searching woman to see if she was with
> child before she was whipped ... three of them ...   ... 2 *shillings*.

There seems to be a particular concentration upon the whipping of
women, which no doubt derived from Puritanical fear and hatred of sex.
Disease also furnished a plausible excuse for indulgence in the national
pastime of whipping.

> Paid Thomas Hawkins for whipping 2 people that had the
> small poxe   ...   .   8 *pence*.

But some entries do not give any reason at all, and perhaps were undertaken merely to keep Mr Hawkins's hand in or warm him up on cold
winter mornings or add to his wages:

> Paid for whipping Goody Barry   ...   .   4 *pence*.
> Paid for whipping Ma Mitchell   ...   .   4 *pence*.

Country architects who designed the edifices of punishment tried to make
multiple combinations, so that the spectators should have all possible
diversions at once, rather like the New York contemporary three-ring
circus. The parish of Coleshill long retained its ancient wooden unit,
which thus combined stocks, whipping-post, and pillory.

In the great country houses punishment was at the discretion of the
owners, who kept their own private stocks on their own grounds, wherein
erring servants could be clapped, to furnish examples to the rest of the
staff. The pillory, however, seems to have been a much more popular
institution, and had a venerable history which preceded the Norman
Conquest. It was used for a wide variety of crimes, including selling short-
weight bread, impure butter, perjury, and prostitution, which last was
known as night-walking. Butchers who sold measled pork were dragged

to the pillory in dungcarts, and bakers had to do penance there for charging too much for their wares. Sexual offences (which included the scolding of husbands by wives and the inability of husbands to stand up to their spouse's henpecking, besides the more serious crimes of profligacy and licentiousness) were expiated in the pillory in a storm of jeering and the throwing of mud and decayed vegetables by the rest of the villagers, who had no other sport to look forward to.

SCOLD'S BRIDLE
English, fifteenth century.

'DRUNKARD'S CLOAK'
English, seventeenth century.

Even royalty found it necessary to use similar punishment to keep its households in order and entertained. The MSS. of Regulations ordering the staff of Henry VIII and Catherine of Aragon, for instance, strictly forbids his Highness' baker from mixing alum in the bread, or rye, oaten or bean flour with the bread-flour, on pain of suffering punishment in the stocks. Similar punishment was the penalty for stealing locks and keys, tables, benches, or other furniture from the houses of noblemen where the King and his court visited. Master cooks were put in the pillory if they did not prevent their scullions from "going about naked or lying all night on the ground before the kitchen fire." And even high-ranking officers of the King's privy chamber risked the pillory if they failed to obey their sovereign's command to be "loving together, no grudging nor grumbling nor talking of the *King's pastime*" (the last a difficult command, indeed, when the whole of England and most of Europe were talking of nothing else).

Outside, in the spacious and lovely gardens of the palaces, stood the ever-ready stocks and pillory, never empty of some erring servant who had broken some regulation such as "romping with the maids on the staircase, by which dishes and other things are often broken," or not taking rightful care of the pewter spoons and carelessly breaking the wooden spoons, or interrupting the kitchenmaids, or putting brimstone in the ale, or using coal in chambers other than those of the King, the Queen, and the Lady Mary.

We may guess with what pleasure the rest of the servants lingered near the stocks to torment the unfortunates doing expiation, for this was not forbidden, but, on the contrary, encouraged, and there was never any edict forbidding servants not to waste time enjoying the misery of their fellow-servants who had the misfortune to be caught.

In the upheavals of the seventeenth century the pillory became a political instrument of religious oppression, and as such often produced undesired reactions, when the mob, instead of jeering and throwing mud, as was required of it, brought hot drinks and sweet flowers to comfort those it considered were voicing its desires, and undaunted preachers continued to preach loudly from the pillory to enormous and sympathetic crowds until they had to be gagged. Daniel Defoe, it may be recalled, who had gallantly given himself up rather than let his publisher be punished for his satire, wrote and lustily sang a hymn he had composed specially for the pillory, all the vast crowds present joining in at the top of their voices.

Among the instruments of punishment continually in use in the sixteenth and seventeenth centuries was the 'drunkard's cloak,' a barrel with orifices for head, legs, and hands. Thus accoutred, imbibers were driven about the village to be pelted and mocked.

Modern psychology reveals that there was a strong sexual flavour attaching to the numerous cruel punishments inflicted on women, especially on supposed witches, who are so peculiarly associated with the Puritan seventeenth century in England that their traditional dress is the ordinary country dress of that time. To-day we have learned to understand better what impulses lay behind their supposed levitationary powers, demoniac possession, and familiarity with black cats. At a time of general superstitious terror in the witch-hunting provinces any outspoken and unafraid woman or, on the other hand, any secretive woman was suspect. By no means all the women put on trial and tortured as suspect witches were old women. Many were quite young and beautiful, and some were mere girls. Significantly enough, there seems to have been much less fear—if, indeed, any at all—of wizards.

It is sad to have to relate that some of the instruments of torture or repression originally employed in the Inquisition were used later in England on suspect witches, and even on refractory women not so suspect. The brank, or gossip's bridle, was a muzzle of iron and leather into which husbands could lock recalcitrant or merely irritating wives. One surviving brank in Stockport is furnished with a barbed gag to pierce the tongue, the gag being forced into the woman's mouth by the action of locking the brank, so that the severest pain was inflicted and all movement of the head impossible. Branks of this kind and various other kinds were in use in the home for centuries, and no doubt afforded relief, if not active pleasure, to husbands who only thus had the satisfaction of turning the key on their unco-operative partners. Since the punishment of the brank was essentially domestic and private it is impossible to know just what the goaded husband did regard as penal, but the name suggests that gossiping, instead of getting on silently with the domestic work of the house, was a traditional offence, and Chaucer himself is the reputed author of

> But for my daughter Julianne
> I would she were well bolted with a bridle
> That leaves her work to play the clack
> And lets her wheel stand idle.

In country districts husbands kept the brank hanging on a hook by the fireplace ready for immediate action. Other punishments visited on women for scolding or gossiping included 'riding the stang,' which consisted of being tied to a chair fastened to a long post which was repeatedly lowered into the village pond.

In the cities a popular entertainment for centuries was to go and laugh at the antics of lunatics kept chained in the Tower of London, and public hangings always drew eager spectators from all ranks of society.

Fisticuffs became an art as distinct from a common pastime as soon as it was taken up by the English gentry at the end of the eighteenth century. Instead of vulgar brawling strict rules were instituted, suitable dress and gloves devised, and approved stances developed, the new gentlemanly sport being assiduously practised in newly opened London gymnasiums. Lord Byron lent the sport the prestige of his name and fame, for he was a passionate devotee, though it was in his case not disinterested love of the art, but a frantic determination to sweat off his tendency to fat, and it was his custom at Newstead Abbey even in the hottest weather to box with one of his servants, enveloping himself first in a heavy Turkish pelisse to encourage perspiration. To demonstrate how refined and useful a pastime boxing had become ladies were invited to watch special displays of the art. Here is an extract from a poster advertising a "sham contest" staged in 1799:

MANLY SPORT 253

Mr Mendoza, the celebrated pugilist, will exhibit (in a sham contest with a practised pupil) his whole system of self-defence. They will appear in the same dress and muffles as worn by them when appearing by repeated desire in the presence of their Majesties and the Royal Family.

Ladies are most respectfully impressed that there is neither violence nor indecency in this Spectacle that can offend the most delicate of their Sex.

To the gentlemen it may ultimately prove *more than amusing* by initiating them into such Principles of the Science by which the Weak and Inoffensive are sometimes preserved from the Ruffian Assaults of the powerful Vulgar.

Most of the young London dandies who frequented the boxing gymnasiums came merely to stare and gossip and drink brandy with their friends. It was firmly believed in France, however, by the Anglophile enthusiasts that every moment when not actually on horseback the English gentleman spent in the gymnasium boxing furiously, and the dandies of Paris hurried to learn to chatter boxing jargon. Some, intent on acquiring all socially elevating pursuits of low life in the English manner, even went so far as to smoke pipes, according to Chateaubriand.

Béranger scored a bull's-eye with his parody on Anglomania and the cult of the boxing-glove:

> Quoique leurs chapeaux soient bien laids,
> God Dam! moi, j'aime les Anglais:
> Ils ont un si bon caractère;
> Comme ils sont polis et surtout
> Que leurs plaisirs sont de bon goût!
> > Non! Chez nous point
> > Point de ces coups de poing
> Qui font tant d'honneur en Angleterre!
>
> Anglais! il faut vous suivre en tout
> Pour les lois, la mode, et le goût,
> Même aussi pour l'art militaire!
> Vos diplomates, vos chevaux,
> N'ont pas épuisé nos bravos!
> > Mais NON, chez nous POINT
> > POINT DE CES COUPS de POING
> Qui font tant d'honneur en 'Angleterre!

Boxing never caught on in France, having nothing to catch on by. The dress or undress was of no interest either to the ladies or to the *tailleurs.* The régime and the rendezvous alike made no appeal to fashionable Paris society, and the dandies were glad to escape into other activities which they could do better—dancing, for instance, for in the art of dancing England still learned from France.

It was essential for the sons and daughters of successful English tradesmen to become socially adept at sports which admitted no suspicion in the minds of critical beholders that these young people were of vulgar origin. Aristocrats might consort with low-caste boxers in smoky saloons, but something more refined was essential for those whose foundations were less socially secure. Dancing was such a sport. It was safe, helpful in the storming of coveted social portals, and not so very difficult to learn how to do. It gave middle-class young ladies a chance to show off their expensive new gowns and middle-class young gentlemen a chance to show off their refinement and the modishly genteel fancy steps learned at considerable expense from one of the many establishments set up for this purpose all over England. They were of necessity very snobbish establishments, for on this depended their appeal. All claimed royal, or at least noble, patronage in their handbills. Here is Mr Duval's Academy advertisement from the Liverpool *Mercury* of 1817. Mr Duval, it may be mentioned, was no more French than his city.

> The QUADRILLES in the most fashionable stile of grace and Elegance as they are now danced in London, Bath, Paris, etc. *N.B.* Young Gentlemen who have not acquired a proper method of dancing he will engage to perfect fit for the First Assemblies in SIX LESSONS.

Dress was all-important. A gentlemen's manual of etiquette published in 1834 advises aspiring gentlemen:

> Always wear your gloves to a ball. Do not wear black or coloured gloves. Dance only from the hips downwards and lead the lady as lightly as you would tread a measure with a spirit of gossamer.

There was danger also in dancing too correctly, a practice which smacked of the six lessons from Mr Duval or one of his *confrères*:

> Don't dance *too* neatly either, unless you are ambitious of being taken for a dancing-master, between whom and to dance like a gentleman there is a great difference.

A little *tremolo* sentiment was not out of place in the ballroom:

> If a lady refuses to dance with you and dances with another do not be offended with her. We cannot always fathom the hidden springs which

influence a woman's actions and there are many bursting hearts within white satin dresses.

Precisely because dancing was such a helpful step in social climbing the leaders of English Society went to extreme lengths to keep their clubs exclusive. Almack's, the goal of every social aspirant, was the hardest nut to crack of the lot. It was, declared Captain Gronow,

> the Seventh Heaven of the fashionable world. Only 6 out of the 300 Foot Guard Officers managed to gain admittance and all sorts of intrigues were practised to get past the clique of ladies who ruled supreme.

Obligatory dress at Almack's in the year of Waterloo was knee-breeches, white cravat, and *chapeau bras,* a uniform already becoming *démodé* outside those sacred portals. As is well known, even the great Duke of Wellington himself was once denied admittance when he presented himself at the door dressed otherwise.

At Almack's they danced Scottish reels and English country dances, until in 1815 Lady Jersey introduced a sensational new dance from Paris called "the mazy waltz," which sent a shudder of horror through England, because the couples performing it danced in an embracing position. Lord Byron was one of the first to denounce it as an open invitation to outrage and rapine and wrote a satirical poem against it. It was generally felt that if the sexes did not learn to keep to their proper places in the ballroom neither would the classes keep to them in society. Anarchy was prophesied.

The history of nineteenth-century social life, indeed, is one long battle in the ballroom between those struggling to get in and those, having got in, struggling to keep the other strugglers out. Never are bonds drawn tighter than in times of social uncertainty, and in England these bonds were sometimes tangible.

"Nowhere," declares a book on etiquette published in 1884 (written by "a member of the aristocracy" and which quickly ran into eleven editions), "is class brought into more prominence than at a County Ball. At some balls a cord is drawn across the ballroom to render the upper end unassailable."

The author considered it a reflection on society that the cord should be necessary, adding, more kindly, "This extreme exclusiveness is not often resorted to, 'clique' or *class* being thoroughly maintained without its aid." Not only the dancers, but the dances were either 'in' or 'out.' "Some dances are of lower social rank than others. The *only* dances danced by *society* are Quadrilles, Lancers, Valses, the Highland Schottisch, the Highland Reel and the Polka." The rest were out. "Such dances as the Caledonians, the Mazurka, and the Prince Imperial Quadrilles are unknown in good society."

To make all quite clear the author indicates, in an elaborate note, the precise social divisions of 1884. It makes interesting reading, and should be compared with lines of social demarcation of different periods. First royalty, then the nobility, then the gentry (the progress of nineteenth-century industrial fortunes may be gauged by the detail the author feels it necessary to add at this point).

> By the word GENTRY is included the LANDED GENTRY, all those belonging to the ARMY, the NAVY, the CLERGY, the BAR, the MEDICAL and other PROFESSIONS, the ARISTOCRACY OF ART, the ARISTOCRACY OF WEALTH, MERCHANT PRINCES and the leading CITY MERCHANTS and BANKERS.

The other ranks he specifies as being rigorously excluded from good society include the "lower professional classes, the middle classes, the lower middle classes and the lower classes."

This was a clear trumpet-call to the other ranks to make haste to make enough money to qualify as *leading city merchants* if not actual *merchant princes*, and to spare no effort to bring up their sons in the expectation of slipping in quietly by the professional back door, as rectors or doctors.

UNKATAHE, PROPHYLACTIC
GODDESS
North American Indian.

ETHIOPIAN GOOD-LUCK
CHARM
Cross with divine face.
Contemporary.
Musée de l'Homme, Paris

Among the high-ranking diversions enjoyed by men seeking distraction, drinking, smoking, and gambling occupy perhaps the premier place. Brandy and *chemin de fer* in a cloud of cigar smoke or mild-and-bitter and football pools in a fug of cheap tobacco—the same instinct obtains. There is no doubt that men love to get away from women and relax among themselves in their own way, and this is their favourite way.

Gambling appears to have been commonly practised in "ordinaries" in England in the reign of James I, gallants and men of the town using these ordinaries as clubs, and it was later precisely in the famous London clubs that the gambling mania of the eighteenth century reached its zenith. White's, the Cocoa Tree, Boodle's, and the rest, all kept heavy betting books. The acme of distinction was to stake an enormous bet on the most trivial incident and lose—or, indeed, win—without displaying the slightest emotion. It was an exercise in futility and self-control, and as such made an immense impression on visiting foreigners, so much so that the Jockey Club later on modelled itself and its betting manners exactly on these examples of English sangfroid.

When General Scott (father-in-law of the politician George Canning) won £200,000 at White's, playing whist on one occasion, by keeping sober and using his brains, two points which his adversaries neglected, it was regarded as not quite gentlemanly. Marshal Blücher, a confirmed gambler, lost even more caste for failing to behave like a gentleman, because he looked daggers at the croupier and swore in German when he lost at the gaming-tables.

Gentlemen dressed meticulously for their nightly gambling bouts, though such addicts as Charles James Fox and his particular cronies often turned their fine coats inside out, and sometimes darkened their faces as well, to cheat a run of bad luck.

Gambling brought many wealthy aristocratic English families to bankruptcy, a process which went all the faster because it was modish for ladies to gamble as well as gentlemen, if separately no less passionately. Most of the English nobility were obliged, therefore, to keep their finest jewels in pawn, only redeeming them temporarily for important social occasions. Lord Thanet, whose income was never less than £50,000 a year, lost every farthing of it at the gaming-tables. In Paris in 1815 he used to play on at the tables at the Salon des Étrangers long after the rooms had closed down for the night. He would play on with anybody who would bet with him on anything, chicken hazard or écarté for preference. One night he lost £120,000 at a single session.

When Parliament passed an Act in 1739 prohibiting by name faro, basset, hazard, and ace of hearts, Bath, then the fashionable gambling centre for Society, was outraged. It was soon found quite easy, however, to evade the gambling laws by the invention of different games with different names, and these served admirably until Parliament passed another anti-gambling Act in 1740, this time forbidding all games of chance involving numbers, and this time involving the inventor also in the penalties incurred in breaking the law. But England is never more

I

ingenious than in circumventing restrictions on her liberty to gamble, and the reply to this piece of legislation was the invention of two new gambling games which did not need numbers, one being known as "Roly-poly" and the other "Marlborough's Battles." These two games of chance brought a gush of life back to Bath, which lived largely on its gaming-tables.

Most popular of all the new games which took the place of those forbidden by law was one known as E O (Even and Odd), which simply substituted letters for numbers, the bank taking $2\frac{1}{2}$ per cent. of every bet.

But the Puritanical element in England was sufficiently strong in Parliament to make itself heard, and in 1745 still another anti-gambling Act was forced through, forbidding all games of chance *except card games* and making keepers of gambling-houses, and every one there present, equally guilty in case of contravention of the law and equally liable to be convicted.

At this cruel blow to their favourite recreation the nobility withdrew into their town houses and behind the windows of their London clubs, there to gamble wildly in privacy on such subjects as the Act could not cover, as, for instance, the virtue of a certain lady, the colour of hair of the next man to pass the club windows, and the sex of the next child to be born into the family.

If Bath was undone without its gaming-tables, foreign cities were in a happier situation, and then began the long story of English gambling in casinos abroad, a story which has not yet reached an end. Card games after 1745 had to suffice gamblers in the London clubs, and they managed to lose their fortunes well enough this way. The great Duke of Wellington, for instance, almost sacrificed his military career, for in his youth he lost so much money by gambling that he was about to sell his Army commission and retire from the military life in an effort to pay off his card debts. He was, in fact, only able to remain in the Army because Lord Camden settled his gambling debts for him and gave him enough money to go abroad, and he wisely took himself off to study profitably at the military college at Angers.

Dandies bored with card games bet on anything at all. Ball Hughes managed to lose immense sums of money at battledore and shuttlecock. In the years of the Regency the only exercise a London dandy took was from the card tables of White's to the card tables of Crockford's, and from Crockford's back again to White's. And it was gambling that eventually ruined that shrewd and hard-headed leader of the London dandies, George Brummell, not the disfavour of the Prince of Wales, for at the time of his ruin Brummell was actually considered of more social importance than the Prince.

Gamblers, like sailors and bull-fighters, are particularly prone to superstition, and superstitions connected with gambling are numerous and very deep-rooted, concerning themselves with numbers and colours that reach backward into the beginnings of astrology. Clothes are also of immense significance to gamblers. Certain garments, by association, are lucky or are unlucky, and accordingly must or must not be worn. So are charms and coins. Brummell blamed his ruin on the fact that he had lost his lucky sixpence.

Present-day American gamblers traditionally hate a two-dollar bill. They call it a *deuce* (slang for "devil"). To take away the curse they tear off a corner, thus making a triangle which equals three, a lucky and beneficent number regarded as excellent counter-magic. Sometimes gamblers tear off all four corners, the better to propitiate unkind Fate, or take another way out by passing the bill on quickly to another person, thus making a hand-on chain of magic, the fifth recipient being supposed to destroy the unlucky money-bill. But often cashiers in restaurants who are given two-dollar bills kiss them instead to kill the bad luck, saliva being universally regarded as a powerful magic disinfectant against the Devil.

EGYPTIAN AMULET: EYE
OF HORUS
Blue stone.
Fitzwilliam Museum, Cambridge

CORAL CHARMS AGAINST THE EVIL EYE
The extended fingers represent the devil's
horns. Italy and Switzerland.
Contemporary.
Musée de l'Homme, Paris

Gambling is no less popular to-day if the means are different. Football-pools entries choke the post-offices on sending-in day, necessitating the engagement of extra staff to avoid the delay of regular mail. Fruit-machines absorb the wages of millions of the Western world's youth, and the proprietor of a contemporary Californian slot-machine parlour told me recently that some of his regular clients were so hypnotized by the practice that they habitually gambled with two fruit-machines at the same time, using both hands simultaneously. Even family Monopoly or Ludo with the children takes on a brighter aspect the moment some one introduces, as some one always does sooner or later, stakes of match-sticks or boiled sweets.

The traditional and habitual accompaniment of gambling is drinking, and in the eighteenth century and a good part of the nineteenth every gentleman got drunk.

Even the Muslims, whose religion forbids alcohol, enjoy drinking-bouts, and Sir Richard Burton noted that they dressed up specially for such occasions.

When Easterns sit down to a drinking-bout, which means getting drunk as speedily and pleasantly as possible, they put off dresses of dull colours and robe themselves in clothes supplied by their host of the brightest he may have, especially yellow, green and red of different shades.

At the same time that a village lout was clapped into the stocks or the 'drunkard's cloak' for being intoxicated it was regarded as positive bad form in the top ranks of English society for two centuries after the Restoration for gentlemen not to drink to excess. Port-drinkers in the eighteenth century were then four- or even five-bottle men, and the only thing that prevented more deaths from alcoholic poisoning than actually occurred was the fact that port was customarily drunk slowly and from small glasses.

This addiction to port and brandy gave a smart impetus to smuggling, affected the shape of bottles and containers and even the cut of certain articles of male dress, for smugglers (some of whom were gentlemen themselves or parsons or other respected members of the community), employed such devices as double-containers of flattened Bristol glass, which could be carried inconspicuously inside a fold in the shirt or inside hidden pockets specially sewn in the rear thigh of the breeches or into the tail of the coat. Walking-sticks too, which were of all shapes, high and elegant and shorter and thicker, were often made hollow to contain smuggled brandy.

The lower classes liked their alcohol too, and one of the chief grievances they nourished against the Puritans was the forcible closing down of the village taverns, which after the Restoration reopened to brisk business again. By the nineteenth century the amount of alcohol consumed in England from the top of society to the lowest dregs was prodigious. Harvest Home was a favourite occasion in the country for intemperance, and Hogarth's Gin Lane had changed only in so far as the city gin-shops had turned into gin-palaces, where there were glitter and mirrors, warmth and raucous music, to console the wretched for the misery outside them. Even in respectable middle-class families the amount of alcohol consumed was amazing. Mrs Beeton is lavish in her daily family quotas of every kind of beer, wine, and spirit. There also appears to have been a considerable amount of secret drinking by respectable married English women during the greater part of the nineteenth century, and no doubt the frequent medicine-bottles were laced with alcohol.

The Earl of Athlone, gallantly undertaking the task of reforming the alcoholic propensities of the Eastern counties of England in 1855, declared:

> The great stain on the social life of England among the humble classes has been drunkenness. It is the bottle which is the cause of three-fifths of the crime and poverty and misery perpetrated or endured by the English peasant or artisan.

ETRUSCAN WINE-GOBLET
Clay.
Louvre

His Grace then quoted the opinion of eminent judges (themselves doubt-less no strangers to the pleasures of the best vintages) who vowed that at least three-quarters of the crime which came before them was caused by drinking. He proceeded to say:

> The East Anglians have hitherto been in the habit of displaying their gratitude to the Almighty for His abounding mercy by getting beastly drunk. It seems possible, however, to give another direction to the simple piety of these grateful rustics.

This direction, after much earnest consideration, his Grace decided, would best be achieved by gathering some thousands of agricultural labourers together for a gigantic tea-drinking, after which the noble Earl himself addressed them at length on the evils of alcohol. Not a few of the grateful rustics, however, proved to be of the same opinion as William Cobden, who denounced tea-drinking as utterly poisonous.

The Times, declaring the following year that "drinking lies at the base of the British Constitution" and that "the drinkers of strong drinks will always outnumber, outwit, outface, and outdo those who do not drink and will always dominate over the tea-drinkers," reported with much satisfaction that Mr Barkeley, M.P. for Bristol, had received from his constituents "a box of church oak, set with brilliants and worth a thousand guineas, for the zeal and ability he had displayed against a Bill for the further closing of public-houses on Sunday."

SMOKING

"Tobacco is essential to the proper enjoyment of
drinking." From *Illustrierte Flugblatt* (seventeenth
century).

There are people alive to-day who can remember wild, gin-drunk fights which took place almost nightly outside the city public-houses, fights in which not only men, but also women took part, using their long hatpins as weapons, so that the police were afraid to interfere. To-day some public-houses do not admit women, not because they fear it is no place for them, but rather to keep the club atmosphere free from female intrusion, for the essential quality of the English pub is its clubbability, and men do not go there to get drunk with all speed, but to pass a pleasantly relaxed evening with their friends.

Correct male wear in the pub is the hat, whether it be the bowler of the city man or the cap of the labourer. Even with shirt-sleeves rolled up and no jacket, the hat should stay on the head.

The pleasures of smoking are such that the consumption of tobacco to-day all over the world is nothing short of stupendous, and even dire warnings by the medical profession that heavy cigarette-smoking is likely to end in lung cancer are apparently making no difference whatever to the sales of cigarettes. Cigarettes have become an essential opiate no less than an essential manual fidget impossible, it appears, to give up in our nervy atom era.

Sir Walter Raleigh, introducing tobacco into England from America, where the Redskins had taught the practice of smoking to the early colonists, incidentally supplied the British Exchequer with one of its most profitable taxable imports. James I, who loathed the habit of smoking but needed the money, soon issued a proclamation forbidding tobacco to be grown in England or imported from anywhere else but Bermuda and Virginia, his object being not to help the struggling colonists, but to facilitate the Collection of the Revenue.

Charles II followed this up by enacting legislation directing the sheriff of every district to root out any tobacco plants found growing, for tobacco, as many English people found during the deprivations of the Second World War, is not at all difficult to grow in England, despite the lack of dependable sunshine, though it is not easy to cure, and can as easily be grown even in moist Ireland, where agents of the Crown forcibly stopped its cultivation in 1837.

The English revenue in tobacco tax in 1688 was above £400,000, and by 1857 had grown into more than £5,000,000, though women then scarcely smoked at all. To-day it has risen to somewhere near £670,000,000. It would be reasonable to suppose that so widespread and deep-rooted a social addiction would have developed its own distinctive dress, and in former times, especially the nineteenth century, this was indeed so.

In the early nineteenth century smoking was a romantic male pastime, but one or two daring and outstanding women such as George Sand were smokers too. George Sand liked small cigars and even enjoyed a pipe.

Smoking was regarded as romantic in the extreme, and it was not Virginian but Turkish tobacco that was preferred, hookahs, when procurable, being the extremist *chic*. In *Endymion*, published in 1880, Benjamin Disraeli described a contemporary cigar-divan thus:

> ... a capacious saloon well lit and fitted up with low broad sofas fixed against the walls, on which were seated or reclining persons, chiefly smoking cigars but not a few practising with the Hookah or other oriental modes.

Naturally, such cigar-divans, attracting away eligible young men, were not very popular with the other sex, who were, of course, excluded, and to build up the prestige and attractions of domesticated life married ladies hastened to install a smoking-room for husband and sons and friends in their houses. They declared that it was in order to spare the drawing-room curtains from the ravages of tobacco smoke that they did so, but, since the drawing-room curtains, like all the other curtains and upholstery in the house, were continually subjected to much worse damage from ordinary city smog and the smoke from domestic fires, we may guess that it was a subterfuge, intended to keep their men at home somehow. Now that they had a room to smoke in, the question of what costume to smoke in became of deep concern, and all the fashion-books of the nineteenth

SMOKING-PIPE OF CARVED
FISHBONE
Yakonta tribe (Arctic). Contemporary.

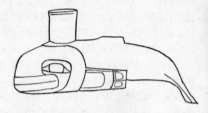

PIPE CARVED IN FORM OF WHALE
Tlingit Indians, Alaska.
Museum of Natural History, New York

century devote pages to fancy designs for smoking-*peignoirs* for modish gentlemen, smoking-jackets, smoking-waistcoats, smoking-slippers, and especially smoking-caps, for not only was tobacco smoke declared harmful to the hair, but the Oriental association of the *tubeteka* proved irresistible. A smoking-cap was the perfect present for a young lady to embroider for her fiancé or intimate relation of the male sex, or even for the curate.

Instructions in 1880 for embroidering one such smoking-cap in an all-over pattern of writhing tobacco leaves included the use of twenty-four skeins of green silk, sixty yards of heavy gold thread, besides "a ball of twine such as is usually used for tying up parcels and a handsome green and gold tassel." To be correctly attired for a session in his smoking-room, either alone or in the company of a crony or two, a gentleman would get himself up in a long exotic 'Persian' robe, a heavily embroidered and tasselled smoking-cap, and rich Turkish slippers with toes turned up. For two generations this mode persisted, and in the eighteen-nineties we find Sherlock Holmes and his familiar, good Dr Watson, retiring together into the Doctor's smoking-room, muffled in *peignoirs* and caps, to indulge in a bout of their favourite weed.

The smoking-room, indeed, did not fade from English domestic life until women began to smoke seriously themselves, which happened during the 1914 War, when so many former social taboos were flung aside. Since then not only do as many women appear to smoke as men, but smoking has become incessant, so that no office, factory, theatre, cinema, or home is free from the narcotic. Men and women alike smoke in the street—and even in railway carriages reserved for non-smokers; he who has the courage to point this fact out to cigarette-puffers will merely provoke an outraged stare. There is no longer any dress for smoking in, since every dress is used, from nightgowns and pyjamas for smoking in bed, through every change of the day's clothes for work or play; and every room in the house has become the smoking-room.

This must be regarded as still another defeat for man, for where has he left to go now to escape from women, an essential escape if he wishes to assert his masculinity? No smoking-room, no immunity from women in pubs, nor in universities, nor in the House of Commons. Even the sacrosanct Inns of Court have no longer been able to stem the tide, but have had to admit women members.

There are practically no sports to-day in which women do not join. The most popular sports, say Lillywhites, of London, are archery and underwater diving. Archery is popular because it is not too expensive for modestly paid employees to keep up, and has the further advantages that it can be practised all the year round, has satisfactorily romantic associations and agreeable dress which doesn't cost too much. The green suit with white shirt pleases both sexes, and the jargon is splendidly esoteric.

Deep-sea diving is still an expensive sport, as British waters are too cold and too cloudy, so that the would-be diver must take a journey to warmer coasts before he can begin. The equipment too is expensive compared to that of archery. Nevertheless deep-sea diving is an exciting sport rapidly increasing in popularity, for equipment may be hired, and the seabed, once attained, is free to all comers. The costume is simplicity itself, the merest bathing-slip and goggles, to which must be added an air-supply and perhaps flippers, a harpoon, or a movie-camera. The very simplicity of the costume has worried the sports-dress manufacturers, who have already been instrumental in introducing all-over rubber costumes to keep out the cold and to add to the complication whereby prestige and cost are simultaneously raised.

The once barbarously cruel British now lead the world in animal-observation societies, whose deadliest weapon is a camera. Of all these societies the British Birdwatching Society has the greatest number of members. We can also claim flourishing Butterfly and Fish Societies and an honourable Society of Snail-watchers. None of these societies so far has required a special sports dress, old tweeds being preferred, but not tweeds so old as to be remarked, the ideal being to slip unnoticed into the bosom of Nature without the creatures to be watched being alerted to watch their watchers.

The growth of spectator sports, stimulated by radio and T.V. is enormous. Instead of dozens of people watching a cock-fight we now have thousands watching greyhound-racing, and millions watching

THE ESSJEE 'AQUALUNG' STANDARD MODEL
(now modified to give improved performance)
"The 'Standard' Aqualung consists of a single 1200 litre (40 cubic feet) cylinder, with the demand valve (reducer unit mounted directly on the cylinder valve) incorporating the well-known Cousteau Gagnan patents. This set has an endurance for normal light activity in 10 or 12 ft. water of approximately 40 minutes. The apparatus consists of one steel cylinder, one demand valve/reducer unit, breathing pipes, mouthpiece and noseclip, carrying harness, pressure gauge and tube and a standard set of tools and spares.

By courtesy of Lillywhites, Piccadilly Circus, London

boxing, racing, and ice-sports. Instead of playing football themselves for their old school club, or cricket on their village green, a generation has grown up whose sport is all done for them by others and whose rôle is not merely to look on, but to look on from a long distance away.

The remotely controlled mass sport of looking on is becoming a world phenomenon. Crouching in darkness in stuffy living-rooms (and families living in only one room often have television), our youths to-day are enjoying vicarious triumphs of bodily skill and manly courage. It is a dream existence for millions who take absolutely no exercise themselves beyond the couple of steps necessary to reach the television set and the action of stooping down to turn the knob.

CHAPTER ELEVEN

MILITARY GLAMOUR

Cavalry has always been celebrated over the Infantry for its advantage in screening and new-fronting a bad figure, a reason why the younger branches of noble families intended for the army always go into it. There an insignificant head is hidden under a martial plumed helmet. The coat, padded well in every direction to sit perfect, whilst it is rendered small at the waist by means of stays or a belt, as the former term should never be uttered by ears polite.

Manual of Dress and Deportment, by a Cavalry Officer (1830)

BIOLOGISTS tell us that the branching antlers of the stag are not sexual lures, but are purely aggressive in Nature's intent. They tell us that the doe, far from patiently awaiting the outcome of the battle between two of her suitors and then meekly following the victor, takes no notice whatever of the battle, not infrequently, indeed, trotting off during the progress of the battle with a third suitor, who may well be an undersized stag with but a poor spread of antlers. The stag, in fact, gives battle, not for the female he wants, but for his territorial rights.

Once firmly established on his undisputed terrain, the stag will then devote his attention to the task of satisfying his urge to mate. But not until then. Similarly with birds, fish, insects — all living creatures except reckless man. The very plants in the earth are impelled by natural forces to struggle to overcome other

HANNIBAL CROSSING THE ALPS
French, Middle Ages. Illuminated manuscript.
Yale University Library

claimants to their fragment of soil before seeking to propagate themselves.

We two-legged biological specimens must rid ourselves of much cherished sentiment if we wish truly to understand Nature. The divine song of the nightingale on summer evenings, contrary to poetic belief, is not the yearning plaint of the lover at all, but the warning cry of the aggressive cock-bird on patrol. The scarlet buttocks of the male baboon are so painted by Nature, not to entice female baboons, but to intimidate other male baboons who venture near his bit of the jungle.

The gorgeous spread of the peacock's lavish-eyed tail, intensified by the characteristic *frison* ruffling the iridescent plumes, is not provoked by the presence of the pea-hen, who remains unmoved by his display even when she happens to be present, but by the presence of another peacock near his home ground. The peacock, in fact, is trying, not to attract a wife, but to frighten his enemy off his territory, and his gorgeous panoply is not a wedding garment, as Darwin was inclined to think, but a gladiator's vestment.

The pea-hen takes absolutely no notice of his displaying. We do not even know, it may be observed, what the pea-hen sees when she looks at the peacock. Her vision is certainly not the same as human vision, nor is she in the slightest degree likely to be affected by what humans understand as beauty in the same way as are humans. What we do know for certain is that until the peacock has established a secure home she will not be approached by the peacock with intention to mate. For in the animal world the acquisiton of territory always precedes the desire to satisfy the instinct to procreate, the natural order being first the home, then the babies.

In this respect the animal world is considerably more prudent than the human world, which, after thousands of years of experiment, has not yet solved this tricky problem. There is no Welfare State in Nature, no foundling hosptals, no deliberate exposure of female babies to save dowries. Parents must prepare all beforehand. Den, lair, nest, must all be ready waiting for the offspring, and before all else the potential father must struggle for *Lebensraum*. This is a wise provision on the part of Nature, ensuring, in a world of terrible hazard, enough living-room for the home and the provison of food for the babies before they are summoned into the world.

Nature, however, in providing male animals with aggressive weapons to win themselves necessary living-room, not infrequently overreaches herself. Sometimes the branching antlers of the stag grow to such magnificence that they wear down and exhaust their owner. Often enough such splendid antlers become inextricably locked in combat with the equally splendid antlers of a rival, so that both warriors starve to death. The proudest peacock can be seen to falter and stagger beneath the weight of his aggressively spread fan, which, if it has not frightened off the enemy peacock by its display, will certainly prove to be an active impediment in physical battle.

So too man, when he girds himself for battle (which, whatever the official pretext, is always to acquire territories and loot or the political power which will confer them), tends to embellish himself to the detriment of his military performance. Like the lesser creatures, his military dress is intended to make him look like a conquering hero and frighten his enemy.

HATS WORN WITH ARMOUR
Portugal, fourteenth century.

Battle dress, as we have known it in the last two world wars, is a machine-age phenomenon concerned with camouflage, not aggressive display, and as such has never been popular either with the troops or with the civilians. Since he is asked to offer his life the soldier would prefer a handsomer sacrificial garment. Modern wars, moreover, are waged equally against civilians and women and children no less than against men. It would be logical, therefore, to clap all the civilians as well as the troops into handsome uniforms to bolster up morale in modern wars; and it will be recalled that the tin hat in the 1939 War became no less essential civilian than military wear.

Protection of the fighting-man is not the real purpose of military uniform, as every sergeant knows, and it can, if this aspect is too greatly stressed, even be highly destructive of morale. The valiant soldiers of the crack regiments in the English Civil War scoffed at cuirass and helmet as effeminate, and preferred to fight without them. The cavalry, who sometimes weakened so far as to protect their heads with iron skull-caps, were careful to hide them inside their hats. The odd bits of old armour the Roundheads sometimes conjured up were, it would appear, worn for *panache*, not for protection. Similarly the High Command of the German Army did eventually produce bullet-proof vests for its troops towards the end of the First World War, but not until its manpower was running desperately low.

The high morale every army officer would like to see in his troops consists of disdain of death, not reliance on safety precautions, and the historic recipe for this high morale has been to dress the part by emphasizing martial swagger. The classical plumed helmet (for show, not for real protection) worn above the sword-defying naked breast remains our ideal of the gallant warrior. For if the gallant warrior is too well protected where is his gallantry? According to Pliny, the pre-Roman Briton wore a rough coat and trousers of brightly striped and chequered stuff over which he flung a felt cloak so hard and closely woven as to be all but sword-proof. When he fought, however, protective cloak and jacket were thrown aside, and he hurled himself upon the Roman invader naked from the waist up, fearsomely tattooed with patterns in blue woad.

Armour, when it was introduced into warfare, was certainly worn more for prestige than protection, and *had to be vulnerable somewhere*, at its highest point of development, in order to get wars started at all, for two warriors facing each other, each encased in armour so perfected and chink-proof as to be utterly invulnerable, would have meant stalemate. When armour, in fact, did reach a high degree of protection new weapons, such as gunpowder, were introduced to overcome this impasse.

From all historic records, however, it is clear that armour, though satisfactory in presenting an aggressive appearance, was often more of an impediment on the field of battle than a saviour. Armour was hot and heavy. It rusted. It was difficult to get into and sometimes impossible to get out of. It frequently had the effect of doubling instead of parrying the force of a blow. And there was no armour ever worn which could not be penetrated. Yet because it was costly, a noble vestment capable of the most grandiose embellishment, and a glittering prize for looters, it occupied a high place in the panoply of war.

The corpse of Charles de Blois, taken from the battlefield after the battle of Auray in 1364, was dressed in a padded pourpoint gorgeously embroidered with ducat gold thread and fastening with thirty-four buttons made from precious stones, looped into green silk buttonholes, each sleeve separately attached with elaborate jewelled points, and this handsome dress was soaked through with blood from the sixteen severe wounds his costly armour, worn over the dress, had not saved him from receiving.

It must be remembered that in wars earlier than those of our own times no one was in a hurry. Show-off was an essential element, and the feasts of colour and brave display were at least as important as the actual fighting. The slow preparation of silken tents and splendid banners, the organization and the fastidious erection of whole cities of showy paraphernalia, held up the moment of engagement for months and even years. Prestige was the first consideration, and prestige demanded princely show-off on both sides. History records one bravely decked Italian battle, fought during the Middle Ages, which lasted seventy-two hours, finally producing a total of eight casualties, of which three were caused by knights suffocating in their own armour.

BATTLE DRESS IN ACTION
Battle of Judas Maccabeus with Timotheus. Wall-painting. Fourteenth century.
St Stephen's, House of Commons

GERMAN SOLDIER, LATE FOURTEENTH CENTURY
From painted wooden altarpiece of Apocalypse.
Victoria and Albert Museum

Only the greatest nobles and richest lords could afford to wear the finest armour, which at its peak of glory was, indeed, worth a king's ransom, gold, silver, and precious jewels being lavishly employed in its artifice. Lesser lordlings wore plainer armour, and often only portions of armour—sometimes inherited and thoroughly out of date. The rabble of soldiery often fought barefoot, and frequently without proper weapons.

While the desire for sport and manly distraction spurred on the noblemen engaging in these wars, the hope of ransom money and loot also played a considerable part. The chance of looting rich armour and costly horse-armour, the capture of many prisoners, who could be profitably sold into slavery if not important enough to be ransomed, made wars a profitable risk, and for the younger sons of great families offered their only chance of earning an honourable living, since war (and hunting, which is mimic war) was the only occupation not considered beneath their social status.

Captured commoners had been sold as slaves since history began. British slaves were sold in the Roman slave-markets in Cæsar's time, and English slaves in the eleventh century tilled the ground in Scotland and France, and vice versa. There were enough Christian slaves captured by Turks in the long religious wars to form entire regiments, for these Mamelukes were esteemed as good warriors by their captors.

Captured nobles, on the other hand, though they had to be treated with the respect and dignity due to their rank, were the greatest haul. The actual amount of ransom demanded being a delicate question necessitating much jockeying and adjustment, with prestige overbalancing prudence, noble captives had to be ransomed often enough for more than they were actually worth in the eyes of their ransomers. It is recorded that Du Guesclin, on being taken prisoner, proudly fixed his own ransom at a fabulous figure, replying, when the Prince of Wales expressed a doubt whether so vast a sum could be raised in France to ransom him, that he looked to the Kings of France and Castile to open their coffers, plus a hundred friends who would sell their estates to raise the money, vowing that not a woman in all France but would be honoured to spin for his deliverance.

Sometimes the ransom was not forthcoming, or delayed for years, and French lords wilted in chilly English castles, an irritation to their host no doubt, if a source of lively interest to their hostess, and vice versa; English barons fumed and grumbled in remote French castles, imbibing something of the Gallic way of life willynilly. In such devious ways does culture spread and gentlemen copy secrets of dress and adornment from one another.

Ransoms were worth waiting years for, and laid the foundation of many fortunes, not a few famous French and English estates being set up and handsomely equipped with castles and furnishings during the long years of war between the two countries—Sudeley Castle, in Gloucestershire, for instance.

By a Statute of Henry V, the booty of war was ordered to be carefully divided between the participants; one-third was to be given to the King's officers, of which one part had to be set aside towards the ransoming of prisoners, and the remaining two-thirds was to go to the Crown. The amounts involved were enormous, £10,000 (then worth fantastically more) being the basic ransom for a fairly important personage (King John of France, had he been captured at Poitiers, was marked at £20,000), and national economies could be upset by the many districts sweating unprofitably to raise the huge sums demanded as ransom for their captured lords, after a defeat.

Armour is an admirable illustration of the objective of military dress, which is to make the wearer look taller, stronger, and more frightening than he actually is, *and to make him feel so himself.* It boosts the wearer's own morale at the same time as it undermines the morale of his opponent.

The fortunate fact that armour outlasts silk, velvet, and leather has enabled us to see for ourselves the many extravagances of fancy that generations of skilled European armourers lavished on the armour they forged, for use both on the field of battle and in the tilting-yard. Every

SARACEN BRONZE HELMET DAMASCENED
IN SILVER WITH PERSIAN MOTIFS
Wadi Keren.
Acre Museum, Israel

foible in the male fashions of the day was faithfully repeated in steel. Slashings, cuttings, apple-pie borders, piked shoes, duck-bill toes, the cod-piece, the peascod belly, all found their way into armour. In an age when engineering was still in its infancy highly technical skill was employed in the forging and embellishing of steel which was sometimes enriched with inlays of silver and, for the glorification of great personages, whole suits of armour were worked entirely of silver inlaid with gold, and even precious jewels.

Articulated joining demanded a particularly high degree of technical skill, and was employed both for human and equine armour, the latter often being far more costly than the former. Worn together with stately valances brightly emblazoned with the lord's heraldic bearings, it made a brave show, and also offered an excellent target, which was considered to be of less importance than the brave showing.

The theatrical element could not be too greatly stressed, and extravagances were admired in proportion to their exaggeration. King Henry VIII, in one of his many military helmets wore plumes four and a half feet long, plucked from the tail of an Indian bird.

Helmets offered a perfect opportunity for braggadocio, and were wrought in rich and fanciful styles. One made in Milan in 1540 embodies a gold-embossed visor in the form of a lion's head. A steel morion of Italian make (1580) now in the Fitzwilliam Museum in Cambridge is not only embellished with a high steel cockscomb, but also etched all over with military trophies. Part of the boasting was the plume, which added to the height of the wearer and at the same time, by its dancing movements, added a touch of arrogance and *panache*. All the helmets, until right at the end of their history, were forged with a special tube at the back to hold the plume or plumes.

If Italian armourers excelled at handsome shapes and delicate inlay, German armourers preferred weight and solidity. One German two-handed sword forged in 1550 is seven feet high, and must have been difficult even for two men to lift. A German conceit, too, is a double-edged sword, undulated like the edge of a bread-knife, richly gilded and engraved with a gallows, for special use in military executions.

Such armour and such equipment, together with extravagant arms, tents, and furnishings, made wars no less bedevilled with debt in the Middle Ages than they are to-day, though it is true they offered more of a treat for the eyes, and did much less damage. King Henry V spent so much money on the equipment of his wars that his army was often never paid at all, and the very carrier of his splendid banners at Agincourt, according to Hobbes, was obliged to petition the King's successor for reimbursement of the great expenses he had incurred during the campaign, having received not a farthing either of salary or of reward for his pains.

Until the mechanized wars of the twentieth century protection always took second place to display, as we have seen, and camouflage in military dress hardly existed. Military uniforms were worn in battle which were not only so eye-catching as positively to invite sword-thrusts and bullets, but were in addition so non-functional as actively to hamper the soldier from fighting properly. Such impossibly gallant dress, we may be sure, was approved in the shrewd belief that danger is the best stimulant to courage; that the more a soldier's dress made him visible to the enemy the greater determination would he therefore feel to acquit himself bravely; and the more his dress hampered his movements in action, the greater exertion would he make to surpass himself in gallantry.

To the luxurious dress of the French nobility on the field of battle the Church attributed their defeat at Crécy, the chronicler of St Denis declaring:

> We must believe that God suffered this to happen because of our sins, for pride had grown so swollen in France, above all amongst the nobility. Arrogant also the immodesty of the dress seen everywhere about the Kingdom.

Some of the garments they chose to trail on to the field of battle, he protested, were so heavily pleated on hips and thighs that they made their wearers look like women; others had over-long sleeves dragging on the ground, better suited to jugglers than honest men; and some of the youthful noblemen wore tunics so short that they did not even reach, still less cover, the buttocks. "And for this it is no marvel that God desired to chastise the excesses of the French by his whip, the King of England."

The chronicler omitted to mention one important point about the defeat, and that was that the English noblemen were wearing garments just as extravagant, immodest, and impractical. In the opinion of another, perhaps more cynical French writer, there was another purpose than display in the abbreviated tunics worn by both sides. "These *seigneurs*," he scoffed, "had themselves dressed short and light the easier to flee before the enemy." Philippe de Mésières protested that the extravagant costumes worn as uniforms by Gallic noblemen "upset the digestion, compressed the stomach, and let in the cold." Urban V added his papal disapproval to the condemnation by the Emperor Charles of long piked shoes. "still more of a menace to reason and modesty on the field of battle than off it," denouncing them as "a deformity conceived in derision of God and the Holy Church."

But all these condemnations were of no avail. Though they lost battle after battle, and believed God chose to take sides with the English because He was angered at their finery, they did not moderate their flaunting dress. On the contrary, the fashions were pushed to still greater extremes, for there is no more conspicuous place for gentlemen to feel themselves the cynosure of all eyes than the field of battle.

Officers, whose special task it is to set an example of cool courage to their troops, have always worn notably showy uniforms. On the other hand the common soldier, whose duty it is to obey orders and ask no questions, has been obliged to wear whatever his lord, or C.O., or reluctant War office could be induced to provide, and frequently he has worn what, strictly speaking, can not be described as uniform at all, but simply odds and ends of unrelated items of dress which he has looted for himself, or cobbled from enemy banners, or stripped from the dead after the battle.

It was not until the noble commandants of the eighteenth and early nineteenth centuries came to look upon their regiments as private play-things and amused themselves designing dashing uniforms to look splendid on parade that some of the rank and file at last achieved smart uniforms. The resulting eye-catching uniforms pleased the ladies and may have helped recruiting. What Swift called the "passion for a scarlet coat" made uniform a social asset totally unconnected with the boredom and danger of actual military engagement. James Boswell, who for long had tried by every means in his power to get himself a commission in the Army, so that a dashing uniform could help him to conquer London socially, abruptly ceased to do so on learning that such a commission might necessitate his being sent into action overseas—just as Beau Brummell, perhaps the worst officer the British Army ever had, resigned his com-mission as soon as his regiment was ordered to serve in a North-country town, away from the delights of the London season.

So long as soldiers were not actually fighting there seemed no limit to the fantasy permitted and even encouraged in their uniforms; indeed, as English dress for men became dull and uninspiring it was precisely in the Army that the sartorial glamour, suppressed outside it, displayed itself most imaginatively. What was impossible and in bad taste to wear in civilian dress was not only possible but positively gentlemanly to wear in uniform, and the brilliant colours, tassels, and gold braid the Industrial Revolution swept out of everyday life were swept into military uniform, the last stand of gallant British male dress.

This worked admirably and still works, until there is war, and it is in between wars, when brilliantly clad soldiers have little to do except dazzle and escort the ladies, that military uniforms blossom like hot-house flowers—grow brighter, tighter, more heavily braided and tasselled and gallooned and buttoned, until they seem only designed for the last act of *opéra bouffe*. It is in between wars that military trousers are cut progres-sively tighter until they are impossible to manœuvre in, uniform sleeves cut narrower and narrower until the soldier wearing them cannot raise his rifle, military caps shrink until they become too small and too flat to remain on the head at all, or so enormously swollen out that they fall over the eyes and obscure vision.

The brave dress of the Household Brigade, which pleases the tourist no less than it pleases every British citizen, is essentially peace-time uniform. The bearskin headdresses of the Brigade of Guards, properly worn, cover the eyes so that their wearer cannot see in front of him, as does the splendidly plumed brass helmet of the Household Cavalry. The costly

COMBINATION PEACE PIPE
AND TOMAHAWK
North American Indian.

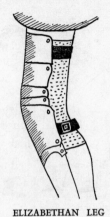

ELIZABETHAN LEG
ARMOUR
Method of fastening over pads.
Painted marble effigy, 1570.
Ely Cathedral

crimson jackets are so little intended for serious action that parades in the Park have been cancelled by the prudent authorities when the weather has been inclement, lest they be damaged in the rain. The dress the Grenadier Guards wear today on the battlefield is something quite different, for to wear parade dress for fighting in would be courting not merely personal suicide, but military disaster.

But practical battle dress is something new in history and belongs, like camouflage uniform, essentially to our own machine age. In the past it has been only on the battlefield itself, in the red-hot exigencies of action, that extravagant and impractical military uniform has suffered sensible mutation. It has been during the clamour of the actual fighting that too cumbersome armour has been struggled out of, blinding helmets flung aside, false curls tossed off, and hampering lace ruffles torn out. It has been in the heat of combat that the elegant falderals that dazzled the duchesses in London drawing-rooms, no less than the simple country wenches on the village green, have been abandoned as so much impedimenta. In action the desperate soldier has burst through his unsuitable finery, tearing and hacking at his sartorial bonds in order to free himself bodily to be able to tear and hack at the enemy, and this has resulted in strange things being done to his uniform, which he has ended the battle wearing in a way quite different from what the military tailor intended.

If his side happened to win the battle the soldier found himself unwittingly having set a new fashion in dress, his frantic sartorial innovations quickly becoming world-renowned and proudly copied, not only by

MILITARY DISCIPLINE (DECAPITATION BY SWORD)
From *Coutumes de Toulouse* (1296).
Bibliothèque Nationale, Paris

GERMAN PEASANT SOLDIER
After Holbein. Sixteenth century.

other soldiers in other armies, but by the civilians on both sides. Not a few popular fashions in civil life have thus been born on the field of battle.

This is how slashing arose and spread through Europe like a disease, lasting for more than 150 years, when in 1477 the victorious and ragged Swiss troops seized the fine banners of their retreating Burgundian enemies and tore them up to stuff the holes in their own ragged garments. The Steenkirk cravat, worn half undone or negligently slipped through a ring, owes its origin to the fact that French officers, taken by surprise in a skirmish in 1692, tumbled out of their tents and into battle half undressed, without having delayed long enough to knot their cravats properly.

It is, it must be noted, only the winning side that can rightly set such fashions, for no one wishes to be associated in any way with defeat. Even the German soldier's song *Lili Marlene* was taken up by the British soldiers at a time when the German army was more than holding its own. While Napoleon was the unconquered hero every army in Europe modelled their uniforms on the Grande Armée, and, as Napoleon allowed his favourite officers to design their own uniforms, the most grandiose conceits flourished—tall, nodding plumes, sashes, panther-skins, bullions, buttons by the hundred, swinging capes, death's-head-braided jackets worn over one shoulder, glamorous gold braid, and swinging tassels, all proliferated.

After Napoleon's defeat it was English military dress which even France copied, because it was associated with victory and luck. And it is the wish to invoke luck which influences the dress of soldiers and sailors to an enormous extent, although other reasons are always given for the choice of certain shapes and colours of uniform. For example, the close military throat-wrapping of the late seventeenth and eighteenth and early nineteenth centuries (wrapping at last so tightly drawn that both officers and privates regularly fainted during manœuvres) was tenaciously retained by soldiers throughout Europe because the rumour had gone round that it afforded special protection in battle, magically stopping enemy bullets or sword-thrusts. (This was an old superstition which had persisted ever since the cravat was permitted to Louis XIV's mercenary Croat troops on their insistence, since they believed that it afforded magic protection to the heart.)

The element of magic in all dress, and more especially in dress for dangerous occupations such as war, may well be underestimated by social historians. The most rational men, in the most rational times, tend to wear what they secretly, even unconsciously, believe will bring them luck, do them good, grant them prosperity in their undertakings, and stave off failure and disaster. If this is so in times of peace, how much more strongly does it hold in times of war, when the element of luck suddenly becomes openly important, as the uncertainties of life are suddenly intensified. Success and survival must then be courted by every magic aid and device that can be invoked. Uniform that has already been 'proved' by successful troops is the uniform every soldier, and his womenfolk, want above all others.

Common soldiers grow stubbornly attached to certain traditional items of their uniform, to which they attribute magic properties. Pigtails were not abolished in the British Army until 1800—wigs later still—and the troops thereafter greatly mourned their loss, though the tedium of powdering and the fuss and bother of powder-drill had previously provided a fruitful source of grumbling. Flashes are tenaciously clung to as if they were mascots, and buttons tend to remain on uniform cuffs long after they have ceased to button anything, because neither the War Office nor the regular soldiers want to start a run of bad luck by altering anything.

Such a deprivation (of something on their uniform they don't need and that serves no practical purpose) seems to them like a castration, though the Imperial War Museum archly suggests that the reason for the retention of cuff-buttons was probably merely to prevent the lower ranks wiping their noses on their sleeves.

Louis XIV, who set the sartorial fashions for all the courts of Europe, is known to have spent a good deal more money on his fabulous military manœuvres than on actual fighting, and no doubt such exhibitionist displays in an exhibitionist era enabled him comfortably, in the early part of his reign at least, to retain his military prestige without wasting his wealth and his armies on actual battlefields. This tradition was respected by some English noblemen who continued to model themselves on Versailles, and might well have lost England certain battles of decisive importance, owing to incompetent amateur command by aristocrats, had it not been for the efforts and stubborn common sense of despised N.C.O.'s and unprivileged professional officers.

Captain Gronow has much to tell us on this subject about the Napoleonic campaign in which he served as a young officer. He was a rich Welshman of noble birth, who, fortunately for historians, survived the ardours and dissipations of a military youth to dwindle into a dandified old gentleman with dyed hair, who, in the eighteen-sixties, continued to ogle passers-by from the discreet bow windows of his St James's Street Club, and suck the knob of his clouded cane as he had done in his Regency youth, while he recalled with nostalgic precision his young days in the Army and in Society.

Like so many other young officers who fought against Napoleon, Gronow received his commission without any preliminary training, and went straight from Eton into the Grenadier Guards as ensign, to command men who were called upon to fight against one of the most skilled and experienced armies the world has ever known. Nobody troubled about teaching him how to be an officer, and his superiors only bothered about sartorial discipline.

Here is the typical obligatory equipment ordered for field-days for the Castlemartin Yeomanry Cavalry in 1807, much more modest than most army units:

Helmet and feather
Black stock
Uniform jacket
Blue overalls (leather breeches when ordered)
Gloves
Boots and spurs
Sword and belt
Sword knot

Military bridle
Collar
Holsters and straps
Pistols
Goatskin
Cloak and cloak-case
Feeding-bag, folded and strapped to cloak-case
Pad and straps
Crupper
Sashes (to be worn by officers)

More equipment could be and usually was carried, but these few items in this far-off corner of the British Isles were basic for both officers and men.

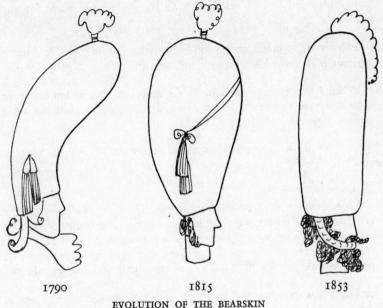

1790   1815   1853

EVOLUTION OF THE BEARSKIN
Grenadier Guards.

This early nineteenth-century military uniform aimed at elegance, and was rigidly uncomfortable to wear even on manœuvres. The regulation cravat is thus described in the sartorial handbook:

It is of so unyielding a nature that no force of the neck can bend it. The *tout ensemble* of this fashion expresses plainness and dignity with neatness and hauteur to an infinite degree.

So successful was it in achieving absolute rigidity, that officers were warned to loosen it after luncheon to avoid suffocation, several casualties of this nature having occurred and the danger being constantly present.

Despite the fact that England was fighting a life-and-death battle against the most powerful tyrant in Europe, all the high official care and surveillance was expended on petty supervision of uniform and hair-powder, and no military instruction was given to green young officers before they were thrust into action. "I joined in February, 1813," recalled Gronow,

and cannot but recollect with astonishment how limited and how imperfect was the instruction which an officer received at that time. He entered the army without any military training whatsoever. We were so defective in our drill even after we had passed out of the hands of the sergeant, that the excellence of our non-commissioned officers alone prevented us from meeting with the most fatal disasters in the face of the enemy.

Gronow's superior officer was too busy with what he considered more important matters to bother about military drill.

When I first entered the Guards the annoyance to which we were subjected was constantly being obliged to seek the assistance of a *coiffeur* to powder our hair.

Hair-powder at this date was almost completely out of fashion except in high Tory circles, which no doubt was why the Duke of Cambridge was so adamant.

I remember when on Guard incurring the heavy displeasure of the late Duke of Cambridge for not having a sufficient quantity of powder on my head. I received the strongest reprimand from H.R.H. and he threatened even to place me under arrest should I ever again appear on guard in what he pleased to call so slovenly and disgraceful a condition.

England was starving, and hair-powder was a voracious consumer of flour; nevertheless, "Two powder dressings a day were necessary at least; three if going out in the evening."

Generals who knew what was going on, and how unprepared the army was, were aghast, and could only pray for a miracle and rely on the solidity of the N.C.O.'s. General Sir Thomas Picton, *en route* for Waterloo, declared:

Why, damn it, where is our military education? Where our military schools and colleges? We have none, absolutely none. Our greatest

Generals, Marlboro' and Wellington, learned the art of war in France. Nine French officers out of ten can command an army whilst our fellows, though as brave as lions, are totally and utterly ignorant of their profession.

General Sir Thomas Picton, unlike the Duke of Cambridge, unlike Wellington himself, believed that on the field of battle the aristocratic principle in itself was not enough. "Damn it, sir, they know nothing." And he could only cross his fingers and rely on the N.C.O.'s.

But even the N.C.O.'s could not work miracles against the dangerous enemy that oversmart uniform had become, uniform too tight to permit the soldiers to fight properly. Marshal Exelmans later on gave his British conquerors a fatherly word of advice on the subject:

Permit me to point out a gross error as regards the dress of your cavalry. I have seen prisoners so tightly habited that it was impossible for them to use their sabres with facility.

The British troops openly envied the French their more battleworthy uniform.

The clothing of the French soldier was roomy and enabled him to march and move about with ease. No pipeclay accessories occupied their attention. In a word their accoutrements were infinitely superior to our own.

The young English aristocrats, commissioned from Eton or from the gilded dissipations of the London season, where Brummell was still god, believed that war would be no different, and expected to live elegantly and have plenty of sport, exactly as in England. "The Hon. W. Dawson," recalled Gronow,

had innumerable hampers of wine, liqueurs, potted meat and other good things brought out from England. His cooks were the best in the army, and besides he had a host of servants of all nations, Spanish, Portuguese, French, Italians, who were employed scouring the country for provisions [a costly enterprise]. He had only a younger brother's fortune; his debts became very considerable and he was obliged to quit the Guards. He and his friends had literally eaten up his little fortune.

The campaign against Napoleon was bedevilled by elegant and wealthy amateur officers, who treated the professional officers with the utmost contempt. There was the case of the rich young officer in the eighteenth Hussars, who brought with him to the war his three English grooms and his two carriages to transport his silver plate and linen. This officer, disillusioned at not finding the comforts and the sport he had expected to enjoy with the British army in the field, abandoned his first outpost duty and simply galloped off. He ordered his servants to pack his things and hired himself a special transport back to England, remarking that campaigning was not intended for gentlemen. This behaviour, not altogether surprisingly, was not looked upon too kindly by his superior officers, but he arrived back in England before his Commander-in-Chief's dispatch, and had time to sell out his Commission in his regiment, and so escaped all censure.

KNUCKLE-DUSTER
FINGER-RING
Khevsur tribe, Caucasus,
U.S.S.R.

ARCHAIC GREEK
BRONZE HELMET
Louvre

THE DUKE OF
WELLINGTON'S
CAMPAIGN NIGHTCAP
White knitted wool.

Wellington himself, unlike many of his high-ranking officers, preferred that the dress of his troops should be reasonably comfortable and battle-possible, but, since he himself was partial to the aristocratic principle and the unmilitary accessories that proclaimed it, he delayed putting his foot down until the last possible moment on the sartorial excesses of his noble officers. Being himself as inseparable from his umbrella as a modern man-about-town, he did not forbid them to his officers until the action of November 10, 1813, near Bayonne, against Marshal Soult. Gronow reported:

> His Grace, on looking round, saw to his surprise a great many umbrellas with which the officers protected themselves from the rain which was then falling. Arthur Hill came galloping up to us saying, "Lord Wellington does not approve the use of umbrellas during the enemy's firing, and will not allow the gentlemen's sons to make themselves ridiculous in the eyes of the army."

A few days afterwards Wellington observed to Colonel Tyling, "The Guards may in uniform when on duty at St James carry them if they please, but not in the field."

But not even the great Wellington managed to stop the gallant Spanish troops carrying parasols and using fans on the battlefield, and even when entering Hamburg in triumph in 1807 all the Spanish soldiers were seen to be bearing sunshades.

Gronow never forgot the ghastly realities of the actual Battle of Waterloo:

At four o'clock our square was a perfect hospital, being full of dead, dying and mutilated soldiers. The surgeon, Mr Gilder, had much difficulty in using his knife, having blunted it and all his other weapons by amputation in the earlier part of the battle. . . . When I call to mind [forgetting for once his gentlemanly detachment] how ill-rewarded our noble soldiers were for their heroic deed my heart bleeds for them. Under the cold shade of aristocracy men whom France would have promoted for their valour to the highest grades of the army, lived and died 20 and 30 years after the battle with the rank of Lieutenant or Captain. As to the private soldiers, their stubborn endurance, desperate courage, their indomitable pluck were but ill-rewarded by a shilling or two a day and a refuge in Chelsea or Kilmainham Hospital.

All in all, as Wellington remarked, it was a damned near thing—and it appeared that Napoleon deserved to win. The French journal which circulated in Paris after the French disaster at Waterloo actually reported that the Great Imperial Army of Napoleon had in fact gained the victory. When the truth at last leaked out the Paris mob, disenchanted with their hero and weary of having their menfolk killed off in his continual wars, fastened ropes to his column in the Place Vendôme and tried to haul down his triumphal statue, pulling and struggling vainly till nightfall.

Occupying Paris after the victory at Waterloo, British regiments bivouacked in the Bois de Boulogne, where the dress of the Scottish soldiers upset the women of Paris as much as it did the German soldiers of 1914, "their peculiar uniform," says Gronow, "creating a considerable sensation amongst the Parisian women, who did not hesitate to declare that the want of *culottes* was most indecent."

It is familiarity which decides morality, and the skintight pantaloons of the non-Scottish regiments occupying Paris, pantaloons whose tightness and lightness of colour, thrown into relief by the extremely high-waisted and abbreviated jackets, outlined the vital organs with the utmost precision, seemed to them perfectly respectable.

If any lessons were drawn from the military inefficiencies revealed in the long campaigns against Napoleon they were shelved and soon forgotten. The last battle had been won somehow in approved British fashion, and the great Duke busied himself receiving the homage of Europe and arranging for the accommodation of the many gilded tea and dinner services ordered by the remaining crowned heads of Europe in his honour, for show-cases by the score were required for their display and for his collections of jewelled batons of honour and jewelled orders. He continued to hold on firmly to the aristocrat-amateur principle of officering the British Army (a principle of which he himself was the brilliant denial), with trained N.C.O.'s to do the real management and impressed troops to perform the fighting, for he feared democratic ideas might lead to revolution.

Thus the same inefficient and untrained aristocratic-officer class nearly wrecked the conduct of the Crimean War (as Cecil Woodham-Smith has so ably described). The young ignorant aristocrat officers had grown into old ignorant aristocrat officers, or else were succeeded by their sons, whose only difference from their fathers in lack of professional military experience was one of years. And the same mistakes were made. This time much worse, for the conditions of the campaign were climatically much more severe, and the weapons of war had become much more destructive.

Military trousers, if changed in colour, were no less tight; helmets, if of different shape, no less awkward and unwieldy; and uniform sleeves had become still tighter. Indeed, the greatest achievement of British uniform in the Crimean War was in roasting the troops in the heat of summer as successfully as it froze them in the snows of winter.

Bickering between jealous generals, lordly disregard of advice from experienced professional officers, neglect of the most elementary sanitary precautions, neglect of the supply of food and of arms, were worse than ever. The passionate preoccupation of high-ranking officers was with finicking details of dress and grooming. Dress and grooming were, in truth, the only aspects of soldiering with which they were familiar, and if victories depended on the precise mathematical angle at which whiskers should be worn they would have proved the greatest of generals.

This time the disastrous state of affairs was made known to the British public in a blistering series of dispatches from the *Times* war correspondent, and if little change was actually made in the high command at least Florence Nightingale was permitted to go out and organize care of the wounded. The best thing to do with a bad job was to ignore it. Tennyson wrote his *Charge of the Light Brigade*, and *The Times*, at the end of the campaign, merely commented that the fearful conditions, accentuated by administrative blundering, gave the British troops a perfect opportunity to display their traditional pluck.

Yet the aristocratic-officer tradition still lingered in the British Army into the next century, and enabled certain high-ranking officers in the mud and blood that was Flanders to uphold feudal estate in the great *châteaux* and inspired the bitter pen of Siegfried Sassoon:

If I were old and fat and short of breath. . . .

This time there was no glamour and little pretence at glamour. The saucy pillbox hats of Kipling's day had gone the same way as the braided glories of Waterloo and the plumed shakos of the Crimea. The uniform

ENGLISH SUBALTERNS, WORLD
WAR I
Drawing by Fish.
These drawings originally appeared in
The Tatler.

ETRUSCAN WARRIOR
Bronze. Five inches high.
Louvre

of the 1914 War was uglier and drearier than any other uniform in history—not even successful, despite the innovation of the colour khaki, as camouflage. The destructive power of the huge new guns was so great that it was unnecessary for them to be selective.

Though the magic pen of 'FISH' lent the baby-faced hero subalterns, with their jodhpurs and little canes, a certain girlish elegance, the real look of the 1914 uniform may better be seen in Bruce Bairnsfather's "Old Bill," with his ill-fitting jacket, shapeless trousers, and ill-rolled puttees. The tin hat, like a demented bowler, persisted into civilian life in the form of the female toque. The ominous tin hat was the true emblem of the First World War, symbol of the increasing danger from the skies.

Typically the tin hat never fitted. It did not fit then, nor does it fit to-day. *The Times* of May 19, 1954, reporting progress in this item of military dress, said:

> The steel helmet which is issued to the three services is to be partially re-designed following complaints that it is cumbersome and unstable. The chinstrap of the present standard helmet is attached to its interior harness at a point so high on the side of the head that the helmet itself is not firmly held. During the demonstration assault landings being made on Eastney Beach, near Southsea, this week soldiers running from their landing craft can often be seen clutching rifles with one hand and holding their helmets steady with the other.

To-day anodyne buttons make life easier for the unenthusiastic youths called up for their military service, but they are detested by officers racking their brains to think up new methods of combating the eternal ennui that comes from idleness, and which they consider more demoralizing than the ennui which comes from polishing brass buttons.

The American influence even in contemporary military life is worth noting. It is frequent to-day among youths doing their two years' service in the R.A.F., for instance, to loosen up by bending and breaking the visor of their caps, so that they take on a limp, unstarched appearance more like the American cap. Martial erectness and stiffness is similarly discarded, whenever they can or dare, for a transatlantic loose and easy slouch which they associate with freedom and the delights of jazz. At the same time there is much jealousy of American soldiers because their pay is so much higher.

Civilians too are influenced by American service dress, especially in North Africa and Italy, where looted or discarded uniform is bought, sold, trafficked, or fiddled freely among Arabs, Sicilians, Neapolitans, and Tunisians, so that the peculiar olive-green khaki associated with the United States may be seen on the least military of men, and the peculiarly tight seat of the G.I. trousers has long ceased to excite mirth or embarrassment.

Americans do not take kindly to militarism, as is natural in a country where their own wars have largely been fought by irregulars. The brilliantly coloured yellow or green silk kerchief, first worn as a sweat-rag by the Eighth Army in the desert, to hide its unbuttoned shirt-top, has been developed as a recruiting bait, and aglets enticingly added to walking-out dress. But more than this is needed, and American army command found it necessary to introduce a new military chic into the army by redesigning its uniform entirely. Green uniforms came into force in October 1956, in place of the former olive-khaki, and black shoes and

socks replaced the former brown. As a special bait to recruitment it was
laid down that officers and privates must wear exactly the same uniform,
distinguished only by military ensigns.

In the age of the hydrogen bomb is it possible to make military dress
fetching? Every soldier, no less than every civilian, cannot but feel
helpless when informed that

> To-day we talk in terms of megatons, the equivalent of millions of
> tons of TNT. That first A-bomb is not even fit to be used as a trigger
> for the multimegaton hydrogen bomb. The world has entered the
> megaton age in which one plane carrying just one bomb can deliver
> on a target a cargo of destructive force equal to about five times the
> total load of explosives dropped in the whole of the Second World War
> by the air forces of all the combatants.[1]

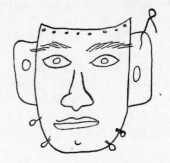

SPANISH SOLDIER
Tile-painting. Eighteenth
century.
*Hermitage of St Sebastian
Cadaqués, Catalonia*

INCA MASK OF GOD OF WAR
Silver.

What uniform can make a soldier feel brave and manly when such
weapons are in question?

The British Army Council, however, is unshaken. Here is a letter to
The Times written in 1954:

> In the midst of the present public anxiety about atomic warfare
> readers of *The Times* will doubtless be relieved to know that the
> British Army remains unruffled. This last week-end I attended Terri-
> torial Army Training ... the morning was passed with lectures on the

[1] William Lawrence, *American Weekly*, 1956.

K

use and effect of the atomic bomb; in the afternoon we practised sword-drill.

Old soldiers do not all agree with new soldiers that Army uniform is uninspiring to-day. Here is another letter to *The Times* (September 26, 1956):

> As a former sergeant-major, I read with great interest the letter published on recruiting in your issue of September 20th . . . I do feel that battledress is not so bad as the writer describes it. In my opinion and experience, for what they are worth, battledress, properly fitted and pressed, with shoulder titles, formation signs, and badges of rank clean, and decently polished and blancoed web belt, can look very smart. The man must hold himself more or less erect as well.
> Again I have heard No. 1 dress described as "looking like a bus driver's uniform," but I disagree entirely. The wearer of any uniform, however gorgeous, makes all the difference. I am equally convinced that the modern Regular Soldier would not wish, with a few exceptions, to go back to the complicated full-dress uniforms of before the 1914–1918 war, or anything like it. If anything was laughable, the ridiculous pill-box hats of the Edwardian era were.

All Great Britain, however, felt the shock when a group of young Australian National Service soldiers went on strike in Australia (January 1957) because they were posted to the Black Watch Regiment, and could not endure to wear the kilt, which they thought ridiculous and certain to be laughed at in their home town.

Modern wars cost enormously more than the wars of the past, and many more people, both military and civilian, are killed in them. The first atomic bomb dropped on Hiroshima killed 100,000 Japanese at a cost of approximately £5000 a head. But, now that we have megatons, such figures are already well out of date.

If, in the exceptional circumstances of our present scientific era, military authorities are perplexed as to how best to dress their soldiers, at least fashion experts in civilian life have lost no time in adapting themselves to the new jargon. Marc Tushnet, State President Emeritus of the New Jersey Association of Master Hairdressers, has declared:

> Colours seen in the A-bomb detonations will be apparent on women of all ages before long. Flame symbolizing the fiery red core of the blast is second only in popularity to the topaz shade of the outer edges of the familiar fireball.

It may be that our world will only be saved from itself by an international army of the United Nations, of all colours and speaking all tongues, policing awkward danger-spots in the world until tempers quieten down, and hopeful souls see in the blue helmets of the token U.N. force sent to Suez in November 1956 an augury of sanity for the future.

BRITISH NAVAL DUFFLECOAT
"The man who began by saying, 'I can't stand those ridiculous Montgomery-style coats'." Italian cartoon.

STEEL TASSETS AND
COD-PIECE
German, 1560.
Fitzwilliam Museum, Cambridge

Despite centuries of fuss over the design of military uniform the fact remains that the British Navy, Britain's senior Service, has only very recently managed to achieve any sort of uniform at all, and that has suffered a most chequered career.

Until 1856 British seamen in the Royal Navy had no definite uniform, but had to be content with whatever bits of clothes they themselves could manage to provide. As late as 1830 the British Admiralty was obliged constantly to keep pestering the British Treasury for compensation due to sailors who had damaged their own clothes on naval duty. During the periods of Britain's greatest glory sailors in the Royal Navy made do with whatever bits and pieces they could muster, just as pirates had to do on their ships, and there was no attempt at uniformity.

Rowlandson's drawings of naval types in 1777 shows the cabin boy dressed in a low-crowned straw hat and wide Dutch petticoat breeches (unchanged in style for over a century); some ordinary ratings in pink-striped cotton pantaloons, others in white canvas trousers; the quarter-master in a top-hat of yellow straw with flowing black ribbons, blue shirt, and black waistcoat; the warrant officer in a black top-hat with a wide brim, a blue coat with a high black stock, and rows of brass buttons on his jacket.

In the mercantile marine there was no attempt whatever at any kind of uniform, and the entire crew simply wore whatever came to hand. Herman Melville mentions the ship's doctor on an English whaler in 1851 wearing a faded blue frock and patched trousers, and considered the frock-coat as seaworthy garb to be rated above most other forms of naval dress. "They laugh at long-togs so; but it seems to me that a long-tailed coat ought always to be worn in all storms afloat. The tails tapering down that way to carry off the water, d'ye see." Cocked hats too had this unintended advantage: "Same with cocked hats, the cocks form gable-end eaves troughs. No more monkey jackets and tarpaulines for me. I must mount a swallow-tail and drive down a beaver so." As to the tattooed Redskin harpooner of the American whaler, given pride of place because of his skill, he had crowned himself with feather plumes of such height that they swept the cabin ceiling even when he was sitting down.

On ships of the British Royal Navy it was customary for the captain to make his own regulations as to what wear he considered proper for gentleman officers, but in all cases swords were obligatory, and most captains insisted on cocked hats as well, though the prestige they conferred and the drainpipe virtues Melville has indicated were liable to be counterbalanced by the fact that they always blew off in a high wind at sea. Cloaks and light slippers were also essential, the more vulgar top-boots being strictly forbidden to officers until after 1795.

Epaulettes, so dear to the Army, were not introduced into the Royal Navy until Captain Seymour, a British naval commander, failed to be saluted by French sailors in Toulon in 1783. This indignity he immediately took steps to remedy, despite Lord Nelson's well-known dislike of epaulettes, which he considered ridiculous. But then Lord Nelson, small, fragile, so delicate in health that he was always seasick, even in harbour, was in love with daring and glory of a kind which depended on spiritual gallantry and had little to do with show-off. All the ships he ever commanded were known not to be dressy ships, and he himself dressed somewhat on the old-fashioned conservative side—and even at Trafalgar was still wearing a pigtail, an out-of-date stock of black velvet, three inches wide, fastening at the back with a four-pronged buckle, and huge shoe-buckles of outmoded shape, adorned with crystal.

Valour and indifference to comfort are the standards he himself set and they have since become watchwords in the British Navy. It is therefore not surprising that the same dress should have been regarded as suitable service wear both for the tropics and the Arctic, in which latter climate the wearing of gloves was scorned as effeminate. With the passing of time, nevertheless, certain modifications gradually crept in. One ship's

GODDESS OF WAR,
WA-HUN-DE-DAN
North American Indian.

GODDESS OF PEACE
Ceramic design. Picasso.
Contemporary.

officer, on duty near the equator, daringly introduced a white top-hat into his naval dress. Other officers ventured to have their uniforms tailored in thin, blue material as more suitable wear for the great heat, an unfortunate experiment as it turned out, because they proved to be not merely cooler, but also transparent as well, revealing braces underneath. White drill uniform for tropical wear was never seen until 1865.

Swords continued to be regulation wear for naval officers, are still always worn on dress occasions, and were last used at sea officially in 1918 in a sea-fight against a German destroyer. Admiral Beatty in the same war made another sort of history by wearing six buttons on his tunic instead of eight.

Mr Arthur Wilson (the Liverpool carrier of seaman's luggage), in applying in 1956 for an extension of his licence to permit him to carry miscellaneous goods, remarked, "The days are gone when sailors came in laden with boxes, bags, and a parrot in a cage. They dress smartly, like stockbrokers, now, and all they carry is a small leather week-end case."

We must not close this chapter on military uniform without showing another aspect of English military life, no whit less English in its downrightness and its belligerent anti-belligerency. The Quakers had their uniform too, an austere and workmanlike dress, which they insisted stood for peace and defied war.

In 1660, somewhere about the time that Charles II, having got hold of Bunyan's fiery pamphlet *Sighs from Hell*, amused himself by having it bound within the covers of a lascivious French *conte*, the English Quakers presented him with a solemn Declaration.

To understand the temerity of their gesture we must visualize them, not as they now are, a highly respected and prosperous world community, but as they then were, a mere handful of despised outcasts, chiefly of poor journeymen, mostly in gaol for their opinions, and generally regarded as dangerous lunatics.

Here is their Declaration:

We utterly deny all outward wars and strife and fightings with outward weapons for any end or under any pretence whatever. This is our testimony to the whole world. The spirit of Christ by which we are guided is not changeable so as once to command us from a thing as evil and again to move unto it. And we certainly know and testify to the world that the spirit of Christianity which leads us all into truth will never move us to fight and war against any man with outward weapons, neither for the Kingdom of Christ, nor for the Kingdoms of this world.

CHAPTER TWELVE

JEWELLERY FOR MEN

I frown the while, and perchance wind up my watch or play with some rich jewel.

WILLIAM SHAKESPEARE, Malvolio in *Twelfth Night*

JEWELLERY and the proper enjoyment of it do not belong to an age of push and bustle, and the prettiest watches were those made when time did not count. Love for the magic beauty which is inherent in jewels has to-day given place to concern for their value as transportable investments,

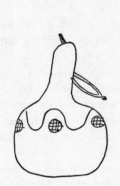

CALEBASSE JEWEL-CASE
Brazil.
Musée de l'Homme, Paris

JEWELLED BUDDHA,
AFGHANISTAN
Painted clay.
Musée Guimet, Paris

and diamonds are now bought not because they radiate rainbows like the dew on dawn grass, but because they will bring their price elsewhere in the troubled world of to-day.

The beauty of jewellery, which depends on the design of the jewel and the skill with which it has been wrought, has little to do with the market

295

price of the material employed. Some of the most beautiful jewels ever made have been created in inexpensive paste. Conversely some world-famous jewels are and were not beautiful at all, though fabulously costly. Such was the historic diamond necklace which helped to bring Marie-Antoinette to the scaffold, a heavy *parure* of perfectly matched large diamonds, with no pretensions to grace in its ponderous loops and monstrous tassels.

The work of the famous firm of Fabergé cannot be called beautiful either. This highly successful firm of clever brothers had the honour of designing costly jewels for the last Tsar of Russia, his friends, and his Court. It was not a period of good taste in Europe, and the firm of Fabergé employed wonderfully skilled craftsmen to carry out ingeniously vulgar ideas to please their patrons.

Since a profusion of male jewellery was already regarded as not altogether gentlemanly, they made the Tsar costly toys from precious stones and expensive metals, such as Easter eggs of gold and valuable enamel, encrusted with huge rubies, enormous diamonds, and great sapphires. These Easter-egg baubles opened to display a treasury of extravagant miniature toys, such as minuscule railway-trains made of platinum and diamonds and the like.

Ingenuity was prized above good design, and jewels which moved by clockwork were most admired of all, though such an attribute has nothing whatever to do with the intrinsic beauty of a fine jewel, and is the antithesis of a work of art. Thus a round enamel brooch with a rocking balance in diamonds, which on being wound up would go on oscillating for ninety minutes without stopping. As jewellery such regal toys were extremely costly and necessarily limited, and as such their price has enormously increased since they were made. But they never were, are not, and never can be beautiful.

On the other hand we find simple-minded Kikuyu tribesmen putting together beautiful and original earrings from ordinary trade safety-pins, and truly lovely torcs daily being woven by natives of the Ghats of Western India from rattan and growing creepers.

In our present Western society commercial values obtain to the detriment of more lasting values, and wealth is rarely to be found in the hands of those who either understand or care greatly for art, which is why commercially valuable diamonds are the preferred jewels of Western society. When aluminium was first invented and very expensive, a wide bracelet was made from it by a famous firm of jewellers precisely because it was so costly a substance. If radium lent itself to the making of jewellery it would be an ideal material for the commercial market, being scarce, light in weight, easily transportable, and fantastically expensive.

Colette has perfectly described this standard of values in the little scene at the turn of the century where the schoolgirl Gigi is looking through the jewellery of her Aunt Alicia, a retired courtesan, and, to the old lady's indignation, mistakes a yellow stone for a topaz.

A topaz! I have endured many humiliations but this is the worst. A topaz amongst my jewels! Why not an aquamarine or a peridot? It is a yellow diamond, little goose, and such as you will not often see.

Whereat the experienced old lady proceeds to instruct her how to and what to choose to wear most usefully as jewellery.

"Never wear artistic jewellery; it devalues a woman completely," enumerating among such disastrous jewels mermaids wrought in gold with eyes of chrysoprase, Egyptian scarabs, large engraved amethysts, bracelets which are not very heavy but said to be wrought by the hand of a master jeweller, lyres, brooches in the form of stars, encrusted tortoises, cameos, baroque pearls and family jewels. The only permissible jewels, she declares, are "Diamonds and pearls. White diamonds, yellow, blue or rose. . . . Don't speak of black diamonds. They are not worth the trouble." Rubies are passable if one is quite certain of them. Sapphires will do provided they come from Kashmir, and emeralds if they are of the very top quality. But best of all, she advises, is to stick to large perfect diamonds and the most expensive pearls, which keep up their market value.

It has happened in culturally high periods in the world's history—alas, not to-day—that exquisite jewellery has been made out of exquisite precious materials. Then the results are indeed miraculously beautiful.

We must never forget that it is not until our own sad times of "a higher standard of living" (which has been needlessly accompanied by a low standard of art) that men have stopped wearing jewels. Motor-cars, stocks and shares, luxury hotels, alimony, private aeroplanes, and fast yachts — these are what the wealthy Western man of to-day spends his money on. He no longer ornaments his dress with jewels, nor wears glittering necklaces, nor hangs a large pear-shaped pearl in his ear, nor loads both hands with handsome rings. But as far back as the earliest traces of human life can be excavated on this earth his male ancestors spared no pains to adorn themselves with jewels.

We know that mammoth-hunters made ivory beads into necklaces and chipped ivory pendants which they laboriously engraved with magic patterns. A male skeleton of the Ice Age was unearthed wearing a necklace of mixed fossil-shells and pierced fragments of mammoth tusk. Of two skeletons dating back to 25,000 B.C. the male was the one which was adorned with a necklace of deers' teeth and fish vertebræ.

Among primitive peoples to-day both sexes wear jewels, but it is the male who wears more and larger jewels than the female. Andaman islanders wear no clothes, but fashion for themselves manly necklaces from twelve different kinds of coral, from shells, and from human finger-bones. The Kootzmahoo Indians of Alaska decorate their dancing-shirts with ceremonial patterns made from three-inch puffin-bills, and

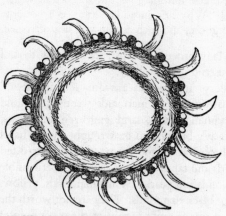

MALE JEWEL: MINIATURE
OF EYE, 1803
Smithsonian Museum,
Washington

NECKLACE OF OTTER-SKIN AND GRIZZLY-
BEAR CLAWS WITH LIGHT AND DARK
BLUE TRADE BEADS
Family heirloom of Fox tribe, North
American Indian.
Natural History Museum, New York.

weave fascinating straw and rope necklaces adorned with trade pearl buttons. Centuries before the Romans landed on English shores the natives of this country were wearing magnificent necklaces fashioned out of coal. Material is never lacking, it is clear, when the desire to make and to wear jewellery is strong. It is only to-day that Western man, surrounded by so much too much of so many things, has forgotten, or is ashamed to remember, that jewellery enhances manly beauty.

Men have worn, and in some parts of the earth still do wear, jewels not only on all their clothes, but also on their heads, in their ears, noses, lips, on their foreheads, round their necks, on their breasts, backs, arms, legs, hands, feet, on their buttocks and on their stomachs, on their sexual organs, and even inside their mouths. They wear these jewels to give themselves prestige and beauty, and for magic protection against danger and evil. The unusual places where jewellery is worn on the body are precisely those places which, they feel, require most magic protection because most vulnerable.

In the minds of primitive men use, beauty, and magic protection from danger are inseparable. Traders from Europe were always able to dispose of their trade beads at high prices to the American Indians, who worked the beads for magic protection into their traditional diagonal patterns on their dress, their headdress, the carrying-basket of their papoose, and the protective turtle guarding his first moccasins.

The Blackfoot Indians were particularly eager to purchase white or sky-blue beads, which for them had strong magic associations, so that an ordinary trade necklace of blue beads, on which there was a meandering pattern, such as sold and still sells to-day in Venice for practically nothing at all, could be readily bartered for a good horse or magnificent buffalo robe. The Hudson's Bay Accounts show that in 1749 half a pound of milk-white beads of large size were valued at one beaver skin. By 1833 the American Fur Company was doing brisk business selling ordinary trade beads to the Indians for furs, at a profit to themselves of several thousand per cent. on each deal.

In primitive societies the male always wears more jewellery than the female, not only because he is considered to be more important, but also because, in his rôle of hunter of food and military protector, his life is likely to be in more peril and therefore in need of more magic protection.

Such considerations as difficulties of materials, inclemencies of climate, scarcity of material hard enough for tools, lack of time and place to work do not count at all when man desires to adorn himself. On the contrary, every difficulty seems to act as a greater stimulant. Eskimoes in the bitter wastes of the Far North carve themselves enchanting buttons from seal-tusk, fashioned in the shape of baby seals, which are wondrous little works of art. Lovely jewellery is wrought by most primitive people living in the tropics, from fragile flowers and leaves and seeds, jewels which take longer to make than they do to decay, so that fresh jewels are made each day with the same interest and delight in making.

The American continent has been a rich source of splendid male jewellery. The Aztecs esteemed gold purely for its beauty, having no conception of Western ideas of coinage, and were eager to exchange priceless gold necklaces for the cheap glass beads the Spaniards offered them on their first encounters. Montezuma, it was recorded, believed these glass beads to be extremely precious stones, for deception was no part of the Aztec way of life, and it did not occur to him that the courtly Spaniards would have taken the trouble to come so far merely to bring rubbish. When Cortés gave Montezuma a common necklace of musk-scented glass beads Montezuma in return gave Cortés a very rich and elaborate necklace worked in the shape of golden crabs.

We shall never know the full list of treasures of golden jewellery

Cortés collected with such ease from the Aztecs, for it was so little esteemed by the Spaniards, except for its commercial value as metal, that they melted it all down in order to cast it into more portable gold chains, the easier to carry off to Spain. There was so much of this jewellery that the task of melting it down took three whole days, and all the resulting gold loaded suddenly on the Spanish market as soon as they got it back to Spain upset the whole economy of the country.

From the Aztecs, with their gold and precious stones and carved stone jewels, through the plains Indians with their gorgeous feathers and silver jewels and their splendid beadwork, right up to the woods Indians with their simpler but no less beautiful ornament, their ritual masks, bead and quill patterning, and corn-husk fantasies, still farther North to the Alaska Indians with their strong, strange decoration, America, whether she will or no, inherits one of the world's finest cultural endowments of ornament and jewellery.

Even the Puritan deadly fear of ornament, grafted uneasily on top of all this savage luxuriance, has not been able altogether to kill the passionate instinct to adorn engendered by those wild woods, wondrous deserts, brilliant blue skies, those fearsome tornadoes and merciless winters. Nature *needs* propitiating in America. The eagle-feather headdress of the Sioux chief, worn together with two buffalo horns to grant him the magic strength of both creatures, has to-day given place to insurance policies and mighty dams, scientific talismans against the same fears; but do the worried business executive who directs the insurance companies and the busy engineer who works on the dams never wear a lucky silver ring to make just a bit more sure?

The instinct to wear jewellery is far from dead, happily, in the modern American male, who is much less self-conscious about wearing rings, medals, silver buttons, and fancy metal-studded belts than the modern Englishman. Respect for tough physical work is still present in America wherever the tough pioneer spirit lingers, and it was precisely the cowboys, the gauchos, and the loggers, sweating long hours at arduous and dangerous jobs for miserable pay, who in the past have most delighted in jewellery.

Massive silver rings, gaily decorated horse-trappings and saddles, richly ornamented belts, ornamented riding-boots, scarf-rings, brooches, even earrings and bracelets, were never regarded as effeminate, since the men who delighted to sport them were so patently tough. Such men, with no home and often no other clothes than those on their backs, invested their hard-earned wages in male jewellery just as gipsies to-day often use silver or even gold coins to adorn their clothes. Otherwise the wages perhaps would have vanished without trace in the bar-rooms and brothels and gambling parlours at the end of each job, for Owen Wister has recorded that the cowboys were a race of men apart, who made few contacts outside their work, and rarely married.

Certainly the American male has less sales-resistance to jewellery than the modern Englishman, and it is a pity that modern male dress offers no scope for the introduction of jewellery as an integral part of its ensemble, as former dress for men has done. "The addiction of our men to wide gold wrist-watch straps," says the American dress-designer Elizabeth Hawes, "is clearly an indication of the fact that they too would like to brighten up that corner where they are with some glitter."

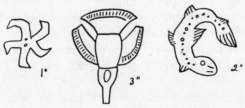

INCA DRESS ORNAMENTS (SILVER)

Before men abandoned bright dress and the wearing of jewellery, in despair at the ugly shape of the industrial civilization they were dedicating themselves to, they not only decorated their own bodies with manly and with magic-protective jewellery, but they also decorated their animals and their vehicles. Horse-trappings have glittered with gold and silver and even precious stones in noble European courts, and even poor peasants still adorn their donkeys' reins and eye-shades with fancy stitching and patterns of brass studs. The pack-straps of certain North-eastern woodland tribes of American Indians, woven skilfully of milk-weed fibre, were carefully sewn with geometric designs of coloured trade beads in black, white and scarlet, to invoke the protection of pagan deities on journeys. Redskin warriors of proved bravery were entitled, besides gorgeous paint on their bodies and feathers in their headdress, to adorn their horses also with paint and with eagle feathers, to grant swifter speed.

Persian coracles, carrying cargoes of sand and melons, still bear two blue beads and two cowrie-shells in their rim for magic protection, and the Greek taxi-driver in Athens makes sure of the safety of his vehicle and himself by hanging two blue beads beside the speedometer. Indian elephants wear the richest caparisons their owners can afford, and the trappings of elephants in the service of the great rajahs have been, and sometimes still are, gorgeous indeed, the very elephant goads being wrought of ducat gold enriched with great emeralds, and the howdahs of magnificent velvets and brocades elaborately enriched with gold and precious stones, swinging gold fringes, and tinkling golden bells. Not so fast as a modern Rolls-Royce no doubt, but certainly more of a pleasure for eyes and ears. The luxurious motor-cars used to-day in India on State occasions (such as visits of the Dalai and Panchen Lamas) are gorgeously decorated with festoons of flowers and bright ornament.

In Europe the increasingly rare horse traffic means so much less opportunity for horse finery. But horse-brasses still jingle on shining harness and forelock, carrying in their stylized moons and stars occult Saracenic symbols for magic protection from ancient fears, unchanged since the Crusaders brought them back to England from the Holy Land.

Even in our own atomic age the streamlined motor-car frequently carries a good-luck figurehead on the bonnet, and the car-owner is curiously willing to spend more than he really means to on this figurehead, thus propitiating fate, though he may not be consciously aware of it.

Among the exquisite Greek jewellery used by both sexes, which Roman soldiers took back into Rome, were bracelets and finger-rings, earrings, brooches, buckles, dress-borders, and toilet-boxes and mirrors and coronets and delicate little toilet accessories. From ancient Britain Roman soldiers looted gold rings and torcs, beads of amber and jet and coal. British rings became so fashionable in Imperial Rome that connoisseurs collected them in cabinets for display, and elegants wore several rings on each finger, just as two thousand years afterwards French æsthetes collected Egyptian jewels and Roman coins, in the wake of Napoleon's conquests.

As Rome grew more decadent the number and size of the rings increased, and the wearing of huge, often hollow and paste, gold bracelets enabled the dealers in false jewellery to extend their trade hugely in "authentic British jewels," cobbled quickly in Rome. As the power of Rome declined the overt display of luxurious jewels intensified, and the traffic in paste and bogus increased. Martial poked fun at Charinys for wearing six rings on each of his ten fingers, but such had by then become the common practice. Anything to show off. Entire couches were veneered in tortoiseshell for no other reason than that it was expensive, just as millionaires to-day sometimes order their bathroom taps to be made in solid gold.

The early Christians had no particular jewellery. Extreme in their austerity, their Kingdom being not of this world, they included the poorest and humblest people, many of whom were slaves. Their early symbols of a fish or a cross, cut roughly on the stone tombs in the Catacombs, later lent themselves to the most elaborate decoration both in Eastward and Westward ritual. The Greek Orthodox Church, which the converted Emperor Constantine established with Oriental splendour—aided by such technical tricks, to impress the devout, as the mechanical elevation of the Imperial throne and jewelled tears mechanically weeping from the painted eyes of monster seed-pearl-clad Madonnas—savoured perhaps more of the pagan past than the simple original Christian doctrine of Galilee, and Russian Greek Orthodox Churches derived thence are mostly unchanged to-day.

ST PETER WITH JEWELLED
HALO
Arras Tapestry, 1460.
Musée de Cluny, Paris

THE INFANT JESUS PROTECTED
BY CORAL JEWELS
From an altarpiece by Luca di
Tommé, 1366.
Fitzwilliam Museum, Cambridge

The Church of Rome also soon became richly adorned and jewelled, altar, vestments, and ritual alike blazing with colour and glitter. Naturally, much of earlier pagan beliefs still clung to the new religion. Simple minds confounded the Virgin Mary with the older mother goddesses, some Greek, some Egyptian. The mother-and-child symbol is common to nearly all religions, for what men must first worship is continuity. The mother goddess has always been particularly dear to Mediterranean peoples, and soon a multiplicity of saints arose to split the conception of one God uniting the whole world, a conception so starkly simple and necessary that men have still not come to accept it and abide by its meaning.

Pagan belief in the magic powers of precious stones received ecclesiastical blessing, and took on a fresh lease of life under Christian authority. The jewels of the Middle Ages were all a blend of religion and magic, the Church having the first right to all jewels, which, if not actually owned by the Church, had to be made in Divine images under its care, rosaries, reliquaries, crucifixes, and the like.

Rich nobles, however, presently began to scatter their fine apparel with jewels and precious embroidery, by no means all of which was directly inspired by religious meaning and imagery. Neither was the precious jewellery which enriched priestly vestment all of holy inspiration either, for luxury swept many prelates into frenzied displays of earthly riches, which drew sharp reproof from the Vatican on many occasions.

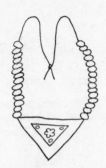

AMULET TO PROTECT
ANIMALS AGAINST
THE EVIL EYE
Blue glass beads, leather,
and silver. Turkish.
Musée de l'Homme, Paris

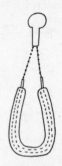

MENYT, ANCIENT
EGYPTIAN PROTECTIVE
JEWEL
It was slung between the
shoulders at the back for
magic preservation from
an unseen blow. The god-
dess Hathor gave it power.

Holy Christian jewels were worn for holy-magic-protective purposes, just as pagan jewels had been worn, as a health-insurance, and worn in exactly the same places, especially over the heart. Emeralds, blessed by Holy Church, were sold to cure eye disease, elk-horn to cure epilepsy, sharks' teeth (known as the tongues of asps) to cure snake-bite. Pious pilgrims took their savings and treasure to the great shrines of Europe, receiving in exchange spiritual receipts in the physical form of small lead *enseignes*, believed to possess such powerful magic for preserving and curing the owner that an immense traffic quickly sprang up, the *enseignes* passing from hand to hand at continually increasing prices.

Kings and powerful nobles owned specially important relics of holy origin, or so believed to be, such as prickles from the crown of thorns, splinters from the true cross, a hair or toenail, or even a finger, of one of the saints. These precious relics were mounted in sumptuous jewelled settings and enshrined in gorgeous and important reliquaries. They were believed to grant absolute protection from physical and moral harm. Sometimes such relics were embodied in finger-rings or worn as amulets.

As a medical precaution gentlemen as well as ladies carried pomanders (*pomme d'ambre*), which were incised hollow balls made out of rich metal to keep at bay the infection bad odours were believed to carry. This new form of amulet soon became enormously popular, and they were made in many shapes and sizes, often in the form of rosaries worn strung from the finger, together with the crucifix for added protection.

Pomanders were new to England in the Middle Ages, but they were not new to history, for the Etruscans had developed the use of a similar protective jewel worn on the upper arm. Nor were they confined to Europe, for the jewels of India were frequently used to protect or cure the wearer. Thus an Indian Mogul necklace of seventeenth-century workmanship in grey jade, beautifully inlaid with gold, emeralds, and rubies, was "a specific against palpitation of the heart."

Thornwood was believed by good Christians to exercise holy powers on account of the crown of thorns, and as such counted as a jewel, rosaries of thornwood being in great demand. One such thornwood rosary, made in the fourteenth century, had each bead carved in a different pattern, and was worn slung from a waist-chain carved from the same wood.

Such was the craving for jewellery that the Church was no more successful in preventing her prelates from wearing fine jewels than were the prelates from preventing wealthy and noble laymen from doing the same. Men of much lower degree too longed to parade in gold- and silver-embroidered dress like their betters, and, though lack of means and stringent sumptuary laws alike prevented this, they painted common fabric with designs in gilt and silver paint in imitation of the costly brocades they coveted, just as four centuries later American colonists who could not afford carpets painted carpet patterns on their bare wooden floors. For to look grand is a deeply human urge—almost the deepest.

Sumptuary laws (and jewellery figured largely in most of them), could never wholly prevent merchants from copying nobles, nor servants their masters, though such copying was bitterly resisted. It is a deeply inherent trait in the English people not to accept class barriers as insurmountable, but rather to welcome them as a challenge. English people, it may be observed, are not democratic in the American sense, nor revolutionary in the French sense. They neither want their society levelled down nor levelled up. They like to climb.

Buttons as jewels began to appear as an aristocratic luxury on men's dress in England in the reign of Edward I, and were frankly ornamental.

They were known as "queintise," for no one even pretended they had anything to do with holy worship, and they quickly became a craze. One and a half dozen buttons sewn down the front of a cotehardie, where they fastened nothing, jewelled buttons sewn all over purses in an ingenious pattern, a long row of jewel-buttons tightly packed from wrist to elbow of tunic sleeves; in such ways were ornamental buttons disposed.

King Francis I of France wore one suit of black velvet which was ornamented with no fewer than 13,600 buttons of gold. Early handkerchieves, another great luxury having nothing whatever to do with blowing the nose, were carried like banners, entirely for display, and offered an unrivalled opportunity for the exhibition of clusters of jewelled buttons sewn all over the fabric. In those days the King could command unpaid service from any of his people, and not only were masons, bricklayers, singing-boys, and soldiers thus impressed into the King's service, but goldsmiths also, as was the case with King Edward IV, who kept one jeweller thus entirely occupied making precious buttons for his adornment.

Sumptuary laws were speedily enacted to prevent people of lower degree from wearing buttons to which their rank did not entitle them, and though transgressors were fined, gaoled, deprived of their fine buttons, and beaten into the bargain for their impudence, they went on transgressing. Like rosaries, buttons were wrought in gold and in silver, carved in ivory and amber and coral, set with emeralds, rubies, sapphires, and presently diamonds and fine enamels as well. Entire garments were 'powdered' with buttons, and the button-mania persisted for centuries through many other changes of mode.

The first serious opposition to them was started in the seventeenth century by the new sect of Quakers, followers of George Fox. To signify their dislike of worldly show the Quakers wore simple drab dress from which all buttons were banished, keeping their garments attached by overfolding, or hooks and eyes, or tied strings, or slotted points, or just plain fit. In fact, the dress of luxurious non-Quakers was also fastened with points, the buttons being there for show, not use. Even points, however, could be fashioned into a sartorial extravagance and laden with jewels. The portrait of Charles I in the London National Portrait Gallery shows him wearing elaborate points gathered up in decorative bunches like tassels, the *dégagé* dress being cunningly devised to display them to best advantage.

The Tudor courts had provided men of rank with unrivalled opportunities for displaying a profusion of gems, and no monarch has loved jewels more or worn so many as Henry VIII, who squandered much of the careful savings of his pinch-penny father thus, all his clothes for sports or mourning, no less than for State occasions, being sewn all over, shoes included, with precious stones, besides wearing quantities of rings, earrings, necklaces, and suchlike. The inventory of his jewels is impressive indeed, including rings, buttons, devices, *enseignes*, holy jewels of every kind, jewels to wear on hats, on shoes, on garters, as cod-piece ornament, jewels to powder on his gowns and gloves and hose, besides a tremendous collection of wide jewelled collars. He was reputed to be caught by glitter like any jackdaw, without being at all expert on authenticity, and Cellini recounted, not without malice, how easily he had been sold a large fake emerald made of green glass.

LEAD STUDS FOR BELTS
Worn by commoners. Fourteenth and fifteenth centuries.
Musée de Cluny, Paris

In his day watches were still a rarity in England. The very few known here had been bought at enormous prices as fancy toys. Noblemen squandered their patrimony rather on wide rich necklaces (simultaneously worn with other necklaces) worn in a shallow ellipse from shoulder to shoulder, where they were pinned with special pins as mayoral collars (dating from Tudor times) still are pinned to-day. Courtiers followed the king's lead, and wore as many as eighteen rings on their hands, and an additional one hanging from a jewelled chain. It was elegant to wear rings between the finger-joints and to have gloves slashed or 'cutted' to show the rings through the slashes, the gloves themselves being also sewn thickly with jewels.

All these fashionable joys were continued and intensified in the brilliant reign of Queen Elizabeth I, and it is impossible to conceive of a court which glittered and sparkled with jewels more than hers. It was an upstart and proudly ambitious period, where there was every encouragement to display and a vast amount of new treasure to peacock with from the looted Spanish treasure-ships, which display served the double purpose of show-off and truculent patriotism. Elizabeth's courtiers were tricked out in doublets so thick-sewn with jewels that sometimes the fabric beneath could not be seen at all. Sir Walter Raleigh's dresses were especially sumptuous. He wore garments with fine pearls worked into solid rivers of ornament, embroideries sewn with rich gold bullion, and every rare and precious stone he could find, loot, or buy enriched his elegant court dress—and not only his court dress, for he dressed no whit less gorgeously on his voyages. This proud display was part of his very being, and his silver sword blazed with such a profusion of diamonds that beholders recorded how it hurt the eyes merely to look at him. His hose was enriched with jewels to match his doublets, and the roses of his shoes were reputed to be worth a fine estate. Earrings, or often just one splendid earring, swung slowly from the tip of his ear, size being more important than purity of shape or texture.

He would often carry, like other Tudor courtiers and fine gentlemen, a large jewel loose in his beringed hands, to play with in public—perhaps a mermaid fashioned from a huge irregular baroque pearl, or a dolphin or Triton contrived from a fine emerald. Pagan themes were more admired than holy imagery in this court, though there was plenty of both.

It was, of course, not only men who wore so much jewellery at this time, though they often wore more than their women, who, when they wore a lot of jewellery, seemed to be showing off their husband's riches, much as is done to-day. Such certainly was the case with Gabrielle d'Estrées, mistress of Henry IV of France, who, famous for his own austere dress, saw to it, for the sake of his prestige,that she should be jewelled as befitted his station, and one of her gowns, made of black atlas, was so loaded with pearls and precious gems that she was unable to stand upright in it without assistance.

Jewels, in truth, are disproportionately heavy for their size, and bullion embroidery greatly adds to the weight of the fabric on which it is embroidered. As recently as 1910 the richly worked ceremonial dress of the Russian Ambassador at the Court of St James's was so heavy that it took three valets to lift it to dress their master.

Elizabeth's was the age of the pomander, curious and enormous rather than lovely or elegant jewels, the gorgeous and gross being always preferred. Yet such was the dash and *élan* of the period, that the *nouveau-riche* flavour seems washed clean by the sea, which brought them its looted treasures and upon which the great Armada was so gallantly defeated. It was a rich, vulgar, dishonest, blatant period, but it was even more a period of passionate interest in life and in living, of manly daring and scientific curiosity, of rich and pulsating language, and the grossly audacious, glittering dress succeeds in impressing by its very audacity.

New Year presents were given and received at the Court of Elizabeth, and jewels, set in buttons, in toothpicks and ear-picks, and in little prayer-books and in pomanders, were all much in demand. Watches, and sometimes little portable sundials, were already more in evidence and greatly admired. They were designed in all kinds of fancy shapes: spherical (or *œuf de Nuremberg*), hexagonal, oblong, walnut-shaped, square, skull-shaped, and lily-shaped, as well as round, and they hung on a chain from the neck or waist instead of, or sometimes in addition to, the pomander. Sometimes they chimed. The Emperor Charles V owned an earring containing such a tiny chiming watch. Watches, in fact, were becoming so popular that cheaper ones began to find their way into the possession of less important people. The London play *Antipodes,* which was staged in 1638, contains the gibe: "Every puny clerk can tell the time of day in his pocket." In rural districts, however, they were still a rarity, and Aubrey recounts how a certain Mr Allen's housemaids, entering his bedroom in order to make his bed, heard his newly bought watch ticking, and, believing it to be possessed of the Devil, grasped it with a pair of tongs and threw it out of the bedroom window into the moat below. The watch, however, was caught by its chain on a branch of elder-tree before it reached the water, which convinced the maids that it was indeed the Devil.

One portion of men's dress which offered a steady excuse for the display of rich jewels was the hatband. Fashionable were gold medallions engraved or cast in relief, with classical themes, which now superseded the earlier *enseignes.* Stowe recorded in his annals of 1592: "As well as women men did wear borders of great crystal buttons as hat bands as worthy garment to distinguish between the gentry and others." Endymion Porter, determined not to be outvied at a grand ball at the British Embassy in Madrid, borrowed his wife's diamond necklace to wear round his hat.

Peter the Great of Russia, that strange giant who preferred the company of low sailors to that of noble courtiers, and who in his childhood had learned how to use his hands skilfully from the peasants he frequented, liked to design and cast his own buttons. There still exists one of his coats, of quite extraordinary length, sewn with metal buttons of his own manufacture. This monarch was a good century before his time in delighting in manual dexterity, for in his day only the lower orders were expected to take any interest in a useful occupation. Manual skill, however, is no respecter of rank, and the ill-fated Louis XVI of France was an excellent natural locksmith, who, had he not suffered the ill-luck to be born to the throne, a profession for which he was ill-adapted, would certainly have lived a longer and happier life.

Next to the Court of Elizabeth I of England, perhaps the most bejewelled was that of Louis XIV, wherein the King took good care to outvie all his courtiers, one of his magnificent waistcoats containing no less than 816 gems. Saint-Simon reported that on one occasion the King's coat was sewn with so many diamonds that he faltered and could not keep upright beneath the weight of them. Since show-off is the object of such display, the Duke of Buckingham was perfectly logical in carrying this one stage farther, and ordering his tailor to attach by a loose thread some of the fortune of gems sewn on his Court dress, so that he could suddenly scatter a profusion of jewels all over the parquet in the King's drawing-room.

BUTTONS OF INCISED MOTHER-OF-PEARL
Polynesia.
Musée de l'Homme, Paris

The Puritan reaction to this sort of show-off was to set their faces like flint against any kind of 'bauble,' the least of gems being condemned as a manifestation of the Devil. Yet they too did not disdain one form of jewel—death-reminders. These were not invented in the seventeenth century, but had originated in the Middle Ages. They were so much to the taste of Puritans, however, that tiny death's-heads and skeletons in coffins were even permitted in precious metals, to remind the wearers of the Day of Judgment. Also permitted were mourning rings of hair, often bequeathed by friends in their wills. A strong flavour of this mortality jewellery persisted in English middle-class life, and mourning rings and hair jewellery continued to be worn in tradesmen's circles for more than two centuries afterwards.

Despite the wholesale disposal or melting down of family jewellery during the Civil War—for funds had to be raised somehow—and the loss of carefully concealed treasures from hiding-places that proved not to be safe, male jewellery at the Restoration was soon profuse if rather more elegant. Earrings were now out of fashion for men, because the perukes gave no opportunity for them, and, because of the distraction of lace cravats, male necklaces also became redundant. Instead, rings and costly shoe-buckles, fan-handles (in summer), and muff-chains (in winter) provided gentlemen with sites for jewels. The cases for their fans were often so magnificent that they cost far more than the fans themselves, and a new profession arose, specialized craftsmen devoting their lives to the making of richly jewelled fan-cases alone.

Muffs were contrived from any rich and expensive material, fur only being employed if sufficiently precious. Mink, then plentiful, was disdained as mere vermin, but otter was highly regarded. William Penn mentioned collecting three fine otter skins from the Redskins of his colony in Pennsylvania for a present to the King of a "muffe." These muffs were large—large enough at least to contain a little dog, and in Paris there was a special shop which sold nothing else but these *chiens-manchon*. It was the Maison Guenon in the Rue du Bac.

It was not only French muff-dogs that English noblemen were now so eager to import into England, but all kinds of French luxuries and elegancies, for they felt they had lost face during the Commonwealth. The Duke of Norfolk, at a *levée* of the Pompadour, observed an article of furniture he had never seen before which excited his curiosity no less than his admiration. It was an octagonal vase, elegantly wrought in gold and engraved with her arms. From her maid he learned that it was a *pot de chambre*. Hearing of his interest in this utensil, Mme de Pompadour ordered her goldsmith to copy it exactly and have it engraved with the arms of the Norfolk family. She then graciously had this copy sent off to England to the Duchess of Norfolk. The Duchess, delighted with her present, took it to be a soup tureen, and had it brought to table in triumph filled with mutton broth at the dinner of welcome offered for the Duke on his return home from France.

Toothpicks still continued to be fashionable, and sword-handles, shoe-buckles, scabbards, little combs, and scent-bottles were all modish forms of male jewellery throughout the eighteenth century. France set the fashions, and good taste, if continually talked about, was not always in evidence. The scent-bottles, for instance, were often as improper as they were costly, moulded in the finest china or precious metal in the shape of human figures in indecent attitudes, or with the perfume sprinkling, like a prep school joke, from the other end of the torso from the jewelled head. Watches continued to be a favourite jewel-toy. The Comte d'Artois, for instance, wore watches on his fine Court dress instead of buttons. And the buttons themselves became larger and larger and steadily more extravagant, or else they became extremely tiny and intricately costly. Family pride dictated the large buttons painted like

FOLDING TOOTHPICK AND EAR-PICK
Chinese. Bone. Contemporary.
Author's collection

SILVER BUTTONS FOR MAN'S
COTTON SHIRT. 1½ INCHES
North American Indian.
*Museum of the American
Indian, New York*

miniatures with family portraits, and the taste for *chinoiserie* dictated the ordering from Peking of minute buttons delicately embroidered in fine silks.

Elegants had to have something to fidget with, and the snuffbox was the perfect solution, offering in small compass an excellent occasion for costly show-off and at the same time an unrivalled opportunity for the display of fine manners. In the manner with which a gentleman offered, or refrained from offering, and took or refrained from taking, snuff the whole gamut of social language could be demonstrated. The snuffbox and its manipulation was a fine art which had to be studied, and many gentlemen were eager to pay handsomely in order to learn.

Though older ladies were often as greatly addicted to the snuffbox as gentlemen (and Queen Charlotte for one was so unable to refrain that her chin and the bosom of all her gowns were stained brown with dropped grains of snuff), it was essentially regarded as a male habit, the snuff being brought to the dining-table with the wine-bottles after the ladies had left. In London to-day Fribourg and Treyer still sell the famous brands of snuff which tickled the palates of the Prince Regent (though he only pretended to take it) and Brummell and Sheridan and Byron and London high society. The same Masulipatam, High Dry Toast, Macouba, and Brown and Black Rappee are still savoured to-day after more than 250 years of unchanged formulæ.

For the goldsmith the snuffbox offered a satisfactory medium for the display of his art, and every London elegant possessed a collection. Besides knowing how to handle a snuffbox elegantly, it was just as socially elevating to understand how to select the right kind of snuffbox for each social occasion. Not a few dandies sported snuffboxes in summer and winter weights, besides keeping different ones for different days of the week.

Snuffboxes were made in all sizes and shapes and from every kind of precious substance—enamel, ivory, gold and silver, amber, alabaster, fine porcelain, vernis martin, and often several of these at the same time. It was the height of good taste to carry several different snuffboxes about the person, hidden in various different pockets, so that the mood and time of day, the friend and the conversation, might be exactly accommodated.

Some dandies went so far as to design their own snuffboxes. This was less of an innovation than a reversal to an earlier whim. Frederick the Great, for instance, liked to have his snuffboxes made after his own fancy, usually embodying such Teutonic themes as pug-dogs, frogs, and snails, and with indecent pictures painted inside the lid.

The Regency was a famous period for fidgeting and fiddling, and snuffboxes were ideal for this purpose. Even the stern Napoleon was not immune from the general passion for little boxes, though he preferred to use his for *bonbons* instead of snuff. Besides snuff boxes, there were seals and trinkets for elegant fingers which needed something to play with in public. They had to tinkle pleasantly and with a studied nonchalance that not a few English gentlemen went specially to Paris to learn from experts who taught the art of noble tinkling for a hefty fee. Tinkling their seals, offering comfits from little comfit-cases, and snuff from smart snuff boxes, whiled away the long idle hours not at table or in the gaming-booths, and offered an opportunity to display fine breeding in the graceful manipulation of these social accessories.

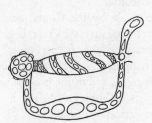

THE DUKE OF MARLBOROUGH'S
DRESS-SWORD HILT
Silver set with diamonds.

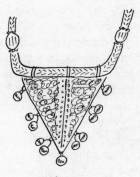

BOY'S PECTORAL
Silver filigree with eleven bells.
Yemen. Contemporary.
Musée de l'Homme, Paris

Napoleon had no natural tastes in any of the arts except that of war. Nevertheless he could well understand the rôle of jewels in propping up prestige, and he had the great French Crown Jewels set in his military hat and his sword-hilt. At Waterloo he had the mortification of losing them all to the Prussians, together with a half-buckle containing twenty-two huge solitaires and twenty-one brilliants. He was, at the time, also wearing the famous Sancey diamond, once the pride of Cardinal Mazarin. This too was appropriated by the Prussians for the embellishment of the Prussian Crown Jewels.

Why did Napoleon take these treasures into action with him? He was as superstitious as any scullery-maid, and he was following a pattern of behaviour which reaches back into remote antiquity, for with them he was invoking magic protection from defeat, though he was doubtless also thinking in terms of a possible getaway.

Jewellers and goldsmiths, like any other artists, must have patrons, which means they must work for the top layer of society. In times of revolution their patrons change dramatically, and new themes, exactly the opposite to preceding themes, are demanded of them, though the settings themselves may remain. In the Carnavalet Museum in Paris we may see politics in action, as the aristocratic large buttons of the mid-eighteenth century painted with proud family miniatures, delicate scenes from a highly artificial nature framed with gold rims, or ingenious and costly puzzle-buttons which once had strutted in Versailles change their theme yet keep their shape. During and after the French Revolution precisely the same-shaped buttons were made by the same jewellers, but the *motifs* were transformed into trees of liberty, masonic symbols of equality such as the triangle and the eye, swords, scythes and swathes of corn, caps of liberty and the triumphant tricolour.

The delicately enamelled gold watches made by the Court jewellers suddenly display tiny guillotines and such slogans as "Vivre libre ou mourir," or "Vigilance and justice characterize a free people," or "Fraternity unites men and makes their happiness." The spate of snuff-boxes did not decrease. Only the *motif* changed, and in the procession of new *motifs* we may read the burning pages of history. On the lids of exquisitely turned snuffboxes are painted caricatures of Louis XVI and his Queen, slogans such as "Death to the tyrants!" "Long live our brave sansculottes!" together with the inevitable cap of liberty and two attendant nymphs, the latter very like the fashionable pre-Revolutionary nymphs, but intended to symbolize the new sentiments which proliferate in the endless slogans. "Peace to the cottages, war to the *châteaux*!" declares a jewelled gold snuffbox, clearly belonging to the latter and not to the former. One silver snuffbox is exquisitely engraved with a scene in perspective of the King being brought back to Paris by the mob. Like the documentary fans steadily printed through those stirring days, the buttons, the snuffboxes, the watches and trinkets, reflect stage by stage every political development of the period.

Goldsmiths must work for somebody, and they are artists in a peculiarly difficult situation, as the raw material for their craft is so costly. Doubtless, like artists in other mediums, the kind of society they would prefer would be that which honoured their profession, offered them a stable place, paid them promptly, and protected them from the misery of having to satisfy vulgar whims or sheer bad taste.

The same generation of French jewellers, having had to switch the *motifs* on their snuffboxes from aristocratic portraits to caps of liberty and cannon, had to switch again in the eighteen-thirties to romantic themes such as mourning nymphs drooping over classic urns beside weeping willows. The nymphs remained the same nymphs as before their two separate metamorphoses, merely being given a more melancholy expression. Rising suns, trees of liberty, and sheaves of corn, however, were now completely *démodé*, for the new *motifs* had all to do with death and decay, unrequited love, and hopeless yearning for nothing in particular.

Seals were now in fashion, and pairs of watches, one of which was a dummy; and human hair was so popular in this fetish-ridden period that it was worked into chains and rings and buttons and framed in fancy lockets, and even used for tapestry-work and sampler-embroidery. Romantic young gentlemen found it modish to wear a tooth from the jaw of their beloved, expensively set into a tiepin, more especially if their beloved had died young and unwed, and best of all if she had so died from consumption.

The craftsmanship of the jewels of this period was already beginning to decline, and insincerity as well as uncertainty is apparent in many of them. The Industrial Revolution and intensifying machine civilization was the reality always in the background, a reality repugnant to the romantic movement, but which, however resolutely it closed its eyes, it was unable to dismiss.

There was a general falling off in male jewellery, for the dead hand of Brummell lay heavy over male dress in England. Austere clothes meant no jewellery either, or almost none. Scarf-pins of diminutive size, a modest signet-ring, a prosaic watch-chain, these were soon as far as a 'gentleman' cared to go. The peacock's tail was folding up in dejection, and most Englishmen, even while they secretly read Oriental romances and dreamed of exotic dress, now pushed aside jewels as irreconcilable with their counting-house existence. When Disraeli wore his diamond rings outside his gloves, as he took his seat in Parliament in 1837, he caused a scandal, and no one dreamed of copying him.

'Taste' had already dwindled to mean dour sobriety, the denial of colour and glitter. Riches could no longer be expressed in male jewellery, for men no longer wore any jewellery. Wealth now meant substantial bank balances and might only be displayed in jewellery in the shape of heavy female *parures* and expensive, unhappy female brooches, and costly diamond manacles on the wrists of the wives of successful businessmen. Even Army officers in civilian clothes had to watch their step, or lose caste.

Lady Harriet Howard, in a letter to her sister written in 1830, related with indignation how a certain Colonel Craddock had the effrontery to attend an evening reception at which she was present in the *beau monde* wearing an embroidered shirt and coat-buttons of diamonds and opals. They were real diamonds and real opals, but that was no help. He should not have been wearing jewelled buttons at all. She described him scornfully as attracting general hostility by his "dreadfully bad taste." The eighteenth century was dead indeed.

ESKIMO BUTTONS

Incised fishbone carved in the form of
baby seals.

Musée de l'Homme, Paris

Since, like the English Puritans of the seventeenth century, the principal business in life of middle-class Englishmen of the nineteenth century was to make money, gaiety and male display of glitter were out of place, and might suggest that the man was not 'serious'—an unenviable imputation, implying that he had no serious purpose in life, since the serious purpose in life was precisely to make money, not to waste precious time being interested in anything else.

A century later English businessmen are still thinking on these lines. Even those men who trade in jewels, and through whose fingers pass the priceless treasures of the world of precious stones, wear the horrid uniform of the Stock Exchange, and are the first to deny to their own sex the pleasure of wearing jewels or more beautiful dress. There has been one distinguished exception, to whom people from all over the world are grateful, for adding something important to London life in this way. Mosheh Oved, the interesting owner of Cameo Corner, that treasure-trove of antique jewels, for years brightened his jewel-shop by wearing at work a splendid long gown of purple velvet.

Today, though England boasts goldsmiths and jewel-makers of such fine quality that Oriental potentates send their regalia to London to be cared for and added to, Englishmen are quite out of the picture. Even the semi-precious waistcoat buttons, still just permissible in the early years of the twentieth century, for special occasions, are now forbidden by the best tailors as vulgar and prestige-lowering.

To-day gentlemen who wish to remain gentlemen in England may wear no other jewellery than cuff-links and evening shirt studs. And these must be of an extreme austerity, which should be costly but must not be showy. An extremely thin flattened gold watch is also permitted. Nothing more.

Of course, the popular 'Charing Cross Road' gents' outfitters stubbornly sell bright waistcoats of imitation brocade and gay cheap face-cloth, fastening with very-imitation-semi-precious-stone buttons, or horsy corduroy with brass buttons, which appeal specially to unrural city youths. These waistcoats are not cheap for their purchasers, though by Savile Row standards they are teeth-grittingly inexpensive, besides being unspeakably vulgar.

The man out of the top drawer, however, must have nothing whatever to do with any dress or jewellery which looks as though it could be cheaply imitated. So, in this age of general paste, he must totally renounce jewels. To-day he may display his wealth and high position only in the jewels of his wife or his mistress (and the latter, in our prudent society, must be done so surreptitiously that it is really not worth the effort of doing it at all). The great days of the great courtesans of the nineteenth century are over now. Such women to-day earn far more money, directly, by displaying their sex allure on the screen. It may also be observed that the increasingly important 'first nights' in our day are those not of the theatre any more, but of the cinema, and it is a contradiction in terms to dress up in a blaze of real jewels in order to sit afterwards in black darkness. The momentary flash of the Press-camera bulbs in the foyer is unselective, jewellery not taking kindly to the strait-jacket of photography.

It is a gruesome vision to look into a future where the only jewels men will ever receive will be lumpy silver memorial cigarette-boxes from their firms on retirement. Such a prospect is as lethal to the dignity of men as it is to the future of the jewel trade.

The question remains. On what jewels can a wealthy man to-day spend his money if he wishes to spend his money on jewellery? He may, of course, collect jewels, not to wear himself but merely for the sake of collecting something. Or he may seek novel forms of using precious stones. Thus £15,000 was recently expended on a jewel-encrusted roll of honour made by an English firm of goldsmiths for the 7th Regiment of New York. It was the same firm which made, before the First World War, the richly jewelled binding of a special edition of Omar Khayyám, a binding containing no less than 1051 gems worked in a design of grapes, poppies, and peacocks entwined with deadly nightshade. This binding took seven years to complete, the book being then dispatched to its American purchaser in 1912 on the *Titanic*, with which it now lies at the bottom of the Atlantic. The insurance money enabled an exact copy of this binding to be begun again in 1932, the work again taking exactly seven years to complete, being finished in 1939 just on the outbreak of the Second World War. On this occasion the jewelled masterpiece was prudently placed in a City strong-box for safe keeping during enemy action. The building containing the strong-box and the strong box itself were totally destroyed by bombing, however, during World War Two. The same firm is now engaged on a third attempt to execute the commission.

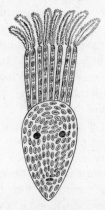

FERTILITY DANCE MASK
Cowrie shells on wood, surmounted
by plumes of blue feathers.
Bambara, French Sudan.
Musée de l'Homme, Paris

Jewellery has its history of techniques no less than industry of a heavier nature. In making jewels first plain gold was used. Then the secrets of enamels were discovered and elaborated. Next the combination of precious stones in settings of precious metals was perfected. At first the precious stones were set at wide intervals, until, by the seventeenth century, the goldsmith's skill had so far advanced that he could set them safely close together. Three centuries have passed since then, and there has been no further development. Why? Because to-day the mind of man turns ever farther from self-adornment towards self-destruction. And the jeweller's skill lies idle and unwanted.

CHAPTER THIRTEEN

TATTOOING, BODY-MUTILATION, AND BODY-PAINTING

Mort aux flics!
Body-tattoo used by French criminal in 1956

BESIDES jewellery, which can be put on and taken off at will, there are other forms of decoration involving the use of the flesh itself. Besides body-painting, a widespread practice and one that involves designs which can be removed and altered to taste, there are two other kinds of flesh-decoration, more or less permanent. These are tattooing, which involves the injection of coloured patterns into the flesh, and which does not affect the contours of the surface of the flesh, and scarification (known as keloid marking by anthropologists), which involves the induction of raised cicatrices on the flesh, and which is usually employed where the colour of the skin is too dark to show up tattooing proper.

There is, in addition, induced body-deformation in the interest of prestige and beauty. This last is perhaps the most widespread of all, and as frequently found in one form or another in Christian countries as in pagan. Gentlemen's corsets or belts are waist-suppressors, therefore body-mutilators, no less than elongated ear-lobes or noses pierced for the reception of barbaric ornament. So also are tight shoes, more frequent in Christian countries than any other regions, and hats so hard that they cause a mark on the wearer's forehead.

Long before the days when anthropologists took to measuring skulls early peoples decided for themselves which shape of head looked most aristocratic, and took steps to alter the soft heads of their babies by artificial pressure, so as to induce them to conform to this ideal. 'Round-head' was as offensive an epithet to early Aztecs as to seventeenth-century Royalists. The early Aztecs wished their babies to have 'moon-shaped' heads, as distinguished from lesser tribes and from slaves, and so they altered the shape of their babies' heads by compression between boards, a practice strictly forbidden to their slaves and servants.

They regarded it as especially important, in this effort of racialism, to ensure that the child's forehead should slope well backward, a sugar-loaf head tilting to the rear being highly esteemed. Slaves were never permitted this privilege, the slaves themselves and their children and children's children being required to grow up to be and to look like slaves, therefore round-headed. Such sugar-loaf head-binding is still practised in some corners of Melanesia.

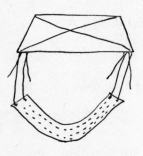

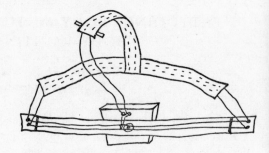

SOUTH AMERICAN HEAD-
FLATTENING BOARD
Sipiho.

SARAWAK MELANAU APPARATUS FOR
BROADENING HEAD OF INFANTS

It has been suggested, as explaining why some African tribes practise crippling self-mutilation, that this may have begun as a safety-measure in order to protect tribal women from the slavers by making them look undesirable. This point of view is hardly more tenable than that which assumes that the pea-hen is impressed by the beauty of the peacock's tail. What the Western mind regards as beautiful rarely is so regarded by Eastern or Oriental minds. Moreover, the mutilations are often found to be practised both on men and women or men alone, and also in tribes which the Arab slaver never reached.

What appears as a frightful disfigurement in modern Western eyes does not so appear at all in African eyes, which may rather regard it as a token of great endurance or brave distinction. Peasants and poor people in Europe, unwilling to fight in wars they felt were no concern of theirs, have been known to injure themselves deliberately in order to render themselves useless as soldiers. It may be that these African mutilations were undertaken with precisely the opposite objective in mind—that is, in order, by a display of stoic bravery under pain, to please the pagan gods, who, thus propitiated, would grant the victim magic strength and invincibility against his enemy in battle.

This aspect of voluntary suffering in the ordeal of being tattooed or marked with keloid pattern, or suffering mutilation for decoration, should not be underestimated. American Indians, we know, did not count as braves until they had proved their manhood by public self-torture. They were required to endure their agony in silence, or sing while inflicting it on themselves, if they wished to win the respect of their fellows and the approval of their gods. The marks of such self-torture counted as honourable wounds, as physical medals of bravery, a permanent testimonial marked on the body of the examinee.

Every one can see such a mutilation or scarification, and the sufferer's reputation is thereby so enhanced that others hasten to do the same, or suffer still worse agony, in order to win 'face.' Thus, in the competition to show who is the bravest, we find ear-lobes hanging down to the waist, underlips grossly stretched by plugging with enormous metal roundels, the nose heavily perforated in several places, the neck extended by rows of brass rings, the whole body tattooed completely or keloid-marked all over. What may have begun as a small pattern of tattoo round the wrist, or simple prick to allow the ear or nose to receive a minor jewel, has run riot in the cause of show-off, exactly as the wearing of jewellery has sometimes run riot for the same purpose. It is even possible that both tattoo and scarification originated in the accidental entry into a wound of foreign matter, which became infected and healed with the foreign matter inside, like the blue scars on the faces of old European miners. It is certainly true that in primitive societies, where masculine bravery is all-important, the men are always more elaborately tattooed than the women.

Women in such societies are tattooed to establish their social position, and sometimes also suffer scarification to give pleasure to their lovers. Thus some African tribeswomen undergo scarification on the zone of the small of their backs to please their lovers, who declare that the feel of the raised lacework of flesh on their caressing hands adds greatly to their amorous satisfaction.

It is a common belief among sailors, soldiers, and people of little education that tattooing acts as inoculation against such diseases as yellow fever, smallpox, and syphilis, and the tattoo parlours of London and every British seaport flourished mightily during the major cholera epidemics in London in 1832, 1848, and again in 1853, epidemics which raged for more than a year each and killed nearly half a million people altogether. (These were the major epidemics. Mayhew says that there were certain London dosshouses so dirty that cholera always thrived there, general epidemic or no.)

In point of fact not only was a visit to the tattooist's parlour useless in those days as a precaution against infection, but it enormously increased the chances of picking up infection, the tattooist's needle never being

L

cleaned between customers, so that venereal diseases were readily transmitted from one client to the next.

The pain suffered in modern tattoo parlours, where electric needles are now employed and hygiene is greatly improved, is relatively slight, especially as very large designs are worked in several instalments. The desire to prove manly bravery by fortitude under suffering is thus not

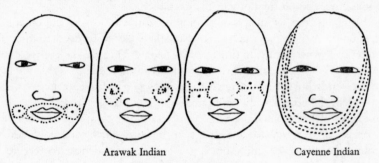

Arawak Indian   Cayenne Indian

TATTOOING PATTERNS

satisfied, and modern fans come to the tattoo parlours because their pals do, or to record some emotion permanently, usually connected with love of mother or pal or sweetheart, or admiration for some religious or martial hero.

Tattooing is still regarded as a manly embellishment by those who undergo it, and it is preferably sited where it may be displayed and by those whose work enables them so to display it. Navvies, sailors, dockers, and soldiers are the chief clients of tattoo parlours to-day. There is also a sprinkling of criminals, who wish to be marked with their own tattoo language to give themselves a sense of unity and purpose.

Tattooing is a very old practice in history, favoured not only by primitive peoples, but also during periods of high culture. It was used by the Greeks to mark their slaves, and by the Romans for the same purpose, a practice revived by Nazi Germany in the concentration camps of the 1939 War. As an old-established identification of slaves it may thus have become the recognized stigmata of the social outcast and the voluntary badge of the criminal, keeping its brooding defiance of authority in the race-consciousness of the uneducated and downtrodden through the centuries.

Cesare Lombroso, the Italian founder of modern scientific criminology, has declared that in the Western world tattooing is more frequent among criminals than any other professions. An American woman journalist, reporting on the female reformatory of Los Guilucos (*Collier's*, 1953), records spontaneous outbreaks of self-tattooing and mutual tattooing among these young teen-agers, performed by means of ordinary sewing-needles dipped in ink, and sited on faces, arms, hands, and anywhere at all on the body. "One girl," she reported, "had a brief Anglo-Saxon word tattooed across her *derrière*." The girls, she explained, told her that they were utterly bored and pent up, needed release from emotional tension, and did it for 'kicks.'

TURTLE EMBLEM
Polynesian tattoo.

FACIAL TATTOO
Chaco tribe,
South America.

To-day tattooing is still commonly found both among petty thieves and the more important members of the underworld such as pimps. They have their own recognizable tattoo insignia, marks of their particular *métier*. An eagle bearing aloft a naked woman is the internationally recognized emblem of the pimp, the butterfly no less widely known as the emblem of the professional thief. Field-Marshal Montgomery, no doubt, was unaware of this association when he had his arm tattooed with a modest lepidopter.

More respectable crafts also like to have the trademark of their work tattooed on their forearms. Tailors, coopers, carpenters, were once proud to bear the tattooed emblem of their skilled profession where it could be seen and recognized. To-day, as we have said, most of the clients are labourers, dockers, men in the Army or Navy (the Air Force does not seem to feel the same passion for the tattoo needle); a considerable number are good Roman Catholic Irishmen, and they like to display symbols of their faith in their tattoos. The Vatican, which originally forbade the practice to believers, has now withdrawn its veto.

As body-decoration of a pious nature Roman Catholics prefer crucifixes and holy pictures, often in combinations with tattooed memorials to "dear Mother," or "my dear comrade killed in battle," or "dear Jim drowned at sea," or the usual pledges of undying love coupled with a particular female name. There is a pretty general belief in the magic protection of religious symbols thus tattooed, and old salts in the Navy recall the stubbornly held belief of ratings that an enormous crucifix tattooed on a sailor's back would prevent him from ever being flogged. American sailors to-day, of whom at least 90 per cent. are tattooed, believe that a pig or rooster tattooed on the left instep is an infallible charm against drowning.

The races in whom the art of tattooing has been carried to its highest degree of delicacy and intricacy are the Maoris, the Polynesians, and the Japanese. In all these people the largest and most elaborate designs were strictly reserved for persons of the highest social rank. Curiously enough, colour prejudice exists in its own way among coloured races no less than among white, and the precise point at which tattoo will no longer show up against a coloured skin, but must be abandoned for keloid marking, is delicate. London tattoo parlours often have West Indians coming in to be tattooed, to make sure that their skin is light enough to show up the blue patterns.

In Europe generally, although Edwardian England took a strong interest in tattooing, the cult has generally come to be associated with poor and unsophisticated people. The great dragons, writhing geishas, and twining serpents of the high Japanese periods in the art of tattooing have on the whole dwindled into simple affirmations of patriotic zeal or amorous pledges, more particularly amorous pledges. Among these latter one aspect is noticeable in the designs offered by the tattoo parlours. The naked women who still sometimes feature thereon, as mermaids or flag-bearers or pin-up girls, are noticeably of the rather coarse and physically heavy type, who might be expected to be found in the cheaper brothels. This unexotic atmosphere, adapted to the sailor or soldier client, is reminiscent of the Greek fairy-tales with which modern Greek prostitutes used to while away the tedium of imprisonment—which tales always began, with a cosy familiarity: "Once upon a time there was a ravished Queen. . . ."

There are always a few independent or masochistically-minded clients who prefer to tattoo themselves, and for these clients special 'do-it-yourself' tattoo outfits are manufactured to-day, and there are even correspondence courses for instruction in designing *motifs* and patterns. To-day tattooing is done with an electric needle dipped in vegetable dyes mixed with alcohol. A firm rather greasy skin is preferred as giving a better surface than a dry skin which might tear under the needle.

It is important to note that men most likely to visit the tattoo parlours— navvies, agricultural labourers, sailors, furniture-removers, for example— are those whose heavy jobs ensure that the tattoos will be seen, because they have their arms tattooed in order to display them when at work, and they habitually work with their sleeves rolled up. For the purpose of tattooing cannot be said to be completed until the tattoo is seen and admired by others, more particularly by the opposite sex. This is why some forms of tattooing are definitely sexual in intention and character, and are sometimes located on parts of the body normally not in vision except in conditions of extreme intimacy.

Among the thousands of "Ever True" enclosed in roses, or "Mother dear" in laurel, or "Game to the end" with crossed British flags, sometimes different themes are demanded. Thus one old man insisted on having his bald head tattooed with the name "Emily," and not a few clients from the U.S.A. have demanded tattooed socks, covering their feet and ankles.

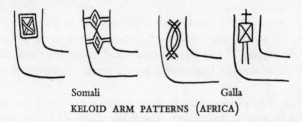

Somali   Galla

KELOID ARM PATTERNS (AFRICA)

In general it is found that American customers prefer larger and more grandiose tattoos, which take up more time and are more expensive and more painful. Enormous eagles and dragons, immense stars and stripes, and the "Statue of Liberty above the Waves" are *motifs* much in demand in the American Navy. American-Irish like to be tattooed with scenes from the Scriptures with elaborate detail. The descent from the cross and the Resurrection are most popular. Best loved of all is the *Rock of Ages*.

Next to religion, patriotism no less than politics is one of the most frequent themes demanded in the tattoo parlours: the British or American flag, the tricolour, the bust of Queen Victoria or King Edward, the assassination of the Duc de Guise, the arrest of Louis XVI at Varennes. Indeed, we may be not far wrong in detecting a link here between the recording aspect of these tattoos and of the snuffboxes, a desire somehow to ensure permanency for such important news.

The sailing-ship days still live vividly in the older tattoo patterns. Old-fashioned cannon, fully rigged sailing-ships, "Death before Dishonour," are still being tattooed on manly chests and arms to-day. The machine age does not yet seem to have penetrated into the London tattoo parlour. No motor-cars, no aeroplanes, are seen; no tractors or modern machine-guns; there is rather the timeless fancy of great dragons and mythical serpents, and the most recent type of female dress used on the tattoos, when there is dress at all, dates from the early days of the 1914 War.

Another aspect of tattooing is that of souvenir, not of mother or sweetheart or perished friend, but of places visited, almost like an insurance against disbelief in travellers' tales. Tourists no less than sailors like to return from their voyages with tattoos of geisha girls, pyramids, palm-trees, dragons, which they have collected in the tattoo parlours on their visits to Cairo and New York, Tokio, London, Cardiff, and New South Wales. It is more interesting and more permanent than a bit of brassware or china.

Not a few distinguished men have been attracted into the tattoo parlours besides Field-Marshal Montgomery, among them the King of Denmark, who has an elaborate large dragon tattooed on his chest.

I have suggested that body-mutilation appears to be associated with desire to raise social status. Head-deformation was known in the ancient world and practised both by Egyptians and Sumerians, with the same intention of rendering babies of superior birth a different shape from their slaves.

Methods of head-deformation vary as much as do the shapes sought for in the process of deforming. Carib Islanders and Cheyenne Indians press small boards to their babies' heads to ensure a narrow backward-inclined forehead, to them the summit of physical beauty and racial pride. Other races used other methods, such as tightly rolled bands of stuff or leaves to press the head width-wise, and one African tribe uses weights and pressures to make the top of the head flat, the better to carry loads.

Other mutilations are suffered in order to admit jewellery. Araquoua Indians of Cheyenne of noble rank pierce the cheeks of their infants at birth, in order later to be able to adorn the child with socially distinguished ornaments of parrot feathers, forest seeds, green and yellow pebbles, and silver trinkets. None of these ornaments may be worn by commoners. The Lango in East Africa knock out two lower front teeth in order to hold the lip-plug, without which they would lose face.

Nor may we, in our Western civilization, pride ourselves on being free from such efforts to achieve social superiority. To many people of good education and for many centuries in the West ordinary rude health has appeared obnoxious and an infallible sign of low birth. Careful breeding and distinguished birth being the desired goal to indicate by a certain fragility of appearance, physical steps have been taken to suggest delicate health and a refinement of body incompatible with rude health and vulgar manual toil. Thus a very small, corseted waist in a gentleman suggests that the muscles of the diaphragm are hardly being used. Small hands crushed into gloves a size too small advertise the fact that the gentleman does not work with his hands. A pale and delicate skin announces that he does not work out of doors like a navvy, though his pale skin may in fact have been achieved by the use of bleaching lotions.

Certain diseases are aristocratic and may be pretended to win social prestige. Gout, for instance, devalues no English gentleman socially, but quite the contrary. On the other hand, such low-ranking ailments as housemaid's knee or waiter's flat feet are socially calamitous.

Painting the body for the purpose of self-aggrandisement is an art practised by all primitive peoples, and Red Indians are still so called not because of the coppery tone of their flesh, but on account of the carmine paint they were originally so fond of using on their bodies. The possibility of completely changing the colour of the skin is a metamorphosis that has always fascinated men, and the Indians of India worship their deity Krishna, in one of his many manifestations, in the form of the blue-painted god.

Selfish king   Upright official   Crafty statesman   Stern judge

FACE-PAINTING, CHINESE OPERA

Parts of the body are also painted for particular effects of pride. Henna is widely used by Persians and Arabs on hair, nails, palms of hands, and soles of feet, and sometimes on the feet themselves, painted on in the form of sandals. Eye-painting, too, is another elegant means of displaying social exclusiveness, blue, white, or red kohl being still commonly employed for this purpose in the East. Only those of great social superiority can afford to mix the antimony used as eye-paint with expensive powdered pearls.

All primitives paint themselves, and especially their faces, in precise patterns which have symbolic meanings. The National Opera of China retains to-day its highly stylized face-painting, an art which has descended unchanged from remote history, and therefore offers invaluable clues as to how the mind of early man conceived the symbols and associations which seem to need so much explanation to the different understanding of modern man.

In Chinese opera, which has been performed unchanged for thousands of years, because the peasants know and love every detail of each opera, each particular character may instantly be recognized for what he is by the colours and patterns painted on his face. Thus he arrives on the scene with his future behaviour clearly marked on his countenance, and the audience knows exactly what to expect from him.

These painted patterns (*lien pu*) began as actual masks, which, however, proved awkward when speaking and singing were introduced into Chinese opera in the thirteenth century. The painted patterns were then transferred from the masks on to the faces of the performers. Each colour has its meaning. Red in Chinese face-painting represents loyalty and courage. A preponderance of black denotes uncompromising integrity. A preponderance of white denotes cunning. Yellow indicates a quiet, calculating nature, green or blue a hot temper, and pink or brown mixed with red the tender weakness of old age.

Cultured Europeans have also taken face-painting seriously. In the eighteenth century in England it was thought no shame, but quite the contrary, for male elegants to powder and paint their faces as lavishly as did the Society ladies, nor did such male face-painting imply homosexual tendencies. An observer in 1754 describes gentlemen in Society who "will spend the whole morning scenting their linen and arching their eyebrows. They have their *toilettes* too, as well as the ladies, set out with washes, perfumes and cosmetics."

The dandies took their appearance even more seriously than the beaux, looking upon it as a full-time job, requiring the strictest discipline. A French traveller named M. de Jouy, staying at a London hotel in 1821, recorded hearing a stream of orders to his valet issuing from the dandy in the adjacent room, for his busk, corset, toilet oils, scents, cosmetics, and skin lotions, and how, after hours spent upon his person, he at last emerged from the hotel, when M. de Jouy observed him to be dressed in the height of fashion, stiff-backed, stiff-necked, small-waisted, his cravat so large as to hide chin and mouth, his hair bunched forward and shining with scented oil, *and his cheeks brilliantly rouged.*

For decades afterwards Englishmen went on painting their faces, though within twenty years it was fashionable to look pale, not red. "Young men of fashion," affirmed Captain Gronow, used to come out of the hands of the *coiffeur* "romantically pale or delicately tinted." All the hand-books on social guidance for gentlemen in the nineteenth century devote pages to cosmetics, and the standard American book on male-etiquette (published in New York in 1850) advises the use of hair-dye, paint, face powder, and eye-shadow for dashing democrats who wished to cut a figure in the social world.

It is true to say that to-day the male beauty-parlour is not only still alive, but flourishing. Gentlemen, no less than ladies, who are dissatisfied with the shape of the nose God gave them do not hesitate to seek expert surgical help to have it remodelled according to their fancy. If

COSMETIC BOX FOR MEN
Silver filigree kohl-container.
Two inches high. Yemen.
Musée de l'Homme, Paris

TATTOO MARKINGS ON LIBYAN
FIGURE FROM TOMB OF SETI
Symbols of goddess Neith, mother of
sun-god Re.

they do not paint their faces the artificial red and white of the eighteenth century, or the phthisis-white of the eighteen-thirties, they still do change the colour of their faces in order to acquire prestige. To-day it is desirable for gentlemen to look as though they had just returned from basking on the beach at Cannes or Capri. "Handsome men," declares the contemporary advertisement, "are slightly sunburned."

Men are invited to achieve this appearance of enjoying a carefree life of open-air idleness in fashionable resorts, by the use of a special sun-lamp, or a particular lotion, or the application of special tanning fluids, designed to sell to junior clerks suffering from sedentary life and office pallor. The wording of this cunning invitation should be noted—"*slightly* sun-burned." Only sunburned enough, that is, to suggest the leisured gentleman, not so sunburned as to suggest the farmer working out of doors in all weathers. The tan must look like a holiday tan, not like an occupational tan.

The precise degree of tan required for the best social effect needs careful consideration, even in England. In such countries as South Africa it is imperative for a white man not to look too tanned, in order to avoid painful situations, for a white man who is tanned a shade too much risks being mistaken for a native, and driven from the white section of train or town. For the avoidance of such situations, since the sun shines with equal vigour on both races, white South Africans wear a strip of ribbon on their wrists which will protect enough of their skin from the sun's rays to display to the authorities in case of doubt.

This preoccupation with colour of skin has a necessarily destructive effect on the self-respect of those born Negro in a climate for which nature designed dark skins. John Gunther has reported how Negroes themselves have learned to discriminate between 'good' hair and 'bad' hair, the good hair being that which is less Negro in texture, therefore more valuable for the owner. By continual pressure of social opinion Negroes even come to prefer those of their children whose skins are lightest in hue.

It is one of to-day's tragedies that so much of the imagination, music, and poetic fervour of the dark-skinned races is being channelled into hysterical self-protection from the white man's traditionally superior attitude, especially tragic now that this attitude is at last changing. A Southern Rhodesian Negro sums it up in declaring, "I have sometimes thought that I am not a human being," describing, in words of Biblical significance, a dream he had experienced in which a dead friend reappeared to him, prophesying:

The day is coming when both black and white shall be white, when the skin and the flesh shall be eaten by worms and your white bones shall be the only symbol of your person. There and then shall equality be yours. Only in death will there be no selection.[1]

[1] Reprinted in *Concord*, April, 1956.

CHAPTER FOURTEEN

DRESS REFORM

The English are the most aristocratic democrats in the world, always endeavouring to squeeze through the portals of rank and fashion and then slamming the door in the face of the unfortunate devil who may happen to be behind them.

An etiquette book, 1830

WHAT is the meaning of fashion? Why do styles change? Why in our day do styles change so much more slowly for men than for women? What hope is there for an improvement in male dress?

To answer these questions—and they are questions of the utmost significance, going down to the roots of every social system—we must remember that society and the individual are constantly at war with each other. Society desires the individual to stay put in his allotted place, whereas the individual desires to elevate himself from his allotted place into a higher social place. It is no accident that the etiquette book quoted above speaks of "rank and fashion," for dress is the most powerful single aid in this historic game of social snakes and ladders.

During the thousands of years when their society remained static dress in China remained correspondingly static; it did not evolve, but stayed put. In India the same thing happened. Each class and each caste wore its ordained garb; each member of the community knew his particular place, and recognized every one else's place. Nothing changed. The dress, like the system, stood still.

In African primitives, whose social system is tightly regulated and unchanging, their dress is carefully regulated down to the minutest details, each age-group carrying its own social status, which is defined in its particular dress, from new-born infant right up to the revered position of tribal elder. The woman who has given birth immediately proclaims her changed status by assuming different ornaments from those she wore before she gave birth. The young lad signifies that he has passed his initiation test by the assumption of certain articles of dress previously taboo to him. The man, at each stage of his life, puts on certain garments which proclaim exactly what niche he is filling in his society at that time. Nothing is casual or haphazard. All his clothes and ornaments have meaning and magic significance, for Africans, like all primitives, cannot live a life without significance. To them meaninglessness equals death, for it is the opposite of life and living as they understand it. The meaning of clothes, in particular, is of such importance to African tribesmen that they cling to sartorial symbolism even in periods of transition.

Here is Father Grévisse's account (reported in *Le Centre Extra-Coutumier d'Élisabethville*) of a ceremony in the Congo concerning an African worker about to retire from his job with the Union Minière in 1951, after completing his term of years.

He came to the ceremony dressed in a European-style jacket and *pagne* (native cotton robe) and a leopard skin. He carried on his shoulders a pick and shovel. After receiving his medal he knelt down and said thanks for it by beating his hands together, and then marched away to the sound of trumpets. Afterwards I asked him what he had intended to symbolize. He replied more or less like this:

"In the service of the Union Minière I did my best until I became a *moniteur* and, thanks to personal sway over my comrades, Judge of the Native Township Tribunal. In this sack I have my employment books and the proofs of my service, to show how proud I am of what I have become through my work. Yet my heart is not changed, and this I show by wearing the dress of the elders at home, the dress I shall wear again when I return to my village. Two loyalties I have had during my life: to my tribal group and its authority and to my whites and their authority."

Here we see the very roots of sartorial significance, the African making sense out of both kinds of life he had known, each life a stable order in itself.

Similarly in classical Chinese dress the dragon symbolized the powers, at once destructive and beneficial, of the elements: water, clouds, and rain. The Emperor alone was privileged to wear on his robes five-clawed dragons facing to the front. Princes of the first rank might wear five-clawed dragons facing to the front except on the shoulders, where the dragons had to be shown in profile only. Princes of the second rank wore five-clawed dragons in profile. Those of the third rank wore four-clawed dragons facing the front. Those of the fourth rank wore four-clawed dragons in profile. And so on.

In the static East no less than the dynamic West sartorial laws were constantly flouted. Thus, despite the strict religious sumptuary law which insisted that Saracenic women should wear their chemises long, many risked imprisonment and severe punishment by wearing them reaching only to the knees. Saracenic women even dared to flout religious edict by assuming the male prerogative of wearing a turban, and Ibn al-Hâjj, the early fourteenth-century chronicler, describes with disgust double-humped female turbans resembling dromedaries. Despite police inspectors, beatings, and the pillory, Mameluke women contrived to defy the laws framed to keep them modestly dressed and in their proper station. Beneath the shrouded wrap they managed to develop their fashions so as to compete with their neighbours. Al-Hâjj complains that their dresses were too short and too tight, and that their long drawers, which should have been fastened decently at the waist, were being shamelessly worn well below it. And there was a continual outcry by the religious authorities against the luxury of their apparel, which no amount of punishment seemed to curb, despite the fact that the vendor risked having his luxurious wares seized by the Sultan.

SHEPHERD, 1500
French.
Musée Cluny, Paris

EGYPTIAN SOCK (SIXTH CENTURY)
Victoria and Albert Museum

If the secluded and fettered Muslim women of Egypt and elsewhere dared so to defy religion and authority for the sake of fine dress, we may imagine to what lengths their menfolk went.

Fashion, indeed, is born only in social struggle, and it is typical of new and struggling societies and times of violent social change which give birth to new social orders that styles change with equal violence. Violent social change need not, however, entail bloodshed. The bitterest battles perhaps are those which have been fought silently just outside the doors of coveted *salons*. As civilizations grow rich by commerce merchants want to use their wealth to climb into higher social circles, circles as determined to keep them out as they are to enter. Thus clothes are copied in an attempt to reach equality, and those whose dress is copied then change their dress for something different, in order to retain their superiority. And this happens through the whole gamut of classes and sub-classes.

But this is a threat to the stability of the social order, a threat which stable societies try to prevent by laying down the strictest laws regulating who may wear what. During the height of her power Rome decreed every detail of the permitted wear for each of her citizens and slaves. Every Roman wore distinctive garb, of which every item was controlled by strict sumptuary laws, so that, as with an army, a glance was sufficient to learn anyone's exact rank in society.

The *tunica palmata*, traditional Imperial Roman dress, such as Julius Cæsar wore, was an embroidered purple toga worn with a tunic worked in gold thread. This was the gala dress allotted a Roman general celebrating a triumph, and also the distinctive dress of magistrates presiding at games. From Cæsar down to the lowest slave every one was dressed according to plan in a dress designed to make clear his age, rank, profession, social class or lack of social class. Clear-cut regulations affected the very shape and colour of footwear, the number of straps permitted on the permitted footwear, and the kind of ornament permitted on the regulated straps.

It was perhaps the disturbing memory of how the decadence and overthrow of Roman power had been preceded and accompanied by the relaxation and unpunished flouting of her once strict sumptuary laws that impelled the early Popes to re-establish strict new sumptuary laws once the Christian Church of Rome had established itself. For the Church stood upon a rock not merely of spiritual values, but also of temporal values. The stability of society under the domination of the Church was its objective, and no man was to be allowed to imperil this stability by social unrest. Every man must know his place, dress for his place, and stay in his place.

If a man were born into a life of toil and hardship because his parents were peasants the Church assured him of a happier lot in the world to come if he lived a good Christian life and submitted to the authority of the Church in all matters. If a man were born a great noble or emperor, though he lived an earthly life of great pomp and luxury befitting his high station, could not the Church withold its blessing from him and deprive him of hope of life hereafter if he refused submission to the Church?

So it was that when the Church of Rome ruled supreme reform in dress came steadily from above, and took the form of repressive measures regulating socially unsettling luxury in dress, which the Church regarded as wicked not only in its preoccupation with worldly vanity (classed as a sin as grave as lust or gluttony), but because it used up wealth which the Church claimed as its prerogative.

The interesting fact is that, with all its immense power and authority, the Church was never wholly successful in the application of its sumptuary laws. Had it succeeded there would never have been any need for more. Fashions would have remained frozen, and no new ideas would have crept into dress.

On the contrary, however, the unceasing streams of new sumptuary laws issuing from the Vatican show that the previous ones were clearly being disregarded. Though threatened by hell-fire itself, men desired and were determined to dress beyond their rank. That men have been prepared to suffer severe punishment for committing sartorial crime, for flying in the face of all-powerful authority, is the measure of their ambition. This is the whole history of men's dress. The lord changed his style of dress as soon as lesser lords began to imitate it, and as the rank below the lesser lords copied their dress, so did they copy the new garb of their superiors. And so on all the way down the social scale. The struggle was unremitting.

Styles have changed and still change because man has opposed himself to the strait-jacket of his enforced class. However thwarted or down-trodden by harsh social circumstances, man has proved invincible, facing and battling against punishment and even death in the hope of bettering himself. There is, when we come to look closely at the subject, a great deal more than mere vanity in man's desire to wear fine clothes.

As to a certain extent dress depended also on wealth, the gist of most sumptuary laws was that extravagant styles were to be permitted only to the greatest nobles. Indeed, there was no stopping them. Periods of great social misery were also periods of great sartorial extravagance, and the plagues, pestilences, and famines of the Middle Ages were accompanied by aristocratic dress of the utmost luxury and extravagance, despite continual outbursts of wrath from the Church, which enforced acts of penance, but never succeeded in diminishing the extravagance of the dress. The Church, however, though not successful, did not relax its denunciation. Slitters and jags in fashionable dress were denounced as wanton; particoloured hose were denounced as shameless; the long full gown with sleeves which swept the ground (and which critics declared made men indistinguishable from women) was denounced as ungodly; the slit-sided robe was denounced as satanic; and the abbreviated male tunic which displayed the buttocks was denounced as blasphemous. The Church declared that crop-failures and plagues were God's punishment for man's sartorial presumption. But all to no effect.

The real check came, indeed, not from the Church, but from the nobles themselves, who had every reason to try to stop sartorial encroachment on their exalted rank. They were men of immense power, well able to punish the unprivileged for aping their finery, and they were as eager as the Church to enforce the sumptuary laws. Yet even they, despite the steady infliction of fines, imprisonment, and public humiliation of offenders, were unable to ensure that the sumptuary laws were completely obeyed, for the desire to rise in the world and look like some one of importance proved an irresistible incentive to disobey the sumptuary laws.

Century after century an increasing avalanche of new sumptuary laws was enacted and ignored, or half disobeyed. Moreover, the Church was meeting with sartorial rebellion in its own ranks, for no one liked fine feathers better than the prelates. As early as the thirteenth century Matthew Paris, the monk of St Albans, set down his disgust at the excessive foppery he found in the clergy of his time, especially the English clergy. It was so scandalous that Pope Innocent IV ordered several English prelates to send to Rome exact copies of their finest vestments for inspection. They turned out to be thickly embroidered with gold and precious stones worked into fanciful pagan patterns and animals.

This clerical taste for finery had been going on a long time. There were priests who not only let their hair grow to cover their tonsures, but also frisked about in gay gowns of scarlet and green, fashionably "cutted," and with "long pykes on their shoes." There were parish priests who carried weapons in fancy scabbards. And it is well known how Thomas à Becket's sumptuous apparel aroused comment all over France.

If the priests could not control the laity neither could ecclesiastical authority control the priests in this matter, and the mania for fine dress persisted no less than the enactment of unsuccessful laws against it. Gradually the sumptuary laws gave ground. What originally was considered too rich and dashing for any but the nobility to wear slowly came to be legally permitted to men of great wealth, and in time even the merchants managed to get a toe into the social portal they longed to push open.

Thus a typical sumptuary law of 1463 required male tunics to cover the buttocks unless the wearer was entitled by his noble rank to dress as he pleased. A century later a sumptuary law of the time of Queen Mary permitted silk to be worn on any portion of the dress by no man whose income was less than £20 a year, though a gentleman by birth.

As usual, the lawyers who set down the terms of the sumptuary laws made heavy weather of their provisions, so that sometimes no one could understand exactly what they meant. One such sumptuary law, passed in 1565, was so complicated that it caused endless and doubtless very profitable legal bickering for years. By this Act the tailor was directed to "line a slop hose not cut in panes with a lyning of coton stitched to the sloppe

over and besydes the linen lynyng straighte to the legge." The correct
interpretation of this regulation caused much anxiety, for the tailor was
liable to heavy punishment and the seizure of the garment in case of
infringement. A deputation of tailors therefore went to demand of the
Recorder of London if he could explain it. He interpreted it as meaning
that the tailors could so line the slop. But other tailors were still dubious,
and further fruitless discussions took place, after which another deputation
lodged an appeal with a still higher legal authority.

CATALAN MALE CLOAK
Painted wooden panel, *gouache*.
Thirteenth century.
*Palacio Nacional, Montjuich,
Barcelona*

ACTUAL DRESS OF FRENCH
REVOLUTION, YEAR 3
Pregnant woman receiving ration of
bread and rice. Boy in blue coat and
brown trousers.
Musée Carnavalet, Paris

It may be illuminating to glance at the actual working of sumptuary
laws in one little society over a period of centuries, for here in small we
find the same tug-of-war that was taking place all over Christendom.
The Town Council of the little township of Zurich passed a law in
1375 forbidding its citizens under heavy penalty to wear striped hose or
cloth of different colours. Fashion proved too strong for the law. In
1488 they passed another law forbidding the use of silk borders, hooks

and eyes, and metal mountings on any dress except that of the nobility and the prostitutes, both, for different reasons, being outside the law affecting ordinary people. This law was not properly obeyed.

Bitter complaints about the decay of good Swiss simplicity and honesty formed the preamble to each new set of sumptuary laws.

> Swiss citizens are accused of wearing shag hats, clothes from London and Lombardy, whole inner and outer coats, silver buttons front and back, and the colour yellow, formerly a Judas colour, has become fashionable.

The wail that a new vanity "has become fashionable" was a wail of despair, for the laws were always weaker than the fashion, no respectable citizens being shamed however low the associations of any new fashion. Thus Bishop Valerius complained in vain that the extravagant new fashion of slashing and pinking had been introduced into Switzerland by the prostitutes following the Swiss army which had beaten the Burgundians. And very likely it had. But the fashion was not prevented from spreading by his exhortation. On the contrary, it was even eagerly adopted by churches and convents as well as by villagers and townsfolk.

In vain did the good bishop denounce all this horrid luxury of apparel, which, he insisted, went hand in hand with "vice, cunning, disbelief, contempt, and pride," and furthermore "caused the gainful arts to expand, which was a sin." How could the Swiss people remain simple and unmercenary if they went as soldiers and learned abroad what they should not? "Many Swiss," he lamented, "went as mercenaries to fight foreign wars and brought back money and luxurious habits."

But the Swiss were not going to be left out of this fascinating new fashion of slashing which their own soldiers had unwittingly begun, and which now raged like a fever throughout Europe. The Great Council of Berne in 1530 enacted laws ordering severe punishment for slashing of clothes, the wearing of clothes slashed at the knee being regarded as especially criminal. (A certain John Mischler, brought to court under this law, only escaped heavy punishment by protesting that his hose were too tight and that, being of an economical nature, he had prudently slashed them to make room, rather than go to the wicked expense of buying new hose.)

The rage for slashing intensified, and the laws against it were disregarded. Seven years after the 1530 Act a peremptory command was read from every pulpit in the country, ordering all citizens to sew up their slashes, one week and not a moment more being given for the accomplishment of this order. But it was apparently not obeyed, for in 1541 there was another command from all the pulpits to the same effect, and these commands continued to be issued without appreciable result for over a century, the clergy themselves finally succumbing to the fashion.

The Town Council had also to turn its attention to the luxurious apparel of the Church, and in 1670 passed a stern law forbidding priests and their families to wear unseemly long hair, large hat-bands, small hats, fringed sword-hangings, double buttons, silk stockings, perforations on their red woollen skirts, shoes with long, pointed toes and large shoe-ribbons. If the clergy could not dress modestly, how were the lower orders going to be kept in their places? The Burgomaster complained bitterly:

Not only are all good ordinances trodden underfoot, but arrogance and pride without shame have been exhibited by more and more from day to day and almost no difference between upper and lower ranks observed.

He thought it timely to remind citizens that God was watching their folly and was rapidly losing patience with them, since the Town Council's "punishments are despised and thrown to the winds: since we do not wish to draw down divine righteous vengeance upon us and the common people, therefore . . ."

Nor was it only by wearing too grand clothes that the erring citizens were trying to appear above their stations. The equivalent of the T.V. aerial above the roof of the modern T.V.-less home had its counterpart in seventeenth-century Switzerland: "When persons owning no horse, or seldom mount another's, constantly jingle about in boots and spurs and appear thus in church."

Society must keep itself in its regulated stations, and once again the sumptuary laws set out clearly who belonged to which station, and precisely what each station had to wear and had not to wear, and precisely how much it might and might not spend on its dress.

These stations formed six classes, and are listed as follows:

1. *The poorest* [respectable] females working for their living [such as sempstresses].
2. *Menservants* working for daily pay.
3. *Handworkers* [100 skills are listed], small tradesmen, inferior musicians, schoolmasters without degrees.
4. *Candidates for doctorates.*
5. *Merchants with a fair trade,* aristocracy of long residence in the town, men living on private means, merchants, upper-grade officials, doctors with degrees.
6. *Government officials,* nobles, city attorneys.

It was the servants whose flouting of the sumptuary laws caused perhaps the most trouble, and the flood of enactments to control them was as unceasing as it was ineffective. They were forbidden sewn hats, and bidden to content themselves with simple felt, and not permitted better hats, even though obtained by gift or inheritance—nor permitted to wear shoes with heels or ornamental perforation, and their shoes were commanded to be made of common, not fine, leather. Repeated attempts were made to restrict all servants to the dress of their original cantons, lest they grow too presumptuous. All these efforts failed. Had the good city fathers understood the springs of the human spirit better they would certainly have produced better results by *forbidding* servants to wear the dress of their native villages. This, indeed, would have ensured their wearing it. Nothing is so successful as a veto in ensuring the preservation of national costume. The Scottish kilt and tartan and Polish peasant dress are typical examples of survival through defiance. When Swiss servants were ordered to wear their own local costume they abandoned it, but when, later, their local costumes were outlawed officially they insisted on wearing them.

Of all the fashions which upset the Town Council ruffs and wigs caused, perhaps, the most trouble, for the Town Councillors themselves were soon caught in their own meshes. At first ruffs were strictly forbidden. Permission was not given for wearing "large wide collars never seen here before and detestable long thick ruffs," except to Government officials and the most important citizens, and these were only allowed "single ruffs," or, if not single ruffs (in case of retreat before the ink on the minutes had dried), then "multiple ruffs only up to as many as five folds and no more," and those five folds might only be "waved or drawn up with the finger, not curled with irons." Neither the citizens nor the Councillors obeyed this order.

The trouble with ruffs was succeeded by worse trouble over perukes. At first they were totally forbidden along with other new fashions, and a law passed in 1637 ordered that

> Young and old, married and single, are forbidden to wear the recently arrived filthy long *alla modo* breeches and indecent long superfluous hairlocks hanging down over eyes, and false curled hair called perukes.

This veto had no success whatever, and by 1708 had been whittled down to the denial of perukes only to "anybody under twenty," with the additional loophole "except in cases of necessity," such cases being at the discretion of the Council. It would be interesting to know just which cases these covered. Perhaps insistent teen-ager relations of the Councillors?

The Council continued stubbornly to fight its losing battle, contesting every inch of ground, even as it retreated. Wigs, if worn, "must not stand high over the forehead or be annoyingly long, or knotted, or bear pigtails." The very details of the successive vetoes furnish us with the most authentic knowledge of the most popular fashions, for the vetoes

AFRICAN CARVING OF CREDO FROM ITALIAN AFRICAN MISSION
Contemporary.

1. Io credo. 2. in Dio Padre Omnipotente. 3. Creatore del cielo. 4. e della terra. 5. Io credo. 6. in Gesù Cristo. 7. suo unico Figliolo. 8. nostro Signore. 9. il quale fu concepito per virtù dello Spirito Santo. 10. Nacque da Maria Vergine. 11. patì. 12. sotto Ponzio Pilato. 13. fu crocifisso. 14. morto. 15. E seppellit. 16. discese all' inferno. 17. il terzo giorno risuscitò da morte. 18. sau'al cielo. 19. siede alla destra di Dio Padre Omnipotente. 20. di là ha da venire a giudicare. 21. I vivi. 22. e i morti. 23. Credo. 24. nello Spirito Santo. 25. la santa Chiesa Cattolica. 26. la communione dei santi. 27. la remissione dei peccati. 28. la Ressurezione della carne. 29. la vita eterna. 30. così è.

were applied just to those extremes of style which, by virtue of their originality, were most costly and prestige-enhancing, therefore, most eagerly sought after.

Hair-powder, banned like wigs, was defiantly used, nevertheless, and the edict condemning and forbidding "the excessive use of powder" was completely ignored from the start.

When the Burgomaster could bear the flouting of the Council's sumptuary laws no longer a few culprits were rounded up and punished, to set an example to the rest. Among the gentlemen of standing thus hauled before the Council and fined for wearing wigs in 1710 were the son of the local parson and the son of the Governor himself.

Despite their ineffectiveness, the Council stubbornly continued to issue its vetoes. No feathers were to be worn save from native ducks; certainly no ostrich feathers. If ostrich feathers were worn, then they were to be reserved for the nobility and Class 6 of the population only. There must be no dressing up for weddings and no dancing to furnish the excuse for dressing up, such being "unseemly and liable to awaken the wrath of God."

And sumptuary laws continued to be enacted and broken right until the outbreak of the French Revolution, after which adjacent upheaval the Swiss prosecutions gradually ceased, leaving the unkept laws still protesting from the statute books.

The Church of Rome took an understandably poor view of the French Revolution and its daring new fashions, denouncing both the pseudo-Greek transparent female mode and the extravagances of the male mode, castigating menfolk for wearing it and for permitting their womenfolk to dress so immodestly. The London *Times* of 1801, not without a touch of malice, details the papal Bull of October 1800:

> His Holiness strictly enjoined his officials, Civil and Ecclesiastic, to repress by fines and corporal punishment these crying enormities.
> Damsels to be punished for wearing transparent robes, voluptuous or magnificent attire, displaying themselves in very seductive or tempting attitudes.
> Heads of families who weakly or negligently permit their wives or daughters and servants to trespass against these rules shall not escape with impunity.

Also involved in this papal denunciation were "tailors, haberdashers, milliners, hairdressers, and man-milliners." And women who dared to go to Mass improperly dressed were ordered "to be driven from church," and if they resisted "higher powers shall be required to lend their aid."

Decency, in the eyes of the Vatican, still requires both men and women to cover themselves up more than contemporary fashion decrees, especially on holiday, where not only is the body usually freer than in everyday clothes, but there is also dangerous leisure to act upon the wanton thoughts such freer dress might stimulate.

A notice posted up outside the village church of the Catalonian fishing village of Cadaqués in 1956 was pointedly, if somewhat inaccurately, written in French (though most of the visitors were English), because it was the French boys and girls who were not obeying the sumptuary laws, not only on the beach, but elsewhere too.

> Remember that this church is the House of God, not a museum or place of entertainment. Therefore, in the name of *élémentaire élégance*, modesty, and politeness, do not enter if you are not properly dressed, men in long trousers and women in a high-necked dress with long sleeves.

It has never been very easy to dress in a way that pleases the Church, whether Protestant or Catholic, and there has never been any period in history when the clergy can be said to have gone on record as declaring themselves satisfied with what their flock were wearing. Either the congregation are wearing too little (immodest) or too much (extravagant), or what they wear is too modish (worldly) or too simple (affectation); or else too feminine (provocative) or not feminine enough (blasphemous); and even the men do not escape censure, though their dress for the last 150 years has become less and less interesting.

Not a few pulpits to-day denounce the wearing of swimming-slips (and even swimming-shorts) by men, not to speak of boys, as indecent, and insist on old-fashioned swimming-suits which reach from the calves to the neck and have sleeves. Such ample male swimming-costume, they consider, is less likely to incite wanton thoughts in the opposite sex.

The revivalist Billy Graham, on the other hand, declared, preaching to a Toronto congregation in September 1955:

> It is as bad as murder to entice others to immorality. Many of you women have dressed in such a way as to bring impure thoughts to the minds of men. May God have mercy on your souls.

He obviously did not consider there was the least danger that the dress of the men could be attractive enough to provoke any wanton thoughts in the minds of the women—a descent indeed (though the preacher, perhaps, considers it a benefit) since the male dress of the Middle Ages, when the Wife of Bath could not take her eyes off the beautiful legs of the young man (shown to such advantage by the long, close-fitting tights) at the funeral of her fourth husband, and eventually made him her fifth husband.

An interesting English dress-reform movement was that undertaken by the Quakers in the seventeenth century. It was a protest against the extravagant fripperies of the fashionable. In outline Quaker dress was not dissimilar from the Restoration dress it rejected, differing chiefly by being made of plainer material, in more sober colours, and entirely without trimming. Quaker colours were drab and grey, of which there were many approved varieties of shade, such as red-drab, brown-drab, and yellow-drab, and several different tones of fawn and slate. These hues were chosen because they were not so difficult nor so expensive to dye as black cloth, which required at least two dippings.

Quakers, then as now, liked to wear simple stuffs of good, serviceable quality which would last them well, and their linen was always spotless. From the beginning they set their faces against such gewgaws as buttons (then modishly worn as jewellery), and against wigs as foppish.

George Fox himself was obliged to defend William Penn against the scandalous gossip that Penn wore a wig, pointing out that Penn had lost his own hair during a nine months' confinement in prison for his Quaker opinions, and had therefore to cover his head with something, that something being but a small and inoffensive substitute.

> He did say that he did ware a little civil border because his haire was come off his head and since I have seen and spoak with William Penn his border is so thin plain and short that one can not well know it from his owne haire.

Fox himself wore his own hair long and uncurled, a plain drab coat, and home-made leather breeches cut to fit close at the waist, as he refused to wear either buttons or points. He was not only handy with his fingers, but obviously interested in dress, making his own breeches of sturdy leather for hard wear and better protection against the vermin which infested the prisons where he was condemned to spend so much of his time.

What Fox wanted dress to do for a man was to make him look like a man. This, he believed, the fashionable dress of his day did not. This is what he thought of the elegant male mode of 1654:

> They must be in the fashion of the world else they are not in esteem. Nay they shall not be respected if they have not gold and silver upon their backs or if their haire bee not powdered. But if one have a store of ribands hanging about his waist, at his knees, and in his hat, of divers colours, red white black and yellow, and his haire bee powdered hee is a brave man, he is excepted, he is no Quaker. And further, if one gets a paire of breeches like a coate and hang them about with points and up almost to the middle a paire of dubbel cuffs upon his hands and a feather in his cap he is a gentlemen because he hath ribands upon his backe and belly and his knees and his haire powdered.

This is ye way of the world but is not this ye lusts of ye eye ye lusts of ye flesh and ye prid of life?

It is instructive to compare this declaration with Samuel Pepys's feverish detailing of his numerous new outfits of lush clothes at the same period. Fox, a man of extraordinarily strong spiritual force and religious insight, was no narrow fanatic, nor was he opposed to bright colour and good

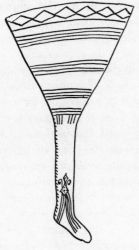

CAVALIER RIDING HOSE, KNITTED
AND SEWN
English, seventeenth century.

TALL HAT OF PLAITED OSIER
French, 1825.
Musée Carnavalet, Paris

shape in dress. It was meaningless sartorial extravagance and its demeaning effect on human dignity that he objected to. The widow of Justice Fell, whom he married, loved vivid colours, and Fox himself bought her a splendid cloak of crimson silk, which expressed her high-spirited and warm-hearted nature as no other mantle could have done. It was good in quality, positive in colour, and simple in cut, without any extra adornment. This, we may say to-day, Quaker or no, is a sound basis for good dressing —indeed, the only sound basis.

In these early days of the Friends the Quakers were nearly all poor, farm-labourers and journeymen and their families for the most part, and their simple attire of plain, buttonless coat and breeches, clean white kerchief, and plain worsted stockings, soon became the uniform of the martyr, for thousands of them were cast into plague-ridden, filthy gaols, after being branded, whipped at the cart's tail, and sometimes also deprived of their ears. William Penn reckoned that no less than 5000 Quakers died in prison over a period of forty years, and so many were incarcerated, out of the tiny Quaker communities, that often there were hardly any adults left to carry on, and for some time in Reading the Meeting was carried on by the children alone. But religious oppression only increased the number of Friends, and Quaker converts and Quaker dress multiplied instead of diminishing.

George Fox and his friends disliked buttons because in the elegant world buttons were then being used not for fastening, but for boastful ornament, and so used in costly materials and in enormous quantities. Fox, objecting to such display as shameful and in bad taste for Christians, objected also to the assumption of privilege by unearned wealth that such display implied. In adopting a clean, plain white collar, instead of the aristocratically limp and unwashed lace cravat, in that the Friends did not use titles or care a fig for class distinctions, they were advocating a more manly dress, and making a stand at the same time for what was to become democracy.

The Quakers looked upon the aristocratic dress of those days as effete and degenerate; and, indeed, it cannot be denied that fashionable dress was studiedly slack in line, soft throughout to the point of limpness, dripping with meaningless ribbons and points, and bedizened with buttons buttoning nothing, so that it was, in fact, decadent in its confusions and aimless meandering. It was broken and fussy (two unforgivable errors in any dress). The shirt was sloppy, the bolero shrunk to ridicule, the petticoat breeches ungainly, the lace boot-frills, three yards at least in circumference (and worn even with riding-boots by truly fashionable gentlemen), grotesque. And the plethora of ribbons suggested a maypole more than a man.

Yet even the logical Voltaire, complacent in his own embroidered court dress and enormous wig, condemned the Quakers, whom he otherwise admired, for their "ridiculous dress."

There was certainly much to be said for George Fox's contempt for the mode, and King Charles II himself was glad to get out of it and into a simpler and more dignified style of dress by October 15, 1666, on which day he put on a long cassock of black cloth pinked with white, worn under a plain coat, and breeches "ruffled with riband like a pigeon's legs," and vowed he had finished with fashion for good.

The next important English dress-reformer was Beau Nash, a big, pompous lawyer of Welsh descent, whose particular genius was a finicking regard for the minutiæ of social observance. He managed to secure the job of Master of Ceremonies for Bath, and succeeded in transforming it from a dreary provincial "kurort" into the most fashionable summer resort in England—and, indeed, Europe—in the eighteenth century.

Previously Bath had utterly lacked social *cachet* of any kind, having had nothing to attract the *beau monde*, whose presence, then as now, was indispensable for success in any such venture. Nash, by appealing to middle-class snobbery, was able to clean up the profanity—that is, the profanity which was merely of the dull kind—improve the boorish behaviour, and enlighten the ignorance of society manners, which, he declared, was keeping Society with a big 'S' away from Bath. Like a relentless nanny, he did not let up on his charges until their manners and their dress had alike been brought up to scratch.

One of Nash's most effective methods of improving boorish behaviour was to display a puppet show in which country squires wore their riding-boots not only all day, but in bed at night as well. He strictly forbade the wearing of swords at Assemblies to avoid the unseemly brawls of the past, and he outlawed riding-hood and morning aprons at Assemblies in the interest of *ton*. Before long, under this new dispensation, rank and fashion began to flock to Bath, and the country gentry, now stiffly got up in their best dress, bootless, whipless, swordless, and exerting all their self-control so as not to laugh vulgarly or even smile, had the privilege of decorously mingling with them.

Foreign visitors, who now also hurried to Bath, the new focus of English High Society, carried back to their own countries first-hand reports of how the English took their pleasures sadly, never relaxing, showing no interest beyond the prescribed solemn performance of precise social ritual, displaying absolutely no animation at dances or concerts or even in the gaming-rooms, which were helping to make Bath so prosperous.

And these foreign impressions lingered on in France to inspire later Anglomaniac French dandies in the following century with an un-Gallic, icy ennui they believed to be truly English *bon ton*. "La mine d'un Trappiste," was the expression Stendhal advised the aspiring young Frenchman to cultivate socially. "To look sad is not *bon ton*. What is essential is to look bored."

Wherein it is clear that the aspiring English middle class had taken Beau Nash's injunctions too literally, and were so anxious not to appear to be vulgarly enjoying themselves at Bath that they had forced themselves to appear not to be enjoying themselves at all.

Nash's legal training and natural love of finnick enabled him to introduce an intricate mass of regulations on the dress and deportment he required in Bath, especially in the Assembly Rooms. He ruled Bath with a rod of iron in the shape of a long white ceremonial stick, which he carried like a sceptre, and he was never seen without his great white hat.

On one famous occasion he publicly chastised the Duchess of Queensberry herself, who had been so imprudent as to come to a ball in Bath in a morning apron. Beau Nash tore the offending garment from her and flung it into a corner of the ballroom. More diplomatic methods were sometimes required for different menaces. When the Wesley brothers descended on Bath to preach in the street on the evils of gambling Nash was able to foil them by hiring three musicians to play French horns at full blast near their outdoor pulpit.

Certainly it was Nash who made Bath, its social *cachet* lasting undimmed for more than a century, and when in 1745 the abolition of licensed gambling by Act of Parliament took away his income the grateful Corporation of Bath voted him an annual allowance of 120 guineas. By supplementing this with the proceeds of the discreet sale of his trinkets he was able to live out his life in decency.

He had aged in that shrivelled, pathetic manner peculiar to those to whom the fusses of society are the breath of life itself. He was described in 1743, at the age of sixty-nine, as "a silly over-lord, a worn-out and toothless old man, crowned with a white hat, and whose face was animated iron-rust, changeless and shameless red," for, of course, Beau Nash used cosmetics.

Another important source of reform in dress is that of revolutionary movements. All revolutions introduce a change of fashion, sometimes from above, often from below, frequently from a foreign country whose politics are momentarily in favour with the revolutionaries. In the excitement of riot and clash of arms a chance colour, an accidental twist of ribbon, a flower or kerchief, becomes a sudden symbol, a rallying point, and a new mode is launched.

It almost invariably happens that the new style of dress which thus develops is nothing like the new style of dress the theorists of the revolution had intended to introduce, and all revolutions have their theorists. At a certain point in every revolution the unconscious it is, not the conscious, which takes a hand.

We have seen how Puritan reformed dress was in its essentials very similar in basic cut to the Royalist dress it scorned. It was the stiff tall hat that the subconscious then thrust forward, a strongly self-assertive demand for power, in no way resembling the pliant, plumed Royalist felt. The American Revolution began attired in buckled shoes like an English gentleman, but ended with guerillas wearing soft-soled Redskin moccasins, useful to creep silently upon the English outpost in the woods, but even more significant as a native symbol of American independence.

The French Revolutionary theorists, who for long years beforehand had been brooding over their plans, commissioned the painter David to design special costumes suitable "for French patriots of every age and condition." David obliged by copying Greek and Roman draperies (because they were beautiful and untainted by royalty) in a series of ambitious designs, which met with complete failure when translated into live dress. A lifetime of arguing and intriguing in stuffy Paris political clubs and taking absolutely

ONE OF DAVID'S DESIGNS FOR
REVOLUTIONARY MALE DRESS
Musée Carnavalet, Paris

YEAR OF THE FRENCH
REVOLUTION
The dress that happened by itself. It was thought to look English.

DRESS REFORM

no other form of exercise had produced in the French Revolutionary leaders neither the figure nor the carriage to wear with dignity drapery which displayed manly limbs in their nakedness and much of the torso as well. One or two impulsive politicians did, indeed, try out David's new dress in public, but beat a hasty retreat. It was clear they had not the right figures for it.

The women fared rather better than the men, for the 'Greek' draperies designed by David for them they managed to rearrange immediately in accordance with their own lively ideas of what constituted Paris 'chic'— which meant an overdeveloped, pushed-up bosom (nothing like the pagan Greek, but curiously akin to the American fixation of the nineteen-fifties), drapery more transparent than the unprurient Greeks advocated, and a waist artificially heightened in a manner totally abhorrent to Greek ideas of the beauty of nature.

David then produced a second set of designs for Revolutionary male dress, in which he abandoned Greek and Roman styles and attempted to combine items from Renaissance dress with other items from Italian dress, English dress, and from military costumes. Though more cautious and more concealing than his first attempts, these second designs had no greater success than the first. Longing though the men of France were for something new to wear which would express their new feelings and ambitions, these designs, they declared, would not do either. David's "patriotic dress for the old," an operatic costume of dark blue and scarlet trimmed with gold lace, worn with elegant shoes with large gold buckles and a huge cockaded bicorne, had no success at all. He tried again with yet another design "proposé pour les vieillards," this time grey cloth with a dark red cloak, lace cuffs, black stockings, a Tudor bonnet with a gold band, and much smaller shoe-buckles. This also failed to please. Nor were any of his carefully thought-out costumes, "suitable for citizens" of every age and profession, ever worn. Renaissance ruffs, Tudor borders, Oriental tassels, Homeric plumes transposed into patriotic red, white, and blue—all met with failure. Simply "On n'a pas voulu."

During the actual Revolution itself military liaison officers did wear what might be described as Revolutionary gloves. They were the same military gloves as before, but smothered with Revolutionary symbols and portents in exuberant profusion, being embroidered on the back of the hand with Liberty, in a Phrygian cap, holding a pike in one hand and scales of justice in the other, in the closest proximity to a lion (symbolizing power) and a cat (symbolizing independence). The Tree of Liberty was only omitted because there was not a centimetre of space left to put it in.

The desire to express freedom by nakedness took a form other than that of Greek drapery. The desire to express aggressiveness took a form other than Roman plumed helmets. The Revolutionary costume that developed itself adopted the English *frac* coat, or riding-coat, and pushed out the shoulders menacingly. It borrowed the new bosom-focus from the women and pushed out a pouter-pigeon front, and it took the *sans culotte* pantaloons and tightened and lightened them in hue, to look like nudity. This costume was easier to wear, because if naked limbs cannot be disguised covered limbs can. French caricaturists of the time made merry with the amount of padding and the number of *fausses cuisses* being employed by dashing young citizens to simulate non-existent manly muscles.

The true dress-reformer of this stirring period in the world's history turned out to be not the Revolutionary painter David at all, but the reactionary English dandy Brummell. For Brummell was the grandson of a valet, and what he really stood for was upstart push. He it was in his sober and prudent dress who expressed best the rising, pushing, fundamentally clean and respectable shopkeeper class. Looking to the pagan past, David had not glimpsed the Nonconformist future.

Fashion is too subtle, too mercurial, too greatly dependent on psychological climate, for a style of dress to be imposed from without, however noble the intentions of the theorists and however distinguished the artists who try to express their theories. The very word 'reform' chills sartorial ardour.

The Russian Revolution of 1917 was fought in such conditions of economic breakdown that it was a long time before the theorists could attempt to give expression to their ideas of 'a suitable dress for the proletariat' to wear. By the nineteen-twenties, however, a Revolutionary dress had made its own appearance, unheralded and unannounced. This costume was a black beret and leather jacket, suggesting the all-important engineer, symbol of the new industry which was to provide tractors and thereby bigger harvests. It was a dress worn by both sexes.

It may be recalled that Keir Hardie, the Scottish miner who became the first Labour M.P., wore his habitual workman's cap when attending the House of Commons, and aroused intense indignation thereby, many other workmen joining in the general Tory disapproval. These workmen felt that Keir Hardie, in continuing to wear what most of them regarded as the badge of their servitude, was not symbolizing their aspirations towards the better conditions he was struggling to obtain for them. In point of fact it was fate that took a decisive hand in this delicate matter. Keir Hardie had decided not to sidetrack the real purpose of his election to Parliament by wearing other than the conventional dress of its representatives, and a friend had offered to lend him a top-hat for this purpose. The top-hat was, however, delayed in delivery, and Keir Hardie had no recourse but to wear his own cap.

The dress of the recent Chinese Revolution is the boiler-suit—the cheap and sexless blue overalls worn by Chinese men and women alike, a dress which Western visitors, who expected something more exotic, have found depressing, but which well-to-do and carefully nurtured Chinese girls wear to-day on the streets of Peking with intense pride. The reason for the social elevation of the humble boiler-suit is the same as the reason for the Soviet social elevation of the leather engineering jacket— that is, the necessity for industrialization, in order to raise the standard of living of the people of the country. Similar garb may be expected to become respected in other Asiatic countries as their inhabitants have to face similar problems in the future.

The Chinese journalist J. Chen writes:

> Immediately after the Revolution the girls wanted to wear boiler-suits because it was what the girls who had taken an active part in the Revolution were wearing. The boiler-suit was a mark of patriotism. It was also cheap.

Mr Chen prophesies a general return to traditional dress with growing material prosperity.

> Now the situation has changed [1956]. Men and women are earning more money. There is the natural desire to be well dressed for the dances and concerts. There are the usual theoreticians prepared to talk and write expansively of the "new dress," "bourgeois influences," etc. The pundits will shout their heads off, and when the clamour has died down we will have lovely traditional dresses and jackets and also elegant Western-style clothes and various styles in between.

The prestige of the Eighth Route Armies and the puritan flavour of contemporary Chinese life are the principal influences on Chinese male dress at this period, which is straight, simple, of plain dark material, and with the traditional high collar. "The men will go on wearing the uniform style for some time yet, though of better materials. It is very convenient and good-looking."

If the Chinese Revolution has produced Western blue boiler-suits as its battle dress Chinese influence in the West is responsible for the high-necked dark sweaters so popular with both sexes in Europe and America; and the flat, easy slippers so typical of modern Western youth, though known as 'ballet,' derive, not from Covent Garden, but from China.

The student of dress will have no difficulty in recognizing in the long, straight, knitted, tubular overcoat launched at the end of November 1956 in England the symbol of the Middle East pipeline no less than the sartorial expression of the Suez Canal, the problem of which was currently racking England. This, buttoning down the front, presented less of a problem to get into than its inspiration. The fashionable 'sack' dress in the autumn of 1957 indicated that the problem of Suez was still unsolved.

Prominent among dress reforms, if transitory, are those hurried in from time to time by sheer panic. There was a French sumptuary law, for instance, passed in 1560 which the King introduced on the insistence of the Guise family, its object being to prevent the possible assassination of

the Cardinal of Lorraine, which an astrologer had predicted. This law
cut down the size of the fashionably large *chausses* then being worn to
such small dimensions that they could no longer conceal a pistol. At the
same time and for the same reason the size of *vertugadins* was equally cut
down.

Pockets were similarly banished in 1563 lest they furnish a hiding-place
for firearms or daggers. James I of England, always in terror of his life,
froze English fashions for a considera-
ble time in a contrary style. Fearing
assassination by the stiletto, he did not
insist that his courtiers should wear
breeches too tight to hold a weapon,
but retained and increased the size of
the already enormously inflated bombasted trunk-hose, a style which elsewhere was already rapidly going out of
fashion. Thus thoroughly padded, he
felt safer from attack, should it come.

Fashions, for a time, can be turned
backward by determination if the dicta-
tor is sufficiently strong. Napoleon,
anxious to re-establish the glories of
the French Court when he became
Emperor, invited back to France the
émigré French nobles who had taken
refuge in England. Those who returned
at this time insisted on wearing their
pre-Revolutionary hoops, powdered
wigs, and silk knee-breeches. They

JANISSARY INFERIOR OFFICER
Turkey, 1802.

established themselves in the Boulevard Saint-Honoré, where they openly
jeered at the Emperor as a Corsican upstart, and irritated everybody
by speaking French with a heavy English accent and introducing English
habits such as tea-drinking at a time when England was France's greatest
enemy.

Napoleon was signally unsuccessful in his plan to use them to embellish
his Court. The skilled craftsmen of the days of Versailles had dispersed,
and the (revived eighteenth-century) Court dress of his era was curiously
clumsy and lifeless. It looked oddly provincial and like an unsuccessful
attempt at fancy dress.

Not until Napoleon's downfall did the rest of the noble *émigrés* return
to France with the Bourbons, when a Treasury grant of a milliard francs

M

(about £40,000,000 then) was distributed among them in recompense for their lost estates "by devotion to the Royal family." This gesture was unpopular with the French people, then extremely impoverished by the Napoleonic wars, and short of men to till the fields, besides being burdened with the cost of an expensive foreign army of occupation.

By all accounts these returning *émigrés* also made themselves generally odious. They wore unchanged the dress of their Versailles youth, and behaved (while the milliard lasted) as though nothing whatever had happened since then—in their determination to show that they had learned nothing and forgotten nothing. Captain Gronow wrote of them later:

> In our day of comparative equality and general civility no one who has not arrived at my age and lived in Paris can form any idea of the insolence and hauteur of the higher classes in Paris in 1815.

Even Captain Gronow, the dandy, no friend to the poor, went so far in his irritation at this behaviour, which in its caricature of English coldness insulted the English aristocracy it admired, as to wear "a white hat, which, I never knew why, was in those days supposed to be an emblem of the very advanced liberal or even republican opinion."

The classic style of male dress in the nineteenth century was due to Beau Brummell; the conflicting romantic style was due to Lord Byron.

In turning his back on the richly coloured brocades and fine silks, the elegant embroideries and costly laces, of the eighteenth century Brummell launched the severe unadorned silhouette which has slackened into present-day male dress. In the process of so doing Brummell established English tailoring and at the same time killed male dress altogether.

History credits Brummell, and rightly, with making English gentlemen clean, a feat which the English Puritans had failed to accomplish. But Brummell did not wash himself all over thrice a day, and concentrate so passionately on the laundering of his linen, because of hygiene or decency, but because he had a terror of dirt which was essentially neurotic. This terror he never ceased to try to keep at bay by continual essence-laden baths and endless changes of under-linen, by having the soles of his shoes polished as meticulously as their uppers, and, when he paid a social call, insisting on having his chair-men carry his white-satin-lined sedan chair right into his hostess's salon, to save him from the necessity of putting his feet on the pavement. He was a compulsive washer, trying all his life to wash something off and to brush something away. Perhaps it was his humble origin.

He spent practically the whole of his day dressing himself for his evening appearance at one of his clubs, or at some noble dinner, and his dressing-room was always crowded with breathless admirers, intent on watching the process, especially the mysteries connected with the tying of his cravat.

Brummell's cravats were twelve inches wide, of delicately starched muslin, and a huge pile of them waited ready for him before he started his solemn ritual. It was less dressing than a well-acted performance of dressing. In a deathly silence, the attendant fans strained and still as marble statues, Brummell's valet reverently eased his shirt over his head, leaving the immensely high collar standing up so that it concealed his head. With pious hands the valet then lifted up a cravat and delicately placed it in position round his master's neck. Brummell thereupon began to persuade the cravat to take the required folds, which had to be absolutely formal and yet appear to have happened absolutely casually. This he achieved by diligently working his jaws until the starched muslin was coaxed down into the precise shape he wished.

Like a trapeze artist drawing attention to a particularly difficult feat by not achieving it purposely the first time, Brummell took care that his first cravat should not always succeed to his satisfaction. His valet would often carry out of the dressing-room an armful of crumpled muslins before his master had performed his trick to perfection. "These," the valet would say to the awed spectators trying to peep round the door, "these are our failures."

Brummell decreed blue woollen coat and drab breeches for day wear, worn with top-boots, and blue coat and black pantaloons for evening wear, worn with varnished pumps. In concentrating upon absolute precision of cut and fit in this bald dress he was doing the only thing left to obtain sartorial distinction, for the dress was so anonymous, so dull and terse, that it made everybody look like everybody else.

Grandson of a valet, Brummell could not, like an English duke of the eighteenth century, strut down Bond Street wearing his ducal riband and garter to proclaim his pride. What he managed to do was even better, for he succeeded in making the duke dress as anonymously as himself. Only in costly perfection of cut and pouter-pigeon carriage could social distinction now be conferred by dress, and in these matters Brummell had the advantage over his social superiors.

This pouter-pigeon carriage was more than just a way of folding the cravat and walking. It was the new look of the nineteenth century, signifying what the Industrial Revolution was bringing to the middle class—money and push. Never in all English history was there so much sickening talk of birth and breeding and gentlemanly *savoir-faire* as at this time, when money was really beginning to provide the magic key to exclusive social portals.

The fact is simple. Brummell was a shrewd young man on the make. He did not need the three barbers he vowed were essential to his hair-dressing (one to attend to the front, another to the back, and the third to the sides). He did not need four different glove specialists (one of whom was expert only in the thumb) to create his beautifully fitting gloves, which clung so closely that the shapes of the fingernails were outlined thereon. It was, however, excellent publicity. Brummell was a modern man. Hollywood is where he really belongs. Nobody knew the news-value of his affectations better than he did, and the legend he was so skilled in creating has lasted successfully into our own times. He could always think up something new. He told infatuated young noblemen that his recipe for boot-varnish was to add champagne to the standard

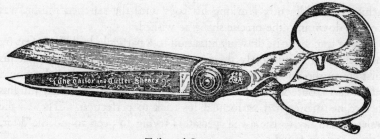

Tailor and Cutter, 1883

recipe. He let it be widely known that he made his valet first wear all his new clothes as they came from the tailors, so that they should not look too vulgarly new when he wore them himself. And so on, endlessly.

Most successful of all his methods of publicity was his outrageous rudeness, which, oddly enough, passed for wit in a period certainly not deficient in wit. Brummell specialized in icy observations at other people's expense, at making his friends and acquaintances hot and uncomfortable by calculated impertinences—about their dress or their birth. He behaved, indeed, like the classic valet of French comedy, dressed up in his master's clothes and overdoing the rôle. In his own neurotic way Brummell was England's second revolution, the valet's revenge on society, valeting it into a cleanliness bordering on mania and at the same time taking all the gaiety and pleasure out of its dress.

Though for France and much of Europe he stood out as uniquely English, in point of fact he was far from English, either in appearance or character. He loathed games, hated sports, detested horses, and thoroughly abhorred the country. Even his famous tailors were not English, but German. He was only himself in London and only at his best at his club. He never loved any woman. He never even loved any man. All his life his one and only love was himself. He did not create anything, for he had no originality. He was unique simply in embodying, a little ahead of his time, the coming shape of England. That is all.

Brummell was no accident. He just had to happen to English society, and to happen just then. He was formed by the social climate of his epoch, an epoch of change, at the end of which birth was going to count, in an industrialized England, less than money. Brummell had audacity, luck, not a bad figure, and he possessed a sour, twisted kind of charm, in addition to a certain austere discrimination. At any other period these not very outstanding qualities, allied to a neglected Eton education and what for those days amounted to but a very moderate fortune, would not have taken him very far. But in the social whirlpool of his own times they carried him to the top.

England and English dress, Brummell's dress, was copied all over Europe, not because all Europe respected Brummell's obsession about washing, but because he symbolized something which foreigners believed to represent England, and England, the nation of shopkeepers, was the great new industrial Power.

Most Europeans, especially the French dandies, who copied Brummell so assiduously, did not in fact think of bathing three or four times a day, though not a few prided themselves on sending their linen across the Channel to Dover in order to be washed by English washerwomen. And the *Strangers' Guide to Paris* (published in 1819)—which aimed to please the English tourists flocking into France now the war was over—felt it necessary to make a special point about the *mystique* of shirt-laundering, since they believed that all Englishmen were slightly unhinged on the subject, like Brummell.

> The linen being washed three miles from Paris *with soap*, and not beaten or brushed as is the custom generally in France, and particular care being taken of it, M. Meurice is obliged to make a trifling addition to the customary charge.

Thus M. Meurice assured his potential customers that he was confidently aware of the ablutionary requirements of English milords.

France took the English dandies much more seriously than did England, building up a great philosophical edifice in their name—and getting most of the facts about them quite wrong—and just as a century earlier Rousseau had fathered Lord Édouard Bompston on to the English nation, so now George Sand invented an English milord dandy—a "typical son of Albion," with "the head of Antinoüs on the shoulders of an Englishman. A type of Grecian of the best period on a bust dressed and cravated peculiarly in the 'British' fashion." In point of fact, on the next page, he turns out to be no milord from London at all but a New York American named Dick Palmer. But the point is made. He *ought* to have been an Englishman, for that was what the French believed an English dandy to look like. That was the copperplate dandy, kept alive by Ouida and still to-day remembered nostalgically in popular romances.

The truth, however, was nothing like the legend. A survivor of their period wrote later of them:

> How unspeakably odious, with a few brilliant exceptions, were the dandies. They were a motley crew with nothing remarkable about them but their insolence. They were generally not high-born, nor rich, nor very good-looking, nor clever, nor agreeable. . . . They were generally middle-aged, some even elderly men, had large appetites and weak digestions, gambled freely and had no luck. They hated everybody and abused everybody and would sit together in White's window, or the pit boxes at the Opera, wearing tremendous crammers. . . . They swore a good deal, never laughed, had their own particular slang, looked hazy after dinner, and most of them had been patronised at one time by Brummell and the Prince Regent. Thank Heaven that the miserable race of used-up dandies has long been extinct! May England never look on their like again.

Unlike George Brummell, Lord Byron became an arbiter of fashion unintentionally. As a young undergraduate he had admired Brummell, and when in London tried to dress soberly in black, and he always maintained stubbornly that he would rather have liked to be one of the dandies himself, had he been able to. But Lord Byron was lame and careless, his valet Fletcher was a ploughboy who was better at the plough. Byron liked swimming and sunshine and travelling in untamed lands better than the ennui of London drawing-rooms. And, for all his neurotic turns and twists, he enjoyed action and did believe in something outside himself. He did believe in liberty. He did want Greece to be free.

Byron caught and held the imagination of the world's youth in a way we find difficult to credit to-day, when publicity is so well organized and the means of impressing a commercially profitable face on the public memory so comprehensive. Byron's romantic poems (which he himself described in a letter to Shelley as "exaggerated nonsense which has corrupted the public taste") were copied out in mauve ink in every girl's album; his satires (snatched from them by outraged mamas); his travels in the Levant and in Greece; his turbulent private life; his extraordinary personal beauty, his crippled foot, his physical prowess—all these were legendary almost from the beginning of his career, for he was one of those men whose lives flare up in an early blaze, and who die old and worn out while still young in years.

Fame and notoriety came to Byron overnight when he was but twenty-four. Within a few days of each other, his maiden speech in the

CAPIDJI BACHI, TURKEY, 1800
Ceremonial Headdress of the Sultan's Carrier
of the Bowstring

House of Lords had a flattering success with the Whigs, and the publication of *Childe Harold* (he had thought so little of the poem himself that he had hardly thought of printing it at all) shot him to world renown.

The year was 1812. Thereafter, until he died of fever in Missolonghi in 1824, whatever he did or said, wherever he went, whatever he wore, was public news and news of major importance. People crowded round him wherever he appeared, and well-bred English ladies were not ashamed to use telescopes to spy on him in Venice. The scandals of his private life only whetted public appetite the more. He was the fashion, and because he was the fashion he set the fashions.

His open-necked shirts were assiduously copied all over the world, and became the particular badge of freedom-loving writers everywhere. Like other sensualists, Byron could not bear the physical irk of constricting clothes, and one day impatiently pulled off his cravat, letting his high shirt collar tumble open about his throat. Thus he unwittingly launched a mode hailed with delight by the young and romantic, and viewed with the deepest distrust by the politically reactionary, to whom it appeared a revolutionary gesture.

As an undergraduate Lord Byron had larked with his college companions about Newstead Abbey (his ancestral home, which he inherited half ruined and could never afford to put in order) in a monk's robe, and had been therefore nicknamed "the Abbot." It is probable that he liked this garb, not only because it was loose and easy, but also because it hid his crippled foot, about which he was agonizingly sensitive.

Forthwith every young poet, when the story spread about, wrapped himself in a similar gown. Byron had beautiful curling auburn hair (his friend Scrope Davies claimed to have seen him in bed late one morning with it still in curl-papers), and he preferred in his portraits to be painted with it wildly storm-tossed against a lowering sky. Abandon forthwith became the only possible *coiffure*. And so persistent was this Byronic cult that as late as 1850 an American book of social advice to gentlemen advises firmly: "When the hairdresser has done his prettiest, passing your fingers through it will be a decided improvement, giving your locks something of the freedom of Nature."

Lord Byron returned from his first visit to Albania with some handsome gold-laced uniforms. "I have some very 'magnifiques' Albania Dresses," he wrote to his mother from Turkey in 1809. "The only expensive articles in this country. They cost fifty guineas each and have so much gold, they would cost in England two hundred." He describes these dresses as "The most magnificent in the world, consisting of a long white kilt, gold-worked cloak, crimson velvet gold-laced jacket and waistcoat, silver-mounted pistols and daggers." He described enthusiastically the dresses he saw everywhere around him, including "Tatars with their high caps and Turks with their vast pelisses and turbans."

One of these Turkish pelisses he carried back to England and used to wear at Newstead Abbey as a boxing dress when he sparred with his page in the heat of the day, hoping thus to help reduce his weight, which, despite continual purges and a starvation diet, persisted in soaring. Something was certainly amiss with his glands.

Unlike Brummell, Byron easily succumbed to the garish in dress. Years of living in Italy at the mercy of fanciful Italian tailors, his horribly fluctuating weight, his magpie attraction to glitter, despite a backwash of well-bred guilt for being thus attracted, all these contributed to Lord Byron's bad dressing. For, despite all the trouble he took, he was a bad dresser. It was not that he did not mind how he dressed. On the contrary, he minded very much. He simply did not know how to. And he never learned. Worse, he unlearned rather than learned, for he had begun under the guidance of what were then considered the world's best dressers, in London. Away from these standards he degenerated rapidly, hanging about himself whatever he came across or was given or happened to pick up. He was easily irritated, and could not have been an easy client for the tailor, nor were what clothes he had ever properly brushed or kept in order, for Fletcher, as a valet, was nothing short of disastrous.

Tom Moore, after a visit to Lord Byron in Venice, told d'Israeli that he had found Byron dressing himself

> very dandified and yet not an English dandy. When I saw him he was dressed in a curious foreign cap, a foreign great-coat, and he had a gold chain round his neck and pushed into his waistcoat pocket.

Lady Blessington, who met him for the first time just as he was about to sail to Greece on his last fatal voyage, and who became a very good friend, was shaken by his lack of taste, lack of dignity, and curiously cheap get-up, resembling "the pride of the parvenue rather than the calm dignity of an ancient aristocrat."

Typically Lord Byron had taken the trouble to design resplendent military uniforms of scarlet and gold, in addition to variegated Homeric helmets, for himself and the two friends who were accompanying him to the campaign in Greece. The helmet he had designed for himself featured, among a mass of other conceits, his family motto, *Crede Byron*, and an immense plume. His colleague Trelawny, however, after one look at the helmet Byron had designed for him, refused point-blank to wear it— which refusal shook Byron's first enthusiasm over his own helmet. In the end, as with so many other of Lord Byron's projects in life, all three helmets were left behind in their pink cardboard boxes, and the order for the scarlet-and-gold military uniforms was cancelled.

With usual Byronic muddle, therefore, his lordship, as his brig approached the romantic, enslaved shores of the Greek islands, on the last and greatest adventure of his life, and with the eyes of the entire world upon him, found himself with nothing to wear. He landed, in fact, to a tremendous military salute, dressed in a cheap green braided cavalry jacket that Trelawny had bought for himself and then discarded as a misfit.

Such were the sartorial habits of the man whose influence on male dress counteracted and in some measure delayed and brightened the deadly uniformity which Brummell had instituted in English dress. It is easy to see Byron's sartorial influence in the nineteenth century. It all looks so curiously un-English, though Byron himself was so very much more English in his habits than Brummell. It seems odd that a man so fond of practical jokes, swimming, singlestick, shooting, and sailing as was Lord Byron should have been responsible for the flood of tasselled, embroidered velvet tubetekas, the flowing Greek cloaks, the upturned Turkish slippers, the Ottoman dressing-gowns, the Indian souvenir jewellery, and the whiffs of strange, un-English perfume. All these Oriental titbits in the nineteenth-century Englishman's wardrobe are due to Lord Byron. They were anathema to Brummell. Brummell had made a fetish of *not* using perfume. Admirers of Lord Byron, on the contrary, sprinkled themselves so generously with extracts of sandalwood, and with such a variety of attars of this and that, that Herman Melville observed that one reason that launched the whaleboats on their dangerous voyages was to hunt for ambergris, because there was such a lively demand for it both in Europe and America, for gentlemen's perfumed pomatums and scented waters.

The wardrobe of an artistic young man in England in 1835, according to Thackeray, comprised "two velvet waistcoats, a pair of braided trousers, four varied satin under-waistcoats, two shirts, half-a-dozen false collars, and a couple of pairs of dreadfully dilapidated Blucher boots."

His studio is furnished with a similar careless Byronic regard for display: "a shabby Spanish hat and cloak and a long Toledo rapier, bits of armour and bits of old damask rags; some unsound Venetian glass, and a guitar with a dirty blue ribbon." And his entire library consisted of *Lalla Rookh* and the Oriental poems of Lord Byron.

Carelessness, looseness as against tightness, the impromptu as against the premeditated, these are the signs of romanticism in dress. In behaviour Brummell's ennui was replaced by Byron's desperation, a new *motif* the volatile French poets seized on with something like relief, for they felt it suited them better. Desperation and an unappeased yearning to travel in far foreign lands made more progress, in point of fact, in France than among the English intellectuals. After all, lots of Englishmen did travel. Few Frenchmen, except those in exile, ever left their Paris cafés for foreign parts. They read Lord Byron instead, and imagined the rest.

It was romantic to wish to be somewhere else, to wish to be some one else. "If I could only transport myself to China," sighs Alfred de Musset's Fantasio. "If I could only escape from my own skin for an hour or two. If I could be that gentleman who is passing by . . ."

Anywhere was better than here. Any time better than now. Anything better than dull certainty. "It is by chance," Fantasio explains precisely. "I say a lot of things by chance. Chance is my dearest confidant."

Chance, luck, the accidental, the unforeseen—in speech, in life, and in dress—these were all carefully courted, for they were modish in the extreme, for abdication of personal responsibility was the very height of fashion to this generation, who talked so passionately about "liberty." Reason and common sense were worse than banal. They were utterly out of date. Instead, the juxtaposition of the planets or the wishes of the Devil

himself determined the actions of these young people, who were infants
at the time of Waterloo. A popular cravat of the period was called
"eternal damnation."

Lord Byron, his trunks all packed, good-byes over, banker's draft all
arranged, stood outside his *palazzo* staring uncertainly at the night sky.
"If that little cloud drifts across the moon I shall go," he said. Every one

ARAB STREET-SWEEPER
(NAZARETH) IN KHAKI SHIRT,
WESTERN CANVAS SHOES, AND
MUSLIM SHALWAR

BEGGAR, TEL-AVIV

He wears an Arab gown under a khaki
army coat and *tembl* cotton hat; he
chants corruptions of Talmudic texts in
Turkish-Arab-Hebrew jargon. Home-
made one-string fiddle. Empty Nescafé
tin for alms. Contemporary.

The small felt cap is worn here without
the *keffiyeh*. The fullness in front of the
shalwar signifies affluence and piety, and
is cooler in the heat. Contemporary.

waited—friends, servants, gondoliers, his major-domo and the Venetian
riff-raff he liked to gather about him, his dozens of pet animals, and his
latest mistress. The little cloud slowly drifted clear of the moon. Lord
Byron went back indoors. The crowd dispersed. His servants started to
haul his trunks and baggages back into the *palazzo*.

This sort of decision made the most exquisite sense to Byron's admirers,
all of whom tried to do likewise at every minor cross-road of their lives.
They made a religion of uncertainty, an art of unreliability, always
fluctuating, never constant in their loves or their opinions.

What made up their minds, when for a moment their minds seemed to be made up, had to be some unforeseen agency. Superstition was taken very seriously, and fate was never more popular. The young men not only liked to wear Oriental gewgaws to feel themselves fashionably in tune with the inertia of Asia, but they decorated their rooms to match their sentiments.

As was to be expected where taking a decision was so painful and unpopular an activity, selection was replaced by profusion in interior decoration. All periods and all styles were jumbled haphazardly together, with a preponderance of the supposed Eastern.

Maria Edgeworth described such a fashionable interior in *Money No Object*. She called it "drawing-room orientalism."

> Bamboo furniture . . . the extensive use of stained glass . . . columns disguised as palm trees. Elaborate fire irons. Frosted glass. An abundance of China ornaments . . . Turkish tent drapery. A fancy of my own in apricot cloth or crimson velvet opposé or en flute on crimson satin. Draperies fanned and enriched with gold fringes en suite . . . intermediate spaces Apollo's heads with gold rays . . . chimeras in the corners covered with blue silk and silver fringe . . . elegantly fanciful. For seats the Seraglio ottomans, paws griffin golden and golden tripods with antique cranes. . . . Alhambra hangings, Trebiz and Trellis paper . . . Chinese pagoda and Egyptian hieroglyph with Ibis border to match.

In short, a super-cinema before its time.

In opposition to the frozen boredom of Brummell, Byron fans cultivated too much emotion, all of a melancholy nature. Provided it had a sad ending, they were ready to follow any suggestion of an adventure. Life was so brief, so sad, the only thing to do with it was to waste it, wishing it were different from what it was. Waste it, preferably, in the arms of a woman, a beautiful married woman much older than oneself and with long black hair. "But the regiment is quartered here for six months," complains Alfred de Musset's handsome soldier in *Le Chandelier*. "One can't spend all one's time in the cafés. The provincial actors are boring. One looks at oneself in the mirror, and one doesn't wish to be handsome for nothing."

Marriage was utterly unromantic and put a man in the wrong. Husbands were poor fish, born to be deceived. Alfred de Musset chose the symbol of gloves to divulge this all too common situation. "They were made of suède of a greenish colour," observes Valentine in *Il ne faut jurer de rien*, describing the gloves of a cuckolded husband, "too large and coming unsewn at the thumb. Whilst he was pushing his hands into them, standing in the middle of the room, an imperceptible smile passed over the corners of his wife's lips."

This Mektoub mistress had always to be dark, mysterious, unpredictable. There were few blonde heroines in nineteenth-century literature.
Beaming black eyes, clustering black curls, a rotundity of arms and bust
more of the Levant than of Europe, were the standard pattern, for Byron's
Orient beckoned the amorous imagination irresistibly. Disraeli's heroines
are all darkly exotic and dressed in the height of fantasy. Nor were
nineteenth-century heroes blond. They too have to have black eyes and
disordered dark hair. There was, indeed, a demon-lover waiting for
Coleridge's wailing woman. He was Heathcliff.

This romantic-Oriental penchant lingered on long after its day was
officially over. Many were the suburban pianos in England that tinkled,
in the eighteen-eighties, *The Fire-worshipper's Cantata* inspired by Moore's
Lalla Rookh, inspired in turn by Byron, though unkind critics sneered at
Sir Granville Bantock, the composer of it, and declared it was made in
Birmingham. Birmingham or not, it was very popular. So was another
enticing composition called *The Pearl of Iran*.

Nor is this Oriental romanticism by any means dead. The general
public flocked to the Cirque d'Hiver in Paris in 1956 to enjoy the
tawdrily spectacular *Perle de Bengale*, which featured a British officer in
the Bengal Lancers as hero, and elephants, a wicked Indian rajah, with a
harem of exotic beauties and limitless treasure, writhing maidens and
writhing snakes, cunning eunuchs, etc., etc. The audience, of course,
loved it. The more the real Asia causes political headaches and economic
breakdowns, the more the public flock to enjoy their dream Asia. "Byron
country" is never out of fashion. It is an escape into that best of fairy-
lands, the *Arabian Nights*, and never more welcome than in our present
troubled era.

Oriental dress has never ceased to hypnotize the English, the highbrows
no less than the lowbrows, and even Mr Cyril Connolly has confessed to
feeling himself dowdy and ill-clad on the streets of Fez in his well-fitting
English lounge suit.... "Like a scene-shifter who had accidentally
wandered on to the stage during a performance of *Chu Chin Chow*."

There was at one point in the nineteenth century a synthesis between
Brummellism and Byronism, the most famous exponent of which was
Count Alfred d'Orsay, a famous dandy in his own right and a man who
managed to combine the miraculous fit of Brummell's dress with not a
little of the fantasy of Lord Byron's.

Byronism was already in the ascendant when he first came to London
from France for the coronation of King George IV, where, among the
festoons and fireworks which pleased the crowds in Hyde Park, the

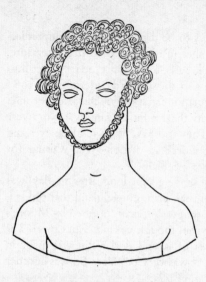

ALFRED GUILLAUME GABRIEL, COUNT
D'ORSAY, 1801-52

Self-portrait marble bust in the possession of
Lord Ilchester.

pièce de résistance was two richly caparisoned elephants, on top of which perched two handsome girls dressed as sultanas.

Unlike the professional dandies, d'Orsay was handsome, an athlete, and charming as a person. This arbiter of elegance, as described by his admirer Captain Gronow, was over six feet in height and beautiful as a Greek marble. No wonder Lady Blessington could not resist him.

His neck was long, his shoulders broad, and his waist narrow, and though he was perhaps somewhat underlimbed, nothing could surpass the beauty of his feet and ankles. His dark chestnut hair hung naturally in long waving ringlets; his forehead was high and wide; his features regular and his complexion glowed with radiant health. His eyes were large and of a light hazel colour. He had full lips and very white teeth, set a little apart.

That was a good start for any dandy. D'Orsay had more than this. "He excelled in manly sports. He was a fine horseman, a good swordsman and a fair shot," which, in the eyes of everybody, gave him the right to be beautiful as well.

He took as much care of his beauty as a woman might have done, perfumed his baths, etc. He had an enormous gold dressing-case which required two men to carry, and wouldn't budge without it.

He was not without wit, which, unlike Brummell's, was never brutally barbed, for the agreeable thing about d'Orsay was that he bore no grudge against anybody, in good times or in bad. Thus, on arranging to fight a duel on one occasion, he suggested good-naturedly:

My antagonist is a very ugly fellow, and if I should wound him in the face he won't look much the worse for it, but on my side it ought to be agreed that he should not aim higher than my chest, for if my face should get spoiled *ce serait vraiment dommage.*

D'Orsay's *éclat* in London Society was tremendous, all the more since he was not at all snobbish and preferred the company of artists and writers to the very rich or the merely noble. He had a sense of humour and invincible kindness of heart, and a steady warmth which lit up his physically splendid appearance. "When he passed in his tilbury," recalled one of his idolizers, "it was as though a splendid dragon-fly was darting through the air."

This peculiar radiance was one of personality no less than of sartorial dazzle, it would seem, for children are rarely deceived by appearances, and Thackeray's daughter, who met him as a little girl when he called one morning on her father in Kensington, remembered all her life the glittering impression he created as he sat chatting to her in her father's study, a glitter which gave out warmth as of the sun.

All London was mad about d'Orsay. Waistcoats, cravats, hats, pantaloons, perfumes, and all sorts of things he had never heard of as well, were eagerly named after him. He had only to put a garment on to make it the rage. Any garment. Once, caught in a shower while on horseback, he beckoned a passing sailor and bought his rough jacket off him to protect his immaculate riding-kit (typically paying the sailor ten guineas for his ragged old coat). Within half an hour ten young dandies appeared in the Park wearing similar rough jackets. The day after all London hurried to buy them.

Brummell had confined himself to fit and precision in dress; d'Orsay, a man of much greater energy and an infinitely wider range of interests, devoted himself not only to fit, but to fantasy and variety of dress as well. Of the six pairs of gloves d'Orsay wore each day every variety had its allotted purpose. He wore a pair of reindeer gloves for his morning drive in a britzka, a pair of shammy gloves for hunting, a pair of beaver gloves for the return to London in a tilbury after the hunt, a pair of braided kid gloves for accompanying Lady Blessington on an afternoon round of shopping, so that he might help her from her carriage, a pair of yellow dogskin gloves for going out to a dinner-party, and for the nightly ball or rout a pair of lambskin gloves embroidered with silk.

He was not afraid of colour and *panache* like Brummell. An American visitor to Seamore Place described him as wearing "a striped waistcoat of a tender shade, light pantaloons, and a brilliantly coloured redingote worn widely open."

D'Orsay's extravagant mode of life ran quickly through both his own fortune and that of Lady Blessington. They tried to earn more by editing sentimental popular albums, such as the *Keepsake*, which could be ordered bound in special silk to match any drawing-room décor, but his debts increased faster than the royalties. Presently he dared not appear on the streets of London, lest duns should arrest him, and had to spend his days asleep at his home and pass his nights gambling at Crockford's.

None of his many talents availed him anything, for he was one of those men who can make everything except money. He even invented a patent alarm signal for use on the new railways, which brought him in precisely nothing. He even tried his hand at alchemy. It was all in vain. With debts which now totalled well over £100,000 there was nothing left for him to do but fly to Paris.

At this point in his affairs a London publisher offered him an enormous sum of money to write his memoirs if he promised to include plenty of gossip about the *beau monde* with which he was so intimate. He refused. (Brummell, in similar straits, had no scruples about sponging on his friends and even the merest acquaintances, some of whom were much worse off than he was; and he spent his time abroad, when not at table or getting dressed, entirely in writing begging letters to England.)

In Paris d'Orsay set himself up in the Rue de la Ville d'Évêque in a bit of a studio, and tried to earn his living as a sculptor, an art for which he had some flair. Though still very handsome, he was ageing; but, though desperately poor and unsuccessful in his profession, he was still rich in the friendship of all the most interesting people in Paris, George Sand, Balzac, Chopin, and Daumier being just as devoted to him as Dickens and Disraeli had been in London.

It was the true gauge of his real character, perhaps, that he not only kept his self-respect and cheerfulness in poverty, but, by all accounts, was able to help other writers and other artists to the right places by introductions, cheerfully and judiciously given. As for himself, it was not until 1851 that he managed to obtain the Directorship of the Beaux-arts, a job for which he was admirably fitted, and which should have been offered him years before. For the first time in his life, to his surprise and gratification, he was able to earn his own living, and a year later he died suddenly before he had had time to get used to the sensation.

Said his friend, the Baron de Plancy, who was with him at the end:

Varnished boots, close-fitting trousers of sky-blue, embroidered shirt, white piqué waistcoat, puce cravat, and curled favourites. . . . Thus he departed from us, and St Peter will surely be astonished to meet him in this fancy rig.

CHAPTER FIFTEEN

THE PEACOCK'S TAIL

A nation arrayed in stove-pipe hats might have built the Pantechnikon possibly, but the Parthenon never.

OSCAR WILDE

BRUMMELL and Byron and d'Orsay between them may have helped a well-set-up man with a proud carriage to make the most of himself during the first half of England's nineteenth century. But many men were not well set up, nor did they move with dignity. Not even the nobility always looked the part. Thackeray, who knew his upper classes, has described the nobleman dandy of 1834 in the character of Viscount Cinqbars, thus:

> A sallow, blear-eyed ricketty undersized creature, tottering upon a pair of high-heeled lacquered boots and supporting himself upon an immense gold-knobbed cane, with his hat on one side and a jaunty air. It was a white hat with a broad brim and under it fell a great deal of greasy lank hair that shrouded the cheekbones of the wearer. The little man had no beard to his chin. He wore a great sky-blue satin stock in which figured a carbuncle that looked like a lambent gooseberry. He had a shawl-waistcoat of many colours, a pair of blue trousers neatly strapped to show his little feet, a brown cut-away coat with brass buttons that fitted tight round a spider waist, a white surtout with sable collar and cuffs and lemon-coloured kid gloves.

It appears more the costume of a second-rate mountebank than a nobleman. It was matter without manner, and, as is well known, it is manner which is crucial in the wearing of any dress. As the century advanced and England gave her attention more and more to industrialization male dress became heavier, more pompous, and gloomier in colour, till it seemed soaked in soot and sententiousness. And as male dress lost its magic, so its wearers grew more and more self-opinionated. Brummell would have met with but short shrift had he appeared fifty years later than he did. Industrialists permitted no word of criticism of their taste. What they liked was law, and only such artists as produced what the factory-owners wanted were tolerated. These new leaders of England, on the crest of the wave of triumphant prosperity, were determined to keep their hands on all the controls of the ship, especially the æsthetic controls.

They would brook no criticism of either their industrial methods or their ideas of beauty, and they were contemptuous of and fiercely hostile to all artists except those they had broken in to paint what they demanded —the enamelled boardroom portraits and the well-varnished travesties of Greek life so appropriate for the gloomy wallpaper of their crowded sitting-rooms. They had the money, and they insisted that it should buy a lot when they exchanged it for anything. Like their sitting-rooms and their dress, their pictures had to be weighty and crammed, so that every one could see they were good businessmen getting their full money's worth. As in their wives' costume and in their own, such considerations as balance and design counted for nothing in their scale of values. Greedy for acquisition, they demanded ostentatious, congested art.

England had been willing to listen to Brummell's criticism of the dress he succeeded in replacing, and had welcomed what she believed to be improvements. Not so the England of the last quarter of the nineteenth century. Oscar Wilde, William Morris, Whistler, Watts, Rossetti—all aroused an outburst of fury at the mere suggestion that English dress (during the ugliest and least hygienic fashions of any period) could be regarded as anything short of perfection.

That a mere handful of unmoneyed Æsthetes should have the effrontery to tell the important people who held the nation's money-bags what was beautiful was regarded as outrageous, even sacrilegious, and the æsthetic movement was damned in England from the moment it started. There were several good reasons why painting should have developed so dazzlingly in France in the nineteenth century and not in England, and the most important reason was that the Juggernaut of industrialism had not overrun France as it had overrun England.

In England it was not enough to make a vulgar joke out of the English æsthetic movement; it had to be ferociously attacked from all angles, especially that of morality. It was, thundered money-bags, undermining the sanctity of the home and the good commercial name of John Bull himself. There was no money in it, to start with; therefore it was not the kind of enterprise they could countenance. The firm of Debenham and Freebody, in a book of fancy dresses recommended for masquerades published in 1884, offers this suggestion for an "Æsthete": "The best colourings are dark blue serge and sun-flowers, white with daffodils, sickly green with passion-flowers."

"Sickly green" meant green made from natural vegetable dye, not the commercial aniline dye.

Even the beginning of higher education for women was bedevilled by fear that the gallant little band of earnest and dedicated girls might be brought to grief by the possibility that people might connect higher education in their thoughts with Æstheticism. There was danger in the fact that some of the dear girls were known to admire Rossetti's paintings. The following disclaimer denouncing æsthetic dress may have been written by the famous Miss Beale herself. It appeared in the *Queen* in 1881.

We see samples of it in the saffron-coloured dress worn by sallow-faced maidens whose first youth has vanished. We see it in the snaky, winding, mystically suspended garments robing the fleshless contours of those whose beauty exists in the approach to the skeleton form; the long thin throats, the bony necks, and the skinny arms, often bare, seem to delight in the scantiness of their charms and the jaundice of their complexions. A perceptible shudder runs through the form of the modern æsthete at the sight of the rosy, healthy-looking, sensibly clad, modern girl.

The sensibly clad English girl, in the same issue, is advised, as the acme of good taste and charm, to choose an outdoor muff of silver fox trimmed with speckled beaver "slung upon gold cords and trimmed with red cords and a large stuffed Oriental bird." She is advised to reject the painting of Mr Whistler currently exhibiting, as he clearly has no conception whatever of the beautiful, being "too French, not suitable for our English tastes, which insists rightly on art which elevates." And she is cheered by the description of the hymn classes and Band of Hope meetings then being arranged in Rome for the salvation of peasant models employed by the "English Ladies" Art Society there, whose elevating conception of the civilizing rôle of artists was to teach Moody and Sankey hymns in English to the illiterate Neapolitans. Nor is the lady reader's own æsthetic development left to chance. Careful instructions are given gratis, in the same number, for painting a plush cover for an umbrella-stand, and there is also "a design for embroidering a canvas sausage-holder."

William Morris was beating his head against the wall when he reproached the women of England in the eighteen-eighties with dressing to look like upholstered armchairs. Watts and Wilde were wasting their breath when they preached against the savage corsetry that was making not only so many women misshapen and ill, but quite a lot of men as well. As to Rossetti, the less he had to say about the vulgarity of aniline dyes, was the general opinion, the better, with an un-English name like that. How dared he?

The only ears prepared to listen to the Æsthetes were those of a few

Society ladies looking for a new sensation to make social capital for their *salons* for a season. When William Morris set up his establishment to produce good carpets, beautiful wallpaper, and better furniture and hangings he made a success of it only by the patronage of a small group of sincere and broad-minded individuals, the type of intellectual England produces a few of, mercifully, in every generation, and who are never

DECADENCE OF DESIGN
Metal inlay on cheap wardrobe, 1890. English.

'GENTILITY'
Vase for church flowers
in white glass. Gordes,
France, nineteenth
century.
Author's collection

afraid to swim against the current. Morris never reached the solid core of middle-class and lower-middle-class English people he most wanted to reach, though he did influence many working-class people, who, how-ever, could not, on their miserable wages, afford to buy his products.

Æsthetic dress, whatever it turned into—and all dress-reforms end up by resembling their own period — was originally a sincere attempt to introduce a softer, more natural line into the dress of both sexes, and to establish the use of more sensitive colour in English dress. Corsets were denounced because they were spoiling the natural lines of the body, and the two cultures singled out for approval were those of eighteenth-century Japan and the Italian Renaissance.

The wives and daughters of Burne-Jones, William Morris, Wilde, and Watts, a notably beautiful group of women, who looked lovely in the Æsthetic dress designed for them, aroused the fiercest antagonism from the non-Æsthetes, who felt, with sudden alarm, that here was competition of a kind they were not used to. If female Æsthetes and their dress were allowed to be regarded as 'beautiful,' then they themselves and their dress could not. So middle-class English matrons brought all their big guns into play in their battle against this threat to their whole way of life. For, from their point of view, with all their daughters to marry off and dwindling dowries, the Æsthetic movement was, indeed, an attack on the sanctity of the home.

Male dress, the Æsthetes also declared, was just as urgently in need of reform as female dress. The Æsthetes, with no great hopes, it must be admitted, turned their attention to English male dress, and tried their best. What they wanted was to introduce something less rigid in line, less wooden-looking, more manly in appearance.

It was difficult to know where to start; everything was moving in the opposite direction to where the Æsthetes wanted to go. The factories, with their sooty chimneys, were spreading all over England, debased standards of workmanship and rapidly produced shoddy stuffs everywhere accepted, and money values all-powerful to the exclusion of all other values. At least, the Æsthetes decided, they would try.

William Morris himself always wore a big grey cloak and a big hat of soft grey felt, comfortable tweeds, and hand-knitted, sturdy stockings. The dress of Englishmen of the nineteen-sixties, however, which in 1890 he forecast in *News from Nowhere*, consisted of an idealized fourteenth-century tunic of blue stuff, girdled with a fine leather belt, whose silver buckle had been tooled by the wearer himself. Morris dressed all his characters in the England of 1960 in bright soft materials fashioned in medieval shapes, which dress they had all taken some hand in designing or making themselves. The most gorgeously dressed man in his merry England (*circa* 1960) is the dustman, who has a taste for rich embroidery, and wears splendid garments "with as much gold as a baron of the Middle Ages." This was Morris's way of saying that all work, however lowly, must be respected if men are to be raised into self-respect ever again.

Unable to conceive a tolerable future except in terms of the past, William Morris stands in history as a mighty protest. Were he alive to-day it is likely that he would accept the machine and teach men to use their leisure better.

Morris dedicated his whole life to protesting in every way he could against the corruption of English taste in proportion as her industrial wealth increased. Like so many English reformers, he himself was of middle-class origin. He was a man of high intelligence and strong integrity. His energy seemed limitless, and he was well balanced by abundant common sense and a deep love for the English countryside. He had learning besides taste, and was an authority on medieval English manuscripts. Best of all he loved making things with his own hands, netting, cooking, painting, gardening, using all kinds of tools. The most vivid picture of him which his friends retained was his appearance at a meeting with his beard stained with bright blue dye, as he had spent the afternoon trying out for himself a recipe for cerulean tincture he had discovered in an old abbey manuscript.

He believed in tools more than machinery, and lamented the passing of England's trade guilds of the Middle Ages because they had given their apprentices a sound training in manual skills. He was the inveterate enemy of the cheap and the shoddy. He wanted everything man handled and looked upon to be carefully designed and carefully made, of the best possible material, and he wanted these good things for everybody. In an important lecture to the Trade Guild he declared:

I do not want art for a few any more than education for a few. . . . A few highly cultivated men who can go often to beautiful places, whose education enables them in the contemplation of past glories of the world to shut out from their view the everyday squalors that most men live in. Sirs, I believe that art has such sympathy with cheerful freedom, open heartedness and reality, so much she sickens under selfishness and luxury, that she will not live thus isolated and exclusive.

These are uncannily prophetic words. The only thing Morris could not visualize was the robot-culture which, within half a century, was to bring the appearance of comfort and prosperity to most of England, a prosperity from which the arts were to be coldly excluded. Morris wanted the arts to make life good to look upon for every one. He believed art to be an essential, not an extra.

No, rather than art should live this poor thin life among a few exceptional men, despising those beneath them for an ignorance for which they are responsible, rather than this I would that the world should indeed sweep away all art for a while (as I said before I thought it possible she might do); rather than the wheat should rot in the miser's granary, I would that the earth had it, that it might yet have a chance to quicken in the dark.

He declared it was greed for money which had corrupted England. Himself the enemy of the pretentious and the bogus, his fiercest battle was against the vandals then busy 'restoring' England's ancient monuments. "Anti-scrape" he called this.

He liked the feel and texture of materials to be honest, and enjoyed the actual handling of tools so much that his workshops were, his employees reported, always happy places to work in. Certainly his workmen got on admirably with him, and took the greatest personal interest in everything that was done there. He got through twenty lifetimes of work without hurry in his life-span—as only a dedicated man can. He was an excellent writer and poet of distinction, a good lecturer, printer, weaver, designer, and painter, and a sound administrator. And he may, indeed, have had some slight influence on male dress, though it took the curious form of inspiring middle-class intellectuals to dress in homespun and corduroy.

SOME IMPORTANT NINETEENTH-CENTURY FACES
From left: Dr Livingstone, Mr Stanley, Disraeli, W. G. Grace, Darwin, Bernard Shaw.

When he died his friends put his bier upon a farm-cart of solid traditional shape such as he loved, the wheels and axle gaily painted in bright blue and bright yellow and scarlet, and thus they followed him to his burial-place. It was the best epitaph for him.

Oscar Wilde, at the beginning of his meteoric career, equally believed he had a mission in life, and that was to awaken the money-making English middle class to the needless and destructive ugliness of their lives and their dress. He started with strong and clear views about beauty in dress. He hated corsets and any form of belted waistline. He loved drapery and clean, simple lines. Of the past dress of England he preferred the costume of the reign of Charles I and Restoration dress (as all men do) and that of the eighteenth century. But best of all he preferred Greek dress. Certainly he did not underestimate the difficulties in the way of developing a new æsthetic standard for male dress in an age when everything was against it. "Perhaps," he argued in a lecture in America,

Perhaps one of the most difficult things for us to do is to choose a notable and joyous dress for men. There would be more joy in life if we could accustom ourselves to use all the beautiful things we can in fashioning our own clothes. The dress of the future will, I think, use drapery to a great extent.

So far this has certainly not happened in the Western world. The stiff dullness he complained of in the male wear of his time has merely dwindled into a limp dullness. As male dress has not to-day even the bolstered pretence of dignity of Wilde's day, we may even say that male dress has actually deteriorated since his time. "At present," said Wilde,

> we have lost all nobility of dress and in doing so have almost annihilated the modern sculptor. And in looking round at the figures which adorn our parks one could almost wish we had completely killed the noble art. To see the frock-coat of the drawing-room done in bronze or the double-waistcoat perpetuated in marble, adds a new horror to death.

Mercifully Wilde died before bronzes of city worthies in lounge suits appeared.

He was not a man of the people, and knew nothing about tools or the actual making of anything except literature. Nevertheless, it is interesting that the group of people he admired most, thought the best dressed, and got on most happily with in his American tour was the Colorado gold-miners. He decided to read Benvenuto Cellini's autobiography to them, since gold was their trade, and got on famously, his readings being received rapturously. At the end of the reading the miners wanted to know why Wilde had not brought the author with him, and on being gently informed that Cellini was dead they asked who had shot him.

Wilde's æsthetic judgment was fundamentally sound and ahead of its time. He foresaw the innate beauty in machinery which is not pretending to be anything but machinery, and he foresaw something that America might create on those lines.

> There is no country in the world where machinery is so lovely as in America. I have always wished to believe that the line of strength and the line of beauty are one. That wish was realized when I contemplated American machinery.

The other two things that impressed Wilde most on his trip, besides the swashbuckling dress of the Colorado miners, were that he found rough Chinese navvies in San Francisco drinking tea out of their traditional exquisitely fragile china cups, and he discovered that the recipient of a plaster cast of the Venus de Milo had sued the railway company when the cast was delivered without arms, and won a handsome sum of money in compensation.

The *New York Herald* reporter who covered Wilde's famous lecture in New York on January 9, 1882, described him as well worth seeing, his short breeches and silk stockings showing to even better advantage on the stage than in the gilded drawing-rooms where the young apostle has heretofore been seen in New York.

The dress-reformer must cry his own wares. Wilde wore velvet jackets with a brilliant orange silk kerchief at the breast. After another lecture in America he was reported as being attired in a

dark brown velvet smoking-suit with lapels of red quilted silk, dark red long necktie, dark brown velvet trousers with red pipings on the outer seams, and patent leather boots with light cloth uppers, and toying with a walking-stick made of olive-wood cut from a famous classical grove in Greece.

In his fight against the "dreadful chimney-pot hat and shocking swallow-tail coat" Wilde used all his weapons of wit and mockery, but, though he liked to wear velvet and enjoyed colours and textures with an artist's relish, he did not himself sponsor any really new form of dress for men to wear. He never got beyond reverting to the velvet knee-breeches and silk stockings of the eighteenth century, which still survives in court dress, and on important occasions later on in his life he did not dress very differently from other well-dressed but conventional men, except in slight detail. On the famous first night of *The Importance of being Earnest*, in February 1895, a spectator described him as

resplendent in a superbly fitting evening dress with a black velvet collar, white gloves and huge scarab ring, a green carnation in his buttonhole, and a bunch of seals dependent from a black moiré guard on his white waistcoat.

The publication of Charles Darwin's *Origin of Species* caused a mighty wave of despair and excitement to pass through England. English people of education began to feel the need of some kind of reformed religion which would admit science. The word 'reform' was on every one's lips. Reformed food. Reformed education. Female emancipation and reformed dress. But it was not to the artists that English intellectuals first looked to set before them a different conception of themselves. They distrusted the artists. 'Æsthetic dress' seemed, according to English puritan conscience, something essentially immoral. What they wanted was *reformed* dress, something with a moral uplift, yet no revolutionary flavour. *Rational* was the adjective that they hit upon. It was sensible and it was sexless. And rational dress was what they demanded and got.

This rational male dress of the eighties ran to deerstalkers (not, however, to stalk deer in, because the exponents of rational dress were vegetarian to a man). Besides this vegetarian deerstalker they wore a Norfolk jacket in homespun tweed, preferably of a loose weave, tightly fitting knicker-bockers, hand-knitted heavy woollen stockings of misty sage green, in honour of William Morris, and home-made sandals—a brief nod to

Above: SANITARY WOOLLEN NIGHT JACKET WITH HOOD
Jaeger Catalogue, 1884

Left: BOY'S SANITARY WOOLLEN SUIT
Jaeger Catalogue, 1884

Tolstoi. They wore an open-throated shirt of limp material, woven with a hygienically wide mesh, to let in the health-giving air and sun, and always carried a stout knotty staff, for pointing out ancient monuments on country walks. In the capacious pockets of their hand-woven tweed jackets they tucked a packet of wholemeal bread sandwiches, a handful of pine kernels, and a volume of Edward Carpenter.

Clear-eyed, tanned by the infrequent but eagerly courted English sun, doggedly upright (if unconventional), in their morals as in their carriage, they may still be seen to-day, healthy and austere old gentlemen, living in Welwyn Garden City on their diminished incomes, surrounded by Kelmscott Books printed in black letter, and cherishing half-forgotten memories of Isadora Duncan and the early days of the Fabian Society.

They it was who began the English cult of Van Gogh's 'sunflowers.' (As far as they are concerned he never painted anything else.) They liked primary colours. One at a time, that is. They it was who first bought

Heal's idealized kitchen furniture for the dining-room, and demonstrated in their dress the beauties of rough tweed and humble corduroy, though their work in life was usually nothing more strenuous than W.E.A. lecturing.

The striking fact is, despite these honourable and intellectual dress-reformers, that English workers hate wearing materials that suggest manual work, feeling these materials to be but the badge of their servitude. Corduroys, rough tweed, like overalls and heavy footwear, have absolutely no æsthetic appeal for them. All they want to do with such reminders of manual toil is to get away from them as fast as they can, in their spare time. It is the middle-class æsthetes, who do not work with their hands, who see the beauty in these homely stuffs, and if English workers ever again consent to wear corduroy it will only be after the material has become so associated with the upper classes (who are even now in the process of taking it over from the artists, for sportswear and week-ending 'rough') that they feel it will confer a distinct social *cachet* on them by wearing it again.

This curiously English form of snobbery is ours and ours alone. French workmen ignore it. American workmen circumvent it by making it general wear and calling it democracy. But English workmen will have none of either of these attitudes. Dickens, over a century ago, complained of the stubborn snobbery which made English workmen disdain the comfortable and suitable "blouse," which French workmen wore for work and for everyday wear—insisting instead on wearing "a frayed and greasy morning coat cut a long way after fashionable Savile Row."

When to-day in London's dockland one sees a collarless shirt, worn with a white knitted silk or a white cotton kerchief, a broad leather belt, cloth cap, and corduroy trousers, it is almost certain to be not an English, but an Irish labourer. English labourers like something with different associations. Indeed, the best way to bring the lounge suit and bowler hat into general disfavour would be to make it an obligatory work dress for labourers to wear.

H. G. Wells, recalling his early days as a young salesman in 1890, wrote:

> When I was a draper's apprentice, the clothing expenditure of the shop assistant's wages were controlled by the fact that the men had to appear behind the counter in a white shirt and collar, black tail coat and dark grey trousers, or some such similar rig. It varied with the establishment.
>
> For shop-assistants living in, this meant that from a quarter to a third of their wages was ear-marked for uniform. In off times there was

nothing for it but to go on wearing the same things. As a natural reaction against this obligation it was the supreme ambition of every assistant to possess a coloured lounge suit. That was the symbol of one's temporary freedom, one's citizenship, one's manhood. One felt when one wore it, no longer a shophand, but a man . . . one might be anyone in mufti.

Wells ventured to forecast that "we may be moving towards a much more varied costume than the world has ever known before."

Alas, the opposite seems to be the case. Far from flowering into more varied dress, English male dress shows a distressing tendency to level up and down into a general miasma of respectable conformity.

Jaeger Catalogue, 1887

JAEGER'S PATENT SANITARY
WOOLLEN KNEE-WARMERS
1884

While the youthful Wells was serving behind the drapery counter a tremendous hubbub was going on in the gentlemen's outfitters', because underwear also was in process of being rationalized. Ardent debates had been taking place for years on what constituted the most hygienic and moral undergarments for men. There was much heartburning on the part of the manufacturers of drawers and vests, who did not wish to be thought behind the stirring times, yet had to take into account the stocks of old-fashioned underwear on their shelves. Reputable firms for long had been selling crimson drawers and combinations for gentlemen, as proof of good faith. For red showed up shoddy by not taking the dye evenly.

It was in the early eighteen-eighties that Dr Gustav Jaeger, Professor of Zoology at Stuttgart University, startled England with his "sanitary woollen system." Dr Jaeger's dislike of vegetable fibre amounted to an obsession. He believed that human beings could only be healthy when clad in animal products, such as hair, feathers, horn, and wool. He insisted that not only must all human underwear and outerwear be made of pure sheep's wool, but also all sheets, pillowcases, tablecloths, furniture upholstery, window-curtains, and even handkerchiefs. He advised the adoption of tight-fitting woollen jackets buttoning up closely round the throat to combat "noxious vapours," and himself designed patent webbing clamps to prevent "updraughts" at wrists and ankles.

Among enthusiastic advocates of his sanitary woollen system in this country were Ruskin, Wilde, and, of course, Bernard Shaw. But it was not only the *avant-garde* intellectuals who wore Dr Jaeger's sanitary woollen combinations, sanitary woollen five-toed stockings, and sanitary woollen patent knee-warmers, but also Society with a capital S. The patronage of one Royal Princess, three Duchesses, two Marchionesses, and five Countesses instantly made wool *bon ton* with the English middle classes as well. Even the War Office was faintly impressed to learn that no less a military personality than Field-Marshal Graf von Moltke himself habitually wore Dr Jaeger's sanitary woollen undergarments and, it was believed, had insisted on the German army doing likewise, a sartorial reform to which advanced military thinkers did not hesitate to attribute the German victories of 1870.

Jaeger Ltd worked night and day producing long, warm combinations of rational wool, some so complete in dimensions as to form a total covering, leaving no inch of flesh unprotected between chin and toes. Engravings of solemnly moustached perfect gentlemen attired in these miracles of hygienic warmth appeared in the firm's brochures, couched in near-Biblical terms and sometimes embellished with texts as well. Thus exhorted, Englishmen one and all bought and wore the new undergarments because hygiene was good for them and for their souls.

There had been little or no attention paid to these matters before. The only garments which had counted had been those that showed, for Brummell had not advocated cleanliness because it was medically desirable, but because he was a neurotic, and the English Puritans had not advocated it because it was hygienic, either, but because they were godly. The nearest Englishmen had ever approached to hygiene before had been when Dr Andrew Boorde published in 1542 his useful little book on how to live and dress healthily.

> Beware [warned the good doctor] of the snoffe of candelles and the savoure of apples for these thynges be contaggyeous and infectynge. Also mystye and cloudye dayes, impetous and vehement wyndes, troublouse and vapourouse wether it is nat goode to labor in it to open the pores to let in infectious ayre. Furthermore bewar of pyssinge in draughtes and permyt no common pyssinge place to bee aboute the hous or mancyon and lett the common hous of easement be ower som water or elles elongated from the howse. And beware of emptynge of pysse-pottes and pyssing in chymnes.

America in the late nineteenth century was not to be left out of this movement for rational underwear. The *Hosiery and Knit Journal* reported in 1885 the invention of a new species of undergarment knit double, the intervening spaces divided into a number of watertight compartments provided with small valves, through which the sawdust, with which the compartments were filled, could be reduced or increased according to the climate. This ingenious insulation worked on the principle of the hay-box or the air-balloon, and was confidently recommended for travelling salesmen.

In our own day male underwear suffers more from embarrassment, to judge by the advertisements, than does female underwear, where no secret is sacred any longer. The latest development for manly men is nothing less than the return to the old-fashioned nightshirt. Perhaps the dignity of the gown is beginning to make some appeal to men again? A popular gent's outfitters advertises thus:

One lives and learns. Last year we mentioned that we had a few nightshirts. But what was this? Everyone wanted nightshirts! More letters. More nightshirt orders. It was only by stealing cloth from the pyjama workrooms that orders were met. Astonishing? But is it? Let us repeat. A nightshirt is voluminous. It will not cut you in halves when you roll about the bed, or bisect you with a cord.

It transpires that the late Bernarr Macfadden, the physical-culture king, a short man with mountainous muscular development, always wore a muslin nightgown. Perhaps men are reverting to gowns, if only for bed, because their womenfolk spend so much of their time awake in trousers.

There have been various sporadic attempts at dress-reform in recent years, always starting among youth. In 1925 'Oxford bags' enjoyed a brief popularity, and not only among Oxford undergraduates. These were extremely large, loose trousers of the palest possible shades of flannel, worn to look as sloppy as possible. They were a gesture for freedom against the previous excessive tightness. To-day the swing is in the contrary direction, the chief quality of Teddy-boy dress being in the extreme tightness and sobriety of colour of the trousers. 'Stove-pipes' are the emblem of the Teddy-boy.

While Savile Row has been worrying about keeping its head above water a new and genuine dress-reform movement has come from below to shake England and bedevil the juvenile courts. The Teddy-boy dress derives originally from the Edwardian waistcoats and faintly Edwardian rig introduced by the Dress Council after the Second World War. In its original form it was a subdued and extremely restrained outfit, expensive and expensive-looking. *Slightly* narrowed trousers, a *slightly* shorter, *slightly* more squared jacket, and a waistcoat of richly sombre brocade. It was not exaggerated, and it was, of course, beautifully tailored and discreet.

To their chagrin, the outfit was enthusiastically copied by the cheap tailors, and taken up, almost overnight, with joy by the post-War youngsters as their own especial uniform, to which they quickly added a shoestring tie and a duck's-posterior *coiffure*. It was theirs exclusively from then on, for Savile Row dropped it immediately and recoiled in revulsion.

It must be remembered that the chief wearers of this dress are now lads in their mid-teens, doing their first jobs, sometimes still at school. They are from poor homes, and for the first time in their lives are wearing a complete suit. Around this Teddy-boy dress these boys have woven a complete personality for themselves, delighted to be in the public eye, behaving with aloofness and an attempted hauteur which scarcely hides a gaucherie they can only cover by keeping together in bands. There are various conceptions of Teddy clothes. Usually the form is a wide-shouldered jacket often coming well over the thighs and worn loose with 'drapes.' Sometimes the coat has a black velvet collar. A 'slim Jim' tie is *de rigueur*. Trousers are worn very tight and black, and often rather short in the leg, the better to show up the socks, sometimes of brilliant yellow or flame-colour, and the clumpy shoes.

What is worth noting is that it is a real attempt at a *gentlemanly* dress, or what these lads imagine it to be, something far more in common with the English dandies of the last century than might have been expected from this generation of youth, brought up entirely on American tough movies and American comics. There is nothing American about Teddy dress at all. It is as English as roast beef, though its exponents are enthusiasts for jazz and rock and roll, having gone through the listless joys of the 'creep.'

"Because of full employment," writes Mary Dunbar in the *Sunday Times* (1953), "uneducated lads of 15 who have never heard of unemployment are earning high wages at unskilled jobs and can afford this distinctive dress. Like an old school tie it gives them an adhesion they would otherwise lack."

The Teddy-boy has his female opposite, and when not going about with his Teddy friends he will keep company with a Teddy-girl, who dresses in a grey, fitted short jacket, worn over an onion-tight black sweater with a high neck. She concentrates above all on a display of bust, inspired by such film-stars as Marilyn Monroe and Diana Dors. With her tight sweaters she wears a tight black skirt, cheap nylon stockings, and very high-heeled shoes, which rarely fit well.

There is no doubt whatever about her attitude to her young man's dress. She is thrilled by it. In her eyes it is a handsome costume, dashing and manly in the extreme. Here are the words of a young girl from West Ham, in East London, describing the ideal attire of her ideal sweetheart, in the 1956 "Leap Year" radio programme:

> Thick crêpe shoes. Spivvy socks. Skintight drainpipes. Stiff shirt collar. Waistcoat. Not a double-breasted coat, a one-button coat. Fingertip drapes. A white handkerchief in the top of his coat. A duffle coat and a cheese cap.

This is a genuine stand for elegant dress as opposed to 'tough' dress, the duffle coat being the darling of present-day youth, of all income groups and postal addresses, and the 'cheese' cap now being O.K. for poor boys to wear again, since it has come back to them sanctioned as gentlemanly wear from a class well above their own income group.

The youths who have already abandoned Teddy-boy dress are not these youths, but the social drifters around Soho, who are never faithful to any dress for long, and who are just now wearing dark polo-necked sweaters and jeans as their riffle-band uniform. But the lads from the mean streets are faithful to their Teddy-boy dress. They have made it their own, and they are well aware that it does something for them.

Though a few Teddy-boys get themselves into trouble now and then for gangster behaviour, such criminal tendencies are no essential part of this dress. Quite the contrary. For Teddy-boy dress is not the dress of the social outcast or the aggressive sloven. The lads who wear it are well washed and tidy and as well groomed as they know how to be. They valet their dress with care, and they brush their careful *coiffure*. Most magistrates, however, see red at the costume, which they believe to be baiting them: "You Teddy-boys!" cried the Chairman of the Hendon Magistrates, to an eighteen-year-old. "Public opinion is getting very strong about you Teddy-boys! They feel you are not being dealt with severely enough!"

But, then, non-Teddy-boy dress also arouses the anger of the Bench. "Don't slop about!" scolded Judge Hodgson at Wandsworth County Court on the hottest day of the 1956 summer. "Fasten up your shirt and have some respect for yourself." The young man in the witness-box was wearing a scarf tucked into his shirt instead of a collar and tie—really not so inappropriate in the sweltering heat as the Judge's own dress.

Much ink has been spilled and many psychological arguments waged to account for the Teddy-boy cult. Dr Macalister Brew suggests that

Teddy-boy dress is a mating lure, necessitated by the post-war phenomenon of an increased ratio of boys to girls. "It is a mistake," she says,
"to think that it is merely the uniform of the young gangster." Mr Ewart
Bell, County Youth Officer of the Surrey County Council, has a different
theory. He has worked out statistics to show that 64 per cent. of youth
are neither aggressive by nature nor especially desirous of collaborating
with authority. All they want is something to relieve their boredom.
"Left to themselves they would get rid of their nervous energy in rock
and roll and other innocent but noisy pastimes." In this 64 per cent. of all
England's youth were the Teddy-boys, "so bored with life that in sheer
desperation they adopted a mode of dress that would at least give them an
opportunity to express their individuality."

These are explanations why youth to-day should want to wear some
kind of distinctive dress. They do not explain why the dress is the
particular dress that it is. There is every reason in the world why it
should rather have taken the form of Western cowboy dress, since youth
is so much more accustomed to seeing such dress on the screens of the
cheap cinemas.

I believe it is a social-climbing dress, like most fine dress. These boys,
I think, want to be somebody, and who they want to be is a real English
gent *who counts for something*. Especially noticeable in Teddy-boys is their
curious gravity of expression. This is surely a pointer. The American
films they see so much of teach them the back-slapping, grinning American
technique of social encounter. Yet this they have rejected. They have
never heard the name Brummell, yet they instinctively put on an aloof
face, with their dandy dress, like any Regency buck. What they are after,
in fact, is not American bonhomie but English dignity.

We are doing the Teddy-boys an injustice to damn them out of hand.
These boys are trying, in the only way they know, to declare that they
want Englishmen to count in the world, to be important people, to dress
up handsomely again, and to enjoy dressing up.

Having lost this round to the Teddy-boys, what can the expensive
tailors do now about dress reform? The *Sunday Times* critic says, "For
the fashionably-minded men, poor creatures, there's only one solution—
back to the humdrum."

But the Men's Fashion Council, the Wool Secretariat, and the best
West End tailors have not accepted final defeat. On the contrary, they
have been racking their brains to conjure up something new for their
clients to wear, something new which will prove too expensive to be
easily copied. Exclusiveness has reached the stage of becoming a handicap.
They fear to launch something really good for the other side again. Timid little

N

adjustments and readjustments, therefore, are all they offer. An *Evening Standard* report of a men's fashion show in 1955 states:

> The tailors favour narrow trousers often without turn-ups. Jacket pockets with crescent-shaped openings instead of the usual straight ones. Waistcoat buttons are spaced in groups of two or three like a guardsman's.

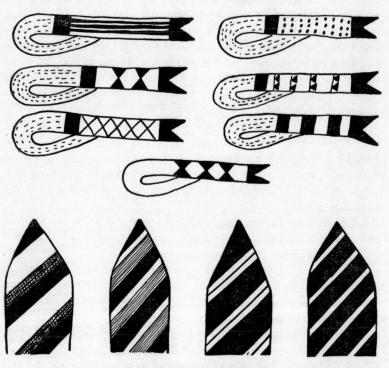

TRIBAL LOYALTIES

Top: Ceremonial penis-wrappers. Painted knotted palm-leaf fibre, with tribal markings. Kejara, Brazil. Contemporary.

Below: School ties. *From left*: Old Etonian, Old Harrovian, Old Rugbeian, Old Tonbridgian. Contemporary.

Not very exciting innovations, if innovations at all. Perhaps not even very tempting to their own clients.

Many men, not having served in the Guards, will recoil from this innovation as they would from wearing a Guard's tie.

Just at this time there was a most interesting series of letters in *The Times* from correspondents all over England, and of all classes, expressing a real interest in the cape, as a useful and beautiful garment worthy of readoption into present English male dress. Here was a strong hint for the Dress Council. But did they take it? Not at all. Capes are so essentially simple, and look so good even in inexpensive material, that they could not remain exclusive. Therefore the hint was ignored. Instead the exclusive designers concentrated on snob appeal.

Two main trends emerged. Brighter colours and light-weight fabrics. New is a *sundown* jacket, a light coloured coat for evening parties, particularly for cocktail parties. One of these jackets was coloured "gold dust." "Why should the ladies have all the pretty colours?" asked Mr Theo Hewitt, secretary of the Men's Fashion Council.

Other jackets were in blue shades named "Cambridge," "Edinburgh," "Bermuda" and "Lavender." One had no buttons, just a tasselled cord like a dressing-gown.

Here we have an attempt to hold on tight to what is intended to represent the aristocratic tradition. "Sundown" is meant to suggest the rich Nairobi gentleman at ease over his pink gin. "Cambridge," "Edinburgh," "Bermuda," suggest expensive education, royalty, and wealthy leisure, not available to ordinary wage-earners. The insistence on special dress for cocktail wear is meant to be a cunning stroke against the known habits of the Teddy-boys, who have moved in on the Espresso bars and drink little if any alcohol (another difference between them and contemporary American youth).

We cannot describe these innovations as dress reform. What they represent is dress deadlock.

What has America to offer, then, to present-day men looking for something better to dress themselves in? America has two kinds of dress to offer, *hard* and *soft*. The 'tough' dress is the gorilla silhouette of the comics criminal, overheavy jacket and limp slouch hat above curiously ineffective, teetering trousers, ending in small and insignificant shoes. The jacket indicates bluster, and its two patch pockets should rightly be bulging with revolvers. The lower limbs are ineffectively clad, because they are not meant for walking in, but riding fast cars in. The hat may be pulled down ferociously, but it is soft. It is bogus tough.

In shape—and we must never forget that it is always the shape that counts most in dress—this tough dress is merely the usual city suit developed into the gangster suit. What it expresses is not manhood, but the pursuit of 'lolly,' at the pistol's point instead of in the broker's office.

American 'soft' dress has tried out lingerie-pink shirts and ready-made cummerbunds with matching clip-on ties, worn with polka-dot frilled shirts, and is now developing glittering garments for men.

American fashion-designers in 1956 showed "sashed smoking-jackets of silver yarn and sapphire-blue worsted" and "sports jackets of fancy tweed threaded with green Lurex." But the actual shape of the dress was the same as before. This, therefore, does not augur a nobler sartorial future, but only indicates a contemporary commercial racket. No more does Liberace's shimmering lavender evening dress nor his silver brocade dinner jacket herald a coming revolution in male dress, for the conventional shape is unchanged. He is merely borrowing female dress materials.

These glittering garments, in the same deadly shape as before, do not announce a new beginning, but a bad ending. They are suitable for well-to-do, middle-aged, unmarried men with mother fixations and most appropriate wear, perhaps, for sessions on the psychoanalyst's couch.

These American styles are not dress-reform either. They also represent dress-deadlock. Perhaps even abdication.

We have seen in these chapters how English male dress went wrong when Englishmen wrenched apart art and science, discarded art and enslaved science, in order to make money. Money is a base objective. If that is all man wants that is all he will get. And that is all Englishmen got, vast wealth, now largely blown up in two world wars. Now we have to start planning our national life again, and we must learn from our big mistake.

This time we must restore the artist to his rightful place beside the scientist in our society, so that both may work together for the good of all. The scientist's wonder machines, if we are to survive, must be controlled to serve man, not to displace him, nor annihilate him. The artist must devote his gifts to making our towns and countryside and homes and dress beautiful, and showing us how to enjoy our increasing leisure creatively. Neither scientist nor artist alone can bring ordered beauty to our modern world; they must work together, as they always should have done, and originally did. Leonardo da Vinci was both artist and scientist at the same time, never dividing truth from beauty. Our English scientists began with exactly the same approach, and they were right.

The Royal Society, to which such early English scientists as Halley, Sir Isaac Newton, and Sir Christopher Wren (a notable example of a man who excelled in both the sciences and the arts) belonged, thus set out its objectives in its Charter of 1662: "For the promotion by the authority of experiments of the sciences of natural things to the glory of God the creator and for the advantage of the human race."

Life is not worth living when men work only 'for the lolly,' whether on the Stock Exchange or in the factory. The unquenchable thirst for knowledge of the real scientist, the endless taking of time and trouble to make something well of the real artist, these are what we need to-day to restore man's self-respect and belief in himself. In England we are not using our artistic resources intelligently, and we must do much better.

We have magnificent museums and libraries, artists, actors, musicians, equal to, sometimes superior to, any in the world. But we are starving and neglecting them. It is nothing short of criminal that the British Museum should be understaffed and its world-famous library in arrears with its catalogue to-day. It is a disgrace that our National Gallery should be obliged to keep a thousand of its masterpieces stored away and deteriorating for want of space to show them. It is shameful that all over the country one theatre after another should close down, and art schools be shut up and artists of value, whose vision and skill we so desperately need, be out of work.

"Most of the men and women of talent or even genius for painting and sculpture are working as clerks or administrators or teachers," says Arthur Giardelli, "yet there are countless walls on which old and miserable or new, shiny, mass-produced pieces of rubbish are hanging."

We are suffering from the false values of our industrialized age. The money is there and is being spent, but not on work of significance and lasting value. One instance will suffice. England to-day can still boast some of the finest graphic artists in the world, and no country can surpass England in the production of fine books. Yet these important skills languish because our publishers fear to take the risk of producing beautiful books with beautiful pictures. They know that the people with money are not interested in such products, and the people who are cannot afford them. At a recent book festival, however, held in London, there was one expensive book, lavishly illustrated regardless of cost, so that the book cost eight guineas a copy. This book was a *Builders' and Decorators' Manual*, explaining exactly how to fake wood in imitation of different marbles, and precisely how to execute simulated wood-graining.

England, it appears, cannot afford both the genuine and the bogus. She can afford only the bogus.

This attitude to life is what has brought England to her present impasse, and we have got to change it to survive in the new world that is taking shape. What practical steps can we take?

First of all our museums and art galleries and libraries must be properly financed and encouraged. They belong to all of us and should not be starved. Our treasures should also be spread more evenly about the country. At present London has too many, the provinces not enough. Millions of English people have no idea what treasures we have, or know anything about them, a deficiency our schools are doing almost nothing to overcome. Why do we not use T.V. and radio more for this purpose? The appetite is stimulated by what it feeds on, and millions of English people who had never heard the word 'archæology' before have become enthusiastic because Sir Mortimer Wheeler has shared his own delight in the subject with T.V. viewers in a popular and scholarly programme.

Our best T.V. programmes and our best radio programmes are splendid. Why do we not concentrate on quality all the time instead of quantity?

DANCING BOY
Egyptian clay tile. Roman period.
Fitzwilliam Museum, Cambridge

We should not underestimate the public. If the best is shown to them intelligently—that is, without condescension and highbrow jargon to baffle and irritate them—they will appreciate it. Here it must be pointed out that the real experts are always simple enough to understand. It is not they who talk mumbo-jumbo and put off the ordinary public, but rather the intellectual middleman, whom the arts can well do without, for in our time the arts have got to become important once more to everybody. They must matter, or we ourselves will not.

The theatre in England must be restored to its rightful place. It is tragic that the land of Shakespeare should produce less Shakespeare than other countries. Our theatres are overtaxed and undersubsidized, and we do not pay enough attention to our amateur theatre. In this respect we have much to learn from other countries. America has thriving little theatres—in fact, it is from here that her best plays so often come. France may well be proud of her Théâtre National Populaire, which takes the best productions out into the countryside, playing, as the old mystery plays were once played, in the open air in town squares and in the courtyard of the Palace of the Popes in Avignon. By such means France has re-created her theatre public, and educated it to demand only the very best.

Compared to the money we squander elsewhere, the subsidies we allow our theatres are pitiable. The little town of Malmö, in Sweden, a town no bigger than Plymouth, gives one subsidy to one theatre alone which is as large a subsidy as that we begrudgingly dole out to all the theatres in Great Britain altogether. Yet the theatre, properly handled, would give the public something worth having for its money.

Our meanness to the arts, which we now need to help us, is founded upon distrust of the common man as much as upon distrust of the arts. Yet how wrong this is may be seen by the results achieved when we reverse this attitude. It is crooked thinking to-day to declare that we cannot afford the arts. The arts are precisely the enterprise we cannot now afford not to afford. They belong to Everyman, and now in his need must be his guide.

Consider the value of the Festival of Britain, which so splendidly showed the world and ourselves what a contribution England can make to all the arts to-day. Not only was it enjoyed by everybody, regardless of class and education, but it stimulated the production as well as the appreciation of much unsuspected artistic effort from below. The street decoration in the poor quarters of Fulham and West Ham frequently surpassed in skill, imagination, and gaiety the professional street decoration of the grander thoroughfares. The arts are not dead in the lower-income groups in England. The seeds are there all right. They need, however, the stimulus of an occasion in which to grow and flower. We ought, in our own interests, to furnish many more opportunities. Fairs and festivals are the traditional mediums for the expression of skills in music and dancing, drama, and handwork.

Edinburgh has done admirably with her Festivals. But they tend to attract mostly the already cultured section of the public. On the other hand, the Welsh people are losing their wonderful miners' choirs because a cultural sullenness has settled over the coalfields. These choirs are part of our national inheritance and must not be allowed to vanish. Here again the radio, T.V., and even the cinema could help. The miners would take the trouble to rehearse if they believed the whole country was eager to hear them—that is, if they believed their singing mattered to-day.

Despite the general production of much that is meretricious and shoddy (products which are sold on the whole to the poorer class of people, though there is plenty of bad taste for sale in the expensive shops too), there are to-day some hopeful signs of a change.

Two brilliantly successful enterprises, based on the conviction that ordinary people will buy the best if they are offered it at a price they can afford, are *Marks and Spencer's* and *Penguin Books*.

Marks and Spencer's has become a millionaire firm by employing the best artists and designers and the best possible materials for them to work on, so that their products, which are profitable because they sell by tens of millions, are frequently in much better taste than the costly snob-products of the really exclusive shops. Penguin Books educated a whole generation of English people who could not afford to buy expensive books, and earned a well-deserved knighthood for the promoter, who started with practically no capital at all and who has resolutely refused to compromise over quality.

These show what is needed and what can be done. But before there can be only good and beautiful products for sale a clean sweep must be made of the rubbish which is being put out, and on which so many people still waste their earnings. Norway and Sweden and Denmark will not allow trash on their markets. They have committees of artists and designers to keep up the quality by refusing to allow inferior designs into production. They help the sculptor by insisting that a small percentage of the costs of every important building shall be devoted to statuary to embellish it. That is why these small Northern democracies, which have such respect for their citizens, have such lovely ceramics, furniture, buildings, and fabrics. The Royal College of Art to-day is hopefully starting a special new course for the art training of industrial designers. But this is not enough. Every new technical college and school should have its own art department to work closely with the technological side.

Ordinary people are the big customers of our time. There are two ways of looking at them. They can be respected or they can be exploited. And it is according to which way we look that men's dress will shape itself in the coming years. Van Gogh, who looked at them the first way, declared that what he was trying to paint in the vibrancy and purity of his colour was the eternal in man, that which the halo symbolized, the spirit itself. The second way of looking is that taken by the well-known Hollywood director who declared, "Don't give me any of these 150-dollars-a-week geniuses. I want a 2500-dollars-a-week writer who has a swimming-pool and is paying alimony."

This director was not out to produce a good film, but merely to exceed the usual 300 per cent. profit.

Whether we like it or not, our age is becoming the age of the common man. Atomic power will make possible enormous international enterprises previously impossible, and automation is going to give more leisure and power to those who previously have had little of either. This new pattern is even now taking shape. The young people of to-day are quite different kinds of people from their parents. They belong to a different age. Their tastes are simpler, and they have fewer prejudices. Even well-to-do youth prefers Espressos and modest meals to the long tedious dinner-parties of fifty years ago. All young people to-day are less snobbish than their parents, and not snobbish at all compared to their grandparents. In England they mix more easily with other classes— indeed, the whole class system is visibly beginning to dissolve. They mix better with other races too than their parents did. In America racial discrimination is being attacked and also beginning to disappear.

English youth as a whole is getting a much better education than it did a generation ago. Most university students are there on grants, and come from homes where there has been no previous tradition of education up to university standard. Conversely we have the phenomenon of Humphrey Lyttelton, old Etonian son of an old Tory family, losing no caste—rather, indeed, gaining it—by playing hot jazz for his living, and boasting of his total inability to read a musical score. England, in fact, is levelling herself out much more in this generation of teen-agers than ever before in all her history.

That is why the Savile Row suit is dying of inanition to-day. It must adapt itself to the times or it will die. The vitality which will shape the coming English dress will be the vitality of the multitude, because that is where the vitality is to be found to-day, however momentarily sulking the English multitude may be. The revolution which seized Edwardian dress from Savile Row and won it for the Teddy-boys has been a bloodless revolution, but it is nevertheless a revolution, in which the bays of victory have been fairly won by the lads from the mean streets.

England has the tradition of always winning her last battle, and sartorially this is her last battle. A good general knows when he is beaten. And a wise general makes the best terms he can. Surely this is the moment for Savile Row to take a hint from such distinguished designers of female dress as Norman Hartnell and Christian Dior, men not too proud to design good clothes for the multitude, since this is the day of the multitude, and privilege can no longer afford to keep the exclusive fashion houses running.

Is it not better to design directly for the multitude (who pay promptly and are appreciative customers) than to continue to design for a dwindling few, and have these exclusive designs copied from below anyway? Not all men can afford to pay a lot of money for their clothes. But there is no reason why inexpensive clothes, if designed by an artist in good faith, and honestly carried out in simple, unpretentious materials of good quality and good colour, should not be truly beautiful.

This calls for considerable rethinking from Savile Row, but would it not be better for them to make a good fresh start now, and give a new lease of life to a respected and highly skilled English craft, which is to-day dying on its feet because it will have nothing to do with the only remedy which can save it? Once Savile Row removes the stranglehold of exclusiveness, which is killing its possibility of real service to more than a dwindling handful (mostly of South American millionaires), English tailoring could again lead the world, and this time in a better direction. For the insistence on careful apprenticeship and fine craftsmanship, and the refusal to be content with anything less than the very best—these Savile Row virtues need infusing to-day into the dressing of the multitude.

Dress historians in our day try to tabulate the vagaries of fashion without personally committing themselves to an opinion as to whether the dress is ugly or beautiful, and, if such a state as absolute impartiality could exist, this no doubt would be as wise as it would be scholarly. For taste swings wildly, biting its own tail every twenty years or so. There are, however, certain standards of beauty which defy, and will continue to defy, the crumbling of time.

The garments hanging from the coat-hanger are dead things until the man who puts them on gives them life. It is his spirit which must inform them, and it is in his spirit that they will shape themselves, for good or for bad. Dress may be sober or sensuous, simple or complicated, tight or loose, costly or inexpensive, and still be beautiful. What dress cannot be and still be beautiful is spiritless. What most quickly kills beauty is emptiness of spirit.

The Greeks, the beauty of whose dress has never been surpassed, believed the body of man to be so beautiful that they did not 'make' his clothes at all, but simply allowed his body to give shape to the few yards of material he wrapped about him, his body always dominating the material, so that his every movement created fresh harmonies of line and folds.

With the same zest for life, Tudor gallants did not disdain false hair, sawdust bombast, and paste jewellery, but they too wholly believed in the glory of man and his value in the eyes of his gods, and they held themselves no less proudly than the Greeks.

Sir Walter Raleigh, that "damnably proud" man, was a courtier who saw through the treacheries of courts to something greater than thrones. That is why he dressed for his shameful death with the perfection of a great artist, knowing that it could not diminish him in what most mattered to him—his personal integrity.

The spirit of the English peacock is not dead. It still lives. It is only waiting for release for the glorious feathers to be displayed as never before.

The grave-faced English youth to-day, in his duffle coat, is England, facing the atomic age with only his belief in himself and his pride. With no more in 1940 his father won the Battle of Britain.

CABIN-BOY, 1777
After Rowlandson.
Greenwich Maritime Museum

SHORT INDEX

The figures in bold type refer to illustrations in the text.

396